PRENTICE HALL

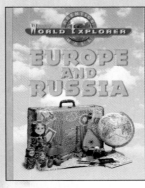

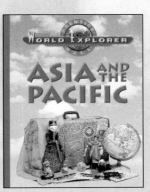

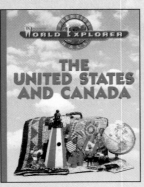

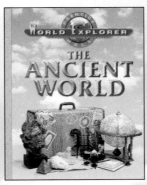

The world studies program that lets you choose.

PRENTICE HALL
Simon & Schuster Education Group
A VIACOM COMPANY

Upper Saddle River, New Jersey
Needham, Massachusetts

ISBN 0-13-424946-1

1 2 3 4 5 6 7 8 9 10   01 00 99 98 97

T1

The only middle grades world that can truly provide the right materials to fit your

Prentice Hall World Explorer lets you choose the right balance of history, geography, and cultures for the regions of the world that you cover in your middle grades curriculum. No more being confined to the contents of a single text. No more having to spend valuable time locating additional resources. All this with hands-on activities and skills; interdisciplinary connections; integrated technology; and manageable resources to support your teaching style.

YOU CHOOSE what's right

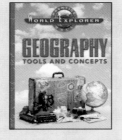  

A few of
the most popular
**COURSE
CONFIGURATIONS:**

	GEOGRAPHY TOOLS AND CONCEPTS	EUROPE AND RUSSIA	AFRICA
Eastern Hemisphere*	GEOGRAPHY TOOLS AND CONCEPTS	EUROPE AND RUSSIA	AFRICA
Western Hemisphere*	GEOGRAPHY TOOLS AND CONCEPTS		
World History			
Western Civilization		EUROPE AND RUSSIA	
Pacific Rim	GEOGRAPHY TOOLS AND CONCEPTS		
World Cultures		EUROPE AND RUSSIA	AFRICA

studies program curriculum.

for your course of study.

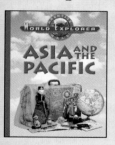 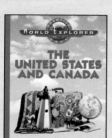   

ASIA AND THE PACIFIC	THE UNITED STATES AND CANADA	LATIN AMERICA	THE ANCIENT WORLD	MEDIEVAL TIMES TO TODAY
ASIA AND THE PACIFIC				
	THE UNITED STATES AND CANADA	LATIN AMERICA		
			THE ANCIENT WORLD	MEDIEVAL TIMES TO TODAY
	THE UNITED STATES AND CANADA		THE ANCIENT WORLD	
ASIA AND THE PACIFIC	THE UNITED STATES AND CANADA	LATIN AMERICA		
ASIA AND THE PACIFIC	THE UNITED STATES AND CANADA	LATIN AMERICA		

Available in single, hard-bound volume

Only World Explorer provides this many management resources— built right into the program.

Designed from the start to have more time-saving resources for middle grades teachers, the World Explorer program has brand-new ways to help you coordinate your program, scheduling, assessment, team teaching, interdisciplinary connections, and other valuable resources.

- **Managing Time and Instruction**
- **Block Scheduling**
- **Assessment Opportunities**
- **Activities and Projects**
- **Resource Pro™ CD-ROM**
- **FYI**
- **Technology Options**
- **Flexible Planning Guide**

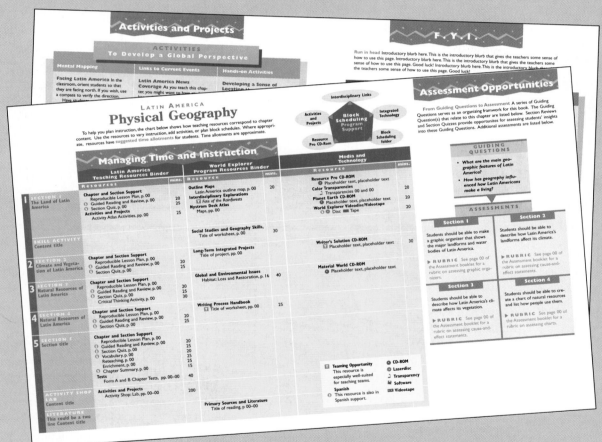

TECHNOLOGY OPTIONS

- Teacher's Edition wraparound with barcodes
- Point-of-use technology references
- Integrated video presentations

Guided Reading Audiotapes *
Computer Test Bank
   (MAC/Windows)
World Video Explorer
   Videodiscs *
   Videotapes
Resource Pro™ CD-ROM
Material World CD-ROM
Planet Earth CD-ROM
Writer's Solution CD-ROM
*available in Spanish

FLEXIBLE PLANNING GUIDE

This key supplement makes it easy to plan, schedule, and coordinate World Explorer's multi-book program.
- Course configurations
- Pacing charts
- Scope and sequence of skills
- Correlations to national standards

Teacher's Flexible Planning Guide
- Guide to Program Components
- Pacing Guide
- How to Use World Explorer in Interdisciplinary Teaching Teams with Activity-Based Learning with Block Scheduling with Technology
- Skills Scope and Sequence
- Correlation to the National Geography Standards
- Correlation to the NCSS Standards

RESOURCE PRO™ CD-ROM

PRENTICE HALL

- Teaching Resources
- Planning Express™
- Computer Test Bank

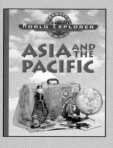
ASIA AND THE PACIFIC

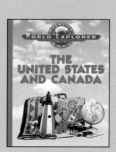
THE UNITED STATES AND CANADA

LATIN AMERICA

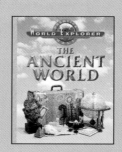
THE ANCIENT WORLD

MEDIEVAL TIMES TO TODAY

Coverage of all World Explorer program skills is provided in the Student Edition and Teacher's Edition.

Skills Activity
Students learn, practice, and apply core social studies skills through the use of hands-on activities.

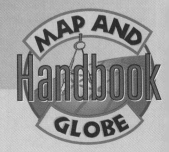

Skills Mini-lessons
These lessons supplement and reinforce core social studies skills that are not formally presented in the student book.

Map and Globe Handbook
Students practice and review basic geography skills that focus on understanding maps and charts.

AFRICA
SKILLS SCOPE AND SEQUENCE

MAP AND GLOBE SKILLS

SKILL	BOOK	PAGE
Using Parts of a Map	STUDENT	188
Comparing Maps of Different Scale	STUDENT	189
Understanding Distortions in Map Projections	STUDENT	186–187
Using Political and Physical Maps	STUDENT	190, 191
Using Regional Maps	STUDENT	104–105
Using Isolines to Show Elevation	STUDENT	146–147
Using Distribution Maps	STUDENT	126–127
Using Route Maps	TEACHER	35

CRITICAL THINKING SKILLS

SKILL	BOOK	PAGE
Expressing Problems Clearly	TEACHER	165
Identifying Central Issues	TEACHER	83
Distinguishing Facts From Opinions	TEACHER	101
Recognizing Bias	STUDENT	58–59
Recognizing Cause and Effect	TEACHER	117
Drawing Conclusions	TEACHER	153

CHART, GRAPH, AND ILLUSTRATION SKILLS

SKILL	BOOK	PAGE
Interpreting Graphs	TEACHER	137
Interpreting Diagrams and Illustrations	STUDENT	26–27
Using a Time Line	TEACHER	43
Reading Tables and Analyzing Statistics	TEACHER	111
Understanding Special Geography Graphs	TEACHER	19

READING AND WRITING SKILLS

SKILL	BOOK	PAGE
Previewing	TEACHER	11
Reading Actively	TEACHER	97
Assessing Your Understanding	STUDENT	86–87
Using the Writing Process	TEACHER	123
Writing for a Purpose	TEACHER	73

STUDY AND RESEARCH SKILLS

SKILL	BOOK	PAGE
Locating Information	TEACHER	39
Organizing Information	TEACHER	173
Organizing Your Time	STUDENT	166–167

Use this daily pacing chart to help plan a nine-week course or a twelve-week course for Africa.

Block Scheduling
Suggested times are for daily class periods between 40 and 50 minutes long. For planning extended blocks or for teachers who wish to vary the pace of instruction, see the "Managing Time and Instruction" charts before each chapter or the Resource Pro™ CD-ROM

	9-WEEK COURSE	12-WEEK COURSE
ACTIVITY ATLAS	2 DAYS	2 DAYS

CHAPTER 1
AFRICA: PHYSICAL GEOGRAPHY

	9-WEEK COURSE	12-WEEK COURSE
Section 1 Land and Water	1	1.5
Section 2 Climate and Vegetation	1	1.5
Section 3 Natural Resources	1	1.5
SKILLS ACTIVITY Interpreting Diagrams	1.5	1.5
CHAPTER 1 REVIEW, ACTIVITIES, AND ASSESSMENT	1.5	1.5

CHAPTER 2
AFRICA: SHAPED BY ITS HISTORY

	9-WEEK COURSE	12-WEEK COURSE
Section 1 Africa's First People	1	1.5
Section 2 Kingdoms and Empires	1	1.5
Section 3 The Conquest of Africa	1	1.5
Section 4 Independence and Its Challenges	1	1.5
Section 5 Issues for Africa Today	1	1.5
SKILLS ACTIVITY Recognizing Bias	1	1.5
CHAPTER 2 REVIEW, ACTIVITIES, AND ASSESSMENT	1.5	1.5

CHAPTER 3
CULTURES OF AFRICA

	9-WEEK COURSE	12-WEEK COURSE
Section 1 The Cultures of North Africa	1	1.5
Section 2 The Cultures of West Africa	1	1.5
Section 3 The Cultures of East Africa	1	1.5
Section 4 The Cultures of Central and Southern Africa	1	1.5
SKILLS ACTIVITY Assessing Your Understanding	1	1.5
CHAPTER 3 REVIEW, ACTIVITIES AND ASSESSMENT	1.5	1.5
ACTIVITY SHOP Interdisciplinary	1.5	1.5

CHAPTER 4
EXPLORING NORTH AFRICA

	9-WEEK COURSE	12-WEEK COURSE
Section 1 Egypt: Hearing the Call of Islam	1	1.5
Section 2 Algeria: The Casbah and the Countryside	1	1.5
SKILLS ACTIVITY Using Regional Maps	1	1.5
CHAPTER 4 REVIEW, ACTIVITIES AND ASSESSMENT	1.5	1.5

CHAPTER 5
EXPLORING WEST AFRICA

	9-WEEK COURSE	12-WEEK COURSE
Section 1 Nigeria: One Country, Many Identities	1	1.5
Section 2 Ghana: First in Independence	1	1.5
Section 3 Mali: The Desert Is Coming	1	1.5
SKILLS ACTIVITY Using Distribution Maps	1	1.5
CHAPTER 5 REVIEW, ACTIVITIES AND ASSESSMENT	1.5	1.5
ACTIVITY SHOP Lab	1.5	1.5
Literature	.5	1

CHAPTER 6
EXPLORING EAST AFRICA

	9-WEEK COURSE	12-WEEK COURSE
Section 1 Ethiopia: Churches and Mosques	1	1.5
Section 2 Tanzania: When People Cooperate	1	1.5
SKILLS ACTIVITY Using Isolines to Show Elevation	1	1.5
Section 3 Kenya: Skyscrapers in the Savanna	1	1.5
CHAPTER 6 REVIEW, ACTIVITIES AND ASSESSMENT	1.5	1.5
Literature	1.5	1.5

CHAPTER 7
EXPLORING CENTRAL AND SOUTHERN AFRICA

	9-WEEK COURSE	12-WEEK COURSE
Section 1 Zaire: Rich But Poor	1	1.5
SKILLS ACTIVITY Organizing Your Time	1	1.5
Section 2 South Africa: The End of Apartheid	1	1.5
CHAPTER 7 REVIEW, ACTIVITIES AND ASSESSMENT	1.5	1.5

	9-WEEK COURSE	12-WEEK COURSE
TOTAL NUMBER OF DAYS	45	60

WORLD EXPLORER

AFRICA

PRENTICE HALL
Needham, Massachusetts
Upper Saddle River, New Jersey

Program Authors

Heidi Hayes Jacobs

Heidi Hayes Jacobs has served as an educational consultant to more than 500 schools across the nation. Dr. Jacobs is an adjunct professor in the Department of Curriculum on Teaching at Teachers College, Columbia. She completed her undergraduate studies at the University of Utah in her hometown of Salt Lake City. She received an M.A. from the University of Massachusetts, Amherst, and completed her doctoral work at Columbia University's Teachers College in 1981.

The backbone of Dr. Jacobs's experience comes from her years as a teacher of high school, middle school, and elementary school students. As an educational consultant, she works with K–12 schools and districts on curriculum reform and strategic planning.

Brenda Randolph

Brenda Randolph is the former Director of the Outreach Resource Center at the African Studies Program at Howard University, Washington, D.C. She is the Founder and Director of Africa Access, a bibliographic service on Africa for schools. She received her B.A. in history with high honors from North Carolina Central University, Durham, and her M.A. in African studies with honors from Howard University. She completed further graduate studies at the University of Maryland, College Park, where she was awarded a Graduate Fellowship.

Brenda Randolph has published numerous articles in professional journals and bulletins. She currently serves as library media specialist in Montgomery County Public Schools, Maryland.

Michal L. LeVasseur

Michal LeVasseur is an educational consultant in the field of geography. She is an adjunct professor of geography at the University of Alabama, Birmingham, and serves with the Alabama Geographic Alliance. Her undergraduate and graduate work are in the fields of anthropology (B.A.), geography (M.A.), and science education (Ph.D.).

Dr. LeVasseur's specialization has moved increasingly into the area of geography education. In 1996, she served as Director of the National Geographic Society's Summer Geography Workshop. As an educational consultant, she has worked with the National Geographic Society as well as with schools to develop programs and curriculum for geography.

Special Program Consultant
Yvonne S. Gentzler, Ph.D.
School of Education
University of Idaho
Moscow, Idaho

Content Consultant on Africa
Barbara Brown
Africa Studies Center
Boston University
Boston, Massachusetts

Content Consultant on North Africa
Laurence Michalak
Center for Middle East Studies
University of California
Berkeley, California

PRENTICE HALL
Simon & Schuster Education Group
A VIACOM COMPANY

Upper Saddle River, New Jersey
Needham, Massachusetts

ISBN 0-13-433685-2

1 2 3 4 5 6 7 8 9 10   01 00 99 98 97

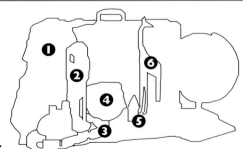

On the Cover
1. West African batik fabric
2. West African ebony statue of a hunter
3. Cowrie shell belt
4. African mask
5. Brass model of a traditional African dwelling
6. Wood carving of a giraffe

Content Consultants for the World Explorer Program

Teacher Advisory Board

The World Explorer Team

TABLE OF CONTENTS

AFRICA

1

OF SPECIAL INTEREST

A hands-on, active approach to practicing and applying key social studies skills

Engaging, step-by-step activities for exploring important topics in Africa

High-interest selections written by African authors that highlight values

MAPS

CHARTS, GRAPHS, AND TABLES

Activating Prior Knowledge

Three sets of reading strategies are introduced on pages viii and ix. Before students read the strategies, use questions like these to prompt a discussion about reading:

- Before you read, what do you do to help you read better?

- How do you figure out the meaning of what you read?

- Do you take a different approach to different kinds of reading, such as a paperback novel or your math textbook?

Discussion of their answers will help students become aware of their own reading processes.

Introducing the Strategies

Point out to students that reading is a process. If students are conscious of their process, they can improve their reading. Point out that there are three sets of reading strategies: **Before You Read, While You Read,** and **After You Read.** Explain that these are the behaviors that good readers exhibit. As students practice these strategies, they too will increase their reading fluency and comprehension.

Be sure to reinforce the idea that students might use several of these strategies at the same time, or they might go back and forth among them. There is no set order for applying them.

READ ACTIVELY

How can I get the most out of my social studies book? **How does my reading relate to my world? Answering questions like these means that you are an active reader, an involved reader. As an active reader, you are in charge of the reading situation!**

The following strategies tell how to think and read as an active reader. You don't need to use all of these strategies all the time. Feel free to choose the ones that work best in each reading situation. You might use several at a time, or you might go back and forth among them. They can be used in any order.

BEFORE YOU READ

Give yourself a purpose

The sections in this book begin with a list called "Questions to Explore." These questions focus on key ideas presented in the section. They give you a purpose for reading. You can create your own purpose by asking questions like these: How does the topic relate to your life? How might you use what you learn at school or at home?

Preview

To preview a reading selection, first read its title. Then look at the pictures and read the captions. Also read any headings in the selection. Then ask yourself: What is the reading selection about? What do the pictures and headings tell about the selection?

Reach into your background

What do you already know about the topic of the selection? How can you use what you know to help you understand what you are going to read?

Ask questions

Suppose you are reading about the continent of South America. Some questions you might ask are: Where is South America? What countries are found there? Why are some of the countries large and others small? Asking questions like these can help you gather evidence and gain knowledge.

Predict

As you read, make a prediction about what will happen and why. Or predict how one fact might affect another fact. Suppose you are reading about South America's climate. You might make a prediction about how the climate affects where people live. You can change your mind as you gain new information.

Connect

Connect your reading to your own life. Are the people discussed in the selection like you or someone you know? What would you do in similar situations? Connect your reading to something you have already read. Suppose you have already read about the ancient Greeks. Now you are reading about the ancient Romans. How are they alike? How are they different?

Visualize

What would places, people, and events look like in a movie or a picture? As you read about India, you could visualize the country's heavy rains. What do they look like? How do they sound? As you read about geography, you could visualize a volcanic eruption.

Respond

Talk about what you have read. What did you think? Share your ideas with your classmates.

Assess yourself

What did you find out? Were your predictions on target? Did you find answers to your questions?

Follow up

Show what you know. Use what you have learned to do a project. When you do projects, you continue to learn.

Point out to students that the sections in this book have a Before You Read feature. Each one is enclosed in a yellow box (see page 9 for an example). It includes Reach Into Your Background, which helps students think about what they already know so that they can apply their prior knowledge to what they're reading. Before You Read also includes Questions to Explore, which focus on the main ideas in the section. Each Question to Explore relates to one of the Guiding Questions for the book. See the list of Guiding Questions on the following page.

Students will also find Read Actively margin notes in every section. Encourage them to respond to these prompts to reinforce their active reading process.

Supporting English Language Learners

Preview and predict Suggest that students look at the title, headings, maps, charts, and photos to guess what the section is about.

Ask questions Tell students that every fact an author writes has a purpose. Have them question the purpose of details as they read them. As they find answers and discover meaning, they can formulate new, deeper questions.

Visualize Have students think how the places they read about would affect their senses. What would it smell like there? What would they see and hear and feel?

Assess Have students review their predictions and see how well they did. What helped them make good predictions?

Introducing the Guiding Questions

This book was developed around four Guiding Questions about Africa. They appear on the reduced Student Edition page to the right. The Guiding Questions are intended as an organizational focus for the book. All of the chapter content, activities, questions, and assessments relate to the Guiding Questions, which act as a kind of umbrella under which all of the material falls. You may wish to add your own Guiding Questions to the list in order to tailor them to your particular course. Or, as a group activity, you may want to ask your class to develop its own Guiding Question.

Ask a volunteer to read the Guiding Questions out loud to the class. These questions will guide students as they learn about Africa.

Introducing the Project Preview

The projects for this book are designed to provide students with hands-on involvement in the content area. On the reduced Student Edition page to the right, students are introduced to the projects. Complete information about them appears on pages 176–177. You may assign projects as cooperative activities, whole class projects, or individual projects. Each project relates to at least one of the Guiding Questions.

The name Africa probably came from the Latin word *aprica,* meaning "sunny." In much of Africa, the sun does shine brightly. It warms cocoa plantations, bakes the deserts, bounces off skyscrapers, and melts the snow on mountaintops. Each morning, the African sunrise awakens one eighth of the world's population in fifty countries. In the chapters that follow, you'll spend the day with some of them.

Guiding Questions

The readings and activities in this book will help you discover answers to these Guiding Questions.

- What are the main physical features of Africa?
- What factors have shaped Africa's cultures?
- Why have many Africans been moving to cities in recent years?
- What connections do African nations have with the United States and the world?
- What factors influence the ways in which Africans make a living?

Project Preview

You can also discover answers to the Guiding Questions by working on projects. Preview the following projects and choose one that you might like to do. For more details, see page 176.

Africa on Stage Create a play about growing up in an African country. Pick out characters, plan a plot, write the script, and present your play for an audience.

Africa in Art Prepare a mini-museum of traditional African mask-making. Research different kinds of masks, how they are made, and what they mean.

Africa 2000 What will life in Africa be like in the twenty-first century? Hold a conference with speakers, ethnic refreshments, and press coverage.

Resource Directory

Teaching Resources

Book Projects, in the Activities and Projects booklet, provides students with directions on how to complete one of the projects described on these two pages. You may wish to assign or have students choose a project at the beginning of the course.

Program Resources

Long-Term Integrated Projects booklet, in the Program Resources Binder, provides opportunities for students to make comparisons across regions through a variety of long-term projects. You may wish to assign or have students choose a project at the beginning of the course.

Left, South African children at school. Above left, a desert-dwelling Tuareg mother and child. Right, twins at a ceremony in Ghana.

EXPLORER'S JOURNAL

A journal can be your personal book of discovery. As you explore Africa, you can use your journal to keep track of the things you learn and do. You can also record thoughts about your journey. For your first entry, write your thoughts on where in Africa you would like to go and what you would want to see there.

Invite students to discuss the three photographs. Use them as a prompt for discussion of what students know about Africa. You may want to begin a K-W-L chart on the board with the headings What We Know About Africa, What We Want to Know About Africa, and What We Learned About Africa. Have students fill in the first column with several things they agree they already know. Then ask them to brainstorm what they would like to know about Africa to add to the second column. Students can fill in the third column as they work through the text.

Using the Explorer's Journal

Have students begin their Explorer's Journal as the paragraph on the student book page suggests. If at all possible, encourage students to use a separate small notebook for their Explorer's Journal entries. They can add to this Journal as they learn more about Africa.

📁 **Teacher's Flexible Planning Guide** includes a guide to the Prentice Hall World Explorer program, a skills correlation, and a variety of pacing charts for different course configurations. You may wish to refer to the guide as you plan your instruction.

💿 **Resource Pro™ CD-ROM** allows you to create customized lesson plans and print all Teaching Resources and Program Resources, plus the Computer Test Bank, directly from the CD-ROM.

Lesson Objectives

❶ Describe the size and relative location of Africa.

❷ Identify some key physical features of Africa.

❸ Summarize the effect of desertification on African lands and peoples.

Lesson Plan

1 Engage

Warm-Up Activity

Show students a U.S. weather map from a daily newspaper. Ask them to describe the weather in various parts of the country. As the class recognizes the climate variations among different regions of the country, discuss other ways in which these regions are different or the same.

Activating Prior Knowledge

Building on the previous discussion, ask students what characteristics Africa may share with the United States. What are some issues facing regions of the United States that may also face parts of Africa?

Answers to ...

LOCATION

The Atlantic Ocean lies between Africa and the United States. Students may say that countries near the Equator probably have hot climates. Students may suggest that Africa's climates are hotter than those of the United States.

REGIONS

Africa is about three times larger than the United States.

ACTIVITY ATLAS

DISCOVERY ACTIVITIES ABOUT

Africa

Learning about Africa means being an explorer and a geographer. No explorer would start out without first checking some facts. Begin by exploring the maps of Africa on the following pages.

Relative Location

UNITED STATES

ATLANTIC OCEAN

Tropic of Cancer

AFRICA

Equator

Tropic of Capricorn

LOCATION

1. Explore Africa's Location One of the first questions a geographer asks about a place is "Where is it?" Use the map to describe Africa's location relative to the United States. What ocean lies between Africa and the United States? Note that the Equator extends through Africa. What role might the Equator play in the climates of nearby countries? How do you think climates of the United States might differ from the climates of Africa?

REGIONS

2. Explore Africa's Size How big is Africa compared to the United States? On a separate sheet of paper, trace the map of the United States and cut it out. How many times can you fit it inside the map of Africa?

Relative Size

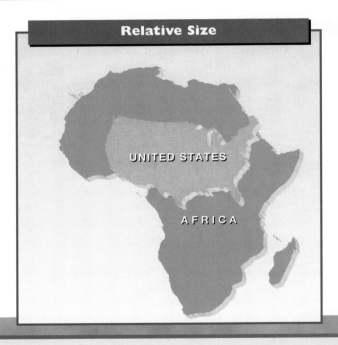

UNITED STATES

AFRICA

2   **AFRICA**

Resource Directory

Teaching Resources

Activity Atlas in the Activities and Projects booklet, pp. 3–5, provides a structure that helps students complete the activities in the Africa Activity Atlas and encourages discovery learning.

3. Find Africa's Lakes There are several large lakes in Africa. Name four of them. What countries do they border? In what part of the continent do you find the most lakes?

4. Predict How Location Affects Economic Wealth Fifteen African nations are landlocked. That is, they do not border any ocean. Find them on the map. Landlocked nations are often poor. How do you think a landlocked location might affect a nation's economy?

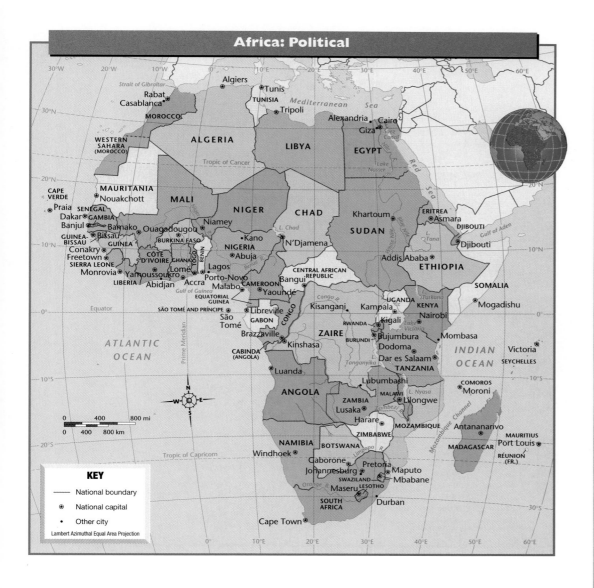

Africa: Political

KEY

— National boundary
⊛ National capital
• Other city

Lambert Azimuthal Equal Area Projection

2 Explore

Have students read the Activity Atlas carefully. Suggest that they create African Explorers' Logs for recording answers to text questions.

3 Teach

Ask students to create a fact sheet for Africa. Headings should include *Location*, *Major Physical Features*, *Key Political Elements*, and *Challenges*.

4 Assess

Fact sheets should note Africa's location between the Atlantic and Indian oceans and its nearness to the Equator. They should also note that the continent is mostly covered by a huge plateau with narrow coastal plains, limited vegetation, rivers, and some rain forests. The continent faces challenges such as desertification and poverty.

Answers to . . .

PLACE

Possible answer: Lake Victoria borders Kenya, Uganda, and Tanzania. Lake Tanganyika borders Tanzania, Zambia, Zaire, and Burundi. Lake Nyasa borders Tanzania, Mozambique, and Malawi. Lake Chad borders Niger, Chad, Cameroon, and Nigeria. Most lakes are in southeastern Africa.

MOVEMENT

A landlocked nation lacks access to oceans, which makes it more difficult and costly to transport goods in and out of the nation.

Practice in the Themes of Geography

Ask students to use the physical map and the natural vegetation map of Africa to find answers to the following questions concerning the five themes of geography.

Location Challenge students to name the major bodies of water that surround Africa (Indian Ocean, Atlantic Ocean, Mediterranean Sea, Red Sea).

Place Prompt students to locate the Serengeti Plain and Lake Victoria on the map. Then ask students to complete the following sentence: *The Serengeti Plain and Lake Victoria are both in the nation of _____*. (Tanzania)

Regions Ask students to name some African nations that have tropical rain forests. (Answers may include Côte d'Ivoire, Ghana, Cameroon, Gabon, Congo, and Zaire.)

Movement Challenge students to identify the key physical feature that makes it difficult for people from Niger, Mali, and Chad to reach the Mediterranean Sea (the Sahara Desert).

Interaction Point out the Suez Canal to students, explaining that it was completed in 1869. Ask students how the canal might affect the economies of the African nations along the Red Sea. (Students should note that the canal gives these nations access to Mediterranean shipping routes.)

Answers to ...

PLACE

The plateau is higher in the southeast.

PLACE

5. Investigate Africa's Physical Features

Parts of Africa's coasts have very narrow strips of flat plains. Cliffs rise steeply from these plains. The interior is high and somewhat flat, forming a huge plateau. Find Southern Africa on the map below. It extends south of 10°S. The cliffs arise where the dark green areas meet the light green areas. Trace these cliffs with your finger. Note that in some places they extend nearly along the coast. Is Africa's plateau higher in the western part of the continent or the southeastern part?

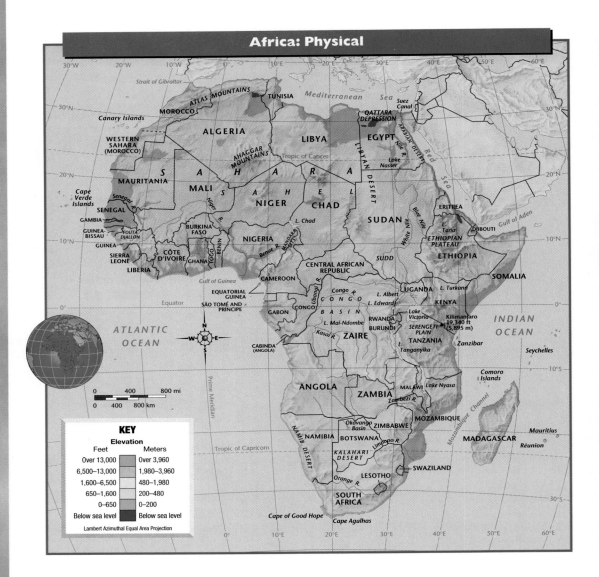

Africa: Physical

KEY
Elevation

Feet	Meters
Over 13,000	Over 3,960
6,500–13,000	1,980–3,960
1,600–6,500	480–1,980
650–1,600	200–480
0–650	0–200
Below sea level	Below sea level

Lambert Azimuthal Equal Area Projection

REGIONS

6. Find Geo Cleo Geo Cleo has gone off on one of her flying trips. This time she's gone to Africa, but she hasn't told anyone exactly where in Africa she's traveling. Read the messages Geo Cleo radioed from her plane. Then use the map below and the maps on the two previous pages to locate the city described in each message.

A. *I'm in a region of tall grasses and few trees, or a savanna. I've landed in a city in Ethiopia near 10°N and 40°E.*

B. *Not too many places in Africa have Mediterranean vegetation. And I'm not even anywhere near the Mediterranean Sea! I am flying over a city on a very narrow coastal plain. The cliffs here are really steep.*

C. *Today, I flew above tropical rain forests growing right along the Equator. Going north, I saw these magnificent forests change into open grasslands, or savanna. I've just landed in a city in the savanna region north of where the Benue River meets the Niger River.*

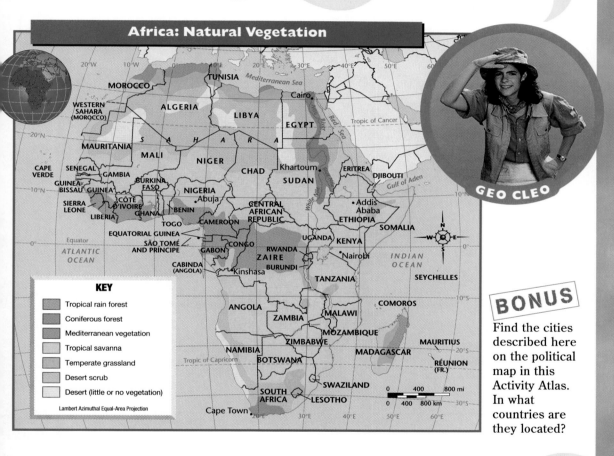

Africa: Natural Vegetation

GEO CLEO

KEY
- Tropical rain forest
- Coniferous forest
- Mediterranean vegetation
- Tropical savanna
- Temperate grassland
- Desert scrub
- Desert (little or no vegetation)

Lambert Azimuthal Equal-Area Projection

BONUS

Find the cities described here on the political map in this Activity Atlas. In what countries are they located?

AFRICA **5**

Background

Biography

Sir Henry Morton Stanley (1841–1904) During the 1800s, European interest in Africa's natural resources grew. A number of European explorers went to Africa to map the continent and assess how Europeans could benefit from Africa's resources. Henry Morton Stanley remains one of the best known of these explorers. Stanley first visited Africa in 1866 as a journalist. He had been hired to find the famous explorer Dr. David Livingstone, who had vanished somewhere in Africa's interior. Stanley succeeded, and upon finding Livingstone near Lake Tanganyika, he uttered the famous greeting, "Dr. Livingstone, I presume." Stanley spent many years exploring and mapping central Africa in the service of British and Belgian interests. Stanley wrote accounts of his discovery of the source and the path of the Congo River as well as several other books about his Central African expeditions.

Answers to . . .

REGIONS AND BONUS

A. Addis Ababa, Ethiopia
B. Cape Town, South Africa
C. Abuja, Nigeria

Interdisciplinary Connections

Art Organize students into groups and assign each group a region of Africa to study. You may define regions by climate, physical features, or political boundaries. Challenge each group to generate a list of their region's physical features. Then have groups design a home in which local people might live. Tell students to consider climate, landforms, available materials, and the need for protection from natural hazards. Invite groups to draw and then build models of their homes. Work as a whole class to compare and contrast the different homes. *Visual, English Language Learner*

INTERACTION

7. Estimate the Impact of Desertification Desertification means a loss of vegetation. In African lands bordering the Sahara, desertification is turning grasslands into deserts. A long period of little or no rainfall may cause desertification. People may cause it, too, by allowing livestock to overgraze the savanna and by cutting trees for firewood. The map on this page shows the spread of desertification in Africa from 1970 to the present. Which countries were affected most by the desertification? How would the loss of all vegetation, including farm crops, affect the people in these countries?

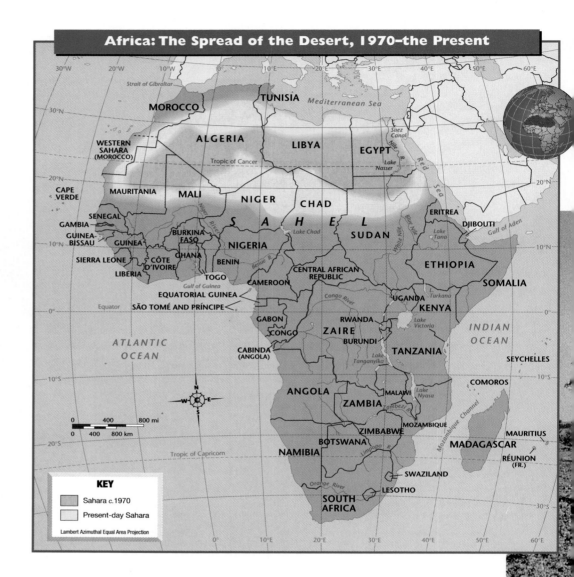

Africa: The Spread of the Desert, 1970–the Present

KEY
- Sahara c.1970
- Present-day Sahara

Lambert Azimuthal Equal Area Projection

Answers to ...

INTERACTION

Algeria, Libya, Egypt, Sudan, Chad, Niger, Mali, Mauritania, Western Sahara, and Morocco all have been affected by desertification. The loss of all vegetation would destroy farmers' and herders' livelihoods and could lead to depopulation and food shortages.

REGIONS

8. Analyze Rainfall in the Sahel The Sahel is a region in Africa just south of the Sahara. The Sahel has been especially affected by desertification. The graph below shows rainfall in Niger, a country partly in the Sahel. What general trend do you see in Niger's rainfall?

In which year did the heaviest rainfall occur? Which year has had the least rainfall? What effect do you think the amount of rainfall has had on desertification?

Rainfall Variation in the Sahel

▼ Very little rain falls in the Sahel.

7

Physical Geography

To help you plan instruction, the chart below shows how teaching resources correspond to chapter content. Use the resources to vary instruction, add activities, or plan block schedules. Where appropriate, resources have suggested time allotments for students. Time allotments are approximate.

Managing Time and Instruction

	Africa Teaching Resources Binder		World Explorer Program Resources Binder	
	Resource	**mins.**	**Resource**	**mins.**
SECTION 1 Land and Water	**Chapter and Section Support** Reproducible Lesson Plan, p. 4		**Outline Maps** The Middle East and North Africa:	
	S Guided Reading and Review, p. 5	20	Physical, p. 28	20
	S Section Quiz, p. 6	25	Africa South of the Sahara: Physical, p. 32	20
			Nystrom Desk Atlas	
			T **Primary Sources and Literature**	
			Readings	40
			Writing Process Handbook	
			Writing an Introduction, p. 29	25
SKILLS ACTIVITY Interpreting Diagrams	**Social Studies and Geography Skills,** Reading a Diagram, p. 56	30		
SECTION 2 Climate and Vegetation	**Chapter and Section Support** Reproducible Lesson Plan, p. 7		**Outline Maps** The Middle East and North Africa:	
	S Guided Reading and Review, p. 8	20	Physical, p. 28	20
	S Section Quiz, p. 9	25	Africa South of the Sahara: Physical, p. 32	20
	Critical Thinking Activity, p. 17	30	**Environmental and Global Issues**	
	Social Studies and Geography Skills,		Topic: Health, pp. 8–13	30
	Reading a Bar Graph, p. 53	30		
	Reading a Line Graph, p. 54	30		
SECTION 3 Natural Resources	**Chapter and Section Support** Reproducible Lesson Plan, p. 10		**Outline Maps** North Africa: Political, p. 31	20
	S Guided Reading and Review, p. 11	20	Africa South of the Sahara: Political, p. 33	20
	S Section Quiz, p. 12	25	**Environmental and Global Issues**	
	S Vocabulary, p. 14	20	Topic: The Global Economy, pp. 20–24	30
	Reteaching, p. 15	25		
	Enrichment, p. 16	25		
	S Chapter Summary, p. 13	15		
	Tests Forms A and B Chapter Tests, pp. 2–7	40		

Block Scheduling Program Support

Block Scheduling Folder
PROGRAM TEACHING RESOURCES

Activities and Projects

Interdisciplinary Links

Resource Pro™ CD-ROM

Media and Technology

Media and Technology

Resource	mins.
🔲 🖸 ⓢ World Video Explorer	20
🖸 Planet Earth CD-ROM	20
🔲 Color Transparencies 49, 50, 92, 93	20
🖸 Planet Earth CD-ROM	20
🔲 Color Transparencies 6, 8, 9, 11, 71	20
🔲 Color Transparencies 9, 10, 15, 17	20
🎧 ⓢ Guided Reading Audiotapes	20
🔲 Color Transparency 174	
(Graphic organizer table template)	20
🖸 The Writer's Solution CD-ROM	30
🖥 Computer Test Bank	30

T **Teaming Opportunity**
This resource is especially well-suited for teaching teams.

S **Spanish**
This resource is also in Spanish support.

🖸 **CD-ROM**

🖸 **Laserdisc**

🔲 **Transparency**

🖥 **Software**

🔲 **Videotape**

🎧 **Audiotape**

Assessment Opportunities

From Guiding Questions to Assessment   A series of Guiding Questions serves as an organizing framework for this book. The Guiding Questions that relate to this chapter are listed below. Section Reviews and Section Quizzes provide opportunities for assessing students' insights into these Guiding Questions. Additional assessments are listed below.

GUIDING QUESTIONS

- *What are the main physical features of Africa?*
- *What factors influence the ways in which Africans make a living?*

ASSESSMENTS

Section 1

Students should be able to create a web of Africa's major landforms.

▶ **RUBRIC**   See the Assessment booklet for a rubric on assessing graphic organizers.

Section 2

Students should be able to write an explanation of how climate and vegetation affect the way Africans make a living.

▶ **RUBRIC**   See the Assessment booklet for a rubric on assessing cause-and-effect statements.

Section 3

Students should be able to create a map that shows Africa's major natural resources.

▶ **RUBRIC**   See the Assessment booklet for a rubric on assessing a map produced by a student.

Activities and Projects

Mental Mapping

Facing Asia In the classroom, orient students so that they stand facing north. If you wish, use a compass to verify the direction.

Have students extend their left arms and point. Tell them they are pointing west toward the Pacific Ocean. Now have them extend their right arms and point. Tell them that they are pointing east, toward the Atlantic Ocean. Have students point straight ahead. Now they are pointing north to Canada.

Have students turn and point in the opposite direction. Ask students what direction they are pointing. (south) Ask them what countries they are facing in the south. (Mexico, countries of Central and South America) Now have students carefully turn two steps to the left. Tell them they are facing southeast, in the general direction of Africa.

Links to Current Events

African News Coverage As you teach this chapter, have students keep a log of African countries covered in the news media. When students see or hear coverage of an African country, they write the name of that country in their logs with a brief note about the topic of the news story.

Encourage students to look for television, radio, newspaper, and magazine coverage of Africa. At the end of the time period, have students bring in their logs. As a class activity, review with students the countries that appeared in their logs most often and the topics covered. Have students speculate on why these African countries appeared in news coverage more than others.

Hands-On Activities

Developing a Sense of Location Have students use a globe to locate the continent of Africa. Point out that Africa includes many countries. Ask students to name some. Be sure their list includes Egypt, Algeria, Nigeria, Ghana, Mali, Ethiopia, Tanzania, Kenya, Zaire, and South Africa. Ask students to locate each of the countries they mention on the globe.

Have students find the Equator, the Tropic of Cancer, and the Tropic of Capricorn. Help students see that most of Africa lies in the tropical latitudes. Have students find other parts of the world in the tropical latitudes. Ask what kind of climate and vegetation students would expect to find in these latitudes.

Cut-Out Map Hang a sheet of poster board on the wall. Use an overhead projector to project an outline map of Africa on the poster board. Have students trace the outline of Africa and make a cut-out map. The cut-out can serve as the base for students to make an illustrated map of the physical geography of East Africa. *English Language Learners*

Rainfall The amount of rainfall varies greatly across most of Africa. This variation affects the vegetation and people of Africa. The Gulf of Guinea, the western coast near the Equator, and eastern Madagascar all receive more than 80 inches of rain a year. The wettest place in Africa is western

Cameroon, which receives more than 400 inches of rain a year. Africa also has desert regions, however. The Sahara, Kalahari, and Namib deserts all receive less than 6 inches of rain in an average year. Have students make a wall chart or graph comparing these quantities of rain and locating the regions that receive these extremes on a map of Africa. *Basic*

Fantastic Food Fair Staple crops of Africa include corn, rice, sweet potatoes, and peanuts. Some of these foods were taken to Africa by Europeans who originally brought them from South America. Others, such as peanuts, were brought to North America by Africans. Ask students to use

library resources to trace the origin of these foods. Students' research findings can be presented as captions for an exhibit of corn, rice, sweet potatoes, peanuts, and products made from these foods. *Average*

Desertification The Sahara desert is growing larger, with a disastrous effect on the lives of the people who live along its edges. Invite students to research the process of desertification. Have them find out what causes a desert to grow and what governments, conservation groups, and others are doing to prevent the growth of the Sahara and other deserts. *Challenging*

F.Y.I.

This page can help you extend your own and students' understanding of the concepts in this chapter. You may want to browse through some of the suggestions in the **Bibliography. Interdisciplinary Links** can connect social studies understandings to areas elsewhere in the curriculum through the use of other Prentice Hall products. **National Geography Standards** reflected specifically in this chapter are listed for your convenience. Some hints about appropriate **Internet Access** are also provided. **School to Careers** provides insights into the practical uses of some of the concepts in this chapter as they might pertain to various careers.

BIBLIOGRAPHY

FOR THE TEACHER

Africa. National Geographic, 1991. Videocassette.

Brandenburg, Jim. *Sand and Fog: Adventures in Southern Africa.* Walker, 1994.

The Dorling Kindersley Geography of the World. Dorling Kindersley, 1996.

Halliburton, Warren J. *African Landscapes.* Crestwood, 1993.

Kreikemeir, Gregory Scott. *Come with Me to Africa: A Photographic Journey.* Golden, 1994.

FOR THE STUDENT

Easy
Kessler, Cristina. *All the King's Animals: The Return of Endangered Wildlife to Swaziland.* Boyds, 1995.

Average
Goodsmith, Lauren. *The Children of Mauritania: Days in the Desert and by the River Shore.* Carolrhoda, 1993.

Waterlow, Julia. *The Nile.* Raintree, 1993.

Challenging
Campbell, Eric. *The Year of the Leopard Song.* Harcourt Brace Jovanovich, 1992.

LITERATURE CONNECTION

Campbell, Eric. *The Place of Lions.* Harcourt Brace Jovanovich, 1991.

Weir, Bob and Wendy. *Panther Dream: A Story of the African Rainforest.* Hyperion, 1991.

INTERDISCIPLINARY LINKS

Subject	Theme: Place
MATH	Middle Grades Math: Tools for Success Course 1, Lesson 1-1, **Making Frequency Tables**
SCIENCE	Prentice Hall Science *Ecology: Earth's Living Resources,* Lesson 3-4, **Grassland Biomes,** Lesson 3-5, **Desert Biomes,** Gazette, **What Became of Africa's Animals?**

NATIONAL GEOGRAPHY STANDARDS

Students explore the 18 National Geography Standards throughout *Africa.* Chapter 1, however, concentrates on investigating the following standards: 1, 3, 4, 5, 7, 8, 11, 14, 15, 16, 18. For a complete list of the standards, see the *Teacher's Flexible Planning Guide.*

SCHOOL TO CAREERS

In Chapter 1, Africa: Physical Geography, students learn about the land, climate, vegetation, and natural resources of Africa. Additionally, they address the skill of interpreting diagrams. Understanding geography can help students prepare for careers in many fields such as history, geography, geology, archaeology, urban planning, and so on.

Interpreting diagrams is a skill particularly useful for engineers, architects, mechanics, builders, and others. The curriculum presented in this book, as in all eight titles of Prentice Hall's *World Explorer* program, is designed to prepare students not only for careers but also for good citizenship—of the world as well as of this country.

INTERNET ACCESS

Many social studies teachers and students use Internet browsers, or search engines, to investigate particular topics. For the best results, use narrow rather than broad topics. Try these for Chapter 1: Great Rift Valley, Mount Kilimanjaro, Congo River, Sahara Desert. Finding age-appropriate sites is an important consideration when using the Internet. For links to age-appropriate sites in world studies and geography, visit the Prentice Hall Home Page at: **http://www.phschool.com**

AFRICA
Physical Geography

Connecting to the Guiding Questions

As students complete this chapter, they will focus on the geography of the African continent. Content in this chapter corresponds to the following Guiding Questions:

- What are the main physical features of Africa?

- What factors influence the ways in which Africans make a living?

Using the Map Activities

Suggest that students find the names of bodies of water and other physical features in each of the regions.

- Central and Southern Africa is the largest region, and East Africa is the smallest. The Nile flows through North Africa and East Africa; the Congo and Zambezi through Central and Southern Africa; and the Niger through West Africa.

Heterogeneous Groups

The following Teacher's Edition strategies are suitable for heterogeneous groups.

SECTION 1
Land and Water

SECTION 2
Climate and Vegetation

SECTION 3
Natural Resources

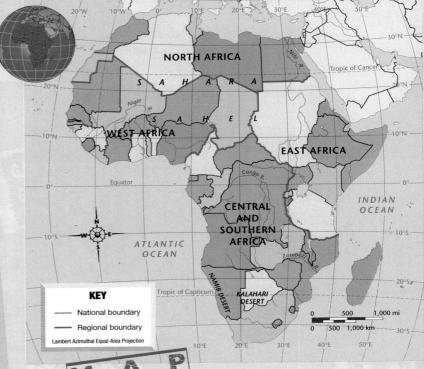

KEY
— National boundary
— Regional boundary
Lambert Azimuthal Equal-Area Projection

MAP ACTIVITIES

This map shows four regions of Africa. Each region contains many different landforms and climates. Start exploring the geography of Africa by doing the following activities:

Study the map
What region of Africa is the largest? Which is the smallest? Through what regions do the major rivers flow?

Consider the geography
Notice that some African nations are much larger than others. As you read this chapter, think about how landforms and climate might have affected the political boundaries of Africa.

Resource Directory

Media and Technology

 Journey Over Africa, from the World Video Explorer, introduces students to the major landforms and climate regions of Africa.

 Geography: The Great Rift Valley, from the World Video Explorer, enhances students' understanding of the geographic factors that make the Great Rift Valley an important location for archaeological study.

Chapter 2

Chapter 3

Land and Water

BEFORE YOU READ

Reach Into Your Background

Think about the state in which you live. What different landforms are in your state? Are there any mountains or valleys? How do these landforms affect your daily life?

Questions to Explore

1. Where is Africa located?
2. What are Africa's most important landforms?

Key Terms

plateau
elevation
escarpment
rift

cataract
silt
fertile
tributary

Key Places

Sahara
Great Rift Valley
Nile River
Congo River
Niger River
Zambezi River

Scientists believe that over 200 million years ago, dinosaurs easily walked from the continent of Africa to the continent of South America. That's because Africa and South America were connected. Find Africa on the world map in the atlas at the back of this book. As you can see, it would be pretty hard to walk from Africa to South America today. How did Africa and South America become separated? About 190 million years ago, forces within the Earth caused South America and Africa to move apart, forming the southern part of the Atlantic Ocean.

The Four Regions of Africa

Africa can be divided into four regions: (1) North, (2) West, (3) East, and (4) Central and Southern. Each of these regions contains many different climates and landforms.

North Africa is marked by rocky mountains and seemingly endless stretches of the world's largest desert, the Sahara. Find the Sahara, which is almost the size of the United States, on the physical map in the Activity Atlas. What countries include part of the Sahara?

▼ Scientists found the bones of this type of dinosaur on more than one continent. This clue made them suspect the continents were once connected.

Teaching Resources

📁 **Reproducible Lesson Plan** in the Chapter and Section Resources booklet, p. 4, provides a summary of the section lesson.

📁 **Guided Reading and Review** in the Chapter and Section Resources booklet, p. 5, provides a structure for mastering key concepts and reviewing key terms in the section. Available in Spanish in the Spanish Chapter and Section Resources booklet, p. 4.

Program Resources

📁 Material in the **Primary Sources and Literature Readings** booklet extends content with a selection from the region under study.

📁 **Outline Maps** The Middle East and North Africa: Physical, p. 28; Africa South of the Sahara: Physical, p. 32

Lesson Objectives

1 Explain where Africa is located.

2 Describe climate zones and vegetation patterns found on the African continent.

3 Identify key geographic features and locate the major regions of Africa.

Lesson Plan

1 Engage

Warm-Up Activity

Give each student a ball of modeling clay (or demonstrate the following activity yourself). Mold the clay inside a pie plate or a flat-bottomed bowl. Turn the resulting shape so that the flat side is on top. Explain that this shape approximates the contours of the African continent. Ask students what they can learn about Africa's lands from studying its contours. For example, how might water flow?

Activating Prior Knowledge

Have students read Reach Into Your Background in the Before You Read box. Ask students to share with the class what they know about the geography of Africa. If necessary, prompt students with questions about rivers, mountains, deserts, and lakes. Record students' responses on the board.

2 Explore

Help students understand Africa's geography by asking them to think about the following questions as they read the section: How might geographic factors influence how people live in different parts of Africa? In what ways might travel be difficult in Africa? Why are rivers an important physical feature?

3 Teach

Have students create a table with four side labels: *North, West, East, Central and Southern.* Top labels should be landforms such as *Plateaus, Rivers,* and *Mountains.* Students should check boxes to correlate side and top categories. Ask students to use their completed tables to write a summary of Africa's main geographic features. This activity should take about 30 minutes.

4 Assess

See the answers to the Section Review. Completed tables can also be an assessment.

Acceptable tables include valid top and side labels.

Commendable tables correctly correlate features and regions.

Outstanding tables include summary statements that outline the variety of landforms in Africa.

Answers to ...
A COASTAL PLAIN IN WEST AFRICA

Students may say that people farm, fish, or work in the tourism industry.

West Africa, the continent's most populated region, consists mostly of grasslands. The soil in the grasslands is good for farming. Find West Africa on the map at the beginning of the chapter. What geographic features border this region to the north and south?

East Africa contains many mountains, and **plateaus,** large raised areas of mostly level land. The east also has areas of grasslands and hills. Find East Africa on the map at the beginning of this chapter. What East African countries have sea coasts?

Much of Central and Southern Africa is flat or rolling grassland. The region also contains thick rain forests, mountains, and swamps. The Namib (NAHM eeb) Desert of the country of Namibia and the Kalahari (kal uh HAHR ee) Desert of Botswana are in this region.

Africa's Major Landforms

Africa can be described as an upside-down pie. If you were to slice Africa in half from east to west, you would see that much of the continent is a plateau that drops off sharply near the sea.

The Plateau Continent Africa is often called the "plateau continent." That is because the elevation of much of the land area is high. **Elevation** is the height of land above sea level.

▼ In the Atlas Mountains of Morocco (below), some people adapt to steep slopes by building houses along the sides of the mountains. Some people living in the lush rain forests of Zaire (inset, upper left) take advantage of the tropical vegetation by gathering honey from bees' nests in the trees.

Resource Directory

Program Resources

Nystrom Desk Atlas

Media and Technology

 Color Transparencies 49, 50, 92, 93

Planet Earth CD-ROM includes satellite images and physical maps of Africa that allow students to view the countries that make up the region, plus World Wonders, Natural: Victoria Falls; and Okavango Delta.

Most of Africa is plateaus and mountains. Africa's few plains lie mostly along its coasts, like this one at Cape Coast, Ghana. In fact, except for two basins in the Sahara, all of Africa's lowland areas lie within 500 miles (805 km) of the coast. **Critical Thinking** Based on this photograph, how do you think people living on Africa's coastal plains might make a living?

Background

Links Across Place

The Great Basin The Great Basin is a 1,200-mile-long (1,900-km) rift in the western United States. Canyons in the Great Basin were formed at thin spots in the Earth's crust. Huge blocks of land sank into the weaker area of crust. The Great Basin has been slowly expanding for millions of years, pushing parts of Utah and Nevada farther and farther apart. It is possible that in the distant future the Great Basin rift will widen so far that a piece of the North American continent breaks off.

Each of Africa's four regions has mountains. The highest are in East Africa. Mount Kilimanjaro is Africa's tallest mountain. It rises to a height of 19,341 feet (5,895 m).

Coastal Plains Edge the Continent Along much of Africa's coast is a strip of coastal plain. This strip of land is dry and sandy at some points. It is marshy and moist at other places. Look at the political map in the Activity Atlas. Find the city of Accra, in the West African country of Ghana (GAHN uh). Here, the coastal strip is only 16 miles (25 km) wide. It ends at a long **escarpment,** or steep cliff, that is about as high as a 100-story skyscraper.

The Great Rift Valley Mount Kilimanjaro is located on the edge of the Great Rift Valley in East Africa. The Great Rift Valley was formed millions of years ago, when the continents pulled apart. A **rift** is a deep trench. The rift that cuts through East Africa is 4,000 miles (6,400 km) long. Most of Africa's major lakes are located in or near the Great Rift Valley.

READ ACTIVELY

Connect What part of the United States contains a deep trench?

Africa's Rivers

Four large rivers carry water from the mountains of Africa's plateaus to the sea. They are the Nile, the Congo, the Zambezi, and the Niger (NI jur). The rivers are useful for traveling. But they are broken in places by **cataracts,** or rock-filled rapids. Cataracts make it impossible for ships to sail from Africa's interior to the sea.

SKILLS MINI LESSON

Previewing
To **introduce** the skill, tell students that previewing what they are about to read can help them develop some expectations about it. List some previewing techniques on the chalkboard: (1) Note the head and subheads. (2) Study the pictures and captions. (3) Relate the subject matter to your own life.

Have students **practice** and **apply** the skill using the text and pictures contained in the subsection *Africa's Rivers.* You might suggest that students develop a one- or two-sentence preview of the text similar to a capsule movie review. (A possible preview might read as follows: This section is about four of Africa's rivers—the Nile, Congo, Niger, and Zambezi. Victoria Falls on the Zambezi River reminds me of Niagara Falls.

Links Across Time

Early Egyptian Civilization
The Nile River was at the center of the ancient Egyptian civilization that flourished between 4000 B.C. and 2000 B.C. The river's floods enriched the soil and made farming possible. The proximity of land to the river also determined land values. Lands that flooded every year were worth more and taxed more heavily than those that flooded irregularly. One of the seasons was even called "flooding." Each year, the Egyptians would try to predict the flood's magnitude. They used special gauges called "nilometers" to measure the rising waters far upstream and then predict how high waters would rise downstream.

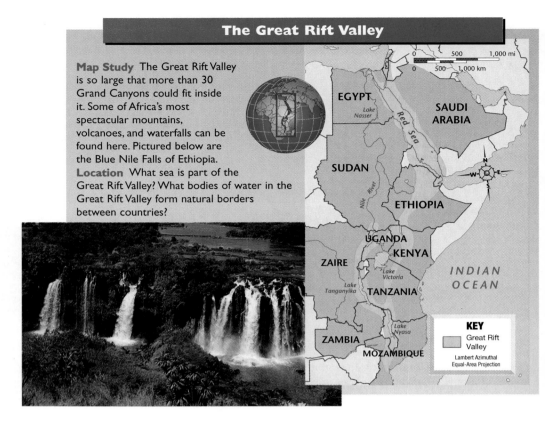

The Great Rift Valley

Map Study The Great Rift Valley is so large that more than 30 Grand Canyons could fit inside it. Some of Africa's most spectacular mountains, volcanoes, and waterfalls can be found here. Pictured below are the Blue Nile Falls of Ethiopia.
Location What sea is part of the Great Rift Valley? What bodies of water in the Great Rift Valley form natural borders between countries?

KEY
Great Rift Valley
Lambert Azimuthal Equal-Area Projection

L I N K S ACROSS THE WORLD

The Mississippi River Like the Nile in Africa, the Mississippi River in North America occasionally overflows its banks. It also leaves behind silt, which fertilizes the farmland along the river's banks.

The Nile River The Nile is the longest river in the world. Its length, more than 4,000 miles (6,400 km), is almost twice the width of the United States. The sources of the Nile are the White Nile in the country of Sudan and the Blue Nile in the highlands of Ethiopia. From these two sources, the river flows north and spills into the Mediterranean Sea.

People have farmed the land surrounding the Nile for thousands of years. At one time, the Nile flooded its banks regularly. Farmers planted their crops to match the flood cycle of the river. The floods provided water for the crops and left behind a layer of **silt,** which is the tiny bits of rock and dirt that build up on the bottoms of rivers and lakes. Silt helps make soil **fertile,** or able to grow a lot of plants.

About 30 years ago, Egypt's government built the Aswan High Dam to control the flooding of the Nile. As the water backed up behind the dam, it created Lake Nasser. Lake waters are channeled to water crops that grow in the desert. Water rushing through the dam makes electricity.

The Congo River The Congo River flows through the rain forest of the country of Zaire (zy IHR) in Central Africa. Look at the map at the beginning of the chapter. What ocean does the Congo River flow into? At 2,900 miles (4,667 km), the Congo is Africa's second-longest river. It is fed by hundreds of **tributaries,** or small rivers and streams that flow into the larger river. People in this region grow grains and cassava to make into porridge. Cassava is a starchy plant a little like a potato. They also catch fish in the Congo with basket traps.

The Niger River   Africa's third-longest river, the Niger, begins its journey in the West African country of Guinea (GIN ee). The river flows north and then bends south for 2,600 miles (4,180 km). The Niger provides water for farms in the river valley. People make a living catching fish in the river.

The Zambezi River   The fourth-longest of Africa's rivers, the Zambezi, is in southern Africa. It runs through or forms the borders of six countries: Angola, Zambia, Namibia, Botswana, Zimbabwe (zim BAHB way), and Mozambique (moh zam BEEK). The Zambezi is 2,200 miles (3,541 km) long. Boats can travel the river's upper section.

A River Without a Delta
The Congo River's current is so strong that the river does not form a delta as it flows into the ocean. Instead, the river has cut a deep, wide canyon beneath the sea for a distance of about 125 miles (200 km).

The Congo River Rushing to the Sea

The Congo River flows very fast—every second, the equivalent of more than 100 swimming pools full of water flows past its mouth.

Activity

Interdisciplinary Connections

Language Arts Provide students with some firsthand accounts of current and historical travel in Africa. Some current examples include *Come With Me to Africa,* by Gregory Scott Kreikemeir, and *From Cape Town to Cairo,* by David E. Duncan. As a historical example, you might choose selections from *Narrative of an Expedition to the Zambezi and Its Tributaries* (1865), by the Scottish explorer David Livingstone. Ask students what these accounts suggest about the difficulty of travel in Africa, both today and in the past. Have them cite specific examples in their responses.

Activity

Critical Thinking

Recognizing Cause and Effect *Suitable as either a whole class or an individual activity.* Begin a cause-and-effect chart on the chalkboard, creating a section for each river. Demonstrate the importance of Africa's rivers by inviting volunteers to add facts about each river and how it affects the land and people around it.

1. (a) large, raised area of mostly level land (b) the height of land above sea level (c) a steep cliff (d) a deep trench (e) rock-filled rapids (f) tiny bits of rock and dirt that build up on the bottoms of rivers and lakes (g) a type of soil that is able to grow a lot of plants (h) a small river or stream that flows into a larger river

2. (a) the world's largest desert, located in North Africa (b) a huge valley that was formed millions of years ago when the continents pulled apart (c) the longest river in the world (d) Africa's second-longest river (e) Africa's third-longest river (f) Africa's fourth-longest river

3. because the elevation of much of the land area is high

4. (a) People fish in the rivers. Rivers are also used for travel, irrigation, and creating electricity. (b) Cataracts make it impossible for ships to sail from Africa's interior to the sea.

5. Answers will vary. Students will probably conclude that more people would live in the area because they would have access to the resources necessary to establish permanent settlements.

6. Students should accurately locate several African landforms and give plausible reasons for visiting.

Waterfalls are a hazard for boats and ships.

Victoria Falls

The African name for Victoria Falls means "The Smoke That Thunders." Victoria Falls lies on the Zambezi River, which crosses 2,200 miles (3,540 km) and six countries. It is broken by many waterfalls. **Critical Thinking** Based on this photo, why do you think the Zambezi River is not used as a major trade route?

People have used the Zambezi's strong current to make electricity. About halfway to its outlet in the Indian Ocean, the Zambezi plunges into a canyon, creating Victoria Falls. People can sometimes see the mist and spray of the falls from up to 40 miles (65 km) away.

SECTION 1 REVIEW

1. Define (a) plateau, (b) elevation, (c) escarpment, (d) rift, (e) cataract, (f) silt, (g) fertile, (h) tributary.

2. Identify (a) Sahara, (b) Great Rift Valley, (c) Nile River, (d) Congo River, (e) Niger River, (f) Zambezi River.

3. Why is Africa called the "plateau continent"?

4. (a) How do people use the rivers of Africa? (b) What makes them difficult to use?

Critical Thinking

5. Drawing Conclusions Most of the people in North Africa live north of the Sahara near the Mediterranean Sea. If the Sahara were a grassland with rivers and forests, would this change where people in North African countries live? Why?

Activity

6. Writing to Learn List several landforms in Africa you would like to visit. Explain why you would like to go there and what you would do on your trip.

Resource Directory

Teaching Resources

Section Quiz in the Chapter and Section Resources booklet, p. 6, covers the main ideas and key terms in the section. Available in Spanish in the Spanish Chapter and Section Resources booklet, p. 5.

Climate and Vegetation

BEFORE YOU READ

Reach Into Your Background

Think about the climate where you live. What kind of weather do you have in the summer? What kind of weather do you have in the winter? What are the months when you have summer? What are the months when you have winter?

Questions to Explore

1. What types of climates and vegetation are found in Africa?
2. How do climate and vegetation affect how Africans make a living?

Key Terms
irrigate
oasis
savanna
nomad

Key Places
Sahel
Namib Desert
Kalahari Desert

A trip to Africa sounds like a great adventure. But packing for the trip might prove harder than you think. What would you pack for a two-week journey to Africa? As you read about Africa's climates and vegetation, see if you would add any items to your list.

What Influences Climate?

Look at the climate map on the following page. Find the Tropic of Cancer and the Tropic of Capricorn. As you can see, much of Africa lies between these two lines of latitude. This means that most of Africa is in a tropical climate region. Notice that the Equator runs through this midsection of the continent. These regions are usually hot.

Many parts of Africa are indeed hot. But much of Africa is not. That is because location near the Equator is not the only influence on climate. The climate of a place may depend on how close it is to large bodies of water. Major landforms also affect climate. So does the elevation of a place.

▼ If you visit Botswana during the rainy season, be prepared to get wet. Floods like this one, on the Okavango River Delta, are common.

Teaching Resources

 Reproducible Lesson Plan in the Chapter and Section Resources booklet, p. 7, provides a summary of the section lesson.

Guided Reading and Review in the Chapter and Section Resources booklet, p. 8, provides a structure for mastering key concepts and reviewing key terms in the section. Available in Spanish in the Spanish Chapter and Section Resources booklet, p. 6.

Media and Technology

Color Transparencies 6, 8, 9, 11, 71

Program Resources

Outline Maps The Middle East and North Africa: Physical, p. 28; Africa South of the Sahara: Physical, p. 32

Lesson Objectives

1. Describe the major climate regions of Africa and the factors that influence climate.

2. Identify vegetation commonly found in Africa.

3. Explain the influence of climate and vegetation on African economic activities.

Lesson Plan

1 Engage

Warm-Up Activity

Ask students to suppose that they have traveled two or three states' distance in any direction from your community. Have them describe the land and climate in the new location and then compare it with the land and climate in your community. Have students hypothesize about why any differences exist. Ask students whether they think both places are in the same climate region.

Activating Prior Knowledge

Have students read Reach Into Your Background in the Before You Read box. After students have considered answers to the questions in the box, have them think about what the answers might be if the same questions were asked about Africa. Have students predict some answers for each question.

2 Explore

As students read the section, encourage them to refer both to the map at the beginning of the chapter and to the climate map. Ask students to look for answers to questions such as the following: How does a place's location in relation to the Equator affect seasons? What effect does elevation have on climate?

3 Teach

Have students create picture postcards that show four distinct climate and/or vegetation regions of Africa. Students should include descriptive caption text with each postcard. This activity should take about 30 minutes.

4 Assess

See the answers to the Section Review. You may also use students' completed postcards for assessment.

Acceptable postcards illustrate four different climate or vegetation regions and include captions that identify each illustration.

Commendable postcards illustrate four different climate or vegetation regions and include captions that identify and locate each illustration.

Outstanding postcards show people engaged in an activity in some of the four different climate or vegetation regions. Captions link climate with human activities.

Answers to ...
MAP STUDY

A tropical climate is most common in equatorial Africa. An arid/semiarid climate is most common near the tropics of Cancer and Capricorn.

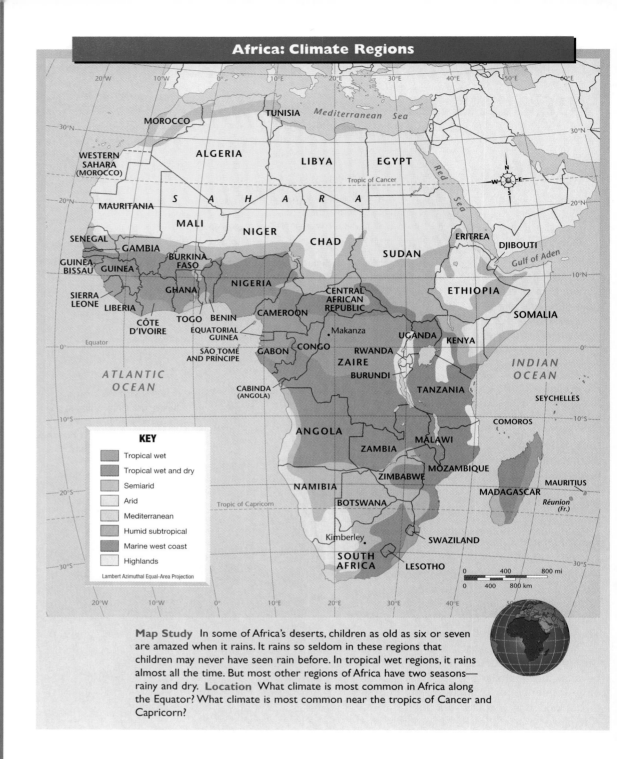

Africa: Climate Regions

KEY
- Tropical wet
- Tropical wet and dry
- Semiarid
- Arid
- Mediterranean
- Humid subtropical
- Marine west coast
- Highlands

Lambert Azimuthal Equal-Area Projection

Map Study In some of Africa's deserts, children as old as six or seven are amazed when it rains. It rains so seldom in these regions that children may never have seen rain before. In tropical wet regions, it rains almost all the time. But most other regions of Africa have two seasons—rainy and dry. **Location** What climate is most common in Africa along the Equator? What climate is most common near the tropics of Cancer and Capricorn?

Resource Directory

Teaching Resources

📁 **Reading a Bar Graph** in the Social Studies and Geography Skills booklet, p. 53, provides additional skill practice.

📁 **Reading a Line Graph** in the Social Studies and Geography Skills booklet, p. 54, provides additional skill practice.

Media and Technology

💿 **Planet Earth** CD-ROM includes satellite images and physical maps of Africa that allow students to view the countries that make up the region, plus World Wonders, Natural: Victoria Falls; and Okavango Delta.

Distance From the Equator Africa's location near the Equator means that most of the continent is warm. A place's location in relation to the Equator influences the seasons. North of the Equator, winter and summer occur at the same time as they do in the United States. South of the Equator, the seasons are reversed. For example, July in South Africa is the middle of winter.

Higher, Cooler: The Role of Elevation Elevation, or height above sea level, also affects climate. The higher the elevation, the cooler a place tends to be. Mount Kilimanjaro, Africa's highest peak, is located very close to the Equator. Yet ice and snow blanket the peak of Kilimanjaro year round.

The countries of Ethiopia and Somalia provide another example. They are about the same distance from the Equator, yet they have different climates. Ethiopia is on a very high plateau. Much of Ethiopia has mild temperatures and much rain. Farmers there grow a wide range of crops—including bananas, coffee, dates, and oats. Because Ethiopia usually gets plenty of rain, many farmers there do not irrigate, or artificially water, their crops.

Somalia is at a much lower elevation than Ethiopia. Its climate is hot and dry. Farming is possible only in or near an oasis, where crops can be irrigated. An oasis is a place where springs and fresh underground water make it possible to support life in a region that gets little rain.

Unpredictable Rainfall Rainfall varies greatly from one region of Africa to another. Along parts of the west coast, winds carry moisture from the warm ocean over the land. Rainfall averages more than 100 inches (250 cm) per year. Compare that to your own height in inches. Forty inches (100 cm) of rain might fall during June alone. But in parts of the Sahara in the north and Namib Desert in the south, it may not rain at all for several years in a row.

Farmers who live in dry regions can never be sure whether there will be enough rain for their crops. Some farmers

READ ACTIVELY

Predict How do you think elevation affects the climate regions in Africa?

▼ What clue in this picture shows that it is Mount Kilimanjaro's high elevation that keeps its snow from melting?

Rain Forests Rain forests like those in Central Africa also exist in South America and Indonesia. These forests, too, are threatened by clearing and pollution. In Indonesia, every six minutes means the destruction of another square mile of rain forest. In South America, however, some efforts are being made to save the rain forests. Venezuela's forests are part of a protected national park system. People who live in the forest and depend on it may remain, but logging and clearing are forbidden.

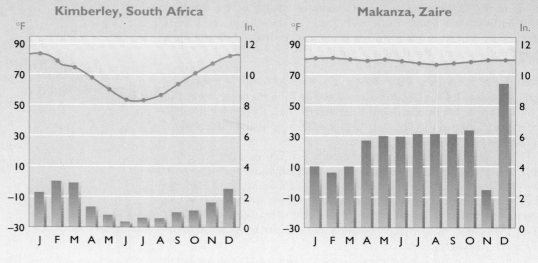

Desert and Rain Forest

Kimberley, South Africa | Makanza, Zaire

Curved lines show temperatures in Fahrenheit degrees. **Bars** show rainfall in inches.

Chart Study The vegetation of Kimberley, South Africa, is mostly desert scrub. Makanza, Zaire, lies in a tropical rain forest. **Critical Thinking** What differences do the climate charts show that would explain why Kimberley is in a hot, dry region while Makanza is in a tropical rain forest?

choose to plant a variety of crops, each needing different amounts of rainfall. These farmers hope they will have at least one successful crop. The charts on this page show rainfall in two cities that have very different climates. Which city do you think would have the best climate for farming?

Vegetation

Look at the vegetation map in the Activity Atlas. Near the Equator are rain forests. Farther from the Equator lies a region of tall grasses, called the savanna.

READ ACTIVELY

Visualize Visualize the rain forest in the country of Cameroon. What might it look like and sound like?

Tropical Rain Forests Tropical rain forests are regions where it rains nearly all the time. The moisture supports a rich environment of trees, plants, and animals. Find the tropical rain forest region on the vegetation map. The tropical rain forest region used to be much larger. It covered much of Central Africa. Through the years, people cut trees from the forest to use the wood or to clear land for farming. Rain forest lands, however, do not make good farmland. Once the trees are cut down, heavy rains wash away the nutrients that make soil fertile.

Answers to . . .
CHART STUDY

In Makanza, it is rainy and hot all the time. The water and warmth support plant growth. In Kimberley, it is dry and the temperatures sometimes dip down almost to 50°F.

Resource Directory

Teaching Resources

Critical Thinking Activity in the Chapter and Section Resources booklet, p. 17, helps students apply the skill of identifying central issues.

Tropical Savannas Much of Africa north and south of the rain forest is tropical savanna. Tall grasses, thorny bushes, and scattered trees grow in the savanna region. Some grasses grow as high as a person's head.

The climate of the tropical savanna is tropical wet and dry. This means that the savanna has two seasons: dry and wet. During the dry season, farming is impossible. Trees lose their leaves and rivers run dry. People use the season to trade, build houses, and visit friends. In the wet season, the land turns green, and farmers plant their crops.

Deserts in Africa Beyond the savanna lie the deserts. The immense Sahara extends across most of North Africa. This desert covers almost as much land as the entire United States.

The southern edge of the Sahara meets the savanna in a region called the Sahel (SAH hil), which is the Arab word for shore or border. The Sahel is very hot and dry. It receives only 4 to 8 inches (10 to 20 cm) of rain per year. Small shrubs, grass, and some trees grow there.

The Namib and Kalahari deserts extend over much of Namibia and Botswana in Southern Africa. These deserts, like the Sahara, feature landscapes of bare rock, towering rock formations, sand dunes, and a few areas of small bushes and grass.

A journalist traveling in the Namib Desert described the region:

> "There was sand everywhere, an impossible amount of sand covering thousands of square miles and heaping into dunes as high as 1,200 feet. The ultimate sandpile. It was uniformly fine and found its way into everything. I blinked sand from my eyes, blew it from my nose, spit it from my mouth and throat."

Nomads make their living in the Sahara. Nomads are people who move around to various places to make a living. Some nomads are traders, and others hunt game and gather food. Most nomads are herders, however. They travel to places where they know they can get water and food for their herds of goats, camels, or sheep.

Some nomadic herders live mainly in the mountainous areas. In spring, they leave their winter grazing grounds in the foothills and head

▲ The acacia tree produces a substance that is used in candy, glue, and ink. It grows in tropical savanna regions.

LINKS ACROSS THE WORLD

The Oldest Sunscreen In the United States, people often wear sunscreen to protect their skin from sunburn. But it is hard to get sunscreen in the Sahara. Instead, desert nomads cover themselves from head to toe in long, loose robes.

Interdisciplinary Connections

Science Tell students that the tsetse fly is not actually the cause of sleeping sickness; it is only the carrier of the disease. The illness is caused by a tiny parasite called a trypanosome. Challenge students to brainstorm methods of controlling sleeping sickness in cattle and humans. These might include fly trap designs or medical methods.

Section 2 Review

1. (a) to artificially water crops (b) a place that gets little rain but where springs and underground water make it possible to support life (c) a region of tall grasses (d) member of a people who move from place to place in order to make a living

2. (a) a very hot and dry place where the southern edge of the Sahara meets the savanna (b) a desert in the western part of Namibia (c) a desert that extends over much of Botswana and part of Namibia

3. distance from the Equator, elevation, and rainfall

4. Rainfall is more important because crops will not grow without water.

5. Students may say that if Mount Kilimanjaro were in Canada, the conditions at its peak would be even colder and more severe as a result of its increased distance from the Equator.

6. Listed items should reflect the many climate conditions a visitor to Africa would encounter.

▶ These Berber nomads are traveling across the country of Morocco, through the Sahara.

up into the mountains. Other nomads live mainly in the flat desert areas. During the dry season, they set up tents near oases. When the rainy season comes, they move their goats and camels to better pastures.

Building Good Health

The climate people live in can affect their health. Throughout Africa there are regions that present health risks to livestock and humans. In rain forest regions, the moist environment is home to many disease-carrying insects. Even in the drier grasslands, disease and illness take their toll.

Nearly one fifth of Africa is home to the tsetse (TSET see) fly, a pest that makes raising cattle almost impossible. The bite of the fly kills cattle and brings a disease called sleeping sickness to humans. African researchers, together with cattle herders, have worked to find ways to control the spread of the tsetse fly. Cattle herders in Kenya are setting traps for flies. Herders in the country of Uganda use netting sewn into a tent that contains poison to catch flies.

READ ACTIVELY

Connect Do you know of any diseases that are spread by insects in the United States? If so, how do people keep the disease from spreading?

SECTION 2 REVIEW

1. Define (a) irrigate, (b) oasis, (c) savanna, (d) nomad.

2. Identify (a) Sahel, (b) Namib Desert, (c) Kalahari Desert.

3. What three factors affect the climate of Africa?

4. What most affects farming in Africa, rainfall or temperature? Explain.

Critical Thinking

5. Recognizing Cause and Effect If Mount Kilimanjaro were located in Canada instead of Kenya, would the climate at its peak be much different? Why or why not?

Activity

6. Writing to Learn Now that you know more about the climate and vegetation in Africa, make your new packing list for a two-week trip to Africa. Explain why you are bringing each item. (Hint: you may want to decide exactly which regions of Africa you will be visiting before you make the list.)

Resource Directory

Teaching Resources

📁 **Section Quiz** in the Chapter and Section Resources booklet, p. 9, covers the main ideas and key terms in the section. Available in Spanish in the Spanish Chapter and Section Resources booklet, p. 7.

Program Resources

📁 **Environmental and Global Issues** Topic: Health, pp. 8–13

Natural Resources

BEFORE YOU READ

Reach Into Your Background

Have you ever heard the saying, "Don't put all your eggs in one basket?" What do you think this saying means?

Questions to Explore

1. What are Africa's major natural resources?
2. How are Africans developing these resources?

Key Terms

subsistence farming
cash crop
economy
diversify

Lesson Objectives

1. Identify some of Africa's key natural resources.
2. Describe some ways in which Africans use natural resources.
3. Point out some challenges facing Africans in balancing the development and protection of their natural resources.

Lesson Plan

1 Engage

Warm-Up Activity

Have students list hobbies and activities at which they excel. Discuss what each requires—for instance, time, money, equipment, or physical effort. Ask students whether they see any conflicts between the various interests. For example, there may be time conflicts or one activity may take the student away from home during an important family activity. Ask students how such conflicts might be resolved.

Activating Prior Knowledge

Have students read Reach Into Your Background in the Before You Read box. Discuss students' interpretations of the saying and how they think the saying could apply to a country's economy.

"**Tete Quarshie:** I have a humble request to make of you, my noble friend. I hope you will not turn deaf ears to my cries. Here, in this load, I bear the seeds of a wonderful tree which, if cultivated in this land, will bless its sons everlastingly with wealth, and people far and near with health. These are the seeds of the cacao tree which I have brought with me from across the sea. . . . Would you, therefore, be kind enough to grant me a mere acre of land in this neighborhood to try my luck, and yours, and that of this country as a whole?"

▼ To make milk chocolate from cacao beans, shown below, chocolate makers grind the beans, and then mix them with lots of milk and sugar.

These words come from a short play, *Cocoa Comes to Mampong*. The play tells the story of cocoa in the West African country of Ghana. Cacao trees, from which cocoa and chocolate are made, used to grow only in Central and South America. As people in the Americas, Europe, and Africa began to trade with one another, they found that cacao trees could be grown in West Africa. In the play, the people granted the land to Tete Quarshie, who raised the first successful crop of cacao in Ghana.

Teaching Resources

 Reproducible Lesson Plan in the Chapter and Section Resources booklet, p. 10, provides a summary of the section lesson.

Guided Reading and Review in the Chapter and Section Resources booklet, p. 11, provides a structure for mastering key concepts and reviewing key terms in the section. Available in Spanish in the Spanish Chapter and Section Resources booklet, p. 8.

Program Resources

Outline Maps North Africa: Political, p. 31; Africa South of the Sahara: Political, p. 33

Media and Technology

Color Transparencies 9, 10, 15, 17

2 Explore

Direct students to read the section. Stop them at intervals to discuss the following questions: How is subsistence farming different from raising cash crops? Why might Africans want to raise cash crops? What are the benefits of a diversified economy?

3 Teach

Have students work in small groups to create a cause-and-effect diagram concerning economic activities in Africa. Allow about 30 minutes for this activity.

4 Assess

See the answers to the Section Review. You may also assess groups' cause-and-effect diagrams.

Acceptable diagrams accurately identify a minimum of three economic activities and the natural resources the activities require.

Commendable diagrams accurately identify four or more economic activities and the natural resources the activities require.

Outstanding diagrams accurately identify four or more economic activities and the natural resources the activities require. Diagrams include positive and negative effects of development.

Answers to . . .

FAMILIES FARMING FOR A LIVING

Accept any reasonable answer. Subsistence farmers and cash crop farmers plant different crops, and cash crop farmers must grow much more than subsistence farmers do.

LINKS ACROSS THE WORLD

Farming Equipment
Corn and wheat farmers in the United States often use heavy machines to work the land. Most African farmers could not use such machines. They would destroy the thin layer of topsoil on most African farms.

Agricultural Resources

Some Africans are farmers living in areas with fertile soil and much rain. But most Africans have land that is hard or impossible to farm because of poor soil or too little rain.

Farming to Live The map on the next page shows how much of Africa's land is used for **subsistence farming.** Subsistence farmers raise crops to support their families. They sell or trade a few crops for other items they need. In northern African countries such as Morocco, farmers raise barley and wheat. They also irrigate fields to grow fruits and vegetables. Farms at Saharan oases in Egypt produce dates and small crops of barley and wheat.

In countries that contain dry tropical savanna, such as Burkina Faso (bur KEE nuh FAH soh) and Niger, subsistence farmers grow grains. In regions with more rainfall, farmers also grow vegetables, fruits, and

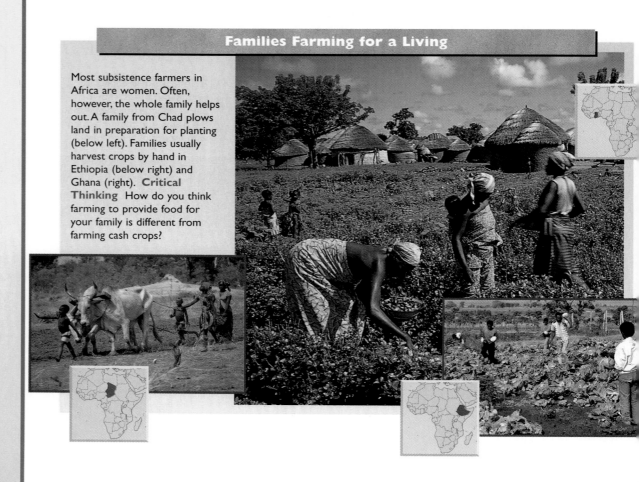

Families Farming for a Living

Most subsistence farmers in Africa are women. Often, however, the whole family helps out. A family from Chad plows land in preparation for planting (below left). Families usually harvest crops by hand in Ethiopia (below right) and Ghana (right). **Critical Thinking** How do you think farming to provide food for your family is different from farming cash crops?

Africa: How People Make a Living

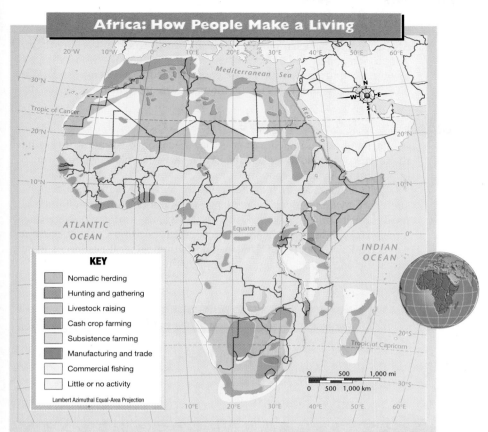

KEY

- Nomadic herding
- Hunting and gathering
- Livestock raising
- Cash crop farming
- Subsistence farming
- Manufacturing and trade
- Commercial fishing
- Little or no activity

Lambert Azimuthal Equal-Area Projection

Map Study Most of Africa's workers make a living by farming or herding. **Regions** In what regions of Africa do workers make a living in other ways? How do workers in these areas make a living? **Critical Thinking** Why do you think that some parts of Africa have little or no economic activity?

roots such as yams and cassava. Tapioca, which is used in the United States to make pudding, is made from cassava. In West Africa, corn and rice are important crops. People in many of Africa's cultures fish or raise goats or poultry.

Crops for Sale In all regions of Africa, farmers raise crops to sell. These are called **cash crops.** Farmers in Côte d'Ivoire (koht deev WAR), Ghana, and Cameroon grow cash crops of coffee and cacao. Farmers in Kenya, Tanzania, Malawi, Zimbabwe, and Mozambique grow tea as a cash crop.

In recent years, more and more farmers have planted cash crops. As more land is used for cash crops, less land is planted with crops to feed families. In some regions, this practice has led to food shortages when cash crops have failed.

Ask Questions What else would you like to know about farming in Africa?

Activity

Cooperative Learning

African Meal Plan Have groups research and plan an African meal. They may focus on a particular region or include a sampling of foods from many regions. Two group members can check with local shops on the availability of ingredients. If possible, prepare some of the recipes. One easy possibility is Banana Fritters (from West Africa).

Ingredients:

1 1/2 cups flour
6 T sugar
3 eggs
1 cup milk
4–5 ripe bananas, pureed
vegetable oil for frying
confectioners' sugar

Mix flour, sugar, and eggs. Add milk gradually, stirring. Add banana puree. Let mixture stand 30 minutes. Heat 2–3 inches of oil in frying pan until very hot. Carefully ladle 1/4 cup of batter into oil, spreading into a round shape. Fry for about 3 minutes until each side is golden brown. Drain on paper towels. Sprinkle with sugar and serve warm. *English Language Learner, Kinesthetic*

Answers to ...

MAP STUDY

Manufacturing and trade are carried out in Southern and East Africa. Off the coasts of Southern and North Africa, people make their living in the commercial fishing industry. In places where little or no economic activity occurs, conditions probably are not suitable for farming, fishing, or herding.

Expressing Problems Clearly *Suitable as an individual activity.* Have students develop a two-minute speech for or against the development of one African natural resource. Speeches should clearly state the effects of development on both people and land. Alternately, students may choose instead to create a persuasive poster depicting their position.

Global Perspectives

Traveling Crops The cacao plant was probably first grown by the Mayas and the Aztecs of Central America. During the 1500s, Europeans who had conquered the Mayas and the Aztecs brought cacao beans back to Europe where they developed processing and refining methods to make cocoa and chocolate. Demand for chocolate and other cacao products is strong throughout the world. Cacao is well-established as a cash crop in Côte d'Ivoire, Brazil, Ghana, Malaysia, and Nigeria.

Answers to ...
MAP STUDY

The western and central parts of Africa produce diamonds. Hydroelectric power cannot be used up.

Harvesting Trees Hardwood trees grow in all four regions of Africa. People can earn money by cutting down trees and selling them. Thousands of acres of these trees have been cut and the wood shipped to other countries. A number of countries, such as Kenya and Côte d'Ivoire, are planting trees by the thousands in order to save the forests.

Mineral Resources

Farming is the major part of Africa's economy. An **economy** is all the things people do to make a living in a particular place. Mining is also important to Africa's economy.

Parts of Africa are rich in mineral resources. In North Africa, nations such as Libya and Algeria have large amounts of petroleum, which is used to make oil and gasoline. In West Africa, the country of Nigeria is a major oil producer. Ghana was once called the Gold Coast because it was a leading exporter of African gold. Other mineral resources from Africa include copper, silver, uranium, titanium, and diamonds.

READ ACTIVELY

Predict How do you think most African countries use their mineral resources?

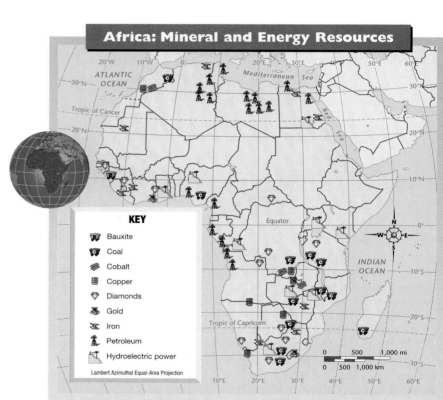

Africa: Mineral and Energy Resources

KEY
- Bauxite
- Coal
- Cobalt
- Copper
- Diamonds
- Gold
- Iron
- Petroleum
- Hydroelectric power

Lambert Azimuthal Equal-Area Projection

Map Study Most of Africa's people work in agriculture, yet most of Africa's exports are produced by miners. **Regions** Southern Africa is famous for its diamond industry. What other regions of Africa produce diamonds? **Interaction** Which resource shown on this map can be used without being used up?

Teaching Resources

Section Quiz in the Chapter and Section Resources booklet, p. 12, covers the main ideas and key terms in the section. Available in Spanish in the Spanish Chapter and Section Resources booklet, p. 9.

Vocabulary in the Chapter and Section Resources booklet, p. 14, provides a review of key terms in the chapter. Available in Spanish in the Spanish Chapter and Section Resources booklet, p. 11.

Reteaching in the Chapter and Section Resources booklet, p. 15, provides a structure for students who may need additional help in mastering chapter content.

Enrichment in the Chapter and Section Resources booklet, p. 16, extends chapter content and enriches students' understanding.

Program Resources

Environmental and Global Issues Topic: The Global Economy, pp. 20–24

Balancing Crops, Minerals, and Industry

Most of Africa's workers are farmers. That makes the economy sensitive to rainfall and to the price of crops. African countries are now trying to diversify their economies. To **diversify** means to add variety. These countries are working to produce a variety of crops, raw materials, and manufactured goods. A country with a diverse economy will not be hurt as much if a major cash crop fails or if world prices for one of its major mineral exports suddenly drops.

Mining requires many workers and costly equipment. Throughout much of Africa, foreign companies mine African resources and take the profits. This system does little to help African economies. In addition, Africa has few factories to make products from its own raw materials. Therefore, many African countries want to diversify their economies to include manufacturing.

▼ All over Africa, people are moving to cities to apply for jobs in factories like this one. These men work on the assembly line at the Livingstone Car Plant in the country of Zambia.

Background

Biography

Jerry John Rawlings (1947–) In 1992, Jerry John Rawlings was elected president of Ghana. Under his leadership, Ghana's economy has improved. Incentive programs have pushed for leaner government, increased exports, better social services, and banking reforms. Rawlings has also offered incentives to foreign investors in order to diversify Ghana's economy.

Section 3 Review

1. (a) raising only enough crops to support a family (b) a crop that is raised to sell (c) all the things people do to make a living in a particular place (d) to add variety

2. to better protect economies against the failure of a major cash crop or a drop in world prices for an important mineral export

3. Both kinds of farming depend on weather conditions. Subsistence farmers grow only enough to support their families. Cash crop farmers grow crops to sell them.

4. fertile soil for farming, trees, minerals

5. Students may list cocoa, coffee, wood, and oil. Students' paragraphs will vary. Accept all reasonable responses.

SECTION 3 REVIEW

1. Define (a) subsistence farming, (b) cash crop, (c) economy, (d) diversify.

2. Why are African governments working to diversify their economies?

3. Compare subsistence farming with farming to raise cash crops. How are they similar? How are they different?

Critical Thinking

4. Identifying Central Issues What are some important natural resources in Africa?

Activity

6. Writing to Learn List some of Africa's natural resources that you and your family use. Then, write a paragraph that explains which you would miss most if you did not have it—and why.

Teaching Resources

Spanish Glossary in the Spanish Chapter and Section Resources, pp. 68–73, provides key terms translated from English to Spanish as well as definitions in Spanish.

Chapter Summary in the Chapter and Section Resources booklet, p. 13, provides a summary of chapter content. Available in Spanish in the Spanish Chapter and Section Resources booklet, p. 10.

Cooperative Learning Activity in the Activities and Projects booklet, pp. 17–20, provides two student handouts, one page of teacher's directions, and a scoring rubric for a cooperative learning activity on making a relief map.

Media and Technology

Guided Reading Audiotapes (English and Spanish)

SKILLS ACTIVITY

Interpreting Diagrams

❶ Describe a cross-sectional diagram.

❷ Create a cross-sectional diagram from a clay model.

❸ Interpret information on a cross-sectional diagram.

Lesson Plan

1 Engage

Warm-Up Activity

Read the opening paragraph with students. Use the information about time and speed to calculate the length and width of Africa in miles and kilometers. Then **introduce** the skill as a volunteer reads the next two paragraphs. Write *cross-sectional diagram* on the chalkboard.

Activating Prior Knowledge

Have students draw cross-sectional diagrams of familiar items such as a peanut butter and jelly sandwich or a cheeseburger. Give students the option of describing the diagram in words.

2 Explore

Direct students to read the text under *Get Ready*. Then model the apple example for students. You may wish to brush paint on the cut surface of the apple and use the painted surface to stamp an image of the cross section. Then have students read the remaining activity text.

A frica is a giant. More than three times bigger than the United States, it covers close to 11,700,000 square miles (more than 30,000,000 sq km). That is about one fifth of all of the land in the world. If you drove across Africa at its widest point going 65 miles (105 km) per hour, without stopping for gas or sleep, it would take you about 72 hours. Traveling north-to-south, the trip would take about 77 hours.

A quick look at a world map will impress upon you Africa's great length and width. But the map will not show you its enormous elevations, or height.

One of the most effective ways to see Africa's elevations is to study a cross-sectional diagram of this gigantic land.

Get Ready

You already know that a diagram is a figure drawn to explain something. A *cross section* is basically a slice of something viewed from the side. For example, if you were to cut an apple in half, and look at the exposed cut, you would be looking at a cross section of the apple. If you drew a picture of what you saw, you would have a cross-sectional diagram of that apple.

You can get a good idea of a cross-sectional diagram by making one of your own—and having some fun as you do it. You'll need:
- modeling clay
- a butter knife
- pen and paper

Resource Directory

Teaching Resources

Reading a Diagram in the Social Studies and Geography Skills booklet, p. 56, provides additional skill practice.

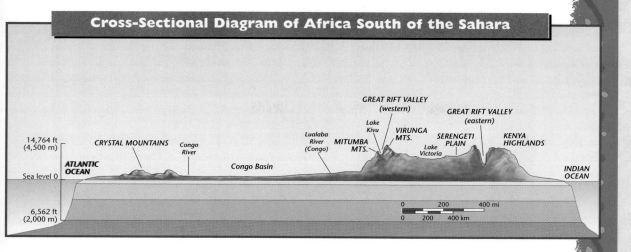

Cross-Sectional Diagram of Africa South of the Sahara

14,764 ft (4,500 m)

CRYSTAL MOUNTAINS

Congo River

ATLANTIC OCEAN

Sea level 0

6,562 ft (2,000 m)

Congo Basin

Lualaba River (Congo)

MITUMBA MTS.

Lake Kivu

VIRUNGA MTS.

GREAT RIFT VALLEY (western)

Lake Victoria

SERENGETI PLAIN

GREAT RIFT VALLEY (eastern)

KENYA HIGHLANDS

INDIAN OCEAN

0   200   400 mi
0   200   400 km

Try It Out

A. Create a continent. Take a fist-sized ball of modeling clay and shape it into an imaginary continent. First, flatten it out. Then mold the continent into any shape you want. Mold mountain ranges, valleys, plateaus, and any other landforms you wish.

B. Cut the cross section. When you've finished, put your "clay continent" flat on a table. Use the butter knife to cut it in half at its widest point.

C. Look at your result. Pick up one-half of your continent and look at the cut side edgewise. You are looking at a cross section of your imaginary continent.

D. Sketch what you see. By sketching a side view of your model, you have made a cross-sectional diagram of your imaginary continent. How does the diagram reflect the vertical shape of the continent? Write the answer on the back of your cross-sectional diagram.

Apply the Skill

The illustration above is a cross-sectional diagram of Africa. Use it to complete the following steps.

1 Understand the diagram. Just as you cut your clay continent at a certain place, the cross-sectional diagram of Africa shows the continent "cut" at a certain place. Does this cross section show Africa from east to west or from north to south? How is elevation indicated on the diagram? What geographic features are labeled on the diagram?

2 Learn from the diagram. What is the lowest point on the diagram? What is the highest point? How large a range in elevation is this? How far below the surrounding landscape does the Great Rift Valley drop?

CHAPTER

1

Review and Activities

Reviewing Main Ideas

1. Why are some parts of Africa cold even though they are near the Equator?

2. List four major physical features of Africa. Choose one and describe what it is like.

3. Explain why there is little or no farming in much of North Africa and parts of Southern Africa.

4. How is subsistence farming in Africa different from farming to raise cash crops?

5. (a) List three cash crops raised in Africa. Where are they grown? (b) Name one mineral resource of Africa. Where is it found?

6. Explain why many African nations are trying to diversify their economies.

Reviewing Key Terms

Use each key term below in a sentence that shows the meaning of the term.

1. plateau
2. elevation
3. escarpment
4. rift
5. cataract
6. silt
7. fertile
8. tributary
9. irrigate
10. oasis
11. savanna
12. nomad
13. subsistence farming
14. cash crop
15. economy
16. diversify

Critical Thinking

1. **Identifying Central Issues** Explain the meaning of this statement. Give an example to support it. "People in Africa tend to live in grassland regions."

2. **Recognizing Cause and Effect** How did the yearly flooding of the Nile affect farmers in the Nile Valley? How did the building of the Aswan Dam affect the farmers?

Graphic Organizer

Copy the chart onto a sheet of paper. Then fill in the empty boxes to complete the chart.

	Amount of Rainfall	Temperature	Crops Grown
Desert	Little or none	Hot	Dates, barley, wheat in or near oases
Tropical Savanna			
Uplands and Mountain Regions			

Reviewing Main Ideas

1. They are at high elevations.

2. the plateau, coastal plains, Great Rift Valley, rivers; descriptions should accurately describe one of the physical features listed

3. because these areas are mostly desert and cannot be farmed

4. Subsistence farmers grow only enough crops to support their families. Cash crop farmers grow crops to sell them.

5. (a) Cacao beans and coffee are grown in Côte d'Ivoire, Ghana, and Cameroon; tea is grown in Kenya, Tanzania, Malawi, Zimbabwe, and Mozambique (b) any of the following: petroleum, gold, copper, silver, uranium, titanium, or diamonds. Libya, Algeria, and Nigeria produce petroleum. Gold is mined in Ghana.

6. Diversification will help African countries protect themselves against problems caused by the failure of a major cash crop or a drop in world prices for an important export.

Reviewing Key Terms

Sentences should show the correct meaning of terms through context.

Critical Thinking

1. People cannot live as easily in extreme climate areas such as deserts and rain forests. The soil in grassland areas is good for farming, so people can grow food for themselves.

2. Yearly Nile flooding brought water and fertile soil to farmlands, enabling farmers to grow crops. The Aswan Dam controls the flooding of the Nile. Water contained in a lake created by the dam is channeled to crops in the desert.

Graphic Organizer

	Amount of Rainfall	Temperature	Crops Grown
Desert	little or none	hot	dates, barley, wheat in or near oases
Tropical Savanna	wet during the wet season; dry during the dry season	hot	grains
Uplands and Mountain Regions	wet	mild	bananas, coffee, dates, and oats

Map Activity

Africa

For each place listed, write the letter from the map that shows its location.

1. Nile River
2. Congo River
3. Sahara
4. Namib Desert
5. Zambezi River
6. Kalahari Desert
7. Niger River
8. Great Rift Valley

Place Location

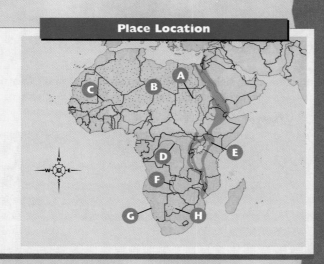

Writing Activity

Writing a Short Report

Describe some problems Africans face that are caused by Africa's landforms or climate. Give some examples of how Africans are solving these problems.

Skills Review

Turn to the Skills Activity. Review the steps for interpreting a diagram. Then complete the following: (a) In your own words, describe what a cross-sectional diagram is. (b) What information can you find on a cross-sectional diagram?

Internet Activity

Use a search engine to find **AfricaOnline.** Choose **Kids Only** and then choose **Learn About Africa.** Scroll to the bottom and click on the **Land** icon. What are the types of climates in Africa? Learn about the land and climates of Africa and then test your brain power with some fun, on-line quizzes.

How Am I Doing?

Answer these questions to check your progress.

1. Can I describe the location of Africa?
2. Do I understand how climate influences farming activity in Africa?
3. Can I identify some mineral resources of Africa?
4. Can I name some large landforms in Africa?
5. What information from this chapter can I use in my book project?

Internet Activity

If students are having difficulty finding this site, you may wish to have them use the following URL, which was accurate at the time this textbook was published:

http://www.africaonline.com/

You might also guide students to a search engine. Four of the most useful are Infoseek, Alta Vista, Lycos, and Yahoo. For additional suggestions on using the Internet, refer to the Prentice Hall Social Studies' Educator's Handbook "Using the Internet," in the *Prentice Hall World Explorer Program Resources.*

For additional links to world history and culture topics, visit the Prentice Hall Home Page at:

http://www.phschool.com

How Am I Doing?

Point out to students that this checklist is a quick reminder for them of what they learned in the chapter. If their answer to any of the questions is *no* or if they are unsure, they may need to review the topic.

Map Activity

1. A	4. G	7. C
2. D	5. F	8. E
3. B	6. H	

Writing Activity

Reports will vary. Accept reports that describe some of the following: difficulties in traveling or transporting goods because of mountains or deserts, food or water shortages due to poor soil or unpredictable rainfall, crop failures due to pests or lack of rain, and the destruction of rain forests. Students may mention that some countries are solving problems by diversifying their economies or that some countries are replanting trees to replace those that have been cut down.

Skills Review

(a) Students should express in their own words the following idea: A cross-sectional diagram shows what something would look like if it were sliced in two and viewed from the side. (b) It can show the highest and lowest elevations.

Resource Directory

Teaching Resources

Chapter Tests Forms A and B are in the Tests booklet, pp. 2–7.

Program Resources

Writing Process Handbook includes Writing an Introduction, p. 29, to help students with the Writing Activity.

Media and Technology

Color Transparencies Color Transparency 174 (Graphic organizer table template)

Prentice Hall Writer's Solution Writing Lab CD-ROM

Computer Test Bank

Resource Pro™ CD-ROM

AFRICA
Shaped by Its History

To help you plan instruction, the chart below shows how teaching resources correspond to chapter content. Use the resources to vary instruction, add activities, or plan block schedules. Where appropriate, resources have suggested time allotments for students. Time allotments are approximate.

Managing Time and Instruction

	Africa Teaching Resources Binder		World Explorer Program Resources Binder	
	Resource	mins.	Resource	mins.
1 SECTION 1 Africa's First People	**Chapter and Section Support** Reproducible Lesson Plan, p. 19 S Guided Reading and Review, p. 20 S Section Quiz, p. 21	 20 25	**Outline Maps** The Middle East and North Africa: Physical, p. 28 Africa South of the Sahara: Physical, p. 31 **Nystrom Desk Atlas** T **Primary Sources and Literature Readings** **Writing Process Handbook** Limiting a Topic, p. 15 **Environmental and Global Issues** Topic: Conflict, pp. 37–42	 20 20 40 25 30
SKILLS ACTIVITY Recognizing Bias	**Social Studies and Geography Skills,** Identifying Assumptions, p. 46 Recognizing Bias, p. 47	30 30		
2 SECTION 2 Kingdoms and Empires	**Chapter and Section Support** Reproducible Lesson Plan, p. 22 S Guided Reading and Review, p. 23 S Section Quiz, p. 24 Critical Thinking Activity, p. 38 **Social Studies and Geography Skills,** Reading a Trade Map, p. 39	 20 25 30 30	**Outline Maps** North Africa: Political, p. 31 Africa South of the Sahara: Political, p. 38	 20 20
3 SECTION 3 The Conquest of Africa	**Chapter and Section Support** Reproducible Lesson Plan, p. 25 S Guided Reading and Review, p. 26 S Section Quiz, p. 27 **Social Studies and Geography Skills,** Understanding Latitude and Longitude, p. 10	 20 25 30	**Outline Maps** North Africa: Political, p. 31 Africa South of the Sahara: Political, p. 38 **Environmental and Global Issues** Topic: Human Rights, pp. 25–30	 20 20 30
4 SECTION 4 Independence and Its Challenges	**Chapter and Section Support** Reproducible Lesson Plan, p. 28 S Guided Reading and Review, p. 29 S Section Quiz, p. 30 **Social Studies and Geography Skills,** Maps with Accurate Directions: Azimuthal Maps, p. 18	 20 25 30	**Outline Maps** The World: Political, p. 5 North Africa: Political, p. 31 Africa South of the Sahara: Political, p. 38 **Environmental and Global Issues** Topic: Conflict, pp. 37–42	 20 20 20 30
5 SECTION 5 Issues for Africa Today	**Chapter and Section Support** Reproducible Lesson Plan, p. 31 S Guided Reading and Review, p. 32 S Section Quiz, p. 33 S Vocabulary, p. 35 Reteaching, p. 36 Enrichment, p. 37 S Chapter Summary, p. 34 **Tests** Forms A and B Chapter Tests, pp. 8–13	 20 25 20 25 25 15 40	**Environmental and Global Issues** Topic: Health, pp. 8–13 Topic: Environmental Destruction, pp. 14–19	 30 30

Activities and Projects

Block Scheduling Program Support

Interdisciplinary Links

Resource Pro™ CD-ROM

Media and Technology

Media and Technology

Resource	mins.
▣ ✎ Ⓢ World Video Explorer	20
⌨ Color Transparency 71	20
⊙ Planet Earth CD-ROM	20
⌨ Color Transparencies 72, 93	20
⌨ Color Transparencies 135, Historical Map Set 5	20
⌨ Color Transparency 51	20
⌨ Color Transparencies 15, 17, 19, 20, 21, 45	20
⌂ Ⓢ Guided Reading Audiotapes	20
⌨ Color Transparency 171 (Graphic organizer web template)	20
✎ The Writer's Solution CD-ROM	30
⊟ Computer Test Bank	30

T Teaming Opportunity
This resource is especially well-suited for teaching teams.

Ⓢ Spanish
This resource is also in Spanish support.

✎ CD-ROM

✎ Laserdisc

⌐ Transparency

⊟ Software

▣ Videotape

⌂ Audiotape

Assessment Opportunities

From Guiding Questions to Assessment A series of Guiding Questions serves as an organizing framework for this book. The Guiding Question that relates to this chapter is listed below. Section Reviews and Section Quizzes provide opportunities for assessing students' insights into this Guiding Question. Additional assessments are listed below.

GUIDING QUESTION

• *What factors have shaped Africa's cultures?*

ASSESSMENTS

Section 1

Students should be able to write a paragraph on the techniques early Africans used to get food.

▶ **RUBRIC** See the Assessment booklet for a rubric on assessing a writing assignment.

Section 2

Students should be able to write an explanation of how trade enriched Africa's kingdoms and city-states.

▶ **RUBRIC** See the Assessment booklet for a rubric on assessing cause-and-effect statements.

Section 3

Students should be able to write a poem that describes the feelings of an African slave.

▶ **RUBRIC** See the Assessment booklet for a rubric on assessing a student poem.

Section 4

Students should be able to role-play a meeting among African leaders who have just gained independence for their countries.

▶ **RUBRIC** See the Assessment booklet for a rubric on assessing a role-playing activity.

Section 5

Students should be able to write a glossary of the key terms in this section.

▶ **RUBRIC** See the Assessment booklet for a rubric on assessing a glossary.

Activities and Projects

Mental Mapping

It's Continental Africa is the second-largest continent on the Earth, containing 11,710,500 sq mi (30,330,000 sq km); or 22 percent of the world's land area. Ask students to draw outline maps of the five largest continents: Africa, Asia, Europe, North America, and South America.

Ask them to use the following figures and observations of a globe to decide whether they have shown the continents in correction proportion to one another. (Remind students that many flat maps distort the sizes of continents, so they should not rely on a flat map to test their estimates.) They may superimpose their outlines one over the other, or they may cut out their maps and place them on top of each other to judge. Asia: 33 percent of the world's land area; Europe: 7 percent; North America: 16.4 percent; South America: 12 percent.

Links to Current Events

History Today As you work on this chapter, ask students to look for articles in newspapers, magazines, or other media that reflect the continuing impact of its history on modern Africa. For example, students may find articles about efforts to rebuild South Africa following the elimination of apartheid, ongoing ethnic rivalries, or military governments that took power once their countries achieved independence.

They may also find articles about the historic legacy of the slave trade, including articles about African Americans who visit Africa to learn more about their own heritage and background, and articles about the role of Islam in Africa. Encourage students to make a bulletin-board display and add to it as they work through the chapter.

Hands-On Activities

Exploration The effort to find a water route to Asia encouraged the exploration and colonization of both North America and of Africa. Have students use a globe to trace the route of Portuguese sailors who began sailing down the unknown west coast of Africa in 1418. In 1441, they reached the coast of Africa south of the Sahara. In 1482, they crossed the Equator and reached the mouth of the Congo River. In 1487, Portuguese sailors rounded the Cape of Good Hope, and in 1498, led by Vasco da Gama, they sailed past the kingdoms of East Africa to India. Ask students to locate each of these spots on the African coast and attach dates to them. Have students note the length of time it took for sailors to move from one point of exploration to the next.

Illustrated Time Line Hang up a long narrow piece of paper with a time line on it marked with dates from 1000 to 2000 at 100-year intervals. Invite students to place illustrations of events or people on the line as they learn about them in this chapter. Students should add and correctly position a specific date or range of dates. Students may make their own illustrations or use illustrations clipped or photocopied from other sources. *Basic*

Graphic Organizer Have students select three or four kingdoms and empires covered in Section 2 of this chapter. Have them create a graphic organizer with one column for each kingdom or empire. Have

students list information about each kingdom in rows of the organizer. For example, they may include information about the location, duration, notable leaders, extent, achievements, and technology of each kingdom. *Average*

Historic Maps Have students make two historic maps of Africa. The first map should show the locations of some of the great African kingdoms and empires of the period before 1500. Have students locate and date each of these. The second map should show the colonial powers in Africa. Have students use colors to show the colonial holdings of France, England, Germany, Spain, Belgium, Portugal, and the

Netherlands in Africa. *English Language Learners*

Human Needs The growth of the kingdoms of East and West Africa are examples of the ways ancient people changed the physical environment to meet human needs. Have students write an essay explaining how the theme of human-environment interaction can be used to examine and understand one or more of these African civilizations. *Challenging*

F.Y.I.

This page can help you extend your own and students' understanding of the concepts in this chapter. You may want to browse through some of the suggestions in the **Bibliography. Interdisciplinary Links** can connect social studies understandings to areas elsewhere in the curriculum through the use of other Prentice Hall products. **National Geography Standards** reflected specifically in this chapter are listed for your convenience. Some hints about appropriate **Internet Access** are also provided. **School to Careers** provides insights into the practical uses of some of the concepts in this chapter as they might pertain to various careers.

BIBLIOGRAPHY

FOR THE TEACHER

Halliburton, Warren J. *Africa Today* series: *African Industries, Africa's Struggle to Survive, City and Village Life.* Crestwood, 1993.

History and Culture of Africa. Queue, 1995. CD-ROM.

Ibazebo, Isimeme. *Exploration into Africa.* New Discovery, 1994.

Koslow, Philip. *The Kingdoms of Africa.* Chelsea House, 1995.

Minks, Louis. *Traditional Africa.* Lucent Books, 1995.

FOR THE STUDENT

Easy
Wisniewski, David. *Sundiata: Lion King of Mali.* Clarion, 1992.

Average
Barboza, Steven. *Door of No Return: The Legend of Goree Island.* Cobblehill, 1994.

Reese, Lyn. *Spindle Stories.* Women in the World, 1990.

Challenging
Feelings, Tom. *The Middle Passage: White Ships, Black Cargo.* Dial, 1995.

McKissack, Patricia and Fredrick. *The Royal Kingdoms of Ghana, Mali, and Songhay: Life in Medieval Africa.* Holt, 1994.

LITERATURE CONNECTION

Hensen, Joyce. *The Captive.* Scholastic, 1994.

Rupert, Janet E. *The African Mask.* Clarion, 1994.

Weaver-Gelzer, Charlotte. *In the Time of Trouble.* Dutton, 1993.

INTERDISCIPLINARY LINKS

Subject	Theme: Change
MATH	Middle Grades Math: Tools for Success Course 1, Lesson 1-2, **Make a Table**
SCIENCE	Prentice Hall Science *Evolution: Change Over Time,* Lesson 3-2, **Human Ancestors and Relatives**

NATIONAL GEOGRAPHY STANDARDS

Students explore the 18 National Geography Standards throughout *Africa.* Chapter 2, however, concentrates on investigating the following standards: 1, 4, 7, 8, 9, 10, 11, 12, 13, 14, 15, 16, 17, 18. For a complete list of the standards, see the *Teacher's Flexible Planning Guide.*

SCHOOL TO CAREERS

In Chapter 2, Africa: Shaped by Its History, students learn about the Africa that is the birthplace of humankind as well as the modern continent. Students also learn about the skill of recognizing bias. Knowing something about the history of Africa can help students prepare for careers in international trade, foreign relations, education, and so on.

Understanding bias is particularly useful for writers, politicians, historians, and others. The curriculum presented in this book, as in all eight titles of Prentice Hall's *World Explorer* program, is designed to prepare students not only for careers but also for good citizenship—of the world as well as of this country.

INTERNET ACCESS

Many social studies teachers and students use Internet browsers, or search engines, to investigate particular topics. For the best results, use narrow rather than broad topics. Try these for Chapter 2: Nubia, Louis Leakey, Quran, Swahili. Finding age-appropriate sites is an important consideration when using the Internet. For links to age-appropriate sites in world studies and geography, visit the Prentice Hall Home Page at: **http://www.phschool.com**

Connecting to the Guiding Questions

As students complete this chapter, they will learn about key events in the history of Africa. Students will also focus on the influence of history on economic, political, and social conditions of modern African countries. Content in this chapter corresponds to this Guiding Question:

● What factors have shaped Africa's cultures?

Using the Map Activities

Direct students' attention to the map. Have them work in pairs to answer the questions.

• Egypt, Mali, Ghana, and Zimbabwe

• Answers will vary. Students may note that rivers and oceans would have aided the development of trade and the exchange of ideas among different peoples.

Heterogeneous Groups

The following Teacher's Edition strategies are suitable for heterogeneous groups.

Interdisciplinary Connections
Language Arts   p. 33
Critical Thinking
Recognizing Cause and
Effect   pp. 33, 43
Expressing Problems
Clearly   p. 51
Cooperative Learning
Mural of the
Slave Trade   p. 44

CHAPTER 2

AFRICA
Shaped by Its History

SECTION 1
Africa's First People

SECTION 2
Kingdoms and Empires

SECTION 3
The Conquest of Africa

SECTION 4
Independence and Its Challenges

SECTION 5
Issues for Africa Today

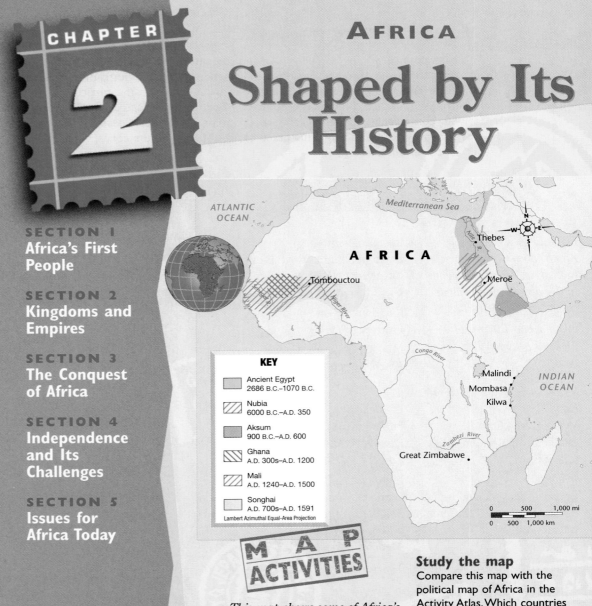

KEY

Ancient Egypt
2686 B.C.–1070 B.C.

Nubia
6000 B.C.–A.D. 350

Aksum
900 B.C.–A.D. 600

Ghana
A.D. 300s–A.D. 1200

Mali
A.D. 1240–A.D. 1500

Songhai
A.D. 700s–A.D. 1591

Lambert Azimuthal Equal-Area Projection

0   500   1,000 mi
0   500 1,000 km

MAP ACTIVITIES

This map shows some of Africa's great empires, kingdoms, and cities. Note that they did not all exist at the same time. Start exploring the history of Africa by doing the following activities:

Study the map
Compare this map with the political map of Africa in the Activity Atlas. Which countries took their names from early empires and kingdoms?

Consider locations
Notice that most of these empires and cities are close to rivers or oceans. How do you think the locations of empires and cities affected their development?

Resource Directory

Media and Technology

Africa's Early Trading Empires, from the World Video Explorer, enhances students' understanding of the trading empires of Ghana, Mali, and Songhai.

Chapter 4

Africa's First People

Lesson Objectives

1. Explain how early humans lived and got food.

2. Summarize the achievements of the civilizations along the Nile River.

3. Describe the possible causes and the effects of the Bantu migration.

BEFORE YOU READ

Reach Into Your Background

What are some of the things you remember from your past? Do you remember your very first day of school? What is the earliest birthday you can remember? All those things are part of your personal history.

Questions to Explore

1. What techniques did early Africans use to get food?
2. How did important ideas and discoveries spread throughout Africa?
3. What civilizations arose along the Nile River?

Key Terms

hunter-gatherer
domesticate
fertile
surplus
civilization
migrate
ethnic group

Key People and Places

Louis Leakey
Egypt
Nubia

Today the dry sands of the Sahara cover most of North Africa. But until about 4,000 years ago, this large area held enough water to support many people and animals. Scientists think that Africa's first farmers lived there. Paintings on cliffs and cave walls tell their story.

But the history of people in Africa is even older. Several million years earlier, the continent's first people lived in East Africa. We know this because of the stones and bones they left behind. These East Africans may have been the very first people to live on the Earth.

Hunter-Gatherers

The earliest humans probably survived by gathering wild fruits, nuts, and roots. These **hunter-gatherers** also hunted animals for meat and clothing. They made tools out of wood, animal bones, and then stone. The first use of stone tools marks the beginning of a period scientists call the Stone Age.

These stone tools worked very well. The scientist Louis Leakey found some of the first evidence of early people in East Africa. He also taught himself to make and use their tools. Using a two-inch, 25,000-year-old stone knife, Leakey could skin and cut up a gazelle in just 20 minutes.

▼ This painting was found in Algeria. The horns on this woman's helmet show that the Sahara may once have supported animal life.

Lesson Plan

1 Engage

Warm-Up Activity

Ask students to imagine that a thousand years from now, archaeologists are studying some of the items in your classroom. Challenge students to speculate on what the scientists might learn about them by studying various items, such as pencils, a globe, student desks, a U.S. flag, and so on.

Activating Prior Knowledge

Have students read Reach Into Your Background in the Before You Read box. Ask students to think about how they know about events that occurred when they were too young to remember. Have they heard them described by family members? Have they seen photographs or home videos? Discuss with the class why people need to remember past events and the different methods for doing so.

Teaching Resources

📁 **Reproducible Lesson Plan** in the Chapter and Section Resources booklet, p. 19, provides a summary of the section lesson.

📁 **Guided Reading and Review** in the Chapter and Section Resources booklet, p. 20, provides a structure for mastering key concepts and reviewing key terms in the section. Available in Spanish in the Spanish Chapter and Section Resources booklet, p. 13.

Program Resources

📁 Material in the **Primary Sources and Literature Readings** booklet extends content with a selection from the region under study.

📁 **Outline Maps** The Middle East and North Africa: Physical, p. 28; Africa South of the Sahara: Physical, p. 31

2 Explore

Ask students to consider the following questions as they read: What have scientists learned about the daily lives of early humans? Why did early Africans begin to farm? What were some characteristics of the civilizations along the Nile? What were some of the results of the Bantu migration?

3 Teach

Organize the class into five teams to compose some answers to the questions given in the Explore part of the Lesson Plan. Observe individual participation. After teams have completed their discussions, call on a member from each team to share their answer to one of the questions. This activity should take about 20 minutes.

4 Assess

See the answers to the Section Review. You may also use team discussions as a basis for assessment.

Acceptable participation includes volunteering some correct information and ideas to the team discussion.

Commendable participation is demonstrated by taking an equal part in group discussions.

Outstanding participation includes insightful contributions to the group and class discussions.

When hunter-gatherers settled down in one area and began farming, they faced longer, harder work days. Farmers spent many hours tilling the soil, planting seeds by hand, tending fields, harvesting crops, and caring for domesticated animals. They used only tools such as these, which they could make by hand. Farmers used axes (left) to clear the land. After butchering a cow, sheep, or goat, farmers used scrapers (top) to clean the hide, and cleavers (bottom) to cut the meat.
Critical Thinking Since farming is harder work than hunting and gathering, why would a hunter-gatherer want to become a farmer?

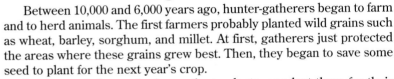

LINKS ACROSS TIME

The Thirst Zone Africa's first farmers probably lived in Algeria, in North Africa. Thousands of years ago, more rain fell in this region. But today, much of North Africa is known as the "Thirst Zone." People need to drink about 2.5 quarts (2.4 l) of water per day. People also use water for washing and farming. All in all, each person needs at least 21 quarts (20 l) of water per day. In the Thirst Zone, only about five quarts (5 l) of water per person is available.

Farming and Herding

Between 10,000 and 6,000 years ago, hunter-gatherers began to farm and to herd animals. The first farmers probably planted wild grains such as wheat, barley, sorghum, and millet. At first, gatherers just protected the areas where these grains grew best. Then, they began to save some seed to plant for the next year's crop.

Later, people began to **domesticate** plants, or adapt them for their own use. They threw away seeds from weaker plants and saved seeds from stronger ones. People domesticated animals by breeding certain animals together.

Domesticating plants and animals meant people could plant their own crops. They did not have to travel to places where grains were already growing. As a result, they could settle in one place. Most people settled where the land was **fertile,** or productive. Some communities produced a food **surplus,** or more than they needed. Surpluses allowed some people in the community to do work other than farming.

Civilizations on the Nile

Over hundreds or thousands of years, some Stone Age farming groups became civilizations. A **civilization** is a society with cities, a government, and social classes. Social classes form when people do a variety of jobs. As a result, some people are rich, some are poor, and others are middle class. Civilizations also have architecture, writing, and art. One civilization arose on the Nile River about 5,000 years ago.

Resource Directory

Program Resources

Nystrom Desk Atlas
Environmental and Global Issues
Topic: Conflict, pp. 37–42

Media and Technology

Color Transparency 71

Answers to . . .

EARLY FARMING

Raising crops provides people with more food.

▲ This Egyptian wall painting shows Nubian princes arriving in Egypt. At first, Egypt ruled Nubia, but later, Nubia conquered much of Egypt.

Egypt   Each summer, the Nile River flooded its banks. It left a layer of fertile silt that was ideal for farming. People began farming along the banks of the Nile by around 4000 B.C. They settled in scattered villages. Over the centuries, these villages grew into the civilization of ancient Egypt.

Ancient Egypt was ruled by kings called pharaohs (FAY rohz). The people believed the pharaohs to be gods as well as kings. When pharaohs died, they were buried in pyramids. People painted murals and picture-writings called hieroglyphics (hy ur oh GLIF iks) on the walls in the pyramids.

Egyptian civilization included more than just the pyramids. The Egyptians were advanced in paper-making, architecture, medicine, and mathematics.

Nubia   Starting in about 6000 B.C., several civilizations arose south of Egypt. This area was called Nubia. The final and greatest Nubian kingdom arose in the city of Meroë (MER oh ee) during the 500s B.C. It thrived until about the middle of the A.D. 300s. Meroë was probably the first place in Africa where iron was made.

READ ACTIVELY

Visualize What does a pyramid look like?

The Bantu Migrations

By about 500 B.C., West Africans had learned to heat and shape iron. They used it to form parts of tools such as arrowheads, ax heads, and hoe blades. The strong iron tools made farming easier and created food surpluses. As a result, West Africa's population increased.

Around 2,000 years ago, a group of people who spoke Bantu (BAN too) languages began to **migrate,** or move, out of West Africa. They were looking for new land to farm. Over hundreds of years, these

Section I Review

1. (a) a person who hunted animals for meat and clothing and gathered wild fruits, nuts, and roots (b) to adapt plants and animals for use (c) productive (d) more than is needed (e) society with cities, government, and social classes (f) to move to a new land (g) a group that shares language, religion, family ties, and customs

2. (a) scientist who studied early humans in Africa (b) area along the Nile River where one of the first civilizations developed (c) area south of Egypt where several civilizations arose

3. The Bantu brought tools and agricultural methods with them as they migrated.

4. Egyptians and Nubians contributed to the fields of writing, papermaking, architecture, medicine, mathematics, and ironmaking.

5. by domesticating plants and animals and forming farming communities

6. Posters should logically illustrate an idea from the section.

Routes of the Bantu Migrations

Map Study Historians are not entirely sure why the Bantu speakers began to move from one region to another. The migrations, however, were the largest in human history. Today, most people in Southern Africa speak Bantu languages.
Movement Notice how the arrows on the map begin in a light shade of orange and become darker. This shows passage of time. Which place did the migration reach first, Lake Victoria or the Orange River?

KEY

Bantu migration route

500 B.C. → A.D. 1500
Lambert Azimuthal Equal-Area Projection

AFRICA

Niger River
Congo River
Lake Victoria
Lake Tanganyika
Lake Nyasa
Zambezi River
Limpopo River
Orange River

ATLANTIC OCEAN

INDIAN OCEAN

0   300   600 mi
0 300 600 km

Bantu-speakers settled in Central and Southern Africa. They introduced farming, herding, and iron tools to these regions. Today, people in this part of Africa belong to hundreds of **ethnic groups,** or groups that share languages, religions, family ties, and customs. But almost all of these ethnic groups speak Bantu languages.

SECTION 1 REVIEW

1. Define (a) hunter-gatherer, (b) domesticate, (c) fertile, (d) surplus, (e) civilization, (f) migrate, (g) ethnic group.

2. Identify (a) Louis Leakey, (b) Egypt, (c) Nubia.

3. How did iron tools, farming, and herding spread to Southern Africa?

4. Name some achievements of ancient Egyptian and Nubian civilizations.

Critical Thinking
5. Drawing Conclusions How did early Africans adapt to their environment?

Activity
6. Writing to Learn Make a poster that illustrates, step-by-step, an important idea from this section. For example, you might show how scientists learn about early people or how ideas spread from one part of Africa to another.

Resource Directory

Teaching Resources

📁 **Section Quiz** in the Chapter and Section Resources booklet, p. 21, covers the main ideas and key terms in the section. Available in Spanish in the Spanish Chapter and Section Resources booklet, p. 14.

Answers to ...
MAP STUDY

Lake Victoria

Kingdoms and Empires

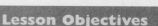

BEFORE YOU READ

Reach Into Your Background

What things do you own or have at home that were made in other countries? What things were made in the United States? Make a short list and share it with a classmate.

Questions to Explore

1. How did trade enrich Africa's kingdoms and city-states?

2. How did the religion of Islam spread to different parts of Africa?

Key Terms

Quran
pilgrimage
Swahili
city-state

Key People and Places

Mansa Musa
Aksum
Ghana
Mali
Songhai
Tombouctou
Kilwa
Zimbabwe

In the year A.D. 1, a Greek writer made a list of things you could buy in Adulis, East Africa. Adulis was the most important city in Aksum, a bustling trade center along the Red Sea. There, you could buy:

 " Cloth made in Egypt . . . many articles of flint glass . . . and brass, which is used for ornament and cut pieces instead of coin; sheets of soft copper, used for cooking utensils and cut up for bracelets and anklets for the women; iron, which is made into spears used against the elephants and other wild beasts, and in their wars. "

▼ These beads are from Zimbabwe, but thanks to the traders of Aksum, they could have journeyed all the way to Europe or India.

Aksum

Aksum was located in East Africa. If it still existed today, it would be in the countries of Ethiopia and Eritrea. Around 1000 B.C., African and Arab traders began settling along the west coast of the Red Sea. They were the ancestors of the people of Aksum. Over time, Aksum came to control trade in

Section 2

Lesson Objectives

1 Describe the Egyptian, Nubian, and Aksum civilizations that grew up along the Nile.

2 Summarize the rise and fall of the kingdoms and city-states of ancient Africa.

Lesson Plan

1 Engage

Warm-Up Activity

Ask students to look carefully at a physical map of Africa and to identify places on the map where they think ancient civilizations might have arisen. Suggest that they begin by listing the things that are needed to build a civilization, such as water and fertile land. Explain that they will be reading about some ancient African civilizations in this section. Encourage them to check their accuracy in predicting where civilizations were established.

Activating Prior Knowledge

Have students read Reach Into Your Background in the Before You Read box. Combine students' lists and record the most frequently mentioned items on the chalkboard. Encourage students to explain their choices.

Using Route Maps

You might **introduce** the skill by telling students that route maps show a route, or path, from one place to another. Point out the compass rose and the lines showing the migration route of the Bantu. Review the use of a scale of miles. Help students **practice** and **apply** the skill by asking them in what directions the Bantu traveled—and how far. Have them calculate the approximate distances traveled south, southeast, and southwest.

2 Explore

As students read the section, urge them to look for specific reasons for the success of each of the kingdoms and empires. Ask them to name some achievements of each, to explain which depended upon trade, and to identify which lasted the longest.

3 Teach

Have students create a chart that lists the six kingdoms and city-states in rows. Have them label three columns: *Time Period, Location,* and *Characteristics.* Urge students to use the chart to compare and contrast the kingdoms and city-states. This activity should take about 25 minutes.

4 Assess

See the answers to the Section Review. You may also assess students' charts.

Acceptable work should include at least one detail in each cell of the chart.

Commendable work will have more than one specific detail in each cell of the chart.

Outstanding charts will provide a comprehensive comparison of the kingdoms and city-states.

Answers to ...

MAP STUDY

West African kingdoms exchanged gold for salt from North Africa. Tombouctou was centrally located between trading kingdoms. The kingdom of Songhai controlled the largest area.

READ ACTIVELY

Ask Questions What questions do you have about trade in ancient Africa?

the Red Sea. Aksum came to power after the Nubian kingdom of Meroë fell. By then, Aksum controlled a trade network that stretched from the Mediterranean Sea to India.

Ideas, as well as goods, traveled along trade routes. The Christian religion traveled to Aksum along these routes. In the mid-300s, many people in Aksum became Christian. Aksum became a center of the early Ethiopian Christian Church. But Aksum began to decline in the 600s. Then Arabs took control of much of the region's trade.

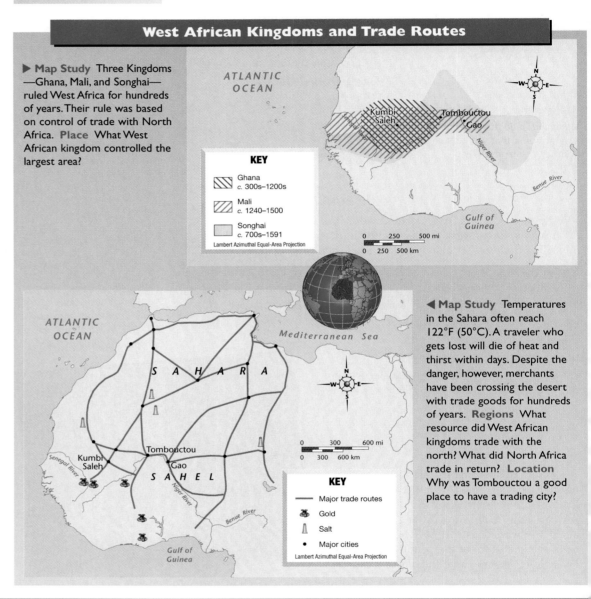

West African Kingdoms and Trade Routes

▶ **Map Study** Three Kingdoms —Ghana, Mali, and Songhai— ruled West Africa for hundreds of years. Their rule was based on control of trade with North Africa. **Place** What West African kingdom controlled the largest area?

KEY

Ghana *c.* 300s–1200s

Mali *c.* 1240–1500

Songhai *c.* 700s–1591

Lambert Azimuthal Equal-Area Projection

0   250   500 mi
0   250   500 km

◀ **Map Study** Temperatures in the Sahara often reach 122°F (50°C). A traveler who gets lost will die of heat and thirst within days. Despite the danger, however, merchants have been crossing the desert with trade goods for hundreds of years. **Regions** What resource did West African kingdoms trade with the north? What did North Africa trade in return? **Location** Why was Tombouctou a good place to have a trading city?

KEY

⎯ Major trade routes

Gold

Salt

• Major cities

Lambert Azimuthal Equal-Area Projection

0   300   600 mi
0   300   600 km

Resource Directory

Teaching Resources

Reproducible Lesson Plan in the Chapter and Section Resources booklet, p. 22, provides a summary of the section lesson.

Guided Reading and Review in the Chapter and Section Resources booklet, p. 23, provides a structure for mastering key concepts and reviewing key terms in the section. Available in Spanish in the Spanish Chapter and Section Resources booklet, p. 15.

Program Resources

Outline Maps North Africa: Political, p. 31; Africa South of the Sahara: Political, p. 33

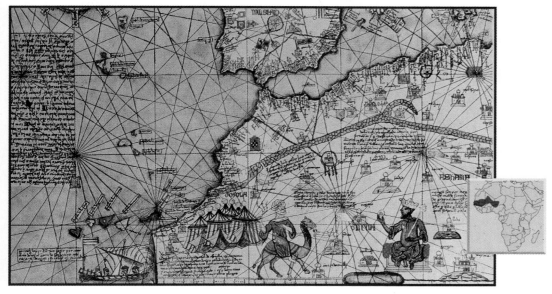

▲ Impressed with Mansa Musa's gold, Europeans included a picture of him on their maps of Africa. He appears in the lower right-hand corner of this map.

West African Kingdoms

As Aksum declined, great kingdoms arose on the other side of the continent, in West Africa. The power of these kingdoms was based on the trade of salt and gold. People need salt to survive, especially in hot areas like West Africa. The people of West Africa had no local sources of salt. However, they had plenty of gold. For the people of North Africa, the opposite was true. They had salt, but no gold.

A brisk trade between North Africa and West Africa quickly grew. Control of this trade brought power and riches to three West African kingdoms—Ghana (GAH nuh), Mali (MAH lee), and Songhai (SAWNG hy).

Ghana   Look at the map on the previous page. Note that the kingdom of Ghana was located between the Senegal and Niger rivers. From this location Ghana controlled trade across West Africa. Ghana's kings grew rich from the taxes they charged on the salt, gold, and other goods that flowed through their land. The flow of gold was so great that Arab writers called Ghana "land of gold." But in time, Ghana lost control of the trade routes. It gave way to a new power, the kingdom of Mali.

Mali and the Spread of Islam   The kingdom of Mali arose in the mid-1200s in the Upper Niger Valley. The word Mali means "where the king lives." Mali's powerful kings controlled both the gold mines of the south and the salt supplies of the north. In Mali, the king was called Mansa, which means "emperor."

Mali's most famous king, Mansa Musa, gained the throne about 1312. His 25-year reign brought peace and order to the kingdom. An Arab visitor to Mali found "safety throughout the land. The traveler here has no more reason to fear thieves than the man who stays at home."

READ ACTIVELY

Visualize Visualize the court of the king of Ghana. How would you know you were in the presence of wealth and power?

Mansa Musa based his laws on the **Quran** (koo RAHN), the holy book of the religion of Islam. Over the centuries, Muslim traders had spread their religion into many parts of Africa. Muslims are followers of Islam. Mansa Musa and many of his subjects were Muslims.

In 1324, Mansa Musa made a **pilgrimage**—a religious journey—to the Arabian city of Mecca. Muslims consider Mecca a holy place. Muhammad, the prophet who first preached Islam, was born there. Mansa Musa brought 60,000 people with him on his pilgrimage. Eighty camels each carried 300 pounds (136 kg) of gold. Along the way, Mansa Musa gave people gifts of gold.

Mansa Musa's pilgrimage brought about new trading ties with other Muslim states. It also displayed Mali's wealth. Hearing the reports, Europe's rulers grew interested in African gold.

Songhai After Mansa Musa's death around 1332, Mali declined. Mali was finally destroyed by a new empire called Songhai. In time, Songhai became West Africa's most powerful kingdom. Songhai's rulers controlled important trade routes and wealthy trading cities.

The wealthiest trading city, Tombouctou (tohn book TOO), also was a great Muslim learning center. People said of Tombouctou:

> "Salt comes from the north, gold from the south, and silver from the city of white men. But the word of God and the treasures of wisdom are only to be found in Tombouctou."

Invaders from North Africa defeated Songhai in 1591. But Songhai people still live near the Niger River, and Islam remains important in the region.

East African City-States

As in West Africa, trade helped East African cities to develop. Around the time that Aksum declined, trading cities arose along East Africa's coast. Traders from these cities used seasonal winds to sail northeast to India and China. They carried animal skins, ivory, and gold and other metals. When the winds changed direction, the traders rode them home. They brought many goods, including cotton, silk, and porcelain.

Trade affected the culture of coastal East Africa. Some of the traders who visited the area were Muslims. Many of them settled and introduced Islam to East Africa. In time, a new language developed in the area. Called **Swahili** (swah HEE lee), it

East African Trade Routes

KEY
→ Trade routes
Lambert Azimuthal Equal-Area Projection

Cairo
To Mediterranean
Mecca
To India
Mogadishu
Malindi
Mombasa
Kilwa
INDIAN OCEAN
To East Asia
Great Zimbabwe
Sofala

0   500   1,000 mi
0 500 1,000 km

Map Study Traders visiting East African city-states could buy gold from Africa, cotton from India, and porcelain from China. **Location** How were the East African city-states ideally located to become centers of trade?

Trade in East Africa

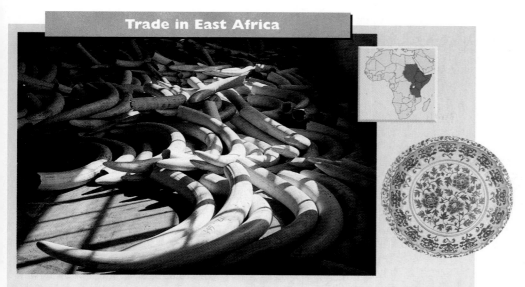

As early as A.D. 1100, traders in East Africa bought and sold goods from many parts of the world. Traders bought animal skins, gold, and ivory, or elephant tusks (above left), from Africa and sold them in India and China.

From India, traders brought back cloth, grain, oil, and sugar. From China, they brought back dishes and vases made of porcelain, a hard substance made by baking clay (above right).

Background

Global Perspectives

City-States The city-state has reappeared again and again throughout history. City-states such as Athens, Corinth, and Thebes were well established by the 500s B.C. These Greek city-states built their wealth through trade and constantly vied with each other for control of the sea. Uneasy alliances among city-states often disintegrated and sometimes led to wars. About 2,000 years later, the lack of a central authority in Italy allowed the growth of a number of self-governing city-states. One of the most powerful of these was Florence, ruled almost exclusively from 1434 to 1737 by the famous banking family, the Medicis. The Medicis were great patrons of artists and intellectuals, and their money and patronage helped make Florence one of the most beautiful and important cities of the Renaissance.

was a Bantu language with some Arab words mixed in. Today, many East Africans still speak Swahili.

Some East African cities grew into powerful city-states. A **city-state** is a city that has its own government and often controls much of the surrounding land. Among the greatest of these city-states were Malindi (muh LIN dee), Mombasa (mahm BAH suh), and Kilwa (KIL wah). Look at the map on the previous page. How do you think the locations of these city-states helped them to become important trade centers?

Kilwa Ibn Battuta (IHB uhn bat TOO tah), a Muslim traveler from North Africa, visited Kilwa in 1331. He had seen great cities in China, India, and West Africa. But Battuta wrote that Kilwa was "one of the most beautiful and best-constructed towns in the world." In Kilwa, people lived in three- and four-story houses made of stone and sea coral.

Kilwa and other East African city-states grew rich from trade and taxes. Traders had to pay huge taxes on goods they brought into the city. "Any merchant who wished to enter the city paid for every five hundred pieces of cloth, no matter what the quality, one gold [piece] as entrance duty," reported one visitor. "After this, the king took two thirds of all the merchandise, leaving the trader one third."

In the early 1500s, Kilwa and the other city-states were conquered by the European country of Portugal. The Portuguese wanted to build their own trading empire.

SKILLS MINI LESSON

Locating Information To **introduce** the skill, mention to students that they are surrounded by a sea of information. In order to locate the information they need, they will need to plan a route through that sea. Help students **practice** the skill by working with them to locate information about the kingdoms or city-states of ancient Africa. Have them clearly define the information they are seeking by formulating a question, for example: *Which goods were most important to traders in Mali?* Discuss with students the best sources for the information they are seeking. Have students **apply** the skill by researching the topic they chose and presenting the information they find in the form of a written report. Be sure students include a list of the sources they used.

1. (a) holy book of the religion of Islam (b) a religious journey (c) Bantu language with some Arab words mixed in (d) city with its own government, which often controls surrounding land

2. (a) Muslim emperor of Mali (b) ancient East African kingdom (c) kingdom between Senegal and Niger rivers (d) kingdom that arose in the Upper Niger Valley (e) West Africa's most powerful kingdom (f) wealthy Songhai city and center of learning (g) East African city-state (h) trading civilization on Limpopo River

3. The city-states were trading centers where metals and other products from Africa were traded for goods from Asia.

4. Traders who were Muslim brought the religion with them.

5. Possible response: Ghana, Mali, and Songhai were powerful empires and trading centers that dominated nearby areas by controlling and taxing trade.

6. Answers will vary. Letters should reflect information provided in the section.

◄The walls of Great Zimbabwe are more than 600 years old. Builders created them without using mortar or cement.

Zimbabwe South and inland from the East African city-states lay another great trading civilization. Great Zimbabwe (zim BAH bway)was located near the bend of the Limpopo (lim POH poh) River in Southern Africa. Great Zimbabwe reached its peak about the year 1300. Today only ruins of it remain. But once, more than 200 gigantic stone buildings covered the area. (Great Zimbabwe means "stone dwelling.")

Upon seeing the ruins in the late 1800s, European explorers did not think that Africans had the skill to build them. They were wrong. The builders were the Shona, a group of Bantu speakers who had lived in the region since the 900s.

SECTION 2 REVIEW

1. **Define** (a) Quran, (b) pilgrimage, (c) Swahili, (d) city-state.

2. **Identify** (a) Mansa Musa, (b) Aksum, (c) Ghana, (d) Mali, (e) Songhai, (f) Tombouctou, (g) Kilwa, (h) Zimbabwe.

3. On what was the wealth and power of the city-states based?

4. How did Islam become a major religion in West and East Africa?

Critical Thinking

5. **Drawing Conclusions** How did Ghana, Mali, and Songhai become wealthy from gold and salt even though they did not mine either one?

Activity

6. **Writing to Learn** You are a traveler visiting one of the West African kingdoms or city-states. Write a short letter home about some of the things you see.

Resource Directory

Teaching Resources

Section Quiz in the Chapter and Section Resources booklet, p. 24, covers the main ideas and key terms in the section. Available in Spanish in the Spanish Chapter and Section Resources booklet, p. 16.

The Conquest of Africa

BEFORE YOU READ

Reach Into Your Background

What actions would you take to get something you really wanted? What would you do to hold on to something that was already yours?

Questions to Explore

1. Why did European contact with Africa increase?
2. What were the effects of European rule in Africa?

Key Terms

colonize

Key People and Places

Olaudah Equiano
Gorée
Cape of Good Hope

On the island of Gorée (gaw RAY), off the coast of the West African country of Senegal, stands a museum called the House of Slaves. It honors millions of Africans who were enslaved and shipped across the Atlantic Ocean. Many Africans passed through this building. Their last view of Africa was an opening called "The Door of No Return." Beyond it lay the ocean and the slave ships bound for the Americas.

Europeans on the Coast

The Atlantic slave trade began in the 1500s and continued through the late 1800s. But contact between Europeans and Africans began long before that. In North Africa, Europeans traded for gold from the empires of Ghana and Mali, and for salt from the Sahara. Why do you think Europeans' first contacts with Africans took place in North Africa?

After 1500, Europe's relationship with Africa changed. It had begun as trade between equals. But it turned into the enslavement and forced migration of millions of Africans. The African slave trade ended in 1860. Then Europeans wanted Africa's natural resources. By 1900, European countries had divided Africa among themselves.

▼ The Door of No Return in Senegal led to a pier, where slave ships were waiting to sail to the Americas.

Teaching Resources

📁 **Reproducible Lesson Plan** in the Chapter and Section Resources booklet, p. 25, provides a summary of the section lesson.

📁 **Guided Reading and Review** in the Chapter and Section Resources booklet, p. 26, provides a structure for mastering key concepts and reviewing key terms in the section. Available in Spanish in the Spanish Chapter and Section Resources booklet, p. 17.

Program Resources

📁 **Outline Maps** North Africa: Political, p. 31;
Africa South of the Sahara: Political, p. 33

Section 3

Lesson Objectives

1. Trace the progress of the European exploration of Africa.
2. Explain the origin and effects of the slave trade.
3. Describe the process of the colonization of Africa by European nations.

Lesson Plan

1 Engage

Warm-Up Activity

Ask students what they would like to do when they grow up. Then ask how they would feel if they were told that they couldn't do any of these things. Instead, they would be assigned a job. It would probably be working in a field or cleaning a house. If they refused to do what they were told, they could be severely punished. Urge students to discuss how they would feel about this future.

Activating Prior Knowledge

Have students read Reach Into Your Background in the Before You Read box. Record students' ideas without judgment or comment. Then open a discussion about the fairness of some of the methods proposed.

2 Explore

Have students read the section. Tell them to look for answers to these questions as they read: What did Europeans learn as they began exploring Africa? In what ways did contact with Europeans change Africa? Why did the slave trade develop?

3 Teach

Have students create a concept web for each of these terms: *European contact* and *slavery*. Have them complete the webs with facts from the section. Have students use their webs to contribute to a follow-up class discussion. You may wish to create master webs on the chalkboard. This activity should take about 25 minutes.

4 Assess

See the answers to the Section Review. You may also want to assess students' completed concept webs.

Acceptable webs include at least six correct key ideas.

Commendable webs include at least 10 correct key ideas.

Outstanding webs include at least 10 correct key ideas plus additional terms or ideas linked to the key ideas.

LINKS ACROSS THE WORLD

Europeans and the Americas Christopher Columbus sailed extensively along the coast of western Africa. He traveled several times to the Portuguese trading post in the Gold Coast. On these journeys, he sometimes found pieces of wood floating from the west. These signs helped to convince Columbus that there was land to the west. Such convictions increased his desire to take the journey westward.

▼ In 1482, the Portuguese built this fort, Elmina Castle, in Ghana to protect and supply its trade with West Africa.

In the 1400s, Portuguese explorers began exploring the coast of West Africa. They wanted to trade directly for West African gold and ivory, instead of dealing with North African merchants. They also wanted to trade with Asia.

Many inventions helped the Portuguese explore Africa's coast. The Portuguese used a lateen sail, a triangle-shaped sail designed in North Africa. The lateen sail allowed ships to sail against the wind as well as with it. And better instruments, such as the astrolabe (AS troh layb), helped sailors navigate at sea. With these improvements, Portuguese sailors became the first Europeans to travel south along Africa's coasts.

At first, both Africans and Europeans traded together as equals. Africans traded gold, cotton, ivory, skins, metal objects, and pepper. In return, Europeans traded copper, brass, and clothing. Europeans brought corn, cassava, and yams from the Americas. These plants became food crops in Africa. Some Africans also became Christians.

But soon this balance was upset. In 1497, three Portuguese ships rounded the tip of Southern Africa and sailed north along Africa's east coast. The wealth of the East African city-states amazed the Portuguese. More Portuguese ships followed—not to trade but to seize the riches of the city-states. Portugal controlled trade on East Africa's coast until well into the 1600s.

The Dutch, French, and English soon followed the Portuguese. They set up trading posts along Africa's coasts, where sailors could get supplies. The Dutch built a trading post on the Cape of Good Hope at Africa's southern tip. Soon, settlers arrived. They moved inland, building homes and farms.

Resource Directory

Media and Technology

 Color Transparency 135, Historical Map Set 5

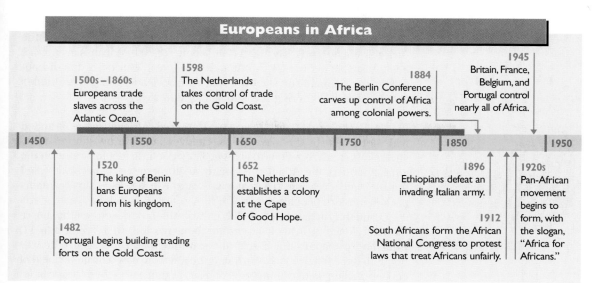

Europeans in Africa

1500s–1860s Europeans trade slaves across the Atlantic Ocean.

1598 The Netherlands takes control of trade on the Gold Coast.

1884 The Berlin Conference carves up control of Africa among colonial powers.

1945 Britain, France, Belgium, and Portugal control nearly all of Africa.

1450 — 1550 — 1650 — 1750 — 1850 — 1950

1482 Portugal begins building trading forts on the Gold Coast.

1520 The king of Benin bans Europeans from his kingdom.

1652 The Netherlands establishes a colony at the Cape of Good Hope.

1896 Ethiopians defeat an invading Italian army.

1912 South Africans form the African National Congress to protest laws that treat Africans unfairly.

1920s Pan-African movement begins to form, with the slogan, "Africa for Africans."

▲ Africans resisted European colonization, but, as this time line shows, Europe slowly took control of more and more of Africa. What year did an African country defeat a European army?

As Europeans spread out, sometimes by force, their relations with Africans worsened. But the growing trade in enslaved Africans poisoned future contacts between Africans and Europeans the most.

The Atlantic Slave Trade

Before the 1500s, slavery was common in Africa. But slaves usually won their freedom after a few years. Some became important citizens among the people who had enslaved them. Slaves could even be bought out of slavery by their own people.

Then the European powers began to build colonies in North and South America. They practiced a new type of slavery there. The Europeans treated slaves like property, not like people. Freedom in the future was out of the question. The African slave trade did not end until the 1800s. By then, millions of Africans had been taken from their homelands, never to return.

The Demand for Slaves Spanish, Portuguese, and Dutch settlers in the Americas needed workers for their plantations and mines. At first they enslaved Native Americans. But many Native Americans became sick and died from diseases or brutal working conditions. Others ran away. To replace them, the Europeans started to import enslaved Africans.

The Europeans thought that Africans would make good slaves. Africa's climate was similar to that of the Americas. Africans were skilled farmers, miners, and metal workers. They also did not know the territory. It would be almost impossible for them to escape.

By the 1600s, Portuguese traders were trading goods for African slaves. Some African groups refused to join the trade. But other groups

SKILLS MINI LESSON

Using a Time Line
To **introduce** the skill, explain that a time line is an illustration of the events that occur over a given period of time. Allow students to **practice** the skill by discussing with them the features of the time line above. Ask students to describe the content of the time line and to identify the basic time interval used (100 years). Have them describe how the time line can help them see the order of events. Encourage students to **apply** the skill by asking them to compose two questions that can be answered using information on the time line. Have students share and answer one another's questions.

Activity

Critical Thinking

Recognizing Cause and Effect *Suitable as either an individual or a whole class activity.* Write the following sentences on the chalkboard. Ask volunteers to circle the cause in each sentence and underline the effect.

- Portuguese adventurers explored the coast of West Africa in order to find a way to trade directly with West Africa.
- The invention of the lateen sail allowed ships to sail against the wind.

Answers to . . .
TIME LINE STUDY

In 1896, Ethiopia defeated the Italian army.

Cooperative Learning

Mural of the Slave Trade
Assign students to work in groups of four, with each group choosing an aspect of the slave trade as a topic. They might choose the journey across the Atlantic Ocean, the slave auction, or family separation. Have students create a mural depicting this topic. Suggest that students divide the work, assigning research to one member, planning the mural to a second member, and creating and presenting the mural to the third and fourth members. Have groups display their murals and share what they learned with the class. *Visual*

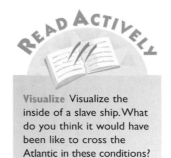

READ ACTIVELY

Visualize Visualize the inside of a slave ship. What do you think it would have been like to cross the Atlantic in these conditions?

sold slaves captured during battles. In return, the Europeans gave the Africans cheap guns. By the 1700s, about 78,000 African slaves were being transported across the Atlantic each year. But even this did not satisfy the demand for slaves. Some African leaders began to kidnap people from neighboring areas to sell as slaves.

The Horror of Slavery   Captured Africans were branded with hot irons. In the slave ships, captives lay side by side on filthy shelves stacked from floor to ceiling. They got little food or water on the journey across the Atlantic. As many as 20 percent of the slaves died during each crossing. To make up for these losses, ships' captains packed in more people.

Olaudah Equiano (oh LOW duh ek wee AHN oh), described this horrible experience in a book he wrote about his life. In 1756, at age 11, Equiano was captured and sold at a slave auction. He was sure he was going to die: "When I looked around the ship and saw a large furnace of copper boiling and a multitude of black people of every description chained together . . . I no longer doubted of my fate."

Equiano proved luckier than most African slaves. In time, he was able to buy his freedom. For most slaves, freedom was little more than a distant dream.

The Cramped Journey Across the Atlantic

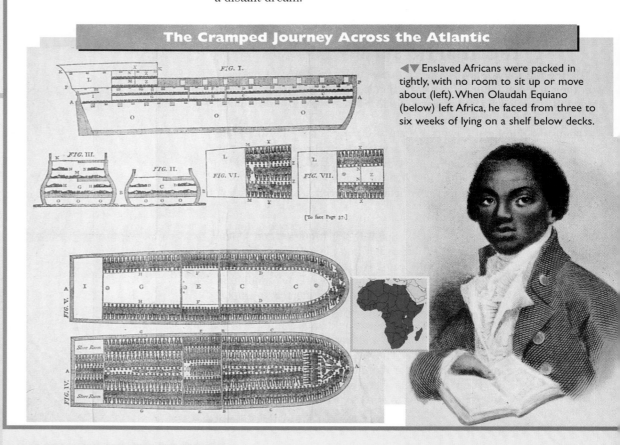

◀▼ Enslaved Africans were packed in tightly, with no room to sit up or move about (left). When Olaudah Equiano (below) left Africa, he faced from three to six weeks of lying on a shelf below decks.

Resource Directory

Program Resources

Environmental and Global Issues
Topic: Human Rights, pp. 25–30

The Effects of Slavery on Africa Some Africans grew wealthy from the slave trade. But the slave trade was a disaster for Africa. The people who were sold as slaves were the youngest, healthiest, and most capable workers from the region. If a country loses its best people, it is hard for it to grow and become strong.

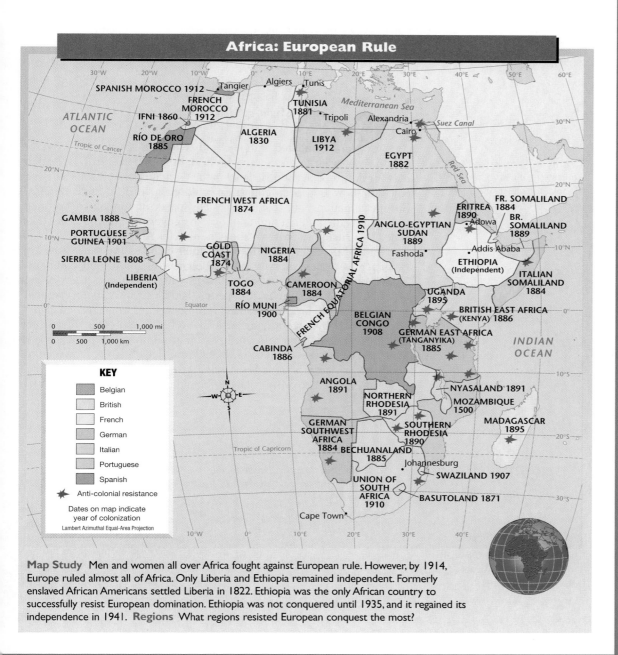

Africa: European Rule

KEY

- Belgian
- British
- French
- German
- Italian
- Portuguese
- Spanish
- ★ Anti-colonial resistance

Dates on map indicate year of colonization

Lambert Azimuthal Equal-Area Projection

SPANISH MOROCCO 1912
FRENCH MOROCCO 1912
IFNI 1860
RÍO DE ORO 1885
ATLANTIC OCEAN
Tangier
Algiers
Tunis
TUNISIA 1881
Mediterranean Sea
Tripoli
Alexandria
Cairo
Suez Canal
ALGERIA 1830
LIBYA 1912
EGYPT 1882
Tropic of Cancer
Red Sea
FRENCH WEST AFRICA 1874
GAMBIA 1888
PORTUGUESE GUINEA 1901
SIERRA LEONE 1808
LIBERIA (Independent)
GOLD COAST 1874
NIGERIA 1884
TOGO 1884
CAMEROON 1884
RÍO MUNI 1900
FRENCH EQUATORIAL AFRICA 1910
Equator
ANGLO-EGYPTIAN SUDAN 1889
Fashoda
ERITREA 1890
Adowa
Addis Ababa
ETHIOPIA (Independent)
FR. SOMALILAND 1884
BR. SOMALILAND 1889
ITALIAN SOMALILAND 1884
BELGIAN CONGO 1908
UGANDA 1895
BRITISH EAST AFRICA (KENYA) 1886
GERMAN EAST AFRICA (TANGANYIKA) 1885
CABINDA 1886
INDIAN OCEAN
ANGOLA 1891
NYASALAND 1891
MOZAMBIQUE 1500
NORTHERN RHODESIA 1891
GERMAN SOUTHWEST AFRICA 1884
SOUTHERN RHODESIA 1890
MADAGASCAR 1895
Tropic of Capricorn
BECHUANALAND 1885
Johannesburg
SWAZILAND 1907
UNION OF SOUTH AFRICA 1910
BASUTOLAND 1871
Cape Town

0 500 1,000 mi
0 500 1,000 km

Map Study Men and women all over Africa fought against European rule. However, by 1914, Europe ruled almost all of Africa. Only Liberia and Ethiopia remained independent. Formerly enslaved African Americans settled Liberia in 1822. Ethiopia was the only African country to successfully resist European domination. Ethiopia was not conquered until 1935, and it regained its independence in 1941. **Regions** What regions resisted European conquest the most?

Background

Links Across Place

Amazing Grace While many ship captains became rich from the slave trade, at least one, John Newton, came to believe that the slave trade was abominable. Newton stopped trading in slaves and began to work to ban slavery in Great Britain. He put his feelings of regret and his hope for forgiveness into words in his hymn *Amazing Grace,* which begins:

Amazing grace, how sweet the sound
That saved a wretch like me,
I once was lost, but now I'm found,
Was blind, but now I see.

Answers to . . .
MAP STUDY

East Africa and Central and Southern Africa

1. to settle an area and take over its government

2. (a) African who was captured and sold into slavery (b) island off the coast of Senegal where there is a museum called the House of Slaves (c) cape at the southern end of Africa where early Dutch explorers built a trading post

3. At first, Africans and Europeans benefited from mutual trade. Later, Europeans began to enslave Africans and carved up Africa into European colonies.

4. Some European nations ran the governments in Africa directly. Other governments were run by Africans who took orders from European officials.

5. Decisions about how to divide up Africa were made without considering existing cultures and ethnic groups. As a result, modern African nations often include ethnic groups that traditionally have been enemies. National boundaries also often divide ethnic groups.

6. Editorials will vary, but should demonstrate an understanding of the different views that would have been held by Africans and Europeans.

Europeans Carve Up Africa

After the slave trade ended, Europeans then began to raid Africa's interior for resources. They wanted the resources to fuel the new factories that were springing up all across Europe. Europeans also saw Africa as a place to build empires.

Africans fiercely resisted European conquest. But their cheap guns proved no match for Europe's weapons. Europeans carried the Maxim gun, the first automatic machine gun. A British author wrote at the time:

“Whatever happens we have got
The Maxim-gun; and they have not.”

Europeans competed with each other to gain African territory. But they did not want to go to war with each other over it. In 1884, leaders of several European countries met in the German city of Berlin. They set rules for how European countries could claim African land. By 1900, European nations had colonized many parts of Africa. To **colonize** means to settle an area and take over its government. One newspaper called this rush for territory "the scramble for Africa."

Not all European countries ruled their colonies the same way. The Belgian government directly ran the Belgian Congo (now the country of Zaire). But Nigeria was run by Africans who took orders from British officials. In all cases, the African people had little power in government.

The scramble for Africa caused lasting harm. Europeans had gained power in part by encouraging Africans to fight each other. Europeans also took the best land to farm. In some areas, they forced Africans to labor under terrible conditions. Finally, Europeans drew new political boundaries. These boundaries divided some ethnic groups and forced differing groups together. These boundaries were to cause much conflict in Africa.

READ ACTIVELY

Ask Questions What questions do you have about the effect of European colonization on the people of Africa?

SECTION 3 REVIEW

1. **Define** colonize.
2. **Identify** (a) Olaudah Equiano, (b) Gorée, (c) Cape of Good Hope.

3. How did relations between Africa and Europe change over time?

4. In what different ways did the Europeans govern their African colonies?

Critical Thinking

5. **Identifying Central Issues** How did the European conquest affect Africa?

Activity

6. **Writing to Learn** Write two brief editorials about the European conference in Berlin. Write one editorial from the point of view of an African. Write the other from the point of view of a European who attended the conference.

Resource Directory

Teaching Resources

Section Quiz in the Chapter and Section Resources booklet, p. 27, covers the main ideas and key terms in the section. Available in Spanish in the Spanish Chapter and Section Resources booklet, p. 18.

Independence and Its Challenges

Lesson Objectives

1. Explain the growth of nationalism in Africa.

2. Describe Africa's role during World Wars I and II.

3. Identify the paths to independence taken by Ghana, Tanzania, Morocco, and Angola.

BEFORE YOU READ

Reach Into Your Background
People have different ideas about what independence means. For some, it means having the freedom to make their own decisions. What does independence mean to you?

Questions to Explore
1. What techniques did African nations use to win independence from European powers?
2. What challenges did new African leaders face after independence?

Key Terms
nationalism
Pan-Africanism
boycott
democracy

Key People
Robert Mugabe
Léopold Sédar Senghor
Kwame Nkrumah

O n April 18, 1980, the people of Rhodesia took to the streets. They had recently elected Robert Mugabe (mu GAHB ee) as Prime Minister. It was the first free election in Rhodesia's history. People waited excitedly through the night. At midnight, the British flag came down for the last time. People cheered loudly. At that moment, the British colony of Rhodesia became the independent country of Zimbabwe.

The fight for independence had been hard and sometimes violent. Now, Prime Minister Mugabe asked all the people to work together. They would have to build a new nation. "The wrongs of the past must now stand forgiven and forgotten," said Mugabe. Zimbabwe was one of the last African countries to win independence. But the movement for freedom in Zimbabwe had begun many years before.

▼ When Zimbabwe's flag went up for the first time, the country became independent of Great Britain.

The Growth of Nationalism

Many Africans dreamed of independence after Europe's scramble for Africa in the late 1800s. In 1897, Mankayi Sontanga (mun KY ee suhn TAHN guh) put this dream to music. His song was called "Bless, O Lord, Our Land of Africa." Sontanga's song expressed the growing nationalism of Africans. **Nationalism** is a feeling of pride in one's homeland.

Lesson Plan

1 Engage

Warm-Up Activity
Encourage students to talk about why they like local sports teams better than teams from other places. Point out that feeling loyalty to local teams is natural. Ask students whether they have these kinds of feelings for other things that are not associated with sports, such as their school, community, state, and country. Tell students that this feeling of pride and loyalty has motivated people in many countries to seek independence.

Activating Prior Knowledge
Have students read Reach Into Your Background in the Before You Read box. Allow students to express their ideas about independence. You may wish to record the most frequent responses on the chalkboard.

2 Explore

Direct students to read the section. Tell them to look for the causes that lay behind the African independence movements. Discuss the different means each nation used to achieve independence and why nations followed different paths toward it.

Teaching Resources

📁 **Reproducible Lesson Plan** in the Chapter and Section Resources booklet, p. 28, provides a summary of the section lesson.

📁 **Guided Reading and Review** in the Chapter and Section Resources booklet, p. 29, provides a structure for mastering key concepts and reviewing key terms in the section. Available in Spanish in the Spanish Chapter and Section Resources booklet, p. 19.

Program Resources

📁 **Outline Maps** The World: Political, p. 5;
North Africa: Political, p. 31;
Africa South of the Sahara: Political, p. 33

3 Teach

Write the following outline heads on the chalkboard.

I. Nationalism
II. Events leading to independence movements
III. Independence

Have students complete an outline of the section as they read, using the listed heads. Ask students to use their outlines in a class discussion. This activity should take about 25 minutes.

4 Assess

See the answers to the Section Review. You may also want to assess student outlines.

Acceptable outlines include at least three subheads under each head.

Commendable outlines include at least four subheads under each head.

Outstanding outlines include at least four subheads under each head, plus additional notes for some subheads.

Activity

Journal Writing

Pan-Africanism Tell students to suppose that they have just attended a rally of a Pan-African movement. It is the evening before they return home, and they are still very excited over all they have heard from speakers like Léopold Sédar Senghor. Ask students to record their feelings in their journal so that they will remember this great event.

The Right to Vote African Americans have also struggled to win the right to vote. By law, African American men received the right to vote in 1870. African American women received the right to vote at the same time as other American women, in 1920. But violence often prevented African Americans from exercising their right to vote. Change came about slowly as the result of a nonviolent social movement. Today, African Americans can exercise their right to vote in peace.

Resource Directory

Media and Technology

 Color Transparency 51

Education and Nationalism Many African leaders worked to encourage pride in being African. The colonial powers had drawn political borders that brought together many ethnic groups. Some of these groups were old rivals. African leaders saw that to end colonial rule, they would have to build a spirit of togetherness.

Nationalism grew during the early 1900s. In 1912, Africans in South Africa formed a political party. Today this party is the African National Congress (ANC). Party members protested laws that limited the rights of black South Africans. Five years later, African lawyers in British West Africa formed the West African National Congress. This group also worked to gain rights for Africans, including the right to vote.

Pan-Africanism In the 1920s, Africans formed a movement called **Pan-Africanism.** This movement stressed unity and cooperation among all Africans. Pan-African leaders tried to unify all Africans, whether they lived in Africa or not. Their slogan was "Africa for Africans." The movement won many supporters.

One of the greatest leaders of Pan-Africanism was Léopold Sédar Senghor (san GAWR) of Senegal. Senghor was a poet as well as a political leader. He encouraged Africans to look carefully at their traditions. They should be proud of their culture, he said. Senegal became independent in 1960, and Senghor became its first president.

Pan-Africanism in the U.S.

W.E.B. Du Bois was one of the first leaders of the movement to gain equal rights for African Americans in the United States. Du Bois also was an early leader of the Pan-African movement. He worked with African leaders, such as Jomo Kenyatta and Kwame Nkrumah, to make plans for African countries to become independent.

These Ghanaians fought in the British army in 1942. Here, they are on their way to defend North Africa against the armies of Germany and Italy. Fifteen years later, they and other Ghanaians achieved independence for their own country. **Critical Thinking** During World War II, Allied armies fought to preserve democracy around the world. How do you think fighting in the war affected Africans' feelings about democracy and independence?

World War II

A major boost to African independence came unexpectedly in the 1930s and 1940s, out of a global conflict called World War II. A group called the Allies included Great Britain, France, and the United States. They fought the armies of Germany, Italy, and Japan, who were invading much of the world. German and Italian forces invaded North Africa.

Africa played a huge role in support of the Allies. The colonies supplied metals for guns and other equipment. Allied planes used their airfields to move supplies into Asia. African soldiers fought and died to help free Europe from conquest. About 80,000 soldiers from Tanganyika, alone, served in the British Army.

Africans came home victorious. Now, they wanted their own freedom. One soldier said, "We have been told what we fought for. That is 'freedom.' We want freedom, nothing but freedom."

Different Paths to Independence

The war not only inspired Africans to win their freedom. It also weakened colonial powers like Great Britain. Many people in Britain felt that they could no longer afford a colonial empire. The United States and the Soviet Union—Britain's allies during the war—began to speak out against colonialism.

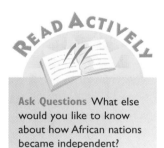

READ ACTIVELY

Ask Questions What else would you like to know about how African nations became independent?

Program Resources

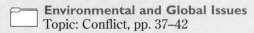
Environmental and Global Issues
Topic: Conflict, pp. 37–42

Background

Global Perspectives

Civil Rights in America
World War II proved pivotal in the push for civil rights of African Americans. During the war, African American men joined the military and fought in all-black units. On the home front, African American men and women were able to get high-paying jobs in the war industry— jobs that would have been out of reach before the war. When the war ended, African Americans were not willing to give up the gains they had made. This determination to achieve equality in the United States led directly to the civil rights advances of the 1950s and 1960s.

Answers to . . .

FIGHTING FOR DEMOCRACY IN WORLD WAR II

Accept any reasonable response.

Global Perspectives

India From 1858 to 1947, India was a colony of Great Britain. The British had almost complete control over India's government and economy. To facilitate their economic interests in India, the British built railroads; they also established schools, courts, and other institutions modeled after those in England. Until 1920, the call for independence was characterized by sporadic violence and the lack of a unified front. In 1920, however, Mohandas K. Gandhi became the leader of the independence movement. He endorsed nonviolent disobedience, such as nonpayment of taxes. Under Gandhi's charismatic leadership, the independence movement soon involved millions of Indians. Independence was achieved nonviolently.

African Independence

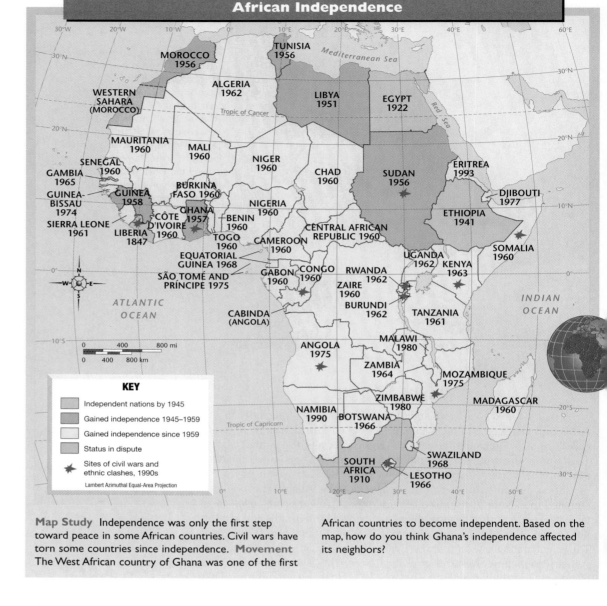

KEY

- Independent nations by 1945
- Gained independence 1945–1959
- Gained independence since 1959
- Status in dispute
- ★ Sites of civil wars and ethnic clashes, 1990s

Lambert Azimuthal Equal-Area Projection

Map Study Independence was only the first step toward peace in some African countries. Civil wars have torn some countries since independence. **Movement** The West African country of Ghana was one of the first African countries to become independent. Based on the map, how do you think Ghana's independence affected its neighbors?

British leader Harold Macmillan realized that Britain would not be able to keep its African colonies. "The winds of change are blowing across Africa," he said. Soon, European countries began to give up their African colonies.

Some colonial powers let go willingly, while others fought to keep power. Ghana won its independence from Britain peacefully. But Algeria, a former French colony, had to fight for its freedom.

Resource Directory

Teaching Resources

Maps with Accurate Directions: Azimuthal Maps in the Social Studies and Geography Skills booklet, p.18, provides additional skill practice.

Answers to . . .

MAP STUDY

Possible answer: Ghana's fight for independence inspired Africans in neighboring West African countries to fight for freedom.

From Gold Coast to Ghana   In the British West African colony of the Gold Coast, Kwame Nkrumah organized protests against British rule in the early 1950s. These protests took the peaceful form of strikes and boycotts. In a boycott, people refuse to buy or use certain products or services. The British threw Nkrumah in jail for his actions. But the protests continued without him. In 1957, he achieved his goal: independence for the Gold Coast. The country took the new name of Ghana, after the great trading kingdom that lasted until the 1200s. It was a name that recalled Africa's earlier greatness. Released from prison, Nkrumah became Ghana's first president in 1960.

War in Algeria   The French people who had settled in Algeria thought of it as more than a colony. To them, it was part of France. Algerians disagreed. They were willing to fight for the right to govern themselves. A bloody war began in Algeria in 1954. The eight-year struggle cost the lives of 100,000 Algerians and 10,000 French. But by 1962, the Algerians had won.

The Challenges of Independence   Africa's new leaders had spent many years working for independence. But they had little experience actually governing a country. The colonial powers had rarely allowed Africans to share in government. And even after agreeing to independence, the colonial powers did little to prepare the new leaders. As a result, some new governments in Africa were not very stable.

In some African countries, military leaders took control of the government by force. Military governments are not always fair. The people often have few rights. Further, citizens may be jailed if they protest. But this form of government has held together some African countries that otherwise would have been torn apart by war.

Other African countries have a long history of democracy. In a democracy, citizens help to make governmental decisions. Some countries have made traditional ways a part of governing. For example, in Botswana, lively political debates take place in "freedom squares." These outdoor meetings are like the traditional *kgotla* (KUHT luh), in which people talk with their leaders.

▼ Children wave goodbye to the British governor shortly after Ghana became independent.

Activity

Critical Thinking

Expressing Problems Clearly   *Suitable as either an individual or a whole class activity.* Have students prepare a two-minute news report titled "Spotlight on African Independence." Point out that their reports should include the challenges that newly independent African countries face, as well as the sources of those challenges. Students may also wish to include some suggestions on how the countries can meet the challenges.

Section 4 Review

1. (a) a feeling of pride in one's homeland (b) a movement that stressed unity and cooperation among all Africans (c) refusal by a group of people to buy certain products or services as a form of protest (d) political system in which citizens help make governmental decisions

2. (a) first prime minister of Zimbabwe (b) poet and political leader of Senegal (c) an early leader of the Gold Coast who helped the colony become independent and became Ghana's first president

3. Possible answer: Ghana gained independence through peaceful protest. Algeria fought a war with France to gain independence.

4. Possible answer: They had little experience in governmental matters.

5. After they fought in the war, Africans felt that because they had been asked to fight for freedom, they should have freedom.

6. Answers will vary. Together, headlines and articles should include the date of independence, how it was achieved, and the names of leaders.

Answers to ...

GAMBIANS CELEBRATE INDEPENDENCE

Both commemorate gaining independence from Great Britain.

Gambians Celebrate Independence

Gambia won its independence from Great Britain through peaceful elections in 1965. Schoolchildren celebrate Gambian independence every year. **Critical Thinking** How is this celebration similar to Fourth of July celebrations in the United States?

READ ACTIVELY

Connect The United States is a democratic country. How does democracy in the United States affect you?

Most African countries are less than 40 years old. In contrast, the stable, democratic country of the United States is over 200 years old. Many Africans feel that building stable countries will take time. One leader commented, "Let Africa be given the time to develop its own system of democracy."

SECTION 4 REVIEW

1. Define (a) nationalism, (b) Pan-Africanism, (c) boycott (d) democracy.

2. Identify (a) Robert Mugabe, (b) Léopold Sédar Senghor, (c) Kwame Nkrumah.

3. Compare Ghana's road to independence to that of Algeria.

4. In what ways did colonial rule cause problems for African countries after independence?

Critical Thinking

5. Recognizing Cause and Effect How did World War II boost the independence movement in Africa?

Activity

6. Writing to Learn Research one African country that won its independence after 1950. Write a headline and a short article for a newspaper that might have appeared on the day your country became independent. Compile all the articles from your class to create a bulletin board display about African independence.

Resource Directory

Teaching Resources

Section Quiz in the Chapter and Section Resources booklet, p. 30, covers the main ideas and key terms in the section. Available in Spanish in the Spanish Chapter and Section Resources booklet, p. 20.

Issues for Africa Today

BEFORE YOU READ

Reach Into Your Background
As you have grown, you have become more independent.

What challenges are you facing as you grow older? How have you met your challenges?

Questions to Explore
1. What challenges do African countries face today?
2. What actions may help Africans meet some of their challenges?

Key Terms
commercial farming
hybrid
literacy
life expectancy

Key Places
Niger
Senegal

In the past, nothing grew during the dry season in the Sahel. Farmers had to travel to cities to find work. Now, the West African country of Niger has a new irrigation program. This makes it possible for farmers to grow a second crop during the dry season. Farmer Adamou Sani (AH duh moo SAH nee) says that raising two crops a year means that he can stay on village land.

▼ Farmers in Niger use irrigation canals to bring water from the Niger River to their crops.

"Dry-season crops are such a normal practice now that everyone grows them. Before, each year after the harvest, I went to the city to look for work. But today, with the dry-season crops, I have work in the village. Truly it is a good thing."

Niger's irrigation program is one way Africans are improving their lives. Africans are also finding ways to meet economic, social, and environmental challenges.

Economic Issues

The colonial powers saw Africa as a source of raw materials and a market for their own manufactured goods. They did little to build factories in Africa. African countries still have little industry. Most economies are based on farming and mining.

Lesson Objectives

1. Describe the economic issues facing African nations.
2. Summarize the social issues encountered by African countries.
3. Explain the challenges posed by Africa's environment.

Lesson Plan

1 Engage
Warm-Up Activity

Ask students to suppose that they have graduated from school and are out on their own for the first time. Tell them that they are excited about their new independence, but also uncertain. Have students write a paragraph about some of the decisions they will have to make and some of the responsibilities that come with independence. Invite volunteers to read their paragraphs aloud. Discuss students' ideas using the context of a newly independent nation.

Activating Prior Knowledge

Have students read Reach Into Your Background in the Before You Read box. Encourage discussion of the challenges they face and the ways in which they address those challenges.

Teaching Resources

📁 **Reproducible Lesson Plan** in the Chapter and Section Resources booklet, p. 31, provides a summary of the section lesson.

📁 **Guided Reading and Review** in the Chapter and Section Resources booklet, p. 32, provides a structure for mastering key concepts and reviewing key terms in the section. Available in Spanish in the Spanish Chapter and Section Resources booklet, p. 21.

Media and Technology

📺 **Color Transparencies** 15, 17, 19, 20, 21, 45

A South African Gold Mine

Have students study the diagram for a few moments. You might explain that the diagram shows a type of mine known as a shaft mine. Shaft mines contain a number of deep vertical shafts, or passages, through which ore is hauled to the surface.

Ask students how gold ore is moved from place to place within the mine (on railroad cars). Discuss with students the advantages and disadvantages of transporting ore in this way.

Have a volunteer identify the first-aid station. Explain that today's mining engineers make complex calculations and plans so that mines will be as safe as possible. Even so, accidents sometimes happen. Ask students what kinds of accidents might happen and why working in a mine could be dangerous.

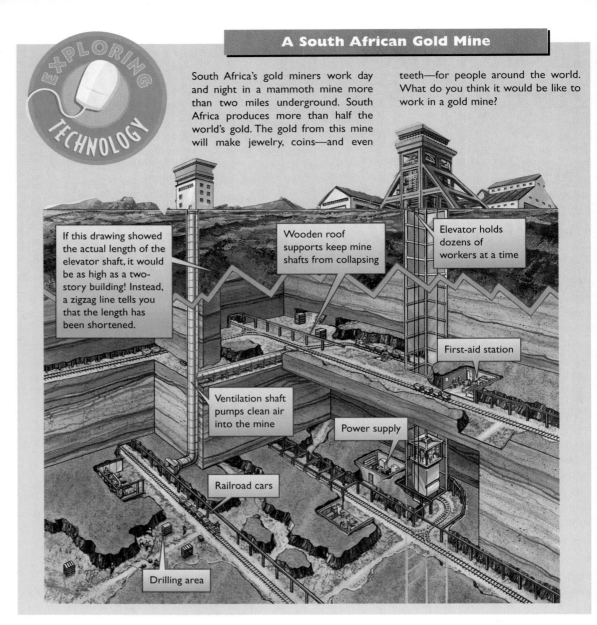

EXPLORING TECHNOLOGY

A South African Gold Mine

South Africa's gold miners work day and night in a mammoth mine more than two miles underground. South Africa produces more than half the world's gold. The gold from this mine will make jewelry, coins—and even teeth—for people around the world. What do you think it would be like to work in a gold mine?

If this drawing showed the actual length of the elevator shaft, it would be as high as a two-story building! Instead, a zigzag line tells you that the length has been shortened.

Wooden roof supports keep mine shafts from collapsing

Elevator holds dozens of workers at a time

First-aid station

Ventilation shaft pumps clean air into the mine

Power supply

Railroad cars

Drilling area

Farming and Mining Farming is the most important activity in Africa. About 75 percent of workers are farmers. And more than half of what Africa sells overseas are farm goods. Africans practice two kinds of farming—subsistence and commercial. With subsistence farming, farmers work small plots of land. They raise just as much food as their families need. **Commercial farming** is the large-scale production of cash crops such as coffee, cocoa, and bananas for sale.

Many African nations have rich mineral resources. They export minerals to other countries. Nigeria has oil and coal. Zaire and Zambia have copper, while South Africa has gold. Look at the diagram on the previous page. How does South Africa produce its gold?

Economic Challenges About 75 percent of African countries have economies that depend on exporting one or two products. Gambia depends on peanuts, while Zambia relies on the export of copper. As a result, African economies are sensitive to the rise and fall of world prices. A fall in prices hurts economies that depend on the sale of one crop or mineral.

African countries are now trying to depend less on one export. They are trying to diversify their economies. For example, Senegal became independent in 1960. At the time, it earned more than 80 percent of its money by exporting peanuts. Today, Senegal has other industries such as fishing, fish processing, and mining. Peanuts account for only 25 percent of the money Senegal makes from exports.

African nations face another economic problem—how to feed a growing population. Many governments are trying to help farmers grow more. One method they use is to develop hybrid plants. A **hybrid** is made by combining different types of the same plant. In the early 1980s, farmers in Zimbabwe who grew hybrid corn doubled their harvests. Today, most of Zimbabwe's corn comes from hybrids.

Social Issues

African nations also must provide social services to a growing population. In the areas of health care and education, many African nations are working to keep their traditions alive while adapting to the modern world.

Education African children must often add to their family's income by working on family farms or selling goods in the market. When girls and boys go to school, families sacrifice. But many Africans gladly make this sacrifice in order to improve their lives.

World Copper Prices

Year	Cents Per Pound (kg)
1990	121.02 (266.27)
1991	106.21 (233.69)
1992	103.72 (228.21)
1993	86.75 (190.87)
1994	104.65 (230.25)
1995	132.91 (292.43)
1996	88.02 (193.66)

Chart Study Zaire and Zambia both rely on copper mining for most of their income. Copper is used to make coins, wire, tubes, and jewelry, like the Tanzanian bracelet at right. **Critical Thinking** Based on these prices, what challenges do you think might face a country that gets most of its income from selling copper?

READ ACTIVELY

Predict What problems do you think can arise when a nation depends on one crop or resource?

2 Explore
Ask students to read the section and, as they do so, to think about the historic origins of the challenges facing modern Africa. Do all of modern Africa's problems stem from historic causes? Which ones? How did the problems develop? How are African nations solving these problems?

3 Teach
Write these words on the chalkboard: *farming, minerals, education, health,* and *environment.* Remind students that these are key topics discussed in this section. Ask students to write a sentence stating the main idea about each topic and then to write at least one detail about it. Have students use their main ideas and details during class discussion. This activity should take about 20 minutes.

4 Assess
See the answers to the Section Review. You may also use sentences as an assessment.

Acceptable work will include accurate information about each topic.

Commendable work will correctly identify the main idea for each topic and include accurate details.

Outstanding work will correctly identify the main idea for each topic and the most important details that support it.

Answers to ...
CHART STUDY

There is no pattern. The unpredictability of copper prices could lead to economic instability for a country that relied heavily upon copper income.

Links Across Time

Disappearing Farms and Herds The Sahara, which encompasses almost all of North Africa, expands and contracts owing to short term variations in rainfall. From 1968 to 1973, a drought caused the Sahara to expand into the Sahel, the semiarid transitional region south of the Sahara. The drought was catastrophic for the people of the Sahel, who subsist by growing crops and grazing livestock. Many people died, and most of the crops and livestock were lost. Because of overgrazing by surviving herds, vegetation has been slow to return to the region.

▶ How is this school in Zimbabwe similar to your school? How is it different?

In South Africa, parents often help to build new schools. The schools are often overcrowded. As a result, students take turns attending. The headmaster at one such school said that students "who couldn't cram into the desks knelt on the floor or stood on their toes so as not to miss a word the teacher was saying."

The number of people who can read and write varies from country to country. But in all countries, since independence, more people have learned to read. When the Portuguese left Mozambique in 1975, only 10 percent of the people in Mozambique were literate. **Literacy** is the ability to read and write. Today about 33 percent of the people are literate. In Tanzania, progress has been even more dramatic. At the time of independence only 15 percent of Tanzania's people were literate. Today, 90 percent of adult Tanzanians can read and write.

Health Like literacy, **life expectancy**—how long an average person will live—differs from country to country. In Mali, life expectancy is less than 60 years. In Botswana, where most people live near health clinics, people are expected to live between 60 and 66 years.

In Africa's tropical climate, insects carry serious diseases. Research has helped control malaria and sleeping sickness. The World Health Organization has worked with African governments to end smallpox and reduce a disease called river blindness. Vaccination programs in Africa have also conquered typhoid. However, Africans are still working to overcome other widespread health problems.

Ask Questions What would you like to know about Africa's environment?

The Environment

Like the United States, Africa faces a number of environmental challenges. About two thirds of Africa is desert or dry land. And more and more of Africa is turning into desert. Forests are being cut down, which causes soil to wash away. This reduces the amount of land on which food can be grown. This, in turn, threatens many Africans with starvation.

Resource Directory

Teaching Resources

📁 **Section Quiz** in the Chapter and Section Resources booklet, p. 33, covers the main ideas and key terms in the section. Available in Spanish in the Spanish Chapter and Section Resources booklet, p. 22.

📁 **Vocabulary** in the Chapter and Section Resources booklet, p. 35, provides a review of key terms in the chapter. Available in Spanish in the Spanish Chapter and Section Resources booklet, p. 24.

📁 **Reteaching** in the Chapter and Section Resources booklet, p. 36, provides a structure for students who may need additional help in mastering chapter content.

Program Resources

📁 **Environmental and Global Issues** Topics: Health, pp. 8–13; Environmental Destruction pp. 14–19

Health Education in Nigeria

This clinic is located in a rural area of Nigeria. Doctors here are teaching women the healthiest foods to feed young children. Health education programs focus on preventing sickness, rather than on curing it after it happens.

But science can help feed Africans and save Africa's environment. Irrigation projects, hybrids, and vegetation that holds water in the ground have all increased crop harvests. To fight soil erosion, farmers in Nigeria now plant food crops such as yams in long rows. Between the rows they plant trees that hold the soil in place. The trees can later be harvested for wood.

African nations still face many challenges. They are meeting them by using their resources, increasing education, and keeping traditions alive in a changing world.

LINKS
ACROSS THE WORLD

Virtual Eritrea Eritrea is a country in East Africa along the Red Sea. It won independence from Ethiopia in 1993. Now, Eritreans are using Internet technology to help them meet the challenges of self-rule. They have formed Dehai, an on-line community. Dehai is an Internet newsgroup. About 500 Eritreans living in other countries use Dehai to discuss issues related to Eritrea's new constitution.

SECTION 5 REVIEW

1. Define (a) commercial farming, (b) hybrid, (c) literacy, (d) life expectancy.

2. Identify (a) Niger, (b) Senegal.

3. Why are African nations trying to diversify their economies?

4. List two challenges African countries face and describe the steps African countries are taking to meet these challenges.

Critical Thinking
5. Drawing Conclusions In what ways have Africans shown the high value they place on education?

Activity
6. Writing to Learn You are the economic adviser to the president of an African country. Write a brief report on some steps the president might take to improve the economy.

Recognizing Bias

Lesson Objectives

1 Define the term *bias*.

2 Identify important clues to bias.

3 Recognize bias in context.

Lesson Plan

1 Engage

Warm-Up Activity

To **introduce** the skill, direct students to read the opening paragraphs. Write the initial statement about African life on the chalkboard or on an overhead projector.

Activating Prior Knowledge

Invite students to respond to the statement about African life. Using their own reactions and the text information, challenge students to define *bias*. Record students' suggested definitions.

2 Explore

Have a volunteer read the text under *Get Ready*. Write the statement *Biased writing takes a side* next to students' suggested definitions. Ask students to compare the text's definition of bias with those they developed earlier, and allow them to revise their definitions as necessary. Together, develop an example of bias that fits the final definition. Then direct students to read the rest of the activity.

When Latisha got to class, she looked at the chalkboard. Every day, Mr. Copeland began class by writing something on the board to discuss:

Life in West Africa is better than life in North Africa.

"Well, class? What do you think about that?" Mr. Copeland asked.

Latisha wondered how someone decided what made life better in one place than another. She raised her hand.

"That statement does not tell the whole story! Whose life are you talking about? And when?"

Mr. Copeland smiled. "Latisha, you've hit the nail on the head. The statement on the board does not tell the whole story—it may even be completely untrue. It shows you an example of *bias*."

Get Ready

To be biased is to lean to a particular point of view. Sometimes, people who write about something only know one side of the story.

Resource Directory

Teaching Resources

Identifying Assumptions in the Social Studies and Geography Skills booklet, p. 46, provides additional skill practice.

Recognizing Bias in the Social Studies and Geography Skills booklet, p. 47, provides additional skill practice.

Other people leave out information on purpose to give their own viewpoint. Biased writing takes a side, even if at first it seems not to.

You need to be able to recognize bias in writing. It is the only way you can know whether you're getting a fair picture. When you read, you can look for certain clues that will point out a writer's bias.

Try It Out

To determine if a writer is biased, do the following:

A. Look for opinions. Opinions are beliefs that cannot be proved. They are the opposite of facts, which can be proved. Biased writing often contains opinions disguised as facts. For example, the statement "Life in West Africa is better than life in North Africa" may sound like a fact, but it is an opinion.

B. Look for loaded words and phrases. Loaded words and phrases carry a hidden meaning. They give a positive or negative impression. Read this sentence: "The coastline of Nigeria is so beautiful it takes your breath away." The words "so beautiful it takes your breath away" are loaded. They give a very positive impression. However, this hidden meaning cannot be proved. It is not fact.

C. Look for what isn't there. Biased writers often leave out information that does not support their bias. For example, the writer might say "the Mali empire failed," but leave out the fact that before it declined, it succeeded for centuries.

◀ Everything you read was written by someone. You need to use your skills to sort out whether to believe what the writer says.

D. Think about the tone. Tone is the overall feeling of a piece of writing. It shows the writer's attitude toward the subject: "From burning desert to steamy tropics, the climates of Africa are unbearable." This sentence gives you the clear impression that the writer has negative feelings about the climates of Africa. Unbiased writing provides the facts and lets the reader form his or her own opinions.

Apply the Skill

The selection in the box is a biased, one-paragraph description of the early African empire of Ghana. To spot the bias, follow steps A through D, at left. Consider these questions: Are there any opinions disguised as facts in the selection? What words give a positive or negative impression of the West African kingdoms? What important facts about West African kingdoms does the writer fail to include? How would you describe the tone of the writing? Positive? Negative? After you have finished, describe the West African kingdoms in one paragraph without bias.

West African Kingdoms

Between the 3500s and the 1500s, West Africa was a terrible place to live. People couldn't even survive without salt. They were forced to trade their most precious gold just to get enough salt to stay alive. In the kingdom of Ghana, the kings forced people to pay money just to carry salt, gold, and other goods through the land. The Ghanaian kingdom became so weak that it fell to the crushing power of the kingdom of Mali.

3 Teach

The steps outlined in *Try It Out* will enable students to **practice** the skill. Urge students to record their own questions as they read through the steps. Then work through each step as a class. After each step, challenge students to identify clues for recognizing bias.

For additional reinforcement, ask students to give an example of each type of bias indicated in *Try It Out*.

4 Assess

Allow students to **apply** the skill to the paragraph contained in *Apply the Skill*. You may **assess** both their written answers and their contributions to a whole class evaluation of the paragraph. Have students identify clues to bias such as the words *terrible* and *weak*.

Reviewing Main Ideas

1. hunting and gathering, farming, herding

2. They had cities, governments, social classes, architecture, writing, and art.

3. Because of the migration, the Bantu language became widely known and is still spoken in Central and Southern Africa. The Bantu also introduced farming, herding, and iron tools to Central and Southern Africa.

4. by controlling trade

5. (a) The European-African relationship began as trade between equals.
(b) Europeans began enslaving and forcing millions of Africans to leave their homelands.

6. Some Africans became rich from the trade, but the slave trade deprived Africa of its strongest, healthiest, most capable people.

7. Education, the growth of nationalism, and World War II helped lead to independence for many African nations.

8. military governments and democratic governments

9. by diversifying their economies, developing industry, and developing more productive crops

10. by making education a priority and by working to eliminate deadly diseases

Reviewing Key Terms

Sentences should show the correct meaning of the term through context.

Critical Thinking

1. The early kingdoms and city-states of Africa grew wealthy through the trade of various natural resources. Later, Europeans came to Africa and began enslaving Africans. The slave traders grew rich and deprived Africa of some of its most capable people.

2. Enslaved Africans were taken to unfamiliar, faraway lands where it was difficult to maintain traditions. Europeans drew boundaries in Africa that did not reflect traditional boundaries. The new boundaries caused much conflict in Africa.

Review and Activities

Reviewing Main Ideas

1. List some of the ways in which early Africans made a living.
2. What were Africa's earliest civilizations like?
3. List several effects of the Bantu migrations.
4. How did Africa's kingdoms and city-states become wealthy?
5. (a) How did the relationship of Europeans and Africans begin? (b) How did it change?
6. Explain two effects of the Atlantic slave trade on Africa.
7. What factors helped lead to independence for many African countries?
8. Describe two types of government used in African countries after independence.
9. How are Africans working to improve their economies?
10. How are Africans working to improve social conditions?

Reviewing Key Terms

Use each key term below in a sentence that shows the meaning of the term.

1. hunter-gatherer
2. fertile
3. surplus
4. civilization
5. migrate
6. ethnic group
7. Quran
8. city-state
9. colonize
10. nationalism
11. Pan-Africanism
12. democracy
13. commercial farming
14. literacy
15. life expectancy

Critical Thinking

1. **Recognizing Cause and Effect** Many of Africa's cities and countries are located along trade routes. How has trade affected Africa's history?
2. **Expressing Problems Clearly** The Atlantic slave trade lasted from the 1500s to the 1800s. Then the "scramble for Africa" began. How did the slave trade and the scramble for Africa affect traditional African cultures?

Graphic Organizer

Copy the web onto a sheet of paper. Then fill in the empty spaces to complete a web of African history.

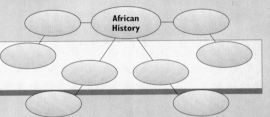

Graphic Organizer

Answers may vary. Possible answers shown.

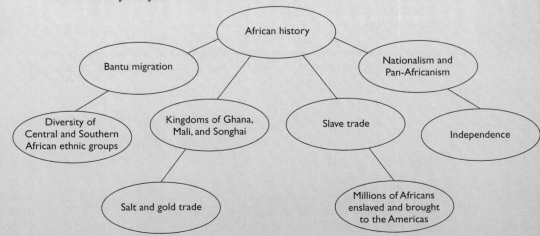

Map Activity

Africa
For each place listed below, write the letter from the map that shows its location.

1. Senegal
2. Great Zimbabwe
3. Tombouctou
4. Cape of Good Hope
5. Kilwa
6. Kingdom of Mali
7. Nubia
8. Aksum

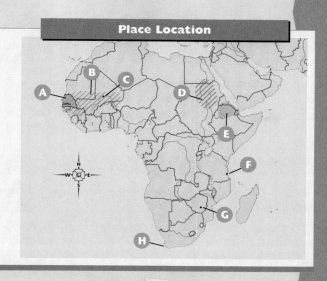

Place Location

Writing Activity

Writing a Speech
In the 1800s, many people in the United States spoke out against slavery. They were called abolitionists, because they wanted to abolish, or put an end to, slavery.

Pretend that you are an abolitionist living in the 1800s. Use what you have learned about the slave trade to write a speech that will help persuade people that slavery is wrong.

Internet Activity

Use a search engine to find **AfricaOnline**. Choose **Kids Only** and then choose **Learn About Africa**. Click on the **People** icon. Read about notable Africans who have influenced Africa's history. Research one person. Send your report and illustration to AfricaOnline to be posted on their website.

Skills Review

Turn to the Skills Activity. Review the steps for recognizing bias. (a) In your own words, explain the difference between biased and unbiased writing. (b) How can you determine whether a writer is biased?

How Am I Doing?

Answer these questions to check your progress.

1. Can I explain how early humans lived in Africa?
2. Can I identify the ancient civilizations of Africa and name their accomplishments?
3. Do I understand how European rule affected Africa?
4. Can I identify the challenges that African nations have faced since independence?
5. What information from this chapter can I use in my book project?

Internet Activity

If students are having difficulty finding this site, you may wish to have them use the following URL, which was accurate at the time this textbook was published:

http://www.africaonline.com/

You might also guide students to a search engine. Four of the most useful are Infoseek, Alta Vista, Lycos, and Yahoo. For additional suggestions on using the Internet, refer to the Prentice Hall Social Studies' Educator's Handbook "Using the Internet," in the *Prentice Hall World Explorer Program Resources.*

For additional links to world history and culture topics, visit the Prentice Hall Home Page at:
http://www.phschool.com

How Am I Doing?

Point out to students that this checklist is a quick reminder for them of what they learned in the chapter. If their answer to any of the questions is *no* or if they are unsure, they may need to review the topic.

Map Activity

1. A	4. H	7. D
2. G	5. F	8. E
3. C	6. B	

Writing Activity

Speeches will vary, but will probably cite the inhuman conditions on slave ships, the moral wrongness of slavery, and the damage done to Africa as a result of the loss of their best workers to slavery.

Skills Review

(a) Biased writing is based on opinions; unbiased writing is based on facts. (b) by looking for loaded words or phrases; by determining if important information has been left out; and by analyzing the tone of writing

Resource Directory

Teaching Resources

 Chapter Tests Forms A and B are in the Tests booklet, pp. 8–13.

Program Resources

Writing Process Handbook includes Limiting a Topic, p. 15, to help students with the Writing Activity.

Media and Technology

Color Transparencies
Color Transparency 171 (Graphic organizer web template)

 Prentice Hall Writer's Solution Writing Lab CD-ROM

Computer Test Bank

 Resource Pro™ CD-ROM

Cultures of Africa

To help you plan instruction, the chart below shows how teaching resources correspond to chapter content. Use the resources to vary instruction, add activities, or plan block schedules. Where appropriate, resources have **suggested time allotments** for students. Time allotments are approximate.

Managing Time and Instruction

		Africa Teaching Resources Binder		World Explorer Program Resources Binder	
		Resource	**mins.**	**Resource**	**mins.**
1	**SECTION 1** The Cultures of North Africa	**Chapter and Section Support** Reproducible Lesson Plan, p. 40 ⓢ Guided Reading and Review, p. 41 ⓢ Section Quiz, p. 42	20 25	**Outline Maps** The Middle East and North Africa: Physical, p. 28 The Middle East and North Africa: Political, p. 29 **Nystrom Desk Atlas** Ⓣ **Primary Sources and Literature Readings** **Writing Process Handbook** Keeping Track of Information Sources, p. 19	20 20 40 25
	SKILLS ACTIVITY Assessing Your Understanding	**Social Studies and Geography Skills,** Connecting Content to What You Already Know, p. 71 Determining If You Understood What You Read, p. 74	30 30		
2	**SECTION 2** The Cultures of West Africa	**Chapter and Section Support** Reproducible Lesson Plan, p. 43 ⓢ Guided Reading and Review, p. 44 ⓢ Section Quiz, p. 45 Critical Thinking, p. 56	20 25 30	**Outline Maps** West and Central Africa: Political, p. 34 **Environmental and Global Issues** Topic: Urbanization, pp. 54–58	20 30
3	**SECTION 3** The Cultures of East Africa	**Chapter and Section Support** Reproducible Lesson Plan, p. 46 ⓢ Guided Reading and Review, p. 47 ⓢ Section Quiz, p. 48	20 25	**Outline Maps** West and Central Africa: Political, p. 34	20
4	**SECTION 4** The Cultures of Central and Southern Africa	**Chapter and Section Support** Reproducible Lesson Plan, p. 49 ⓢ Guided Reading and Review, p. 50 ⓢ Section Quiz, p. 51 ⓢ Vocabulary, p. 53 Reteaching, p. 54 Enrichment, p. 55 ⓢ Chapter Summary, p. 52 **Tests** Forms A and B Chapter Tests, pp. 14–19 **Social Studies and Geography Skills,** Analyzing a Photograph, p. 58	20 25 20 25 25 15 40 30	**Outline Maps** West and Central Africa: Political, p. 34 East and Southern Africa: Political, p. 35 **Environmental and Global Issues** Topic: Human Rights, pp. 25–30	20 20 30
	ACTIVITY SHOP: INTERDISCIPLINARY The Language of Music	Ⓣ Activity Shop: Interdisciplinary, p. 7	30		

Block Scheduling Folder
PROGRAM TEACHING RESOURCES

Activities and Projects

Interdisciplinary Links

Block Scheduling Program Support

Resource Pro™ CD-ROM

Media and Technology

Assessment Opportunities

From Guiding Questions to Assessment A series of Guiding Questions serves as an organizing framework for this book. The Guiding Questions that relate to this chapter are listed below. Section Reviews and Section Quizzes provide opportunities for assessing students' insights into these Guiding Questions. Additional assessments are listed below.

Media and Technology

Resource	mins.
🎥 ⌨ Ⓢ World Video Explorer	20
⌨ Planet Earth CD-ROM	20
⌐ Color Transparencies 51, 52, 70, 92	20
⌨ Planet Earth CD-ROM	20
⌐ Color Transparencies 51, 52, 72	20
⌨ Planet Earth CD-ROM	20
⌨ Material World CD-ROM	20
⌐ Color Transparencies 51, 52, 73	20
⌨ Planet Earth CD-ROM	20
⌐ Color Transparencies 51, 52, 73	20
🎧 Ⓢ Guided Reading Audiotapes	20
⌐ Color Transparency 174	
(Graphic organizer table template)	20
⌨ The Writer's Solution CD-ROM	30
💾 Computer Test Bank	30

T Teaming Opportunity
This resource is especially well-suited for teaching teams.

Ⓢ Spanish
This resource is also in Spanish support.

⌨ **CD-ROM**
🎬 **Laserdisc**
⌐ **Transparency**
💾 **Software**
🎥 **Videotape**
🎧 **Audiotape**

GUIDING QUESTIONS

- *What factors have shaped Africa's cultures?*
- *What factors influence the ways in which Africans make a living?*

ASSESSMENTS

Section 1	**Section 2**
Students should be able to create a chart that names and describes the Five Pillars of Islam.	Students should be able to give an oral presentation on the many ways West Africans make a living.
▶ **RUBRIC** See the Assessment booklet for a rubric on assessing charts.	▶ **RUBRIC** See the Assessment booklet for a rubric on assessing an oral presentation.
Section 3	**Section 4**
Students should be able to write an explanation describing how location has affected the development of East African cultures.	Students should be able to write a short report describing the plight of migrant laborers in Southern Africa.
▶ **RUBRIC** See the Assessment booklet for a rubric on assessing cause-and-effect statements.	▶ **RUBRIC** See the Assessment booklet for a rubric on assessing a report.

Activities and Projects

Mental Mapping

Everything in Its Place List the names of some African countries on the chalkboard. Include Egypt, Algeria, Nigeria, Ghana, Mali, Ethiopia, Tanzania, Kenya, Zaire, and South Africa. Have students draw four columns on a piece of notebook paper. The columns should have the following heads: "North Africa," "West Africa," "East Africa," and "Central and Southern Africa." Ask students to sort the countries into the appropriate columns.

Distribute outline maps of Africa and ask students to locate as many countries on the maps as they can. Tell them to write the names of the countries they can't locate on the water area of the map near the correct landmass. Ask them to keep their lists and outline maps. They may add, correct, or update information as they work through these chapters.

Links to Current Events

African Music African musicians have combined traditional musical forms with the instruments and styles of European and North American music to create a unique style of popular music. Afro-Pop, as it is sometimes known, influences and reflects some of the western musical styles that might be more familiar to students. Obtain and play recordings by artists such as Angelique Kidjo (Benin), Aster Aweke (Ethiopia), Dark City Sisters or Mahotella Queens (South Africa), or Zap Mama (Zaire). The recording *Women of Mali: The Wassoulu Sound* includes a selection of music by West African musicians, in a region in which 90 percent of the musicians are women. Several recordings by Miriam Makeba offer modern folk music influenced by South African folk traditions.

Hands-On Activities

Museum Exhibit Have students use illustrated encyclopedias, large-format illustrated books, and magazines such as *National Geographic* or *Faces* to find pictures of the cultural artifacts of African cultures. These photographs may include structures, clothing, tools, and other objects.

Have students set up four corners or areas of the room, each with a sign labeling it as "North Africa," "West Africa," "East Africa," or "Central and Southern Africa." Ask them to arrange the books and magazines, open to the photographs they have found, in the appropriate area. Students should make themselves "experts" in one or two photographs by reading the article or information about the photograph.

Give students a chance to walk around the room, taking turns visiting displays to ask questions and playing the role of expert to provide answers.

Multilinguists Most Africans speak several languages, since most African countries include people from many language groups. Invite students who speak one or more languages other than English to organize a language fair. Suggest that students who speak the same non-English language work together. Students can make posters that translate certain phrases from English into the other language. They can give lessons to other students in the non-English languages. If the language uses another alphabet, they can write out the words and teach the letters, too. If possible, make sure one or more African languages are presented. You might invite someone from a local college or international company for this purpose if necessary. *English Language Learners.*

Vacation Itinerary Have students plan a vacation trip to one of the four culture areas covered in this chapter. Ask them to list the places they would visit and explain the reasons for their choices. Have them write a brief postcard to a friend back home describing what they see at each site. Each student should produce at least four postcards for their trip. *Basic*

Natural Resources Have students refer back to Chapter 1, where they learned about the climate, vegetation, and natural resources of Africa. Remind them that the geography of a country influences its culture. As students explore the cultures of Africa, have them make a poster showing how some aspect of culture is linked to the geography of different regions. Suggest they create a poster showing each region of Africa with information about the way the geography of that region influences the culture. *Challenging*

At the Crossroads Ask students to create a skit in which people from at least four different areas of Africa (representing the four cultural regions in this chapter) meet and discuss their customs and cultures with one another. The skit might be set in a major airport where the four people are all waiting to catch flights home. *Average*

F.Y.I.

This page can help you extend your own and students' understanding of the concepts in this chapter. You may want to browse through some of the suggestions in the **Bibliography. Interdisciplinary Links** can connect social studies understandings to areas elsewhere in the curriculum through the use of other Prentice Hall products. **National Geography Standards** reflected specifically in this chapter are listed for your convenience. Some hints about appropriate **Internet Access** are also provided. **School to Careers** provides insights into the practical uses of some of the concepts in this chapter as they might pertain to various careers.

BIBLIOGRAPHY

FOR THE TEACHER
Ayo, Yvonne. *Africa.* Knopf, 1995.

Haskins, Jim and Joann Biondi. *From Afar to Zulu: A Dictionary of African Cultures.* Walker, 1995.

Islam: There Is No God but God. Time/Life, 1996. Videocassette.

Moore, Reavis. *Native Artists of Africa.* Muir, 1994.

FOR THE STUDENT
Easy
Angelou, Maya and Margaret Courtney-Clark. *My Painted House, My Friendly Chicken, and Me.* Clarkson Potter, 1996.

Seward, Pat. *Morocco.* Cavendish, 1995.

Average
Heritage Library of African People series: Rosen, 1994.

Bangura, Abdul Karim. *Kipsigis.*

Parris, Ronald G. *Rendille.*

Swinimer, Ciarunji Chesaina. *Pokot.*

Zeleza, Tiyambe. *Maasai.*

Challenging
Knappert, Jan. *Kings, Gods, and Spirits from African Mythology.* Bedrick, 1994.

LITERATURE CONNECTION
Dupre, Rick. *Agassu: Legend of the Leopard King.* Carolrhoda, 1993.

Medlicott, Mary, editor. *The River That Went to the Sky: Twelve Tales by African Storytellers.* Kingfisher, 1995.

INTERDISCIPLINARY LINKS

Subject	Theme: Peoples
MATH	Middle Grades Math: Tools for Success Course 1, Lesson 1-3, **Three Kinds of Averages**
LANGUAGE ARTS	Choices in Literature *The Adventures of Me,* **The Egyptian Cinderella** Prentice Hall Literature *Copper,* **Mufaro's Beautiful Daughters**

NATIONAL GEOGRAPHY STANDARDS

Students explore the 18 National Geography Standards throughout *Africa.* Chapter 3, however, concentrates on investigating the following standards: 1, 4, 6, 7, 9, 10, 11, 12, 14, 15, 17, 18. For a complete list of the standards, see the *Teacher's Flexible Planning Guide.*

SCHOOL TO CAREERS

In Chapter 3, Cultures of Africa, students learn something about the cultures in some countries in different parts of Africa. Additionally, they address the skill of assessing your understanding. Understanding cultures can help students prepare for careers in many fields such as international trade and finance, politics, education, the arts, and so on. Assessing understanding of what you read is a skill particularly useful for attorneys, police officers, editors, and others. The curriculum presented in this book, as in all eight titles of Prentice Hall's *World Explorer* program, is designed to prepare students not only for careers but also for good citizenship—of the world as well as of this country.

INTERNET ACCESS

Many social studies teachers and students use Internet browsers, or search engines, to investigate particular topics. For the best results, use narrow rather than broad topics. Try these for Chapter 3: Islam, griot, Wole Soyinka, African National Congress. Finding age-appropriate sites is an important consideration when using the Internet. For links to age-appropriate sites in world studies and geography, visit the Prentice Hall Home Page at: **http://www.phschool.com**

Cultures of Africa

Connecting to the Guiding Questions

As students complete this chapter, they will focus on how the culture of Africa's four regions has been shaped by political, economic, and geographic circumstances. Content in this chapter corresponds to the following Guiding Questions:

- What factors have shaped Africa's cultures?

- What factors influence the ways in which Africans make a living?

Using the Picture Activities

As a class, discuss the conclusions that can be drawn from studying the pictures.

- Students' responses should be drawn from clues in the picture.

- Accept all reasonable question lists.

Heterogeneous Groups

The following Teacher's Edition strategies are suitable for heterogeneous groups.

Interdisciplinary Connections

Math	p. 67
Art	p. 72
Language Arts	p. 73
Music	p. 84

Critical Thinking

Recognizing Cause and Effect	p. 70

Cooperative Learning

Family Meeting	p. 71
Debate	p. 78

SECTION 1
The Cultures of North Africa

SECTION 2
The Cultures of West Africa

SECTION 3
The Cultures of East Africa

SECTION 4
The Cultures of Central and Southern Africa

PICTURE ACTIVITIES

An African market brings together a wide variety of people and goods. Here you can buy baskets, spices, scarves, or a lamb. You can get a haircut, listen to a storyteller, or watch acrobatic dancers perform. To help you begin to understand Africa's cultures, do the following:

Look for clues
From this picture, what can you tell about how these Africans live? How do they dress? What kinds of products do they make and sell?

Make a list of questions
Pick a person in the picture whose life you would like to know more about. Make a list of questions that you would ask this person if you could. As you read, see if some of your questions are answered.

Resource Directory

Media and Technology

Cultures of Africa, from the World Video Explorer, enhances students' understanding of the many factors of African culture.

Chapter 5

The Cultures of North Africa

BEFORE YOU READ

Reach Into Your Background

Suppose you have been given the assignment of describing your way of life to students in North Africa. How would you answer the following questions: What is a day in your life like? What is your school like? What is your home like? Think about your answers as you read this section.

Questions to Explore

1. What is culture?
2. How does Islam influence life in North Africa?
3. How has its Mediterranean location affected the cultures of North Africa?

Key Terms

culture
cultural diffusion

Key Places

Sahara
Mediterranean Sea

Lesson Objectives

1. Define the term *culture* and explain how it unites people in North Africa.

2. Describe some beliefs of Islam and its effect on life in North Africa.

3. Explain how North Africa's Mediterranean location has influenced its cultures.

Lesson Plan

1 Engage

Warm-Up Activity

Ask students to name a cultural characteristic that they think most Americans share. For example, most Americans speak English. List and discuss some of students' ideas, leading them to the conclusion that Americans have very diverse cultural characteristics. Ask students what they think it would be like to live in a place where almost everyone shares the same religion and many people share the same heritage.

Activating Prior Knowledge

Have students read Reach Into Your Background in the Before You Read box. Ask students to consider how they get to school, the subjects they study, their extracurricular activities, and so forth.

Thirteen-year-old Meena lives in the city of Marrakech (muh RAH kehsh) in Morocco, a country in North Africa. Every morning she works in a factory, weaving carpets. She learned to weave carpets from her mother, who learned the skill from her mother. Carpets play an important role in Moroccan life. They are an export. And in some Moroccan homes, they serve as more than just floor coverings. They are used as chairs, beds, and prayer mats. In the afternoon, Meena leaves the factory to attend school. Her day ends at sunset, when she hears the crier who calls out from the nearby mosque, a Muslim house of worship. Muslims are followers of the religion of Islam. When she hears the call, Meena recites this prayer in Arabic: "There is no God but God, and Muhammad is His prophet."

▼ Moroccan weavers decorate their carpets with intricate designs. Which of these carpets would you buy? What would you use it for?

What Is Culture?

Meena's way of life is different in some ways from yours. That is partly because her culture is different.

Teaching Resources

📁 **Reproducible Lesson Plan** in the Chapter and Section Resources booklet, p. 40, provides a summary of the section lesson.

📁 **Guided Reading and Review** in the Chapter and Section Resources booklet, p. 41, provides a structure for mastering key concepts and reviewing key terms in the section. Available in Spanish in the Spanish Chapter and Section Resources booklet, p. 26.

Program Resources

📁 Material in the **Primary Sources and Literature Readings** booklet extends content with a selection from the region under study.

📁 **Outline Maps** The Middle East and North Africa: Physical, p. 28; The Middle East and North Africa: Political, p. 29

2 Explore

As students read the section text, pause to discuss and answer the following questions: What is the main religion of North Africa and what are some important aspects of that religion? How can the influences of different cultures be seen in North Africa? What are some of the ways North Africans make a living? What effect has North Africa's location on the Mediterranean Sea had on the culture of the region?

3 Teach

Invite students to create a web with *Culture of North Africa* at the center. Secondary circles can contain details about the culture, and tertiary circles can identify cultural influences. Students may explain these influences using supporting facts from the section. This activity should take about 20 minutes.

4 Assess

See the answers to the Section Review. You may also use students' webs as an assessment.

Acceptable webs include a minimum of two details in secondary circles and two influences in tertiary circles.

Commendable webs include a minimum of three details in secondary circles and three influences in tertiary circles.

Outstanding webs include a minimum of three details in secondary circles and three influences in tertiary circles and show how the details and influences are related.

LINKS ACROSS THE WORLD

Building With Adobe
Adobe is an ancient Egyptian word. It refers to a brick made of earth and straw. Arabs brought adobe-making techniques to Spain. Later, the Spanish brought the use of adobe to what is now the southwestern United States. People in the Southwest still build adobe homes.

▼ Adobe bricks fall apart if they are often exposed to cold or wet weather. They can only be used in hot, dry climates. The picture below shows adobe houses in Morocco.

Culture is the way of life of a group of people who share similar beliefs and customs.

Culture has many elements. Culture includes food, clothing, homes, jobs, language, and so on. It also includes things that are not so easy to see, such as how people view their world and what their religion is. These ideas shape the way people behave. Meena, for example, takes time from her activities to pray several times a day.

Cultures in different places have common elements. In many rural villages in Morocco, for example, houses are made of thick adobe, a type of brick made from sun-dried clay. Thick adobe walls help keep out the heat. Across the globe, in Mexico, and in the southwestern United States, many people in rural areas also live in adobe houses.

The Influence of Islam

Religion is an important part of North African culture. Islam is the religion of most North Africans. More than 95 percent of North Africans are Muslims.

Like Jews and Christians, Muslims believe in one God. *Allah* is the Arabic word for God. Muslims believe that Muhammad, as well as the Old Testament prophets and Jesus, was God's messenger. The main duties of a Muslim are outlined in the Five Pillars of Islam, shown in the chart on the next page.

Resource Directory

Program Resources

Nystrom Desk Atlas

Media and Technology

🖭 **Planet Earth** CD-ROM includes interactive political and thematic maps which allow students to investigate the countries and cultures of North Africa.

⚏ **Color Transparencies** 51, 52, 70, 92

The Five Pillars of Islam

Duty	Description
Declaration of Faith	Declaring belief in one God and in Muhammad as God's final messenger
Prayer	Reciting prayers five times a day: at dawn, at midday, in the afternoon, at sunset, and in the evening
Almsgiving	Giving a portion of one's wealth to the needy
Fasting	Not eating or drinking from sunrise to sunset during the ninth month in the Muslim year, Ramadan
Pilgrimage	Making the *hajj*, or pilgrimage to Mecca, at least once in a lifetime if able

Chart Study Actions speak louder than words, so one form of Muslim worship is to do things to please God, like helping other people. Muslims must also perform the Five Pillars of Islam. **Critical Thinking** Which of the Five Pillars do you think is illustrated by the photo on the right?

Five Pillars of Islam

The sacred book of Islam is the Quran. Besides teaching about God, the Quran provides a guide to life. Like the Bible, the Quran forbids lying, stealing, and murder. It also prohibits gambling, eating pork, and drinking alcohol.

The Islamic system of law is based on the Quran. Islamic law governs all aspects of life, including family life, business practices, banking, and government.

Islam Unifies the People of North Africa   Islam and the Arabic language unify the different peoples of North Africa. These peoples are spread out over a large area that includes the following countries: Egypt, Libya, Tunisia, Algeria, and Morocco. People here have many different backgrounds and ways of life.

An ethnic group is a group of people who share language, religion, or cultural traditions. Most North Africans are Arabs. But the region has other ethnic groups, too. The largest of these is the Berbers. About 20 million Berbers live in North Africa, mainly in Algeria and Morocco. Most Berbers speak Arabic as well as Berber. Some live in cities, but most live in small villages in rugged mountain areas. They make their living by herding and farming. The Tuareg (TWAH rehg) are a group of

Background

Global Perspectives

Islam Around the World
In North Africa, most people are Muslims. In fact, more than a third of all Africans are Muslims. Elsewhere in the world, however, Muslims are often a small minority. For example, North America has a population of about 290 million, but only about 3 million are Muslims. Asia, on the other hand, has a total population of 3.3 billion, almost 700 million of whom are Muslims.

Answers to . . .
CHART STUDY
pilgrimage

Links Across Time

Carthage North Africa's cultural interaction with its neighbors has a long history. The city of Carthage, located on the Mediterranean Coast in the modern country of Tunisia, was founded by the ancient Phoenicians in the 800s B.C. The Phoenicians were great sailors and made Carthage into a major trading center. They built sturdy ships to bring people and goods from around the Mediterranean in and out of the city. Phoenician goods were in high demand. For example, the Phoenicians manufactured a unique purple dye that they made from snails and for which they charged a very high price. Purple cloth was worn by high officials of the Roman Empire as a signal of their rank and prestige.

North Africa's Rural and Urban Areas

When the Tuareg travel across the desert, they must bring with them everything they might need, including tents to provide shelter from the sun. North Africa's cities, however, are centers of trade. People who live there can buy things that they need. The city below is in Tunis, Tunisia.

READ ACTIVELY

Visualize What sights might you see if you were walking through an outdoor market in a North African city? How would these sights be different from what you might see inside a modern skyscraper?

Berbers who live in the Sahara, the great desert that stretches across North Africa. The Tuareg herd camels, goats, and other livestock.

In parts of rural North Africa, some people live much as their parents and grandparents did. But traditional and modern ways of life mix in towns and large cities like Cairo (KY roh), Egypt, and Tunis, Tunisia. Like Meena, who weaves carpets, some city people work at traditional crafts. Others are architects, engineers, scientists, and bankers. Some sell baskets in outdoor markets. Others sell television sets in modern stores.

Arab and Berber, urban and rural, architect and herder—the peoples of North Africa live vastly different lives, yet almost all consider themselves fellow Muslims. Islam forms a common bond of culture among North Africans.

Cultural Change in North Africa

North Africa's mix of traditional and modern ways of life shows that culture does not stay the same forever. It changes all the time.

How Culture Spreads Cultural changes often occur when people travel. As they travel, people bring their customs and ideas with them. They also pick up new ideas and customs. In this way, customs and ideas spread from one place to another. The movement of customs and ideas is called **cultural diffusion.** The word *diffuse* means "to spread out."

A Mediterranean Outlook   One factor that has aided the diffusion of culture in North Africa is location. Find North Africa on the map below. North Africans have long viewed their region as a gateway to three continents: Africa, Europe, and Asia. Can you see why? This Mediterranean outlook dates back to early history.

Because of its location, North Africa has been a hub of trade. Throughout history, the people of North Africa have traded with people in Europe, Asia, and other parts of Africa. Thus, they have influenced, and been influenced by, cultures in all these places.

The mixing of cultures in North Africa did not occur only through trade. It also occurred through conquest. North Africa is home to one of the world's oldest civilizations—ancient Egypt. The ancient Egyptians developed trade links with ancient civilizations in both Europe and Southwest Asia. They both conquered and were conquered by other empires. These conquests helped bring about cultural diffusion.

Connect What cities in the United States are centers of trade?

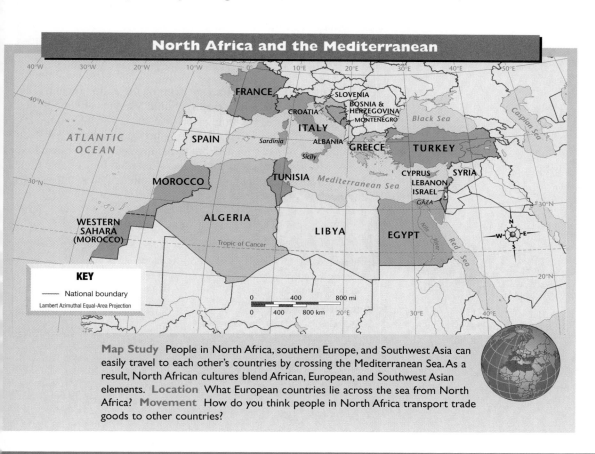

North Africa and the Mediterranean

KEY

— National boundary

Lambert Azimuthal Equal-Area Projection

0   400   800 mi
0   400   800 km

Map Study People in North Africa, southern Europe, and Southwest Asia can easily travel to each other's countries by crossing the Mediterranean Sea. As a result, North African cultures blend African, European, and Southwest Asian elements. **Location** What European countries lie across the sea from North Africa? **Movement** How do you think people in North Africa transport trade goods to other countries?

Interdisciplinary Connections

Math   Have students calculate the distance from Cairo, Egypt, to each of the following Mediterranean cities: Athens, Jerusalem, and Barcelona. (Approximate distances in miles: 750, 250, and 1,800) Then have students use a United States map to measure the same distances in any direction from their own community. Discuss the data, guiding students to see that many Americans can travel distances such as these and still be in the United States. Ask students to suggest some ideas about how the relative closeness of different cultures in the Mediterranean has influenced those cultures and the spread of ideas among them.

Answers to . . .

MAP STUDY

Spain, France, Italy, Greece, and Turkey are some of the countries that lie on the opposite side of the Mediterranean from North Africa.

▶ Muslims often build a large, empty space into the middle of their mosques. Why? In countries with more than one culture and religion, Muslims use mosques as community centers. The empty space can be used for many different kinds of activities, including education.

Preserving Muslim Culture One of the more recent influences on North Africa is Western culture. Some Muslims are concerned that their countries are becoming too Western. More people are wearing Western clothes, buying Western products, seeing Western films, and adapting Western ideas. Some Muslims fear that this will lead to the loss of Muslim values and traditions. They want to preserve their way of life. All over Africa, people face the challenge of how to preserve the traditions they value as their countries modernize.

SECTION 1 REVIEW

1. Define (a) culture, (b) cultural diffusion.

2. Identify (a) Sahara, (b) Mediterranean Sea.

3. How does Islam affect everyday life in North Africa?

4. How has North Africa's location contributed to cultural diffusion?

Critical Thinking

5. Making Comparisons Which aspects of North African culture are similar to and which are different from your culture? Make a list of the similarities and differences.

Activity

6. Writing to Learn What traditions in your culture do you think are worth preserving? Write an essay describing the customs you value most.

The Cultures of West Africa

Lesson Objectives

1 Describe aspects of cultural diversity in West Africa.

2 Explain the role of the family in West African culture.

3 Summarize how West Africans preserve cultural traditions.

BEFORE YOU READ

Reach Into Your Background

How much do you know about different ethnic groups in the United States? Make a list of three or four groups. Jot down notes about each group's culture. Does the group speak a language other than English? What special customs or beliefs does the group have?

Questions to Explore

1. Why does West Africa have such a variety of cultures?
2. What effects do family ties have on West African culture?
3. How has urbanization affected the cultures of West Africa?

Key Terms

cultural diversity
lineage
kinship
clan
nuclear family
griot
extended family

Lesson Plan

1 Engage

Warm-Up Activity

Have students imagine that they are creating a community newspaper. Ask them what languages should be represented in order to reach most readers. Elicit ideas for articles to help readers speaking different languages live, work, and communicate together.

Activating Prior Knowledge

Have students read Reach Into Your Background in the Before You Read box. Invite students to share their lists and ideas with the class. Pool students' contributions to make a class fact sheet about ethnic groups and their cultures, languages, and customs.

In Mauritania, North Africa meets West Africa. Here, the Sahara merges into the savanna, or grasslands. Hamadi (hah MAH dee) is a teacher in a small village school in southern Mauritania. Although the country's official language is Arabic, Hamadi teaches French in the school. But at home, he speaks Poular, the language of the Halpoular, one of Mauritania's main ethnic groups.

Cultural Diversity of West Africa

Being able to speak more than one language is useful in Africa, and especially in West Africa. Seventeen countries make up this region. West Africa also has hundreds of ethnic groups. Because of its many ethnic groups, West Africa is famous for its **cultural diversity**—it has a wide variety of cultures. Unlike the ethnic groups of North Africa, West Africans are not united by a single religion or a common language.

▼ Children in Mauritania do not always have paper and pencils, but that doesn't stop them from learning. Instead, they use slates and chalk.

2 Explore

Have students read the section. Ask students to keep the following questions in mind as they read: Why is West Africa so culturally diverse? Why are young men going to the cities to work? How is life in West African cities different than life in the villages? What problems may result from West Africa's cultural diversity and changing family lives?

Teaching Resources

📁 **Reproducible Lesson Plan** in the Chapter and Section Resources booklet, p. 43, provides a summary of the section lesson.

📁 **Guided Reading and Review** in the Chapter and Section Resources booklet, p. 44, provides a structure for mastering key concepts and reviewing key terms in the section. Available in Spanish in the Spanish Chapter and Section Resources booklet, p. 28.

Program Resources

📁 **Outline Maps** West and Central Africa: Political, p. 34

3 Teach

Encourage students to develop an ad inviting people to visit West Africa for business and pleasure. Ads may include artwork, poetry, or mock quotations or testimonials if their content is plausible. Post the ads in the classroom and use them to begin a discussion about the cultures of West Africa. This activity should take about 30 minutes.

Activity

Critical Thinking

Recognizing Cause and Effect *Suitable as an individual activity.* Have students draw or duplicate images showing some possible effects of West Africa's multilingual culture. For example, students might draw a customer asking a shopkeeper for a certain item. Ask students to write captions explaining the effect pictured. Effects may be either negative or positive.

Answers to . . .

A MARKET IN DAKAR, SENEGAL

The people who buy and sell the fish also benefit.

Predict How do you think the cultural diversity of West Africa affects the lives of its people?

West Africans Speak Many Languages Think about your community. Imagine that the people who live nearby speak a different language. How would you communicate with them? Suppose you wanted to shop in a store, eat in a restaurant, or attend a sports event in the next town. It might seem like visiting another country.

This situation is real for many West Africans. The hundreds of ethnic groups in West Africa speak different languages. Sometimes groups in neighboring villages speak different languages.

To communicate, most West Africans speak more than one language. Many speak four or five languages. They use these different languages when they travel or conduct business. This practice helps unify countries with many ethnic groups.

West Africans Have Many Ways of Making a Living
West Africa's ethnic groups differ in more than just the language they speak. Like North Africans, West Africans have many ways of making of a living. Most West Africans live in rural areas. A typical village consists of a group of homes surrounded by farmland. The village people grow food for themselves and cash crops to sell.

In the Sahara and the dry Sahel just south of the Sahara, many people herd cattle, goats, sheep, or camels. Along the coast, most West Africans make a living by fishing. Some West Africans live in large cities where they may work in hospitals, hotels, or office buildings.

A Market in Dakar, Senegal

At this open-air market in Dakar, Senegal, customers can buy many kinds of groceries, including fresh fish. Dakar is a wealthy port city on Senegal's Atlantic coast. Senegal has built up its fishing industry so much that fish are its most important export. **Critical Thinking** Besides the people who catch the fish, who benefits from Dakar's fishing industry?

Resource Directory

Media and Technology

Planet Earth CD-ROM includes interactive political and thematic maps which allow students to investigate the countries and cultures of West Africa.

Color Transparencies 51, 52, 72

Ways of making a living in West Africa vary from country to country. Most people in Mali (below left) make a living growing crops such as grains, corn, potatoes, yams, and cassava. But in some countries, such as Côte d'Ivoire, almost half the people live and work in cities. The University of Côte d'Ivoire (below right), in the capital city of Yamoussoukro (yahm uh SOO kroh), employs hundreds of people.

Belonging to Groups

Like North Africans, West Africans see themselves as members of a number of groups. Just as you belong to a family, an ethnic group, and a country, so do West Africans.

The Strong Ties of Kinship   One of the strongest bonds West Africans have is **kinship,** which refers to a family relationship. The first level of kinship is the **nuclear family,** which consists of parents and their children. The next level is the **extended family,** which includes other relatives besides parents and children. It may include grandparents, aunts, uncles, and cousins. Many West Africans live in extended families.

Extended families work together and take care of each other. Family members care for the elderly and those who are sick or less well-off. They make decisions together. And they watch over all the children in the village. This custom is reflected in the well-known African proverb, "It takes a village to raise a child." Neighbors always pitch in and help one another. Thus, kinship adds to a strong sense of community.

READ ACTIVELY

Connect How do people outside your immediate family help to raise you?

Teaching Resources

📁 **Critical Thinking Activity** in the Chapter and Section Resources booklet, p. 56, helps students apply the skill of drawing conclusions.

Interdisciplinary Connections

Art Tell students that the Asante people of West Africa are known for their beautifully woven cloth. Weavers make the cloth, called *kente,* from brightly colored silk. Each design is unique and carries its own name. For example, a design made for Ghana's first president is called "One Man Cannot Rule a Country." The name reflects the Ghanaian belief that a leader must be accountable to the people he leads. Prompt students to use markers to design their own *kente.* Tell them to create a design they feel reflects their beliefs, personality, goals, or abilities. Then challenge students to name their *kente.* Display the designs on a classroom wall. *English Language Learner, Visual*

Larger Groups: Lineages and Clans In many rural areas, kinship reaches beyond extended families. A group of families may trace their descent back to a common ancestor. Such a group forms a **lineage.** Several lineages form a **clan.** The people in a clan all have roots back to an even earlier ancestor.

Tracing Lineage Different traditions also govern the way groups trace their lineage. Some groups are matrilineal. They trace their lineage through women ancestors. Property is passed on to children through the female side of a family. In a matrilineal society, if people marry outside the clan, the husband comes to live with the wife's clan. The result is that the village has a core of women who live there. The men they marry are newcomers, who move into the homes of the local women. Most groups, however, are patrilineal. They trace their descent through the male side of a family.

Changes in Family Life

Although traditional family ties remain strong in West Africa, family life is changing. More people are moving from rural villages to urban areas, or cities. This trend, called urbanization, is occurring throughout Africa and the world.

▼ In places like Tombouctou, Mali, where the climate is hot, some families in rural areas do many household chores outside.

Resource Directory

Program Resources

Environmental and Global Issues
Topic: Urbanization, pp. 54–58

Bus drivers must find their way carefully through the crowded streets of Lagos, Nigeria. Like people all over Africa, many of these people have come to Lagos to find work. **Critical Thinking** Why do you think it would be easier to find a job in a city than in a rural area?

Many young men come to West Africa's cities to find jobs. The women often stay in the rural homes. They raise the children and farm the land. The men come home from time to time to visit their families and to share what they have earned.

Keeping Traditions Alive

In West Africa today, people are adapting to change in various ways. But most West Africans still keep strong family ties. People still pass their history, values, and traditions on to the young.

One important way in which West African traditions are being preserved is through storytelling. Traditional West African stories are spoken rather than written. The stories teach children cultural values. A storyteller called a **griot** (GREE oh) passes this oral tradition from one generation to another. The oral tradition of West Africa tells the histories of ethnic groups and kinships. Stories of tricksters, animal fables, proverbs, riddles, and songs are also part of West Africa's oral tradition. This Yoruba proverb reflects the value placed on passing on traditions: "The young can't teach traditions to the old."

L·I·N·K·S TO LANGUAGE ARTS

West African Folk Tales West Africa has a rich tradition of folk tales. One type of tale is the escape story, in which a clever person thinks of a way out of an impossible situation. One tale from Benin is about a cruel king who orders his people to build him a new palace. He tells them that they must start at the top and build down. The people despair. Then a wise old man invites the king to begin by setting the first stone in place. The people are saved.

Background

Biography

Wole Soyinka (1934–)
Wole Soyinka's plays, poems, and novels are strongly linked to his Nigerian heritage. Soyinka's play *A Dance of the Forests* was written for the Nigerian independence celebrations and draws upon Yoruban mythology and folklore.

Section 2 Review

1. (a) wide variety of cultures (b) refers to a family relationship (c) parents and their children (d) relatives such as grandparents, aunts, uncles, and cousins (e) group of families who trace their descent to a common ancestor (f) several lineages who can trace their descent to the same early ancestor (g) a West African storyteller

2. West Africa includes 17 nations and hundreds of ethnic groups.

3. Family members help one another with personal issues, business matters, and decision making.

4. Urbanization has separated men from their families and weakened people's dependence on their extended families.

5. Shared responsibility makes members of an extended family aware of and connected to the community.

6. Possible advantage: support from the extended family. Possible disadvantage: lack of privacy.

When a griot tells a story, it can take all night or even several days. The audience does not mind, because the stories are usually scary, funny, or exciting. This griot, from Côte d'Ivoire, is telling these children a legend from their history. The children pay careful attention, because the griot acts out parts of the story as he goes along.

West African traditions have greatly influenced other cultures, especially American culture. About half of the enslaved Africans who were brought to the United States came from West Africa. They brought with them the only things they could: their ideas, stories, dances, music, and customs. The stories of Brer Rabbit as well as blues and jazz music have their roots in West Africa. Today, West African culture—the stories, music, dances, art, cooking, clothing—is more popular than ever. Griot guitarists and other musicians from West Africa have international followings. In recent years, three Nobel Prize winners for literature have been African. One of them, Wole Soyinka (WOH lay shaw YING kah), is from the West African country of Nigeria.

SECTION 2 REVIEW

1. Define (a) cultural diversity, (b) kinship, (c) nuclear family, (d) extended family, (e) lineage, (f) clan, (g) griot.

2. In what ways is West Africa culturally diverse?

3. Describe the importance of family ties to West Africans.

4. How has urbanization changed the lives of West Africans?

Critical Thinking

5. Drawing Conclusions How has the extended family helped to develop a sense of community among West Africans?

Activity

6. Writing to Learn Imagine that you live in a small village in an extended family in West Africa. Make a list of the advantages and disadvantages of your way of life.

Resource Directory

Teaching Resources

Section Quiz in the Chapter and Section Resources booklet, p. 45, covers the main ideas and key terms in the section. Available in Spanish in the Spanish Chapter and Section Resources booklet, p. 29.

The Cultures of East Africa

Lesson Objectives

1. Describe the influence of East Africa's location on its cultures.

2. Summarize the role of the Swahili language in East African cultures.

3. Explain how ideas about land ownership have changed.

BEFORE YOU READ

Reach Into Your Background

Think about the language you speak. How many words can you identify that come from another language? What about the words *banjo, canyon,* or *succotash? Banjo* comes from an African language, possibly Kimbundu. *Canyon* comes from Spanish. *Succotash* comes from Narragansett, a Native American language. See if you can find other examples.

Questions to Explore

1. How has location affected the development of East African cultures?

2. What role does the Swahili language play in East African cultures?

3. How and why are ideas about land ownership changing in East Africa?

Key Terms
plantation

Key People and Places
Julius Nyerere
East Africa

Lesson Plan

1 Engage

Warm-Up Activity

Ask students who "owns" the Mississippi River, the Rocky Mountains, or the neighborhood parks in your community. Discuss who can use these places. Then ask students who owns the building in which they live and who can use it. Compare the different kinds of ownership. Tell students that in East Africa, traditional views about land ownership are similar to American views about public lands.

Activating Prior Knowledge

Have students read Reach Into Your Background in the Before You Read box. You may want to make available a dictionary that gives word origins so students can compile a list of words that have come from other languages.

Alemeseged Taddesse Mekonnen (ah LEM uh seh ged tah DAY say meh KOH nen) is an Ethiopian who works in a bakery in St. Louis, Missouri. Before coming to the United States, he lived with his extended family in Gonder, a city in northern Ethiopia. His father owned a large store there. Mekonnen speaks three languages: Amharic, Arabic, and English. At home, in Ethiopia, Amharic was his first language. Because he is Muslim, he learned Arabic to study the Quran. And he learned English in school, as other Ethiopians do.

Mekonnen misses life with his close-knit family in Ethiopia. "At home we ate every meal together. If anyone was missing, we waited until they came home," he says. Mekonnen hopes to return home someday. He lives in the United States, but his heart is in Ethiopia.

▼ Shown below is the city of Gonder, in northern Ethiopia. Ethiopia is one of the countries in East Africa.

Teaching Resources

📁 **Reproducible Lesson Plan** in the Chapter and Section Resources booklet, p. 46, provides a summary of the section lesson.

📁 **Guided Reading and Review** in the Chapter and Section Resources booklet, p. 47, provides a structure for mastering key concepts and reviewing key terms in the section. Available in Spanish in the Spanish Chapter and Section Resources booklet, p. 30.

Program Resources

📁 **Outline Maps** West and Central Africa: Political, p. 34

2 Explore

Instruct students to read the section. Discuss with students why peoples from India, Europe, and Southwest Asia might interact with East Africa. Ask: *What is Swahili culture? How does it unify countries in East Africa? How did European ideas about land use differ from those of the East Africans?*

3 Teach

Ask students to create three bookmarks commemorating a lecture series about East Africa. Students should use information from the section to add text or illustrations to the bookmarks that provide information about issues facing the region. This activity should take about 35 minutes.

4 Assess

See the answers to the Section Review. You may also use students' bookmarks as an assessment tool.

Acceptable bookmarks are linked to the lesson objectives.

Commendable bookmarks are each linked to one of the lesson objectives and include decorations or text that illustrate a theme or issue.

Outstanding bookmarks are each linked to one of the lesson objectives and include text or several related decorations that illustrate or explain a theme or issue.

Living Along the Indian Ocean

Knowing three languages is not unusual for an East African, just as it is not for a West African. In Ethiopia alone, more than 70 different languages are spoken. Like West Africa, East Africa has many ethnic groups who speak different languages. The region has great cultural diversity.

East Africa's diversity is the result of its location. Many ethnic groups have migrated to East Africa from other regions of the continent. For example, about 2,000 years ago, Bantu-speaking peoples migrated to East Africa from West Africa. In addition, East Africa has a long coastline along the Indian Ocean. The ocean connects the people of East Africa to people living across the ocean to the east. These people include Arabs, Indians, and other Asians. The connection extends even to countries as far away as China and Malaysia.

This link dates back to early times. Arab traders began to settle in the coastal villages of East Africa nearly 2,000 years ago. They brought Arab culture into East Africa, where it mixed with various African cultures. This mixture produced the Swahili culture.

Lunch Time for a Kenyan Family

Shown above is a family from Kenya. Families in East Africa traditionally eat their meals together, using one bowl or plate. In the traditional style, they use their fingers rather than forks and spoons. **Critical Thinking** What foods do people in the United States share from one plate or bowl?

Kampala is Uganda's largest city and leading trade center. It is a religious center as well. You can find Muslim mosques, Hindu temples, and Christian churches here.

Daily Life

Jewelry and Hairstyles of the Maasai One of East Africa's many ethnic groups is the Maasai of Tanzania and Kenya. Maasai jewelry and hairstyles are quite striking. Women wear dozens of necklaces, bracelets, and earrings made of beaded copper and iron wire. Though the women shave their heads, the Maasai men groom their long hair with clay and grease. Then they braid their hair in tiny braids and loop or drape it about their heads in intricate designs.

Swahili Culture

The Swahili are Africans who have mixed African and Arab ancestry. They live along the east coast of Africa from Somalia to Mozambique. Their language is also called Swahili. It is a Bantu language, but it contains many Arabic words. The Swahili are just one of hundreds of ethnic groups in East Africa. But their language is widely used for business and communication among many ethnic groups throughout the region.

Swahili is the first language of about 49 million people worldwide. It also serves as the second language of millions of East Africans. Swahili is the official language of Kenya and Tanzania. In Tanzania, children are educated in Swahili through the primary grades. Later, they learn English as well. By promoting the use of Swahili, these nations are trying to preserve their African heritage.

A Mixture of Religions

Like languages, religious beliefs in East Africa reflect the cultural diversity of the region. Both Islam and Christianity have large followings in the region. Islam was introduced into East Africa by Arab traders. The Romans introduced Christianity into some of their North African territories. Later, it spread into Ethiopia. In the 1800s,

ACROSS THE WORLD

Kwanzaa Swahili culture and language have also come to the United States. Many African Americans celebrate Kwanzaa (KWAN zah), a holiday based on a traditional African harvest festival. The word *Kwanzaa* is related to the Swahili word for "first." Kwanzaa is based on a set of values that also have Swahili names. These include *umoja* (oo MOH juh), or unity; *kuumba* (koo OOM buh), or creativity; and *imani* (ee MAHN ee), or faith.

Agatha Mbogo Agatha Mbogo wanted to help her rural community of Embu, Kenya. But in her community, it is unusual for women to be political leaders. With little money and no experience, Mbogo ran for a district council seat—and won. That gave her the courage to run for mayor in 1994. Despite facing a veteran mayor, she was elected by the all-male district council.

Europeans pushed into Africa and spread Christianity farther. In addition, traditional religions remain alive in East Africa and throughout the continent.

Changing Ideas About Land

In East Africa, as in the rest of Africa, most people live in rural areas, where they farm and tend livestock. The ways in which they view and work the land are part of the culture of East Africans.

Before Land Was Owned Before Europeans took over parts of Africa in the 1800s, individual Africans did not own land. People did not buy or sell land. The very idea of owning land did not exist. Families had the right to farm plots of land near the village, but the actual plots might vary in size and location over time.

Traditionally, extended families farmed the land to produce food for the whole group. Men cleared the land and broke up the soil. Women then planted the seed, tended the fields, and harvested the crops. Meanwhile, the men herded livestock or traded goods. This division of roles still exists in many parts of Africa today.

The Rise and Fall of Plantations The idea of privately owned land was introduced into many parts of Africa by European settlers. In parts of East Africa, the British set up plantations. A **plantation** is a large farm where cash crops are grown. When many African countries became independent, they broke up the old colonial plantations. They sold the land to individual Africans.

Some land in East Africa is still available to buy. But much of it is poor farmland in areas where few people live. In fertile areas like the Ethiopian Highlands and the Rift Valley,

land for farming is scarce. Many people live in these areas where the farmland is fertile. In densely populated countries, such as Rwanda and Burundi, conflicts have developed over land.

Where Is Home?

Traditionally, Africans feel a strong bond to the land where they grew up. Like the rest of Africa, East Africa is becoming increasingly urban. Yet even people who spend most of their time in a city do not call it home. If asked where home is, an East African will name the village of his or her family or clan. Most people consider their life in the city temporary. They expect to return to their villages at some time.

Tanzania's former president Julius Nyerere (nyuh RAIR ay) is one example. Nyerere continues to be involved in world affairs, but he now lives far from Dar es Salaam, the capital city of Tanzania. After he

READ ACTIVELY

Connect How do you feel when you return home after being away for a long time?

◀ The coastal city of Mombasa, Kenya, began as a trading center in the 1200s. One of its chief exports was ivory. Today, metal arches shaped like elephant tusks memorialize Kenya's ivory trade. While cities like Mombasa can be beautiful and exciting, to most East Africans a city can never really be home.

Activity

Journal Writing

Paying Homage to Home Challenge students to answer the question: Where is home? Explain that students should describe a place where they feel at home, which does not necessarily have to be where they currently live. They may use drawings, poetry, or a narrative to describe the place. Remind students that their journals are private and that no one else will read their entries.

Section 3 Review

1. a large farm where cash crops are grown

2. (a) a former president of Tanzania (b) region in eastern Africa made up of 10 nations

3. East Africa's location on the Indian Ocean made it relatively easy for Arab traders to reach. They brought elements of their culture to East Africa.

4. Many people speak Swahili as a second language in order to communicate with others in a region where many different languages are spoken.

5. European settlers introduced the idea of ownership of land. Traditionally, Africans did not buy or sell land.

6. East Africans did not view land as a commodity to be bought and sold. They farmed land to grow food for their immediate needs. Europeans viewed the ownership of land as a way to earn money. They grew cash crops.

7. Descriptions will vary. Students should define what they mean by "home" and explain its importance to them.

stepped down as president in 1985, Nyerere moved back to his home village. There, he grows corn and millet on his farm. He spends his mornings working in the fields. In an interview in 1996, Nyerere said: "In a sense I am a very rural person. I grew up here, and [working in] Dar es Salaam was a duty. I did my duty and after retiring in 1985, I came back here and said, 'Ah, it's good to be back.'"

Other East Africans feel the same. They may do their duty by earning money in the city. But their homes—and their hearts—are in their rural villages.

◄ On his family farm in Rwanda, this farmer grows potatoes, corn, beans, and cabbage. East Africans sometimes move away from their farms, but they almost always hope to return to them one day.

SECTION 3 REVIEW

1. Define plantation.

2. Identify (a) Julius Nyerere, (b) East Africa.

3. Describe some ways in which East Africa's location along the Indian Ocean has affected its cultures.

4. Why is Swahili spoken by so many people in East Africa?

5. Explain the changes in ideas about land ownership in East Africa.

Critical Thinking

6. Making Comparisons How did traditional East African ideas about land differ from the ideas of Europeans who took over parts of Africa?

Activity

7. Writing to Learn Write a description of the place that you consider home. Tell what it means to you and explain why.

Resource Directory

Teaching Resources

📁 **Section Quiz** in the Chapter and Section Resources booklet, p. 48, covers the main ideas and key terms in the section. Available in Spanish in the Spanish Chapter and Section Resources booklet, p. 31.

The Cultures of Central and Southern Africa

BEFORE YOU READ

Reach Into Your Background

Think of a goal you had to work hard to achieve at home or at school. Why was it important to you to achieve your goal? Think about the plan you made and the strategies you used to achieve your goal. What obstacles did you have to overcome? How did you feel when you finally succeeded?

Questions to Explore

1. How has the country of South Africa influenced the entire region of Southern Africa?
2. How did migrant labor give rise to a new group identity among the peoples of Southern Africa?
3. How does Central Africa reflect the cultural diversity of all of Africa?

Key Terms
migrant worker

Key Places
Republic of South Africa
Southern Africa
Central Africa
Zaire

Section 4

Lesson Objectives

1 Describe the influence of South Africa on the entire region of Central and Southern Africa.

2 Explain Central Africa's cultural diversity and link it to cultural diversity in other parts of Africa.

Lesson Plan

1 Engage

Warm-Up Activity

Tell students that during the 1960s, black Americans joined together to win full political and civil rights. Ask students how they think this fight for rights affected black Americans' sense of community.

Activating Prior Knowledge

Have students read Reach Into Your Background in the Before You Read box. Invite volunteers to share with the class some of their methods for achieving goals.

The African National Congress (ANC), a political party in the Republic of South Africa, played a key role in gaining political and civil rights for all South Africans. Until 1991, Europeans in South Africa had denied equal rights to blacks, who make up a majority of the population. Three countries—Tanzania, Zambia, and Zimbabwe—adopted the ANC anthem for their national anthems. Here are the words to the ANC anthem:

> "Bless, O Lord, our land of Africa
> Lift its name and make its people free.
> Take the gifts we offer unto Thee
> Hear us, faithful sons.
> Hear us, faithful sons."

▼ These teenagers sang the ANC anthem for the opening of Parliament in Cape Town, South Africa.

Teaching Resources

📁 **Reproducible Lesson Plan** in the Chapter and Section Resources booklet, p. 49, provides a summary of the section lesson.

📁 **Guided Reading and Review** in the Chapter and Section Resources booklet, p. 50, provides a structure for mastering key concepts and reviewing key terms in the section. Available in Spanish in the Spanish Chapter and Section Resources booklet, p. 32.

Media and Technology

📽 **Color Transparencies** 51, 52, 73

Program Resources

📁 **Outline Maps** West and Central Africa: Political, p. 34;
East and Southern Africa: Political, p. 35

2 Explore

Draw a cause-and-effect diagram on the board. After students read the section, have volunteers fill in the diagram. You may prompt students by having them think of causes for these effects: *blacks began to view themselves as citizens; transportation links were built in South Africa; migrant workers forged a group identity; Zairians live both very traditional and very modern lives.* Urge students to answer the question "why" as they identify corresponding causes.

3 Teach

After students have read the section, have them develop a Venn diagram showing what things are traditional, modern, and a combination of modern and traditional. This activity should take about 20 minutes.

4 Assess

See the answers to the Section Review. Students' completed diagrams can also be assessed.

Acceptable diagrams include two facts in each cell.

Commendable diagrams include three facts in each cell.

Outstanding diagrams include more than three facts in each cell.

Answers to ...

A SOUTH AFRICAN GOLD MINER

Accept all reasonable responses.

The Pull of South Africa

South Africa is just one country in Southern Africa, but it has ha by far, the greatest impact on the region. Its political and economic infl ence has touched the lives of millions of people.

Ask Questions What questions do you have about South Africa's influence on the rest of southern Africa?

Political Influence of South Africa Until the 1990s, European minority ruled South Africa. In 1923, they separated Sou Africans into categories based on skin color. People of African desce were classified as black, people of European descent as white, ar people of mixed ancestry as colored. Asians, who were mostly fro India, formed the fourth category. Blacks, coloreds, and Asians cou not vote and did not have other basic rights. For nearly 70 years, thes groups struggled to gain their rights.

The struggle for basic rights created a sense of nationalism amor black South Africans. White settlers, not blacks, had established th nation of South Africa. But as blacks struggled to gain political right they began to think of themselves as members of the nation. The wanted to take part as equal citizens in running the nation. The strugg for majority rule in South Africa lasted so long that it inspired simil movements in Namibia and what is now Zimbabwe.

Economic Influence o South Africa South Afric is the richest and most industri ized country on the continent Africa. It produces two fifth of the manufactured goods, half the minerals, and one fifth of th agricultural products of th entire continent. Its econom power and needs have affected a of Southern Africa because i demand for labor has been s great. To provide a labor force f the mines, South African comp nies used workers from throug out Southern Africa.

To get jobs in South Afric hundreds of thousands workers migrated from nearb countries. Workers were allowe to stay in South Africa for only short time. New workers wer always needed. A large force migrant workers, people wh move from place to place to fin work, was soon created.

A South African Gold Miner

This miner commutes to work by crawling through cramped tunnels until he reaches this room, where he does not have space to stand up. **Critical Thinking** What do you think a work day for this gold miner would be like?

Resource Directory

Teaching Resources

Analyzing a Photograph in the Social Studies and Geography Skills booklet, p. 58, provides additional skill practice.

Program Resources

Environmental and Global Issues Topic: Human Rights, pp. 25–30

Media and Technology

Planet Earth CD-ROM includes interactive political and thematic maps which allow students to investigate the countries and cultures of Southern Africa.

In 1912, South African blacks organized the African National Congress (ANC) to fight for equality. The ANC used boycotts, rallies, and work strikes to force the government to reform its laws. Many ANC members, including Nelson Mandela, were jailed for their actions. Mandela spent almost 30 years in jail. The struggle finally paid off. In the 1990s, South Africa ended its discriminatory laws and gave nonwhite South Africans the right to vote for the first time. Mandela became South Africa's president.

Background

Global Perspectives

Migrant Workers The migrant labor system exists in the United States as well as in South Africa. In fact, the American migrant labor system is larger than any other. It exists mostly in farming regions. Many migrant workers are constantly on the move, traveling from place to place as different crops become ready for harvest. Most live in poverty and, because they never stay in one place very long, they don't have reliable access to health care or education for their children. Like South Africa's migrant workers, those in the United States have sought to better their circumstances through group political efforts. The United Farm Workers, under the leadership of Cesar Chavez, achieved some improvements in living and working conditions.

Migrant Workers Form a New Group Identity

Mine workers in South Africa were from many countries. They lived together in compounds, or fenced-in groups of homes. They were far from their families, clans, and ethnic groups. They worked long hours in dangerous conditions for low wages.

A Person Is a Person Because of People The migrant mine workers came to rely on one another. They began to think of themselves as a group—as workers. This kind of group identity was new for Southern Africans. It was not based on family or ethnic group. Group identity is very important in Africa. This is reflected in the African proverb "A person is a person because of people." It means that a person is who he or she is because of his or her relationships with other people. The migrant workers formed a new identity based on how they related to each other as workers.

Mine Workers Form a Union In the 1980s, the mine workers in South Africa formed a union—the National Union of Mineworkers. This union was illegal at the time. But it played a leading role in the drive for equal rights. The union workers sometimes went on strike in support of their causes. Thus, the new identity of the mine workers led them to take group action.

READ ACTIVELY

Predict How do you think South Africa's mines affected its culture?

SKILLS MINI LESSON

Identifying Central Issues

To **introduce** the skill, tell students that one way to understand their reading more fully is to identify main ideas, or central issues, in the text. Suggest the following strategies to help students identify central issues: 1) Check titles and headings for main ideas. 2) Read opening and closing sentences. 3) Think about an idea that all sections of text have in common. 4) Use your own words to restate the central issue. As a class, **practice** and **apply** these steps to the text under the heading *The Pull of South Africa*. Invite volunteers to write on the board their responses to each strategy. Then have students write one or two sentences stating the central issue of the text. (Possible answer: South Africa has had more influence than any other Southern African nation on the politics and economics of the region.)

Interdisciplinary Connections

Music Obtain and play for students some examples of traditional and contemporary music from Central and Southern Africa. Some good choices include: *Mbuti Pygmies of the Ituri Rainforest* (traditional music from Zaire), *Traditional Mbira Musicians & Kevin Volans Ensemble* (traditional and contemporary music from Zimbabwe), and *Soukous Music* (contemporary Zairian dance music played by one of Zaire's most popular musicians, Tabu Ley Rochereau). These and other recordings should be available at libraries and music stores. Many contain informative liner notes and English translations of lyrics. If possible, teach children an African dance or show a videotape of traditional African dance. Alternatively, have students develop their own dances to accompany the music.
Auditory, Kinesthetic, English Language Learner

Barkcloth Art The Mbuti of Zaire use only renewable resources. For example, they make some of their cloth out of tree bark. Men pound the bark with mallets until it is almost as soft as velvet. Then women draw shapes and patterns on the cloth. Many art galleries in the United States and Europe collect Mbuti barkcloth drawings.

Tradition and Change in Central Africa

Like people in Southern Africa and the rest of Africa, Central Africans have gone through many cultural changes in the 1900s. But many people in the region also follow old traditions. Like the rest of the continent, Central Africa displays great cultural diversity. The country of Zaire, alone, has about 200 ethnic groups.

One ethnic group in Zaire is the Mbuti (em BOO tee), who live in the rain forests. The Mbuti are unique because they live much as their ancestors did. In forest camps of 10 to 25 families, they make their dome-shaped houses from branches and leaves. For food, they hunt wild animals and gather wild plants. The culture of the Mbuti is more than 3,000 years old.

In contrast, millions of people live in crowded shantytowns or cinder-block apartments in Kinshasa, the largest city in Zaire. They walk or take buses or trucks to work in factories, offices, and hotels. Some people are Roman Catholics or Protestants. Others practice religions that blend Christian and traditional African beliefs. Still others are Muslims. On Saturday evenings, many people dance and listen to Zairian jazz in city dance halls.

At Work in Cameroon

Cameroon is a country in northwest Central Africa. Most people in Cameroon live in rural areas and make a living by farming or by herding cattle. These men are building farm structures used in taking care of cattle.

Resource Directory

Teaching Resources

Section Quiz in the Chapter and Section Resources booklet, p. 51, covers the main ideas and key terms in the section. Available in Spanish in the Spanish Chapter and Section Resources booklet, p. 33.

Vocabulary in the Chapter and Section Resources booklet, p. 53, provides a review of key terms in the chapter. Available in Spanish in the Spanish Chapter and Section Resources booklet, p. 35.

Reteaching in the Chapter and Section Resources booklet, p. 54, provides a structure for students who may need additional help in mastering chapter content.

Enrichment in the Chapter and Section Resources booklet, p. 55, extends chapter content and enriches students' understanding.

A Modern City in an Old Location

Kinshasa is Zaire's capital. People have lived here since the late 1400s, making a living by fishing or trading on the Congo River. Today, people still fish on the Congo River, and it remains an important source of transportation. However, Kinshasa is also a center of government and industry.

What one writer said about North Africa applies to Southern Africa as well. To define the real North African, he said, "you have to define which one you mean: the rich or the poor, the Berber women of the mountains or the college girls on motorbikes...." Old, new, and mixtures of the two live on in all regions of Africa.

SECTION 4 REVIEW

1. **Define** migrant worker.
2. **Identify** (a) Republic of South Africa, (b) Southern Africa, (c) Central Africa, (d) Zaire.
3. Describe the political and economic effects South Africa has had on the entire region of Southern Africa.

4. What was unusual about migrant workers in South Africa forming a group identity as workers?
5. In what ways are the cultures of Central Africa like those in other parts of Africa?

Critical Thinking
6. **Recognizing Cause and Effect** What positive and/or negative effects might South Africa's labor needs have had on the economies of nearby countries?

Activity
7. **Writing to Learn** Consider the life of a mine worker in a South African gold mine in the 1970s. Write the first verse of a song protesting miners' living and working conditions and wages.

Spanish Glossary in the Spanish Chapter and Section Resources, pp. 68–73, provides key terms translated from English to Spanish as well as definitions in Spanish.

Chapter Summary in the Chapter and Section Resources booklet, p. 52, provides a summary of chapter content. Available in Spanish in the Spanish Chapter and Section Resources booklet, p. 34.

Cooperative Learning Activity in the Activities and Projects booklet, pp. 25–28, provides two student handouts, one page of teacher's directions, and a scoring rubric for a cooperative learning activity on making a relief map.

Media and Technology

Guided Reading Audiotapes (English and Spanish)

1. someone who moves from place to place to find work

2. (a) a country located at the tip of Southern Africa (b) a region in the southern part of Africa made up of 13 nations (c) a region in central Africa made up of seven nations (d) the largest country in Central Africa

3. The struggle for majority rule in South Africa inspired and encouraged similar movements in nearby countries. South Africa has drawn laborers from the entire region and built transportation linking the region to the world.

4. Their new group identity was based on a common experience as workers, not on kinship or ethnicity.

5. There is great cultural diversity. Also, some people live very traditionally while others lead modern, urban lives.

6. Possible answers: Neighboring economies may have benefited from the income earned in South African industry and the worldwide access created by South African transportation. Nearby countries' economies may have suffered labor shortages.

7. Song verses should demonstrate the miners' desire for political acknowledgment and representation.

SKILLS ACTIVITY

Assessing Your Understanding

Lesson Objectives

❶ Explain the process of assessing your understanding.

❷ Practice assessing understanding in a specific context.

Lesson Plan

1 Engage

Warm-Up Activity

After students read the opening paragraphs, **introduce** the skill by writing the word *assess* and its definition (to determine the importance, size, or value of) on the chalkboard.

Activating Prior Knowledge

Ask students to link the definition to the skill title. How might they assess their understanding? (by asking themselves questions about something they have read or learned) Elicit examples of ways in which teachers assess students' understanding (tests, discussion, writing assignments, and so on).

2 Explore

Invite a volunteer to read aloud the *Get Ready* text. Have students then write a one- or two-sentence definition of the skill as it might appear in a book's glossary. Ask them to suggest additional ways that they might apply this skill in or out of school. Then have students read the remaining parts of the lesson.

magine you have a pen pal, a student your age from Africa. In one of her letters, she asks you this question: "What is your school like?" How would you answer?

You might describe it as a large school, or a small one. You could say whether it is in a rural area or in the heart of a big city. You could describe your school building, the classes you take, your teachers, your friends, and so on. This would be easy for you, because school is such a big part of your life. The classes you take, the people you see, and the books you read all seem normal to you.

But have you ever wondered what school is like for a person your age in Africa? You could ask your pen pal. Depending on where your pen pal lives, though, the answer would be different. A school in a big city in Egypt is very different from a school in rural Uganda. But every school in Africa has at least one thing in common with your school—students are there to learn. Like other students, if you want to study new things, you must learn to assess your understanding.

Get Ready

What does "assessing your understanding" mean? It means checking to see how well you understand something you are reading or studying. If you assess your understanding as you go along, you will know what areas you need to read or think more about to make sure you understand. You can concentrate on studying those things. This can help you to get better grades. For example, by assessing your understanding before a test, you can predict what grade you will get on the test. And you will know exactly what you need to study if you want to get a higher grade. It can help you get more out of your reading. If you realize something does not make sense to you, you can use some strategies such as rereading or making a graphic organizer to help you understand the information.

Resource Directory

Teaching Resources

📁 **Connecting Content to What You Already Know** in the Social Studies and Geography Skills booklet, p. 71, provides additional skill practice.

📁 **Determining If You Understood What You Read** in the Social Studies and Geography Skills booklet, p. 74, provides additional skill practice.

Try It Out

A good way of assessing your understanding is to play a simple game called "Do I Understand?" To play, choose one assignment you completed recently. Then ask yourself the questions on the checklist.

1. Do I understand why I was given this assignment? Knowing why you are reading or doing something will help you understand why what you are doing is important.

2. Do I understand the main point of the assignment? Every assignment has a main point or key idea that you should take from it.

3. Do I understand how this assignment relates to what I already know? In school, new knowledge builds on previous knowledge.

4. Do I understand how what I just learned might be useful in the future? For example, think about how this new information might relate to projects you are working on.

Apply the Skill

Practice assessing your understanding with the short reading assignment in the box, "An African School" by David Lamb.

1. Now, reread Question 1 in the list above. Why is it worthwhile to learn about a school in Kenya? What key ideas about the school does the writer try to communicate?

2. Reread Question 2. What do you think is the main point of "An African School"?

3. Reread Question 3. How does the writer's description fit with what you have already learned about Africa? Consider such things as languages, climate, and the condition of the school. Does anything in the reading assignment surprise you, or is it what you expected?

4. Look at Question 4. What are two ways that the knowledge you have just gained could help you in the future?

An African School

The Njumbi primary school [is] not far from the town of Karai in Kenya. . . . The headmaster, Michael Mathini, an energetic . . . man of thirty who rides a bicycle to work, greeted us at the door. He led us into his office and pointed with great pride to a wall graph showing that his students scored above the national average in the annual. . .examination.

The school has 620 students . . . and seventeen teachers who earned from $80 to $135 a month. . . . In the first-grade classroom across from Mathini's office, thirty or forty boys and girls were learning to count. . . They applauded . . . each time one of them gave the teacher the right answer. . . an ancient wooden radio sat on another teacher's desk and the dozen or so teenagers there strained through the heavy static to hear the creative writing lesson being broadcast in English from Nairobi.

Reviewing Main Ideas

1. Islam unified the peoples of North Africa, creating a bond of common religion.

2. North Africa's location just across the Mediterranean Sea from Europe and Southwest Asia has aided cultural diffusion.

3. West Africa has hundreds of ethnic groups that speak different languages.

4. Members of extended families live together, sharing responsibility for one another.

5. East Africa's location along the Indian Ocean encouraged Arab traders to settle, spreading Arab culture along the coast.

6. Swahili aids communication, because it serves as a second language for millions of people speaking various first languages.

7. Before Europeans came to settle, East Africans did not buy or sell land or even have the concept of privately owned land.

8. South Africa has drawn workers from throughout the region of Southern Africa. The struggle for majority rule in South Africa inspired similar movements in nearby countries.

9. It caused them to develop a new group identity as workers.

10. It is culturally diverse.

Reviewing Key Terms

Students' sentences will vary but should demonstrate the meaning of each key term.

Critical Thinking

1. Students might note that relations with other people, particularly family members, are very important in Africa. People are more group-oriented and less individualistic.

2. Students might identify a higher standard of living for some people as a possible benefit. As a drawback, students might cite the loss of close ties among members of extended families.

Review and Activities

Reviewing Main Ideas

1. Describe how Islam has influenced the culture of North Africa.
2. What factor has greatly aided cultural diffusion in North Africa?
3. How is West Africa culturally diverse?
4. What role do family ties play in West African culture?
5. Explain how location has affected East African cultures.
6. How does the language of Swahili help unite the people of East Africa?
7. Why is the idea of privately owned land fairly new to East Africans?
8. How has South Africa affected the cultures of the entire region of Southern Africa?
9. What major effect did migrant labor have on the people of Southern Africa?
10. How is Central Africa like other parts of Africa?

Reviewing Key Terms

Use each key term below in a sentence that shows the meaning of the term.

1. culture
2. cultural diffusion
3. cultural diversity
4. kinship
5. nuclear family
6. extended family
7. lineage
8. clan
9. griot
10. plantation
11. migrant worker

Critical Thinking

1. **Identifying Central Issues** Explain why the proverb "A person is a person because of people" is particularly suited to African culture.
2. **Drawing Conclusions** What benefits and problems have come with modernization in Africa?

Graphic Organizer

Copy the chart onto a sheet of paper. Then complete the chart by describing one or more key features of the cultures of each region.

The Cultures of Africa				
Region	North Africa	West Africa	East Africa	Central and Southern Africa
Culture				

Graphic Organizer

The Cultures of Africa				
Region	North Africa	West Africa	East Africa	Central and Southern Africa
Culture	Islam and the Arabic language unite the peoples of North Africa	hundreds of ethnic groups that speak different languages	Swahili language aids communication among the different groups	South Africa has influenced the politics and economics of the entire region by drawing workers from throughout the region.

Map Activity

Africa
For each place listed below, write the letter from the map that shows its location.

1. Mediterranean Sea

2. North Africa

3. West Africa

4. East Africa

5. Central and Southern Africa

Place Location

Writing Activity

Writing a Dialogue
An exchange student from an African country has come to stay at your home for six weeks. You and your family are sharing your first dinner with the visitor. Write a dialogue in which you ask your visitor about African culture. Use what you have learned in this chapter to write your visitor's answers.

Internet Activity
Use a search engine to find the **Africa Stories Project.** Read about the project. Then read the stories and the African reviewers' comments. Choose a story and research the culture, folk stories, history, and geography of the country where the story was set. Use what you learned about the country or region to write your own fictional Africa story.

Skills Review

Turn to the Skills Activity. Review the steps for assessing your understanding. Then look at the Writing Activity on this page. Ask yourself questions to assess whether you understand the reason for this writing assignment.

How Am I Doing?

Answer these questions to check your progress.

1. Can I describe the cultural diversity of Africa?

2. Do I understand the role of kinship in African cultures?

3. Can I explain how urbanization has changed the way of life of many Africans?

4. What information from this chapter can I use in my unit project?

Internet Activity

If students are having difficulty finding this site, you may wish to have them use the following URL, which was accurate at the time this textbook was published:

http://www.umich.edu/ ~aaps/africa_stories/

You might also guide students to a search engine. Four of the most useful are Infoseek, Alta Vista, Lycos, and Yahoo. For additional suggestions on using the Internet, refer to the Prentice Hall Social Studies' Educator's Handbook "Using the Internet," in the *Prentice Hall World Explorer Program Resources.*

For additional links to world history and culture topics, visit the Prentice Hall Home Page at: **http://www.phschool.com**

How Am I Doing?

Point out to students that this checklist is a quick reminder for them of what they learned in the chapter. If their answer to any of the questions is *no* or if they are unsure, they may need to review the topic.

Map Activity

1. A	4. C
2. B	5. E
3. D	

Writing Activity

Dialogues will vary, but should show a clear grasp of the facts and issues presented in the chapter.

Skills Review

Students might say that the main point of the assignment is to demonstrate their knowledge of African culture by writing a dialogue that incorporates what they have learned.

Resource Directory

Teaching Resources
📁 **Chapter Tests** Forms A and B are in the Tests booklet, pp. 14–19.

Program Resources
📁 **Writing Process Handbook** includes Keeping Track of Information Sources, p. 19, to help students with the Writing Activity.

Media and Technology
🖨 **Color Transparencies** Color Transparency 174 (Graphic organizer table template)

💿 **Prentice Hall Writer's Solution** Writing Lab CD-ROM

💾 **Computer Test Bank**

💿 **Resource Pro™ CD-ROM**

Lesson Objectives

1 Identify and research one type of African drum.

2 Use interdisciplinary skills to build a model African drum and demonstrate its use in a context.

Lesson Plan

1 Engage

Warm-Up Activity

Ask students to write the name of their favorite kind of music on a small slip of paper. Place all the slips in a bowl. Then have volunteers draw slips and copy the information on the chalkboard. Lead a class discussion about the kinds of music listed. Determine together, if possible, which kinds of music contain drum sounds.

Activating Prior Knowledge

Introduce the topic of African drums. Have students identify any music on the chalkboard list that might contain the sounds of African drums. Ask students whether they have ever heard music that featured African drums.

2 Explore

Invite students to read the Activity Shop carefully. Direct them to choose a specific African drum to research. Discuss research ideas, suggesting to students such sources as music schools, large libraries, and the Internet.

INTERDISCIPLINARY ACTIVITY SHOP

The Language of Music

n the United States, you can hear music at parties, in concerts, on the radio, or even in supermarkets. It has many purposes. Music also has many roles in the cultures of African countries. Music may be used to send messages or to tell a story. It may organize work or celebrate a special occasion. In the United States, it is not uncommon to perform music by itself. People in African countries, however, rarely play music by itself. Most often, they combine music with dance, theater, words, games, or visual art.

Traditional African instruments include xylophones, lutes, harps, horns, flutes, clarinets, bells, and drums. Musicians can study for years to master their art, just as they do in the United States. In many African cultures, drums play an important role in traditional and modern music.

Purpose

In this activity, you will research traditional African drums and make your own drum. As you work on this activity, you will learn how Africans make and use drums.

Research African Drums

Traditionally, drums have been the most important instrument in African music. There are many types of drums, including the slit drum, the obodo, and the kettle drum. Use the information on this page to get you started. Then use encyclopedias, the Internet, and other resources to find out more about traditional African drums and how they differ. When you do research, look under subject headings such as African Arts, African Music, and Musical Instruments. You should also search under the names of specific drums.

Write down the names of several African drums. Then choose one drum to model your own after. Learn as much as you can about this kind of drum, including what materials it is made from, how it is played, how it is used, and where it is used.

Resource Directory

Teaching Resources

Activity Shop: Interdisciplinary in the Activities and Projects booklet, p. 7, provides a structure that helps students complete the interdisciplinary activity.

Build Your Own Drum

Once you have chosen a traditional African drum as a model, you can build your own drum. You may want to use items such as buckets, cans, or cartons for the body of your drum. For the head of the drum, you might use cloth, plastic, or paper. Also consider the following questions:

- How will you attach the head of the drum to the body?
- Is one side of the drum open or are both sides covered?
- How will you strike your drum?

If possible, use materials that are similar to the materials the traditional drums are made from. Experiment with different methods to see which sounds best.

Play Your Drum

Figure out how you can use your drum in a way similar to the one you are modeling. For example, if the drum you are modeling was used to communicate messages across a long distance, think of a rhythmic code you can use to play a message to your classmates across the playground. If the drum was used as part of a drum group, you may want to write a short piece of music and play it with your classmates. If the drum accompanied a chant or song telling

the history of a community, write a song telling a story about something that has happened to you or someone you know.

Compare Drums

After you have built your drum and practiced with it, write a paragraph comparing your drum to its African model. You may want to present your work to the class and perform a piece of music.

ANALYSIS AND CONCLUSION

Write a summary that describes how you built and used your drum. Be sure to answer the following questions in the summary.

1. How is your drum similar to and different from the African drum you used as a model?

2. What factors affect the way your drum sounds?

3. How did you adapt the original uses of the model drum?

3 Teach

You may want to organize students into teams. Each team member can focus on a different aspect of the research. Team members can then pool their findings. Once the data are in hand, students may build their models individually, with available materials. Allow class time for students to develop their drums' uses and to write the comparative paragraphs. Encourage students to include a drawing or photograph of the original African drum in their presentations.

4 Assess

Let students display their drums and any text or illustrations they feel are appropriate. Arrange to stage an African music presentation in which students demonstrate each drum's use in an original context. Evaluate the model for accuracy and neatness, the comparative paragraph for insight and clarity, and the performance for originality and creativity.

Exploring North Africa

To help you plan instruction, the chart below shows how teaching resources correspond to chapter content. Use the resources to vary instruction, add activities, or plan block schedules. Where appropriate, resources have suggested time allotments for students. Time allotments are approximate.

Managing Time and Instruction

	Africa Teaching Resources Binder		World Explorer Program Resources Binder	
	Resource	mins.	Resource	mins.
SECTION I **Egypt: Hearing the Call of Islam**	**Chapter and Section Support** Reproducible Lesson Plan, p. 58 S Guided Reading and Review, p. 59 S Section Quiz, p. 60 **Social Studies and Geography Skills,** Recognizing Ideologies, p. 48	 20 25 30	**Outline Maps** North Africa: Political, p. 31 The Middle East and North Africa: Physical, p. 28 **Nystrom Desk Atlas** **T** Primary Sources and Literature Readings **Writing Process Handbook** Editing for Content, Clarity, and Style, pp. 35–36 **Environmental and Global Issues** Topic: Urbanization, pp. 54–58	 20 20 40 25 30
SKILLS ACTIVITY **Using Regional Maps**	**Social Studies and Geography Skills,** Using the Compass Rose, p. 4 Using the Map Scale, p. 5	 30 30	**Outline Maps** North Africa: Political, p. 31 The Middle East and North Africa: Physical, p. 28 **Environmental and Global Issues** Topic: Water, pp. 43–48	 20 20 30
2 SECTION 2 **Algeria: The Casbah and the Countryside**	**Chapter and Section Support** Reproducible Lesson Plan, p. 61 S Guided Reading and Review, p. 62 Critical Thinking Activity, p. 68 S Section Quiz, p. 63 S Vocabulary, p. 65 Reteaching, p. 66 Enrichment, p. 67 S Chapter Summary, p. 64 **Tests** Forms A and B Chapter Tests, pp. 20–25	 20 30 25 20 25 25 15 40		

Block Scheduling Program Support

Block Scheduling Folder
PROGRAM TEACHING RESOURCES

Activities and Projects

Interdisciplinary Links

Resource Pro™ CD-ROM

Media and Technology

From Guiding Questions to Assessment   A series of Guiding Questions serves as an organizing framework for this book. The Guiding Questions that relate to this chapter are listed below. Section Reviews and Section Quizzes provide opportunities for assessing students' insights into these Guiding Questions. Additional assessments are listed below.

Media and Technology

Resource	mins.
◀▶ 💿 ⓢ World Video Explorer	20
💿 Planet Earth CD-ROM	20
▭ Color Transparencies 70, 92	20
💿 Planet Earth CD-ROM	20
▭ Color Transparencies 70, 92	20
🎧 ⓢ Guided Reading Audiotapes	20
▭ Color Transparency 171 (Graphic organizer web template)	20
💿 The Writer's Solution CD-ROM	30
💾 Computer Test Bank	30

GUIDING QUESTIONS

- *What factors have shaped Africa's culture?*
- *Why have many Africans been moving to cities in recent years?*

ASSESSMENTS

Section 1	Section 2
Students should be able to create a map that shows the major cities of Egypt.	Students should be able to write a poem describing life in a Berber village.
▶ RUBRIC See the Assessment booklet for a rubric on assessing a map produced by a student.	▶ RUBRIC See the Assessment booklet for a rubric on assessing a student poem.

T **Teaming Opportunity**
This resource is especially well-suited for teaching teams.

S **Spanish**
This resource is also in Spanish support.

💿 **CD-ROM**

💿 **Laserdisc**

▭ **Transparency**

💾 **Software**

◀▶ **Videotape**

🎧 **Audiotape**

Activities and Projects

Mental Mapping

The Sahara Desert The Sahara is the world's largest desert, but the size of it changes depending on climate conditions. At times it covers nearly 4 million square miles, making it large enough to contain the contiguous 48 states of the United States. Have students make cut-out maps of Africa and the continental United States, made to the same scale, by tracing shapes from a world map in the Atlas or from a wall map.

Have students label the countries of North Africa. Then have students fit their map of the United States into North Africa. Tell them that the Sahara covers about the same amount of territory as the United States. Discuss the size of the United States by talking about how long it would take to drive from one coast to the other. Invite students to imagine how a desert the size of the 48 states would affect life in North America.

Links to Current Events

Ramadan Ramadan is an important Muslim holiday that falls in the ninth month of the Islamic calendar. It celebrates the revelation of the Quran, the holy book of Muslims, to Muhammad. During Ramadan, Muslims all over the world fast between sunrise and sunset. As the size of the Islamic community in the United States has grown, Ramadan has become a more visible holiday here. Point out that just as Christmas is celebrated differently by Christians of different countries, Ramadan is celebrated differently by Muslims in different parts of the world. Therefore, Ramadan in Egypt is celebrated somewhat differently from Ramadan in Pakistan or Indonesia, even though the holiday celebrates the same event in all three countries. Invite Muslim students or adults in your community to discuss the celebration of Ramadan with the class.

Hands-On Activities

The Suez Canal The Suez Canal was opened in 1869. It allowed faster and easier travel between Europe and East Africa as well as between Europe and Asia. For example, ships that sailed from London to Bombay by sailing around the Cape of Good Hope at the southern tip of Africa had to travel approximately 12,400 miles, or 42 percent farther than the 7,270 miles required to travel from London to Bombay through the canal. Ask students to cut out construction paper ships of the same size. Then have them measure, with the ships on a globe or wall map, the journey from different parts of Europe and North Africa to different parts of East Africa, the Middle East, and Asia with and without the canal. Ask them to note their results on a table or chart.

Nile River Tour Have students look at newspaper or magazine travel articles or at travel books about Egypt and the Nile River. Ask them to identify three "sights" they would want to visit on a trip to Egypt. Each student may describe in writing or in an oral presentation the three things they would want to see. *Basic*

Egypt in the News Egypt is an important ally to the United States. Have students look for news stories about meetings between the officials of the United States government and the government of Egypt in the last five or ten years. Students should write a report on these meetings. Whey were they held? What was dis-

cussed? Were representatives of other countries present? What was the outcome of the meetings? *Challenging*

Natural Resources Ask students to find out about the important natural resources of Egypt and Algeria. Suggest they make icons or other symbols to represent these resources. Have them make illustrated resource maps using these symbols. Suggest they research the role of these natural resources on the economy of these two countries. *Average*

Cluster Map About 90 percent of Algeria's people live in the cities of the northern coast. Most of Algeria's land is desert. Ask students to make cluster maps

or web diagrams of details about life in these two environments of Algeria. They may include details from the student text or from other sources. Suggest that they use the details from their cluster maps to make drawings or paintings of life in these two settings. *English Language Learners*

F.Y.I.

This page can help you extend your own and students' understanding of the concepts in this chapter. You may want to browse through some of the suggestions in the **Bibliography. Interdisciplinary Links** can connect social studies understandings to areas elsewhere in the curriculum through the use of other Prentice Hall products. **National Geography Standards** reflected specifically in this chapter are listed for your convenience. Some hints about appropriate **Internet Access** are also provided. **School to Careers** provides insights into the practical uses of some of the concepts in this chapter as they might pertain to various careers.

BIBLIOGRAPHY

FOR THE TEACHER

Ayoub, Abderrahman, Jamila Binous, Abderrazak Gragueb, Ali Mtimet, Hedi Slim. *Umm El Madayan: An Islamic City Through the Ages.* Houghton, 1994.

King, John. *Bedouin.* Raintree, 1993.

Knight, Khadijah. *Islam.* Thomson, 1995.

FOR THE STUDENT

Easy
Tenquist, Alasdair. *Egypt.* Thomson, 1995.

Average
Algeria in Pictures. Lerner, 1992.

Challenging
Hermes, Jules. *The Children of Morocco.* Carolrhoda, 1995.

LITERATURE CONNECTION

Oppenheim, Shulamith Levey. *Hundredth Name.* Boyds Mill, 1995.

Schwartz, Howard, and Barbara Rush. *The Sabbath Lion: A Jewish Folktale from Algeria.* HarperCollins, 1992.

INTERDISCIPLINARY LINKS

Subject	Theme: Adaptation
MATH	Middle Grades Math: Tools for Success Course 1, Lesson 1-5, **Reading and Understanding Graphs**
SCIENCE	Prentice Hall Science *Dynamic Earth,* Lesson 6-6 Connections, **Nature's Gifts From the Nile**
LANGUAGE ARTS	Choices in Literature *The Adventures of Me,* **Aida** Prentice Hall Literature *Bronze,* **How the Animals Kept the Lions Away**

NATIONAL GEOGRAPHY STANDARDS

Students explore the 18 National Geography Standards throughout *Africa.* Chapter 4, however, concentrates on investigating the following standards: 1, 3, 4, 5, 6, 9, 10, 11, 12, 13, 15, 17, 18. For a complete list of the standards, see the *Teacher's Flexible Planning Guide.*

SCHOOL TO CAREERS

In Chapter 4, Exploring North Africa, students learn more about Egypt and Algeria. They also learn the skill of using regional maps. Knowing more about North Africa can help students prepare for careers in many fields such as journalism, international trade, diplomacy, and so on. Skill in locating information is useful for researchers, writers, employment counselors, teachers, and others. The curriculum presented in this book, as in all eight titles of Prentice Hall's *World Explorer* program, is designed to prepare students not only for careers but also for good citizenship—of the world as well as of this country.

INTERNET ACCESS

Many social studies teachers and students use Internet browsers, or search engines, to investigate particular topics. For the best results, use narrow rather than broad topics. Try these for Chapter 4: Egypt, Algeria, casbah, Muslims. Finding age-appropriate sites is an important consideration when using the Internet. For links to age-appropriate sites in world studies and geography, visit the Prentice Hall Home Page at: **http://www.phschool.com**

Connecting to the Guiding Questions

As students study this chapter, they will focus on the countries of Egypt and Algeria in North Africa. Content in this chapter corresponds to the following Guiding Questions:

● What factors have shaped Africa's cultures?

● Why have many Africans been moving to cities in recent years?

Using the Map Activities

Ask students to work in pairs to answer the questions, then discuss students' responses.

• Students may say that Algeria looks the largest and Tunisia looks the smallest. The Mediterranean Sea lies on the region's northern boundary.

• Many major North African cities are on the Mediterranean Coast. Nearness to the sea would have encouraged trade and contact among cultures.

Heterogeneous Groups

The following Teacher's Edition strategies are suitable for heterogeneous groups.

Critical Thinking
Identifying Central Issues
p. 98

Interdisciplinary Connections
Language Arts
p. 101

Cooperative Learning
Travel Brochure
p. 102

CHAPTER
4

Exploring North Africa

SECTION 1

Egypt
HEARING THE CALL
OF ISLAM

SECTION 2

Algeria
THE CASBAH AND
THE COUNTRYSIDE

MAP ACTIVITIES

Six countries make up the region of North Africa. Find them on the map above. To help you get to know this region, do the following:

Size up the region
Which country in the region looks the largest? Which country looks the smallest? What body of water lies on the region's northern boundary?

Consider the location
Find the major cities of North Africa shown on this map. How close are they to the Mediterranean Sea? How do you think that nearness to the sea might have affected North Africa's cultures?

Resource Directory

Media and Technology

Daily Life: Cairo, from the World Video Explorer, enhances students' understanding of daily life in Cairo, including the impact of overcrowding on the city's inhabitants.

Egypt

HEARING THE CALL OF ISLAM

BEFORE YOU READ

Reach Into Your Background

You probably have a favorite holiday that you look forward to all year. Think about what you do during the holiday. What special foods do you eat? What different songs do you sing? Why do you and your family celebrate on that holiday?

Questions to Explore

1. How does religion affect Egypt's culture?

2. How has the role of Islam in Egypt changed in recent times?

Key Terms
bazaar
fellaheen

Key Places
Cairo

At noon, the restaurants in Cairo stand empty. Egyptian teenagers try not to think about pita bread or sweet dates. Only certain people, such as the very young or those who are sick, eat regular meals. Is there a food shortage in Egypt? No, it's the Muslim holiday of Ramadan (ram uh DAHN). Muslims are followers of the religion of Islam. For a month, Muslims fast from dawn to dusk. A fast is a period when people go without food. During Ramadan, Muslims eat only when the sun is down.

But Muslims do more than fast during Ramadan. They also think of those who are less fortunate than themselves. And they try not to get angry when things go wrong.

▼ More people live in Cairo than in any other city in Africa. Most of the people who live here are Muslim Arabs.

Islam in Egypt

Egypt is located in North Africa, where many of the world's Muslims live. Egypt is across the Red Sea from Saudi Arabia, where the messenger of Islam, Muhammad, was born. Islam spread from Saudi Arabia across North Africa. Today, the countries in this area have populations that are mostly Muslim. Look at the Country Profile on the next page. You can see that Islam is the major religion in Egypt. In fact, it is the country's official religion.

Teaching Resources

📁 **Reproducible Lesson Plan** in the Chapter and Section Resources booklet, p. 58, provides a summary of the section lesson.

📁 **Guided Reading and Review** in the Chapter and Section Resources booklet, p. 59, provides a structure for mastering key concepts and reviewing key terms in the section. Available in Spanish in the Spanish Chapter and Section Resources booklet, p. 37.

Program Resources

📁 Material in the **Primary Sources and Literature Readings** booklet extends content with a selection from the region under study.

📁 **Outline Maps** North Africa: Political, p. 31; The Middle East and North Africa: Physical, p. 28

Lesson Objectives

1 Explain the influence of Islam on Egyptian culture.

2 Compare and contrast the lives of urban and rural Egyptians.

Lesson Plan

1 Engage

Warm-Up Activity

Have students list the differences between living in a city and living in a rural area in the United States. Ask them to compare and contrast the kinds of jobs and the types of housing found in the two areas. Record students' responses on the chalkboard.

Activating Prior Knowledge

Have students read Reach Into Your Background in the Before You Read box. Then ask volunteers to name their favorite holidays, and to tell how they celebrate them. Discuss whether the holidays named are shared by most Americans or are specific to certain groups of Americans.

2 Explore

Have students read the section and ask them to explore questions such as these: What are some important teachings and practices of Islam? How has Islam affected the way Egyptians live? Why do some Egyptian women wear veils? Why have many people moved from rural areas to cities? What is life like in rural areas of Egypt?

3 Teach

Ask students to write a letter from the point of view of a rural Egyptian visiting Cairo for the first time. Tell students to include in their letters observations of things that a rural person would find unfamiliar as well as things familiar. This activity should take about 20 minutes.

4 Assess

See the answers to the Section Review. You may also use students' letters as an assessment.

Acceptable letters identify one familiar thing or situation, such as the practice of Islam, and one thing unfamiliar, such as crowds.

Commendable letters identify at least one familiar thing or situation and at least two things unfamiliar, such as crowds and apartment buildings.

Outstanding letters identify at least two familiar things or situations, such as the practice of Islam and the scarcity of land, and at least two things unfamiliar, such as crowds and apartment buildings.

Answers to ...
MAP AND CHART STUDY

Most Egyptians live near the Nile River. Egypt's largest cities are Cairo, Alexandria, and Giza. Because Egypt has an arid climate, most people live near water. Water can be used for irrigation and for transport. The western desert is the least populated part of Egypt. However, there are densely populated pockets, which are probably oases. More Egyptians practice Islam than any other faith.

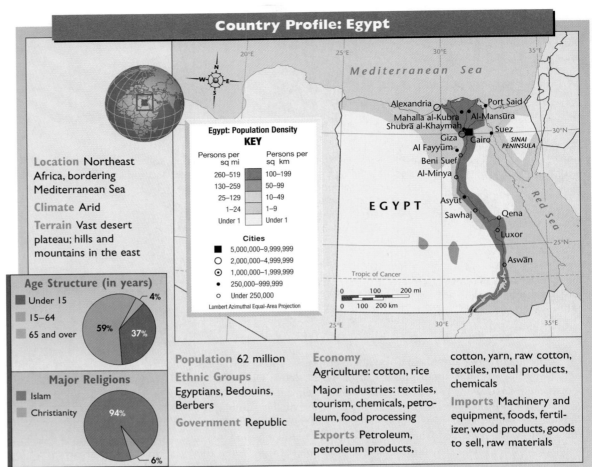

Country Profile: Egypt

Location Northeast Africa, bordering Mediterranean Sea

Climate Arid

Terrain Vast desert plateau; hills and mountains in the east

Egypt: Population Density
KEY

Persons per sq mi	Persons per sq km
260–519	100–199
130–259	50–99
25–129	10–49
1–24	1–9
Under 1	Under 1

Cities
- ■ 5,000,000–9,999,999
- ○ 2,000,000–4,999,999
- ◉ 1,000,000–1,999,999
- • 250,000–999,999
- ○ Under 250,000

Lambert Azimuthal Equal-Area Projection

Age Structure (in years)
- Under 15
- 15–64
- 65 and over

59% / 37% / 4%

Major Religions
- Islam
- Christianity

94% / 6%

Population 62 million

Ethnic Groups Egyptians, Bedouins, Berbers

Government Republic

Economy
Agriculture: cotton, rice

Major industries: textiles, tourism, chemicals, petroleum, food processing

Exports Petroleum, petroleum products, cotton, yarn, raw cotton, textiles, metal products, chemicals

Imports Machinery and equipment, foods, fertilizer, wood products, goods to sell, raw materials

Map and Chart Study This map shows the population density of Egypt. **Place** Where do most people in Egypt live? What are Egypt's three largest cities? **Interaction** Read the information in the Country Profile. Using this information, think of two reasons why people in Egypt live in certain places and not others. **Regions** What part of Egypt is least populated? Is any part of this region densely populated? Explain why. **Critical Thinking** Look at the chart of Egypt's major religions. What religion is most common in Egypt?

Teachings and Practices The Quran is the sacred book of the Muslims. It contains the basic teachings of Islam. Muslims believe that the Quran contains the words of God, which were revealed to Muhammad during the month of Ramadan. Muslims also believe that the Jewish Torah and the Christian Bible are the word of God.

Recordings of the Quran have become very popular in Egypt. As Ahmed Abdel Rahman (AH med AHB del RAHK mahn), a record store manager in Cairo, says, "You can get bored by a song after a few days. But no one gets bored listening to the Quran." During the day, many Egyptians listen to the recordings on audiotapes or on the government radio station.

Media and Technology

 Planet Earth CD-ROM includes an interactive political map of Egypt and thematic maps of Africa which allow students to investigate Egyptian culture.

Color Transparencies 70, 92

Islam's Contribution to Science

Muslim scholars do not limit themselves to studying the Quran. From the 600s on, Muslims have studied art, literature, philosophy, math, astronomy, and medicine. Muslim mathematicians invented algebra, and Muslim astronomers accurately mapped the locations of the stars. A Muslim astronomer drew this illustration of a comet in the 1500s. **Critical Thinking** What practical purpose do you think Muslim scholars may have had for studying astronomy?

"I have two ears," says Saad Eddin Saleh (SAH ahd EH deen SAH leh), a carpenter in Cairo, "one for work, and one for listening to the Quran."

The Quran requires that Muslims pray five times a day. Many Egyptians pray in a mosque, a building used for Muslim worship. During prayer, Muslims face in the direction of Mecca, Saudi Arabia, where Islam's holiest shrine is located. A mosque may also offer religious training for schoolchildren. The young students who attend these schools learn to read and memorize the Quran.

An Islamic Renewal The Quran is one of the main sources of Sharia (sha REE ah), or Islamic law. The Sharia is also based on the words and deeds of Muhammad, and on comments written by Muslim scholars and lawmakers. Muslims in North Africa and Southwest Asia try to renew their faith by living each day according to Sharia.

Praying and fasting are two of the ways that Egyptian Muslims have brought their religion into their daily lives. But the Quran includes many teachings that govern day-to-day life. It stresses the importance of honesty, honor, and giving to others. It also requires Muslims to love and respect their families.

Most Muslims in Egypt agree that the laws of Egypt should be based on Islamic law. In 1978, Egypt's government studied its laws and discovered that most already were in agreement with Sharia. But in recent years, some Egyptians have said that all of Egypt's laws should match Islamic law. And this has led to disagreements among Egyptian Muslims.

READ ACTIVELY

Ask Questions What else would you like to know about the religion of Islam?

Background

Global Perspectives

Feast of Eid-ul-Fitr This feast is celebrated at the end of Ramadan. On this day, which varies from year to year dependng on when Ramadan occurs, Muslim families throughout the world celebrate *eid* (happiness). This celebration marks not only the end of a fast, but also the bond that has been created through shared hardship. Muslims celebrate by exchanging gifts with friends and relatives and sharing holiday meals.

Background

Daily Life

A Call to Prayer One of the sounds of the city is the call to prayer five times each day by muezzins, or criers. From the minarets of Muslim mosques, muezzins repeat the call four times, each time facing one of the four cardinal directions. Muezzins begin the call to prayer with the words, "Allah is most great. I testify that there is no God but Allah. . . ."

Answers to . . .

ISLAM'S CONTRIBUTION TO SCIENCE

Navigators and explorers needed to know the locations of the stars to help them find their way at sea.

Women in Ancient Egypt
The women of ancient Egypt had higher status than women in other parts of the ancient world. Women at the top of the social hierarchy could own and dispose of property as they saw fit, free slaves, and bring about lawsuits.

Biography

Jehan Sadat (1933–)
When Anwar Sadat became president of Egypt in 1970, his wife Jehan Sadat broke with Muslim tradition by taking a politically active role in the presidency. As "first lady," she crusaded for more rights for Egyptian women. In 1979, when President Sadat issued two historic women's rights decrees, they were interpreted as the outcome of Jehan Sadat's persistence. Perhaps Sadat's most important achievement, however, has been her establishment of the Talla Society, an organization that trains women in crafts and provides scholarships to high school and college students. Sadat is internationally recognized for her commitment to "third-world women in their struggle against time-worn barriers."

Answers to ...

CAPTION

Many women veil their faces in obedience to the requirement that Muslims dress modestly. Other women choose not to veil their faces because veiling is not specifically required by Sharia.

King Tut's Clothes
Scientists are studying the clothes of Pharaoh Tutankhamen, the boy who became ruler of Egypt at the age of nine, in about 1333 B.C. They have learned that Egyptian clothing had no hooks or buttons. King Tut had to tuck, wrap, and tie his clothes on. Because of their clothing, ancient Egyptians had to take small steps and walk carefully.

▼ Some Egyptian women veil their faces, while others do not. Why do you think a woman would choose to veil her face? Why might she not?

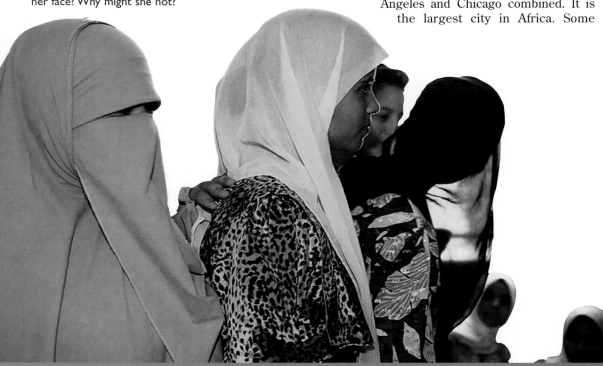

Dressing Modestly   One part of the debate about Sharia has centered on how women should dress in public. Muhammad taught that men and women are equal in the eyes of God. And Islamic law requires that both men and women dress modestly in public. Men and women must wear loose-fitting clothing that covers most of the body. Sharia requires that women cover all parts of their body except their hands, face, and feet.

However, some Muslims believe that women should also veil their faces, except for the eyes. They believe that covering the face is an important way for women to show their Muslim faith. Many other Muslims, including some government leaders, disagree. In 1994, these leaders banned female public school students from veiling their faces. This upset many Egyptians who were not strongly religious. They feel that the kind of veil a woman wears should be a matter of individual choice.

Life in Egypt

People in Egypt's cities and villages alike practice Islam. However, except for the time they spend in prayer, people in the cities and the villages live very different lives.

City Life   About half of all Egyptians live in cities. Cairo, the nation's capital and largest city, is home to about six million Egyptians. More people live in Cairo than in Los Angeles and Chicago combined. It is the largest city in Africa. Some

Teaching Resources

📁 **Recognizing Ideologies** in the Social Studies and Geography Skills booklet, p. 48, provides additional skill practice.

Program Resources

📁 **Environmental and Global Issues** Topic: Urbanization, pp. 54–58

A Traffic Jam in Cairo

Some people think that Cairo is the loudest city in the world because of its honking horns and roar of car engines. More than 13 million people live in the city, but even more drive or take buses and trains in from the suburbs during the day. At night the streets are empty, but it can be difficult to find even one open parking space.

Activity

Journal Writing

A Day in Cairo Ask students to suppose that they are spending the day in Cairo. Have them use their imaginations and the information from the text to write a journal entry about their day. Encourage them to describe the sights and sounds of the city, the different people that live in the city, and so on. If students are keeping an Explorer's Journal, you may wish to do this writing activity as part of that journal.

parts of Cairo are more than 1,000 years old. Other parts of Cairo look just like a Western city. Most people live in apartment buildings with electric fans or air-conditioning. However, they often shop in traditional open-air markets called **bazaars.**

Many people move to the cities from rural areas. They hope to find jobs and better education. As a result, Cairo is very crowded. There are traffic jams and housing shortages. Some people live in tents that they have set up on rowboats on the Nile. Others live in homes they have built in the huge graveyards on the outskirts of Cairo. So many people live in the graveyards that they are considered suburbs of the city, and the government has provided the graveyards with electricity.

Rural Life Most of the people in Egypt's rural areas live in villages along the Nile River or the Suez Canal. In Egyptian villages, most of the people make their living by farming. Egypt's rural farmers are called *fellaheen* (fel uh HEEN). Most of the fellaheen do not own land. Land is scarce because the river banks are so narrow. Some fellaheen farm small, rented plots of land. Others work in the fields of rich landowners.

Many of the fellaheen live in homes built of mud bricks or stones. Most of these homes are small. They have one to three rooms and a courtyard that the family often shares with its animals. The roofs of village houses are flat. The fellaheen use their roofs as places to store food and firewood, spread dates out to dry, and dry wet clothes.

READ ACTIVELY

Connect How does urban life differ from rural life in the United States?

SKILLS MINI LESSON

Read Actively
You might **introduce** the skill by pointing out the Read Actively margin note, which asks students to *connect* their own knowledge of American urban and rural areas to the information given in the text. Point out to students that their own knowledge and experiences can help them understand what they are reading. Tell students that to read actively, they may also *ask questions* about what they are reading, *visualize* something described, and *predict* what will happen as they read. Have students **practice** and **apply** the skill by using one of the four strategies as they read the material under the heading *Rural Life.* Invite students to discuss the strategies they used and to explain how the strategies helped them engage in their reading.

Critical Thinking

Identifying Central Issues
Suitable as a whole class activity. Discuss with students ways of identifying central issues as they read. You might point out that central issues are sometimes stated indirectly and sometimes stated directly. Have students work with a partner to identify the central issue of the last paragraph of the section. "Despite their differences, however, most Egyptians are unified by one thing—their faith in Islam." Invite students to restate the central issue in their own words.

Section I Review

1. (a) traditional open-air market (b) rural farmers

2. Egypt's capital

3. Possible answers: Muslims must pray five times a day. During Ramadan, Muslims must fast from dawn to dusk.

4. Most urban dwellers live in apartment buildings and have electricity. Cities are crowded. Most rural dwellers are farmers and typically live in homes made of mud bricks or stone.

5. by closely following Islamic law

6. Possible entry: In Egypt, people dress modestly in accordance with Islamic law. People also listen to recordings of the Quran. In the United States, some religious leaders dress a certain way, but most people do not dress in a way that reflects their beliefs.

▲ With power from a water buffalo, a fellaheen woman runs a traditional machine that separates the seeds of grain from the plants.

Egypt's people differ from each other in many ways. Some live in cities, while others live in rural areas. Some people make a living by programming computers, while others farm using ancient techniques. Despite their differences, however, most Egyptians are unified by one thing—their faith in Islam. Egyptian Muslims hope that renewing their faith every day will help them to maintain traditional values and customs in a modern age.

SECTION 1 REVIEW

1. Define (a) bazaar, (b) fellaheen.

2. Identify Cairo.

3. Give two examples of how Islam affects everyday life in Egypt.

4. Compare the lives of city and village dwellers in Egypt.

Critical Thinking

5. Identifying Central Issues How have Egyptian Muslims tried to renew their faith?

Activity

6. Writing to Learn In a journal entry, describe how the clothes people wear and the music they listen to may reflect their beliefs. Use examples from your own experience as well as from this section.

Resource Directory

Teaching Resources

📁 **Section Quiz** in the Chapter and Section Resources booklet, p. 60, covers the main ideas and key terms in the section. Available in Spanish in the Spanish Chapter and Section Resources booklet, p. 38.

Algeria

THE CASBAH AND THE COUNTRYSIDE

Section 2

BEFORE YOU READ

Reach Into Your Background

How do you adapt to the climate in your area? How do you change your schedule or your choice of clothing based on the weather?

Questions to Explore

1. What are some differences and similarities between the Berbers and the Arabs of Algeria?
2. How is life in Algerian cities different from life in the villages?

Key Terms

terrace
souq
casbah

Key People and Places

Sahara
Berber
Arab

L ike people in many parts of the world, Algerians adapt to their climate by resting during the hottest hours of the day. Journalist William Langewiesche described part of his visit to Adrar, an oasis city in the Algerian Sahara, as follows:

"We . . . waited out the hot midday hours, drinking brown water from a plastic jug. The water was brown because Miloud had mixed in cade oil. The cade is an evergreen bush that grows in the Atlas Mountains. Saharan nomads use its oil to seal the inside of goatskin water bags. Miloud did not have a goatskin, but he came from a long line of desert travelers. He bought the oil in small bottles and added it to his water for flavor and good health. The mixture smelled of pine sap and tasted of clay. . . . But I would have drunk anything. I had been for a walk."

▼ The Tuareg, a nomadic Berber group, normally relax under tents during the hottest hours of the day. This Tuareg man is brewing green tea.

Teaching Resources

📁 **Reproducible Lesson Plan** in the Chapter and Section Resources booklet, p. 61, provides a summary of the section lesson.

📁 **Guided Reading and Review** in the Chapter and Section Resources booklet, p. 62, provides a structure for mastering key concepts and reviewing key terms in the section. Available in Spanish in the Spanish Chapter and Section Resources booklet, p. 39.

Program Resources

📁 **Environmental and Global Issues** Topic: Water, pp. 43–48

📁 **Outline Maps** North Africa: Political, p. 31; The Middle East and North Africa: Physical, p. 28

Lesson Objectives

❶ Describe the differences and similarities between the Berbers and the Arabs of Algeria.

❷ Compare and contrast rural and city life in Algeria.

Lesson Plan

1 Engage

Warm-Up Activity

Ask students to brainstorm a list of the many ethnic groups that have come to the United States. Encourage students to think of foods, music, dances, art, words, and other contributions various ethnic groups have made to American culture.

Activating Prior Knowledge

Have students read Reach Into Your Background in the Before You Read box. Ask students to brainstorm some ideas about clothing and other items people would need to survive in a desert climate.

2 Explore

As students read the section, have them consider questions such as the following: Where do most Algerians live? What is a typical Berber household like? How do most people who live in Berber villages make their livings? How have the Arabs influenced Berber life? What are some features of Algerian cities?

3 Teach

Ask students to work in groups of four to make a Venn diagram showing similarities and differences between the Berbers and the Arabs of Algeria. Use the diagrams as a basis for discussion of the section. This activity should take about 20 minutes.

4 Assess

See the answers to the Section Review. You may also use students' Venn diagrams as an assessment.

Acceptable diagrams show one similarity and one difference between Berbers and Arabs.

Commendable diagrams show two similarities and two differences between Berbers and Arabs.

Outstanding diagrams show at least two similarities and two differences between Berbers and Arabs and indicate that city-dwelling Berbers and Arabs have the most in common.

Answers to ...
MAP AND CHART STUDY

Northwestern and southeastern Algeria are mountainous. Central and southern Algeria are part of the Sahara. Students may suggest that oases are near Tindouf, Adrar, or Tamanrasset. Arabs are the largest ethnic group.

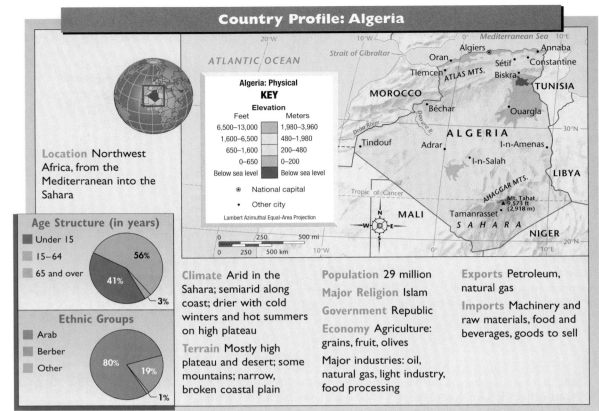

Country Profile: Algeria

Location Northwest Africa, from the Mediterranean into the Sahara

Algeria: Physical
KEY
Elevation
Feet	Meters
6,500–13,000	1,980–3,960
1,600–6,500	480–1,980
650–1,600	200–480
0–650	0–200
Below sea level	Below sea level

⊛ National capital
• Other city

Lambert Azimuthal Equal-Area Projection

Age Structure (in years)
- Under 15
- 15–64
- 65 and over

56%
41%
3%

Ethnic Groups
- Arab
- Berber
- Other

80%
19%
1%

Climate Arid in the Sahara; semiarid along coast; drier with cold winters and hot summers on high plateau

Terrain Mostly high plateau and desert; some mountains; narrow, broken coastal plain

Population 29 million

Major Religion Islam

Government Republic

Economy Agriculture: grains, fruit, olives

Major industries: oil, natural gas, light industry, food processing

Exports Petroleum, natural gas

Imports Machinery and raw materials, food and beverages, goods to sell

Map and Chart Study The map above shows physical features of Algeria. **Regions** What parts of Algeria contain mountains? What areas are a part of the Sahara? **Location** The Sahara is dotted with oases. Cities in the Sahara are often located at oases. Where do you think some of Algeria's oases might be? **Critical Thinking** At one time, only Berbers lived in Algeria. Look at the chart of Algeria's ethnic groups. What ethnic group is the largest in Algeria today?

Algeria's People

The temperature outside while Langewiesche was walking was 124°F (51°C). To survive in that heat, people must drink enough water to produce 2 to 4 gallons (8 to 16 l) of sweat a day. Look at the map in the Country Profile. The Sahara covers all of Algeria south of the Atlas Mountains. Water is in short supply in this area. For this reason, fewer than three percent of Algeria's people live here. But because of their resourcefulness, Berber and Arab nomads have survived in the Sahara for hundreds of years.

The Berbers The Berbers and the Arabs are Algeria's two main ethnic groups. The Berbers have lived in North Africa since at least 3000 B.C. No one knows exactly where they came from, but many

READ ACTIVELY

Predict How do you think people in Algeria make a living?

Resource Directory

Teaching Resources

Critical Thinking Activity in the Chapter and Section Resources booklet, p. 68, helps students apply the skill of making comparisons.

Media and Technology

Color Transparencies 70, 92

Planet Earth CD-ROM includes an interactive political map of Algeria and thematic maps of Africa.

historians think they migrated from Southwest Asia. They settled in the Atlas Mountains and on plains near Algeria's coast. More than 90 percent of Algerians still live near the coast, where the weather is milder than in the Sahara.

Some Berbers live in Algeria's cities. Most, however, live in villages in rural areas. Many Berbers continue to follow traditional ways of life. Berber households form an extended family, which includes more relatives than just a mother, a father, and their children. Each Berber house has an open courtyard in the back. The windows in the house face the courtyard, not the street. Each married couple in a family has its own home, opening onto the family courtyard. In this way, grandparents, parents, sons, daughters, and cousins can all live close together.

Family is so important to the Berbers that their village governments are based on it. The head of each family is a member of the village assembly, which makes laws for the village.

Most families in Berber villages make a living by farming and herding. They get up as soon as it is light. In the middle of the day, when the sun is hottest, people rest for several hours. Then they work until dark. Farmers use wooden plows drawn by camels. They grow wheat and barley and raise livestock. In the mountains, the Berbers build **terraces,** or platforms cut into the mountainside, for their crops. The terraces increase the amount of farmland and stop the soil from washing away when it rains.

The Professional Poet
Many Berber villages have a professional poet. The poet is always a woman who improvises songs in one of the Berber languages. A chorus of women accompany the poet with their voices and with small drums.

A Desert Lifestyle

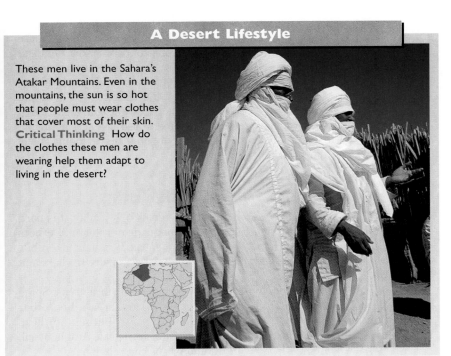

These men live in the Sahara's Atakar Mountains. Even in the mountains, the sun is so hot that people must wear clothes that cover most of their skin. **Critical Thinking** How do the clothes these men are wearing help them adapt to living in the desert?

The Arabic Language
Arabic is the official language of Algeria and the language spoken by a majority of Algerians. It is also the main language spoken throughout North Africa and Southwest Asia. Many Arabic dialects exist. Classical Arabic is the language of the Quran and is considered the ideal. It also is the language in which Arab achievements in science, religion, and literature have been preserved. Because Arabic has been so important in the spreading of Islamic culture, it is a vital link among all Arab countries.

Activity

Cooperative Learning

Travel Brochure Organize students into groups to write and decorate a travel brochure for visitors to Algiers, the capital of Algeria. Ask groups to do research so that they can advise visitors on appropriate clothing, historical sights, food, entertainment, transportation, and so on. Individuals or pairs may do the research and writing. Other group members can assemble and illustrate the brochure. *Visual*

Arabs in Algeria The Berber way of life changed in the A.D. 600s, when Arabs spread across North Africa. The Arabs conquered North Africa gradually, over hundreds of years. Peace in the region came about when most Berbers accepted the religion of Islam.

An Algerian Market

Traditionally, Algerians bought goods in open-air markets. Shopkeepers in Algeria today still put some of their goods outside their stores, so that Algerians can continue to enjoy shopping in the open air. This shop is in the town of El Dued.

Arab traditions are like Berber traditions in many ways. For example, both Muslim Arabs and non-Muslim Berbers traditionally live with extended families. However, Arabs and Berbers do differ.

Muslim Arabs created a central government in Algeria that is based on Islam. The Berber tradition is for each village to govern itself. But Berbers adapted to Arab rule by keeping their own governments along with the new one.

Another difference between the Berbers and the Arabs was that most Arabs were nomads. They usually camped near a well or stream in the summer and herded animals across the desert during the rest of the year. As a result of Arab influence, many Berbers of the hills and plains changed from a farming to a nomadic lifestyle. Sometimes there were conflicts between farmers and nomads. More often, however, they achieved peaceful settlement. Usually, the farmers would let the nomads' herds graze on their land in exchange for livestock and goods. The farmers also sold grains to the nomads. Most Berbers today are farmers, but some Berber nomads still migrate across the Sahara.

READ ACTIVELY

Visualize Visualize yourself walking through a village in rural Algeria. What would you see? What might you see along a city street?

Berbers and Arabs Today

Berbers and Arabs have mixed over the centuries. Today, it is hard to recognize a Berber or an Arab based on language or religion. Berbers and Arabs alike are Muslim. Most Berbers speak Berber and Arabic. Because France ruled Algeria for part of its history, many Berbers and Arabs also speak French.

Most Berbers and many Arabs in Algeria live in rural areas. Some are farmers, while others are nomads. In some rural areas, the Berber way of life has hardly been touched by Arab ways. Berbers in these areas speak Berber languages, and some do not speak Arabic at all. Many have combined Islam with traditional African religions.

Resource Directory

Teaching Resources

Section Quiz in the Chapter and Section Resources booklet, p. 63, covers the main ideas and key terms in the section. Available in Spanish in the Spanish Chapter and Section Resources booklet, p. 40.

Vocabulary in the Chapter and Section Resources booklet, p. 65, provides a review of key terms in the

chapter. Available in Spanish in the Spanish Chapter and Section Resources booklet, p. 42.

Reteaching in the Chapter and Section Resources booklet, p. 66, provides a structure for students who may need additional help in mastering chapter content.

Algiers, the capital of Algeria, has a modern section of high-rise buildings, shown at the left. The old section of the city (above) is called the Casbah. What clue shows that the Casbah was not built in the 1900s?

Life in the Cities Berbers and Arabs who live in Algeria's cities have the most in common with each other. About half of Algeria's people live in cities, and most speak Arabic. Mosques and open-air marketplaces called *souqs* (sooks) fill the cities. Older parts of the cities are called *casbahs* (KAHZ bahz). The houses and stores here are close to each other on narrow, winding streets. Newer parts of the cities look like cities in Europe and the United States. They have tall buildings and wide streets.

The Berbers and the Arabs of Algeria have had many conflicts in the past. However, there have also been long periods during which they learned from each other peacefully. Algeria's future will continue to mix Berber and Arab, old and new.

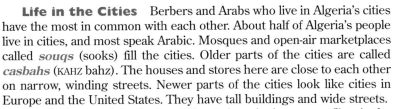

SECTION 2 REVIEW

1. **Define** (a) terrace, (b) souq, (c) casbah.

2. **Identify** (a) Sahara, (b) Berber, (c) Arab.

3. How did the Berber way of life change when Arabs came to North Africa?

4. How are Arabs and Berbers similar today?

Critical Thinking
5. **Drawing Conclusions** What differences might have caused conflicts between Berbers and Arabs? How did Berbers and Arabs sometimes overcome their differences?

Activity
6. **Writing to Learn** Suppose that you were a member of a Berber village assembly at the time that the Arabs first came to North Africa. Write a speech in which you discuss the possible impact of this change on your community.

Enrichment in the Chapter and Section Resources booklet, p. 67, extends chapter content and enriches students' understanding.

Spanish Glossary in the Spanish Chapter and Section Resources, pp. 68–73, provides key terms translated from English to Spanish as well as definitions in Spanish.

Chapter Summary in the Chapter and Section Resources booklet, p. 64, provides a summary of chapter content. Available in Spanish in the Spanish Chapter and Section Resources booklet, p. 41.

Cooperative Learning Activity in the Activities and Projects booklet, pp. 29–32, provides two student handouts, one page of teacher's directions, and a scoring rubric for a cooperative learning activity on making a relief map.

Media and Technology

Guided Reading Audiotapes (English and Spanish)

1. (a) a platform cut into a mountainside that aids farmers by keeping soil from washing away when it rains (b) an open-air marketplace (c) an older part of an Algerian city

2. (a) a desert that covers more than 85 percent of Algeria (b) a member of one of the main ethnic groups of Algeria, a group that has lived in North Africa since at least 3000 B.C. (c) a member of one of the main ethnic groups of Algeria, a group that conquered North Africa beginning in the A.D. 600s.

3. The Arabs created a central government in Algeria based on Islam, and many Berbers converted to Islam.

4. Possible answer: They practice the same religion.

5. Students may suggest that conflicts were caused by different ideas about how to use land. The Berbers usually farmed, and the Arabs were nomadic herders. Berbers and Arabs worked out compromises.

6. Speeches will vary, but should indicate that the Berbers realize the Arabs could pose a threat to their way of life.

Answers to ...
ALGIERS: OLD AND NEW

Students may say that the buildings and street look very old.

Using Regional Maps

Lesson Objectives

1 Describe the purpose of a regional map.

2 Use a regional map to obtain information.

Lesson Plan

1 Engage

Warm-Up Activity

Ask students to read the opening paragraphs. **Introduce** the skill by showing a regional map such as a road map, a bus route map, or a weather map.

Activating Prior Knowledge

Prompt students to name other kinds of regional maps they have seen (state maps, maps of camping sites or train routes). Invite students to explain how they used such maps.

2 Explore

Read and discuss with students the text under *Get Ready*. Ask volunteers to identify the characteristics defining the regions in your sample maps. Explain that most transportation maps are defined by political boundaries, whereas weather maps might be defined by climate features.

3 Teach

Work as a class to **practice** the skill by following the steps in *Try It Out*. Have volunteers identify map elements and answer questions.

For additional reinforcement, ask students to describe an area that could be represented on a regional map.

Have you ever seen anyone try to drive around town with a map of the whole world?

It would never work. A world map is useful for looking at the world as a whole. You can easily see the shapes and locations of the continents and oceans. They do not show you street names, however. Because they cover such a large area, world maps lack the detail to show much about a specific part of the world.

That is why we have regional maps. You already know that a region is an area of the Earth that shares some common characteristics. A regional map is a map of a region. Regional maps are probably the most common type of map. Road maps and bus maps are regional maps. So are the weather maps you see on the news. Throughout your life, you will see regional maps in newspapers and magazines, in textbooks and on television. It pays to know how to use them.

regional maps. But if you learn how to read one type of regional map, you can use your skills to help you read others.

Get Ready

Regional maps focus on one part of the world, showing it in greater detail. Because of this detail, you can learn a lot about the region that is shown on the map. Since regions can be defined by many different characteristics—landforms, economies, political boundaries, and so on—there are many different types of

Try It Out

Follow these steps to read the map in column two on the next page.

A. **Identify the region.** What region is shown on the map? What defines the region?

B. **Use the map key to learn about the region.** What basic information is shown on the map? What do the solid lines represent? What do the single dots represent?

Resource Directory

Teaching Resources

Using the Compass Rose in the Social Studies and Geography Skills booklet, p. 4, provides additional skill practice.

Using the Map Scale in the Social Studies and Geography Skills booklet, p. 5, provides additional skill practice.

C. Use the regional map as a tool. What landforms can be found on either side of the Nile River valley? Where are most cities in the Nile River valley located?

D. Extend your learning. Why might the Nile River be important to people in Egypt? How is the Nile related to the location of Egyptian cities?

Apply the Skill

The map below is a regional map of North Africa. Work independently to apply the four basic regional map reading skills to this map.

1 **Identify the region.** What region is shown on the map? What defines the region?

2 **Use the map key to learn about the region.** What basic information is shown on the map? What physical features are identified on this map?

3 **Use the regional map as a tool.** How many countries are in North Africa? Which countries are they? Do you see any bodies of water in North Africa?

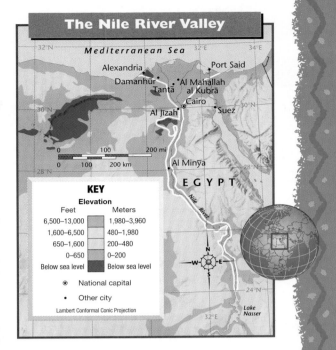

The Nile River Valley

4 **Extend your learning.** Why would this map be useful in learning about the ways of life of this region? How might it help you understand the history of the region? What do you think might have been very important to people of this region?

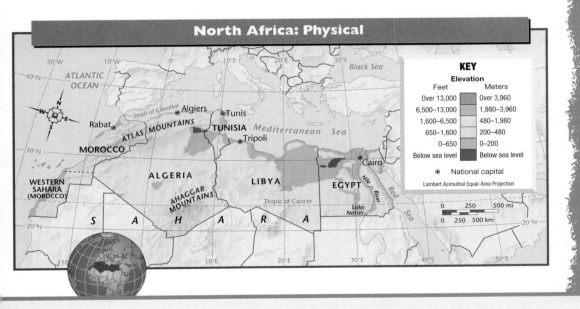

North Africa: Physical

4 Assess

Direct students to **apply** the skill in the final part of the activity. Have them answer the text questions orally or in writing. You may **assess** by evaluating their written answers or oral replies.

Answers to . . .

TRY IT OUT

A. The map shows the Nile River valley. The Nile River defines the region.

B. The map provides information about political and geographic features. The solid lines define the river valley. The dots represent cities.

C. There are mountains on both sides of the valley. Most cities are in the northern part of the valley.

D. The Nile can be used for irrigation and transportation. Most cities are close to the Nile.

APPLY THE SKILL

1. The map shows North Africa. The region is defined by the Mediterranean Sea to the north, the Atlantic Ocean to the west, the Red Sea to the east, and the Sahara to the south.

2. The map shows political and physical features, including mountains, seas, oceans, rivers, and a lake.

3. Morocco (including Western Sahara), Algeria, Tunisia, Libya, and Egypt make up North Africa. North Africa contains the Nile River and Lake Nasser.

4. The map shows the distances between different parts of North Africa and indicates that there are few bodies of water except along the coastal parts of the region. Most cities grew up along the coasts, which probably indicates the importance of water to people.

Reviewing Main Ideas

1. It includes many teachings that govern day-to-day life.

2. by praying five times a day, as required by the Quran

3. The cities are crowded and most people live in apartments. Most rural people are farmers and live in mud-brick or stone houses.

4. Most Berbers and Arabs are Muslims, and many speak Arabic and live with their extended families. Traditionally, Arabs were nomads and Berbers were farmers. Arabs created a central government based on Islam, while each Berber village had its own government.

5. The Sahara covers more than 85 percent of Algeria. A small number of Berber and Arab nomads live in the desert. Berbers who farm in the mountains construct terraces to keep soil from washing away.

6. The architecture of the cities reflects old and new. In the casbah, houses and stores line narrow, winding streets. Newer parts of cities look like American cities, with tall buildings and wide streets.

Reviewing Key Terms

1. bazaar

2. true

3. Terraces

4. souq

5. casbah

Critical Thinking

1. It was more difficult for Arabs to get to these areas, so the Berbers did not receive much exposure to Arab culture or ideas.

2. Because the Quran stresses the importance of honesty, honor, and giving to others, Muslims in Egypt and Algeria probably respect the people of their community.

CHAPTER 4 Review and Activities

Reviewing Main Ideas

1. Why do most Muslims study and memorize parts of the Quran?

2. How do Egyptians show their faith in Islam in their daily lives?

3. How does life in Egypt's cities differ from life in Egypt's rural areas?

4. Explain what Berbers and Arabs in Algeria have in common and what sets them apart.

5. How does Algeria's geography affect the people who live there?

6. How do Algeria's cities blend the old and the new?

Reviewing Key Terms

Decide whether each statement is true or false. If it is true, write "true." If it is false, change the underlined term to make the statement true.

1. A traditional Egyptian open-air market is called a <u>casbah</u>.

2. Egypt's rural farmers are called <u>fellaheen</u>.

3. <u>Souqs</u> are platforms cut into the side of a mountain.

4. In Algeria, an open-air market may be called a <u>nomad</u>.

5. The old section of Algiers is called the <u>Sharia</u>.

Critical Thinking

1. Recognizing Cause and Effect Why do you think that the Berbers who lived in isolated areas maintained their language and traditions after Arabs came to Algeria?

2. Drawing Conclusions How do you think religion affects the way people in Egypt and Algeria feel about their communities?

Graphic Organizer

Copy the web onto a sheet of paper and then complete it. Narrow your focus each time you move to a new level on the web. Fill in the web with as many people and ideas as you can.

Graphic Organizer

Answers may vary. Possible answers shown.

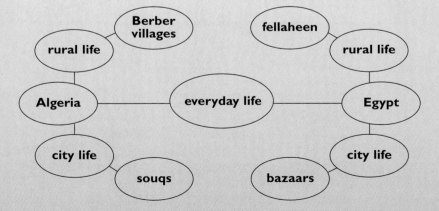

Map Activity

North Africa
For each place listed below, write the letter from the map that shows its location.

1. Cairo
2. Algeria
3. Mediterranean Sea
4. Egypt
5. Sahara

Place Location

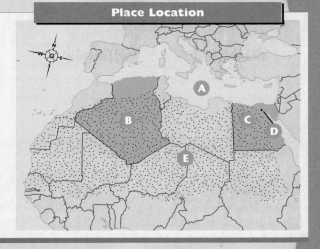

Writing Activity

Writing a Poem
The Berber languages are rarely written down. Most Berber history is preserved by professional poets. Pretend that you are a professional poet living in the 600s, when Arabs first came to North Africa. Write a poem explaining some of the differences and similarities between Arabs and Berbers.

Internet Activity
Use a search engine to find the **Library of Congress Country Studies.** Scroll down and choose **Algeria.** Choose several links to explore. Write a report about what you found most interesting.

Skills Review

Turn to the Skills Activity.
Review the steps for using regional maps. Then answer the following questions: (a) How can you use the map key to help you learn about a region? (b) How can you use a regional map as a tool?

How Am I Doing?

Answer these questions to check your progress.

1. Do I understand how Islam has influenced life in both Egypt and Algeria?
2. Can I identify some historic events that have shaped the modern cultures of North Africa?
3. Do I understand how cultures in North Africa compare to other African cultures I have studied?
4. What information from this chapter can I use in my book project?

Internet Activity

If students are having difficulty finding this site, you may wish to have them use the following URL, which was accurate at the time this textbook was published:

http://1cweb2.loc.gov/frd/ cs/cshome.html

You might also guide students to a search engine. Four of the most useful are Infoseek, Alta Vista, Lycos, and Yahoo. For additional suggestions on using the Internet, refer to the Prentice Hall Social Studies' Educator's Handbook "Using the Internet," in the *Prentice Hall World Explorer Program Resources.*

For additional links to world history and culture topics, visit the Prentice Hall Home Page at:
http://www.phschool.com

How Am I Doing?

Point out to students that this checklist is a quick reminder for them of what they learned in the chapter. If their answer to any of the questions is *no* or if they are unsure, they may need to review the topic.

Map Activity

1. D   3. A   5. E
2. B   4. C

Writing Activity

Poems will vary. Students may mention differences in language, religion, and style of government.

Skills Review

(a) The map key explains what the different symbols and lines on the map represent. (b) It can help people understand more about a particular region.

Resource Directory

Teaching Resources

📁 **Chapter Tests** Forms A and B are in the Tests booklet, pp. 20–25.

Program Resources

📁 **Writing Process Handbook** includes Editing for Content, Clarity, and Style, pp. 35–36, to help students with the Writing Activity.

Media and Technology

🖥 **Color Transparencies**
Color Transparency 171 (Graphic organizer web template)
💿 **Prentice Hall Writer's Solution** Writing Lab CD-ROM
💾 **Computer Test Bank**
💿 **Resource Pro™ CD-ROM**

Exploring West Africa

To help you plan instruction, the chart below shows how teaching resources correspond to chapter content. Use the resources to vary instruction, add activities, or plan block schedules. Where appropriate, resources have suggested time allotments for students. Time allotments are approximate.

Managing Time and Instruction

		Africa Teaching Resources Binder		World Explorer Program Resources Binder	
		Resource	mins.	Resource	mins.
1	**SECTION 1** **Nigeria: One Country, Many Identities**	**Chapter and Section Support** Reproducible Lesson Plan, p. 70 Ⓢ Guided Reading and Review, p. 71 Ⓢ Section Quiz, p. 72 Critical Thinking Activity, p. 83 **Social Studies and Geography Skills,** Analyzing Statistics, p. 64	 20 25 30 30	**Outline Maps** West and Central Africa: Political, p. 34 **Nystrom Desk Atlas** 🅣 **Primary Sources and Literature** Readings **Writing Process Handbook** Writing Effective Paragraphs, pp. 27–28	 20 40 25
	SKILLS ACTIVITY **Using Distribution Maps**	**Social Studies and Geography Skills,** Reading a Population Distribution Map, p. 33	 30		
2	**SECTION 2** **Ghana: First in Independence**	**Chapter and Section Support** Reproducible Lesson Plan, p. 73 Ⓢ Guided Reading and Review, pp. 74 Ⓢ Section Quiz, p. 75	 20 25	**Outline Maps** West and Central Africa: Political, p. 34	 20
3	**SECTION 3** **Mali: The Desert Is Coming**	**Chapter and Section Support** Reproducible Lesson Plan, p. 76 Ⓢ Guided Reading and Review, p. 77 Ⓢ Section Quiz, p. 78 Ⓢ Vocabulary, p. 80 Reteaching, p. 81 Enrichment, p. 82 Ⓢ Chapter Summary, p. 79 **Tests** Forms A and B Chapter Tests, pp. 26–31	 20 25 20 25 25 15 40	**Outline Maps** The Middle East and North Africa: Physical, p. 28 Africa South of the Sahara: Physical, p. 32 West and Central Africa: Political, p. 34 **Environmental and Global Issues** Topic: Environmental Destruction, pp. 14–19	 20 20 20 30
	ACTIVITY SHOP: LAB **Desertification**	Activity Shop: Lab, p. 6	30		
	LITERATURE *The Distant Talking Drum* by Isaac Olaleye			🅣 **Primary Sources and Literature** Readings	 40

Block Scheduling Folder
PROGRAM TEACHING RESOURCES

Block Scheduling Program Support

- Activities and Projects
- Interdisciplinary Links
- Resource Pro™ CD-ROM
- Media and Technology

From Guiding Questions to Assessment A series of Guiding Questions serves as an organizing framework for this book. The Guiding Questions that relate to this chapter are listed below. Section Reviews and Section Quizzes provide opportunities for assessing students' insights into these Guiding Questions. Additional assessments are listed below.

Media and Technology

Resource	mins.
⬛ 🔵 ⓢ World Video Explorer	20
🔵 Planet Earth CD-ROM	20
🖵 Color Transparencies 72, Historical Map Set 5	20
🔵 Planet Earth CD-ROM	20
🖵 Color Transparencies 51, 52, 72	20
🔵 Planet Earth CD-ROM	20
🔵 Material World CD-ROM	20
🖵 Color Transparencies 6, 72, 92, 93	20
🎧 ⓢ Guided Reading Audiotapes	20
🖵 Color Transparency 174 (Graphic organizer table template)	20
🔵 The Writer's Solution CD-ROM	30
💾 Computer Test Bank	30

T Teaming Opportunity This resource is especially well-suited for teaching teams.

ⓢ Spanish This resource is also in Spanish support.

- 🔵 CD-ROM
- 🔵 Laserdisc
- 🖵 Transparency
- 💾 Software
- ⬛ Videotape
- 🎧 Audiotape

GUIDING QUESTIONS

- **What factors have shaped Africa's cultures?**
- **What factors influence the ways in which Africans make a living?**

ASSESSMENTS

Section 1

Students should be able to create a circle graph that shows the major religions of Nigeria.

▶ **RUBRIC** See the Assessment booklet for a rubric on assessing a circle graph.

Section 2

Students should be able to create a web of South African exports.

▶ **RUBRIC** See the Assessment booklet for a rubric on assessing graphic organizers.

Section 3

Students should be able to write a letter to the editor describing the threat of desertification to the Sahel.

▶ **RUBRIC** See the Assessment booklet for a rubric on assessing a letter to the editor.

Activities and Projects

Mental Mapping

West Africa Ask students to locate Ghana, Nigeria, and Mali on an unlabeled outline map. Then have them use a political map as a source of information to check their ideas. Ask them how they might remember these locations in the future.

Using a world map, have students compare the latitude and longitude of these countries with other countries. Point out, for example, that Nigeria and Ghana lie at the same distance from the equator as Colombia and Venezuela, while Mali is at the same latitude as Nicaragua, Honduras, and Guatemala.

Ask students to notice also how far West Africa extends. Observe that the part of Africa where Ghana and Nigeria are situated is by far the widest section of the continent. Have students measure its width by using the scale on the map in the Atlas.

Links to Current Events

African Writers Nigeria has produced some of Africa's most important poets, novelists, and playwrights. They include Chinua Achebe, Amos Tutuola, Wole Soyinka (who won the Nobel Prize for Literature in 1986), Ayi Kwei Armah, and Buchi Emecheta. Invite students to find out about the lives, careers, and writings of some of these writers or others from West Africa. Invite them to share the results by making a bulletin-board display or giving brief oral reports.

Hands-On Activities

Cities of West Africa List the names of these cities on the chalkboard: Ibadan, Accra, Lagos, Kumasi, Bamako. Ask students to use maps in their books to locate these cities. Make a simple graphic organizer on the chalkboard listing the three countries in this chapter (Ghana, Mali, Nigeria) with the cities listed under them in the correct column. (Ghana: Accra, Kumasi; Mali: Bamako; Nigeria: Lagos, Ibadan)

Have students notice whether the cities are located on the coast, a river, or another physical feature.

Regions As students work through this chapter, ask them to think about the geography theme of regions. What makes the countries of West Africa a region? How are they like each other? How are they different from other countries of Africa? Have them write the answers to these questions. *Basic*

Build a Model Suggest that students work in small groups to build three-dimensional models, or dioramas, of some of the cultures discussed in this chapter. Suggest that different groups choose cultures living in different environments. For example, one group might choose a nomadic desert culture; another group might choose a culture living and fishing on a river. Models may be built of papier maché, wood, plastic blocks, cardboard, paper, or whatever materials are available and appealing to students. *Average*

Make a Collage Have students make a picture collage poster of images they associate with one of the countries in this chapter. Encourage students to include pictures that illustrate the geography, history, culture, and economy of the country. Students may photocopy pictures from books and magazines, clip them, color them with highlighter markers, and paste them to create a collage. *English Language Learners*

F.Y.I.

This page can help you extend your own and students' understanding of the concepts in this chapter. You may want to browse through some of the suggestions in the **Bibliography. Interdisciplinary Links** can connect social studies understandings to areas elsewhere in the curriculum through the use of other Prentice Hall products. **National Geography Standards** reflected specifically in this chapter are listed for your convenience. Some hints about appropriate **Internet Access** are also provided. **School to Careers** provides insights into the practical uses of some of the concepts in this chapter as they might pertain to various careers.

BIBLIOGRAPHY

FOR THE TEACHER

Adeeb, Hassan, and Bonnetta Adeeb. *Nigeria: One Nation, Many Cultures.* Benchmark, 1996.

Mali in Pictures. Lerner, 1995.

Reynolds, Jan. *Sahara: Vanishing Cultures.* Harcourt Brace Jovanovich, 1991.

FOR THE STUDENT

Easy

Onyefulu, Ifeoma. *Ogbo: Sharing Life in an African Village.* Gulliver/Harcourt Brace Jovanovich, 1996.

Average

Brace, Steve. *Ghana.* Thomson, 1995.

Challenging

Levy, Patricia. *Nigeria.* Cavendish, 1993.

LITERATURE CONNECTION

Angelou, Maya, and Margaret Courtney-Clarke. *Kofi and His Magic.* Clarkson Potter, 1996.

Bess, Clayton. *Story for a Black Night.* Houghton, 1982.

Olaleye, Isaac. *The Distant Talking Drum: Poems from Nigeria.* Wordsong, 1995.

INTERDISCIPLINARY LINKS

Subject	Theme: Customs
MATH	Course 1, Lesson 1-6, **Constructing Bar and Line Graphs**
SCIENCE	Prentice Hall Science *Ecology: Earth's Natural Resources,* Lesson 2-1, **Land and Soil Resources**
LANGUAGE ARTS	Prentice Hall Literature *Bronze,* **All Stories Are Anansi's** *Copper,* **Osebo's Drum, The Cow-Tail Switch**

NATIONAL GEOGRAPHY STANDARDS

Students explore the 18 National Geography Standards throughout *Africa.* Chapter 5, however, concentrates on investigating the following standards: 1, 3, 4, 5, 6, 7, 8, 9, 10, 11, 12, 13, 14, 15, 16, 17, 18. For a complete list of the standards, see the *Teacher's Flexible Planning Guide.*

SCHOOL TO CAREERS

In Chapter 5, Exploring West Africa, students learn about the countries of Nigeria, Ghana, and Mali. Additionally, they address the skill of using distribution maps. Knowing about West Africa can help students prepare for careers in many fields such as trade, land management, agriculture, mining, and so on. Using distribution maps is a skill used in many careers, including demography, economics, marketing, history, geography, and others. The curriculum presented in this book, as in all eight titles of Prentice Hall's *World Explorer* program, is designed to prepare students not only for careers but also for good citizenship—of the world as well as of this country.

INTERNET ACCESS

Many social studies teachers and students use Internet browsers, or search engines, to investigate particular topics. For the best results, use narrow rather than broad topics. Try these for Chapter 5: Nigeria, Jerry Rawlings, Tombouctou, Sahel. Finding age-appropriate sites is an important consideration when using the Internet. For links to age-appropriate sites in world studies and geography, visit the Prentice Hall Home Page at: **http://www.phschool.com**

CHAPTER 5

Exploring West Africa

Using the Map Activities

Have students work in pairs to answer the questions.

• Many West African countries border the Atlantic Ocean. Bamako, Yamoussoukro, Niamey, and N'Djamena are close to rivers or lakes.

• Most cities are near water. People cannot survive without water.

• Most of West Africa is between the Equator and the Tropic of Cancer and is likely to be hot.

Heterogeneous Groups

The following Teacher's Edition strategies are suitable for heterogeneous groups.

SECTION 1
Nigeria
ONE COUNTRY, MANY IDENTITIES

SECTION 2
Ghana
FIRST IN INDEPENDENCE

SECTION 3
Mali
THE DESERT IS COMING

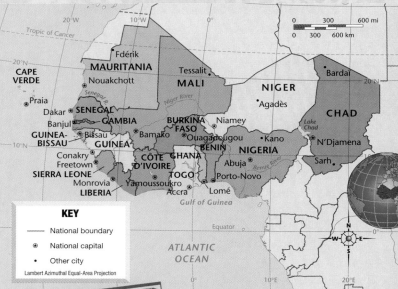

MAP ACTIVITIES

Seventeen countries make up the region of West Africa. To help you get to know this region, do the following.

Consider the location
What ocean do many of West Africa's countries border? What capitals of West African countries are close to rivers and lakes? What cities are far from rivers and lakes?

Think about the cities
Where are most of West Africa's cities? What factors might explain the locations of West African cities?

Consider the climate
Nearness to the Equator is one factor that can influence a country's climate. Where does most of West Africa lie in relation to the Equator and the Tropic of Cancer? Based on West Africa's location, what do you think its climate might be like?

Resource Directory

Media and Technology

A Trip to Coastal West Africa, from the World Video Explorer, enhances students' understanding of the history and culture of coastal West Africa.

Chapter 7

Nigeria

ONE COUNTRY, MANY IDENTITIES

BEFORE YOU READ

Reach Into Your Background
Think about the ways in which you use language in daily life.

How would you communicate with people who do not speak your language?

Questions to Explore
1. What are Nigeria's main ethnic groups?
2. How are Nigeria's main ethnic groups similar to and different from each other?

Key Terms
multiethnic
census

Key Places
Lagos
Abuja
Kano

The language of England is English. The language of Spain is Spanish. The language of Greece is Greek. But the language of Nigeria is not Nigerian. In fact, there is no such language as Nigerian. Nigerians speak more than 250 languages!

The languages of Nigeria match its ethnic groups. Nigeria's three most widely spoken languages are Hausa, Yoruba, and Ibo. There are places called Hausaland, Yorubaland, and Iboland. Most people in Hausaland are Hausa and speak Hausa. Most people in Yorubaland are Yoruba and speak Yoruba. And most people in Iboland are Ibo and speak Ibo. But these places are not countries. In fact, Hausaland and Yorubaland both lie partly in Nigeria and partly in other countries.

Nigeria's History

Why are there so many ethnic groups and languages within one country? Before Europeans arrived, what is now Nigeria was ruled by many ethnic groups, including the Hausa, the Yoruba, and the Ibo. But when Europeans drew Nigeria's borders, they did not think about ethnic groups. Look at the map in the Country Profile. You can see that Nigeria's borders do not match the borders of any one ethnic group.

Nigeria contains so many ethnic groups in part because it is so big. Nigeria is about as big as the states of California, Arizona, and New Mexico combined. More people live in Nigeria than in any other country in Africa. About one out of five Africans lives here. And Nigeria is **multiethnic,** which means that many ethnic groups live within its borders.

Teaching Resources

📁 **Reproducible Lesson Plan** in the Chapter and Section Resources booklet, p. 70, provides a summary of the section lesson.

📁 **Guided Reading and Review** in the Chapter and Section Resources booklet, p. 71, provides a structure for mastering key concepts and reviewing key terms in the section. Available in Spanish in the Spanish Chapter and Section Resources booklet, p. 44.

Program Resources

📁 Material in the **Primary Sources and Literature Readings** booklet extends content with a selection from the region under study.

📁 **Outline Maps** West and Central Africa: Political, p. 34

Lesson Objectives

1️⃣ Identify Nigeria's three main ethnic groups.

2️⃣ Describe the different ways of life of Nigeria's three main ethnic groups.

Lesson Plan

1 Engage
Warm-Up Activity

Have students suppose that they are visiting a country where people speak a different language and have different customs. Ask students to consider what difficulties they might encounter. Would they feel like outsiders? Would they try to find someone who spoke their language? Would they avoid contact with the residents, or would they try to communicate in some way?

Activating Prior Knowledge

Have students read Reach Into Your Background in the Before You Read box. Have students estimate the number of people they have communicated with so far today. Then have them consider whether and how they would have communicated with these people if many of them did not share their language.

2 Explore

Ask students to keep the following questions in mind as they read the section: What are Nigeria's three main ethnic groups? What changes occurred when Europeans arrived? How did the three main ethnic groups and other ethnic groups form the country of Nigeria and how do their ways of life differ?

3 Teach

Have students create a chart with three rows labeled: *Ibo, Hausa-Fulani,* and *Yoruba,* and three columns labeled: *region, culture,* and *history.* Ask students to fill in the chart with facts from the section. Use the completed chart as the basis for a discussion of the differences and the similarities between these groups. This activity should take about 20 minutes.

4 Assess

See the answers to the Section Review. You may also use students' completed charts as an assessment.

Acceptable charts include a correct entry in each cell.

Commendable charts include two or more entries in some of the cells.

Outstanding charts demonstrate an awareness of larger cultural and historical issues, such as the fact that colonialism affected the groups differently.

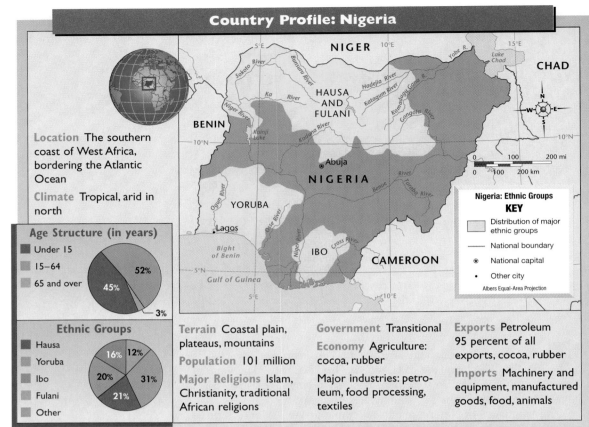

Country Profile: Nigeria

Location The southern coast of West Africa, bordering the Atlantic Ocean

Climate Tropical, arid in north

Age Structure (in years)
- Under 15
- 15–64
- 65 and over

52%
45%
3%

Ethnic Groups
- Hausa
- Yoruba
- Ibo
- Fulani
- Other

12%
16%
20%
31%
21%

Terrain Coastal plain, plateaus, mountains

Population 101 million

Major Religions Islam, Christianity, traditional African religions

Government Transitional

Economy Agriculture: cocoa, rubber

Major industries: petroleum, food processing, textiles

Exports Petroleum 95 percent of all exports, cocoa, rubber

Imports Machinery and equipment, manufactured goods, food, animals

Nigeria: Ethnic Groups
KEY
- Distribution of major ethnic groups
- National boundary
- National capital
- Other city

Albers Equal-Area Projection

Map and Chart Study This map shows the areas where Nigeria's three major ethnic groups—the Hausa-Fulani, the Yoruba, and the Ibo—are in the majority. **Location** Find Abuja, Nigeria's capital, on the map. Based on its location, do you think that any one ethnic group has more influence in the capital than the others? Why or why not? **Critical Thinking** There are many other ethnic groups in Nigeria besides the Hausa-Fulani, the Yoruba, and the Ibo, but these groups are by far the largest. What is Nigeria's largest ethnic group?

The Colonial Legacy The Hausa, the Fulani (FOO lah nee), the Yoruba, and the Ibo were each governing their own regions when Europeans arrived. In the late 1400s, Portugal began to buy slaves in West Africa. Later, Great Britain, the Netherlands, and other countries entered the slave trade.

By 1914, Great Britain had taken over the government of Nigeria. The borders of the British colony of Nigeria included part of Hausaland, part of Yorubaland, and Iboland.

Nigeria became independent in 1960. Ethnic groups that had always lived separately then worked together to create one nation. To help unify the country, in 1991 the government moved the nation's capital from Lagos, in the south, to Abuja (ah BOO jah). The new capital is located in the central portion of the country, where several ethnic groups live.

Resource Directory

Program Resources

Nystrom Desk Atlas

Media and Technology

Planet Earth CD-ROM includes an interactive political map of Nigeria and thematic maps of Africa.

Color Transparencies 72, Historical Map Set 5

Three Different Ways of Life

Making Abuja the capital helped bring Nigeria together, because it meant that the capital would be close to more than one ethnic group. The Hausa, the Fulani, the Ibo, and the Yoruba each live in different regions. Most Hausa and Fulani live in the north. The Ibo live mainly in the southeast, and the Yoruba in the southwest. Many smaller ethnic groups live in central Nigeria and throughout the country.

The Hausa and Fulani: Traders of the North   Both the Hausa and the Fulani built city-states in northern Nigeria. The Fulani conquered Hausaland in the early 1800s. Many Hausa and Fulani have intermarried since that time. The Hausa and the Fulani make up about 33 percent of Nigeria's people. Together, they are called the Hausa-Fulani. Most Hausa and Fulani are Muslims.

For hundreds of years, the Hausa-Fulani have made an important part of their living by trading. Hausa-Fulani traders dealt in goods from as far away as Spain, Italy, and Egypt. The Hausa-Fulani built cities at the crossroads of trade routes. Each of these cities had its own ruler, was enclosed by walls, and had a central market. Kano, the oldest city in West Africa, is a Hausa city. Kano has been a center of trade for over 1,000 years. The Kurmi Market in Kano is one of the largest trading centers in Africa. People from around the world visit its thousands of stalls. These stalls sell everything from fabrics and dyes to electric appliances.

Pidgin How do people talk to each other when they speak different languages? One way is to create a language that includes a little of each language. This kind of language is called pidgin. Nigerian pidgin mixes English words with the grammar of Nigerian languages. Enslaved Africans and their captors may have been the first people in Africa to use pidgin.

Central Mosque in Kano, Nigeria

The Central Mosque in the city of Kano attracts many visitors. This is particularly true on Fridays, when people gather there for services led by a prayer leader called an imam (ih MAHM).

SKILLS MINI LESSON

Reading Tables and Analyzing Statistics Allow students a few moments to study the table shown in the Country Profile, and then **introduce** the skill by telling them that this table shows statistics, or numerical data, and other important data about Nigeria. Point out that the numerical data is presented in the form of pie graphs. Together, these data in the Country Profile provide information about Nigeria's geography, economy, and people. Work with students to **practice** reading the table, identifying how the data are related. For example, the information about climate and terrain can help students visualize what Nigeria's land looks like. Have students **apply** the skill by asking them to write a statement that explains the relationship between two or more pieces of data in the table.

Links Across Place

Yoruban Culture in the United States The Oyotunji African Village in South Carolina was founded by some African Americans to celebrate and preserve the Yoruban culture. People in Oyotunji practice traditional Yoruban religion and learn Yoruban music and crafts. Many visitors come to Oyotunji to learn more about Yoruban culture.

A carver decorates a calabash, or empty gourd, at his stall in Kano's Kurmi Market. A plain calabash makes a light and inexpensive bowl. A highly decorated calabash may, in time, become very valuable. At the Kurmi Market, you can buy crafts from not only Nigeria, but also many other African countries.

READ ACTIVELY

Ask Questions What would you like to know about the differences among the Hausa-Fulani, the Yoruba, and the Ibo?

The Yoruba: Farmers Near the Coast The Yoruba are Nigeria's second largest ethnic group. About 20 percent of Nigeria's people are Yoruba. By about A.D. 1100, the Yoruba had built several city-states. Many Yoruba still live in the city-state they built more than 500 years ago, Lagos. In the 1800s, Lagos was a center for the European slave trade. Many Yoruba were sold into slavery and sent to the Americas. But today, Lagos is a more peaceful center of trade. Its streets are lined with hundreds of small shops that sell many kinds of goods.

Most Yoruba are farmers. They live with their families in large compounds. Each compound has several houses grouped around a big yard. A Yoruba community is made up of many such compounds.

The Ibo: A Tradition of Democracy The Ibo have traditionally lived as rural farmers in the southeast. They have not built any large cities like Kano or Lagos. Instead, they live in farming villages. The people in each village work closely together. Unlike the Hausa-Fulani and the Yoruba, the Ibo rule themselves with a democratic

Resource Directory

Teaching Resources

📁 **Critical Thinking Activity** in the Chapter and Section Resources booklet, p. 83, helps students apply the skill of recognizing bias.

council of elders. Instead of one or two leaders making decisions for an entire village, members of the council work together to solve problems.

The southeast was the first area of Nigeria to be affected by the arrival of Europeans. During colonial times, the Ibo were often educated by Christian missionaries. Many people in the south converted, or changed their religion, to Christianity. During British rule, some Ibo attended European or American universities and became teachers, doctors, and lawyers. Today, many Ibo have left rural villages and work in Nigeria's towns and cities.

Tensions sometimes arise between the Ibo and the other two major groups. In 1967, the Ibo tried to leave Nigeria to start their own country. For two and a half years the country was torn by war. In the end, Nigeria stayed united, and people tried to put the war behind them.

Counting Heads   It is hard to know exactly how many people belong to each ethnic group. Nigeria has tried to count its people. A count of all the people in a country is called a **census.** In Nigeria,

▼▲ Cities like Lagos (below) are not new to Nigeria. The skyscraper below dates from the late 1900s, but the Yoruba built Lagos in the 1400s. The Yoruba traditionally trade in cities and farm (above) in rural areas.

Activity

Critical Thinking

Identifying Central Issues
Suitable as either a whole class or an individual activity. Tell students that because census taking is such a sensitive issue in Nigeria, the government must do everything possible to convince the citizens that the census will be fair. Ask students to write a brief speech that might convince Nigerians of the fairness of the census. Emphasize that students should address the main concerns they believe the citizens have.

1. (a) made up of many ethnic groups (b) a count of all the people in a country

2. (a) Nigeria's former capital, located in the south of the country (b) Nigeria's new capital, located in the central part of the country (c) the oldest city in West Africa, built by the Hausa-Fulani

3. The Hausa-Fulani live in the north. The Yoruba live in the southwest. The Ibo live in the southeast.

4. It reveals which ethnic group is the largest. The largest group will have more political power than other groups.

5. The European slave trade forced many Ibo and Yoruba into slavery. Europeans also brought Christianity to the Ibo and the Yoruba.

6. Possible answer: Nigerians should have one national language because then the different ethnic groups could communicate better. Better communication could help people solve problems and misunderstandings.

▶ Kano's airport was closed for three days during Nigeria's 1991 census. No one could fly in or out of the country.

whenever a census is taken, it causes debate. This is because the largest ethnic group will have the most power in Nigeria's government.

In 1991, Nigeria conducted an unusual census. On November 26, the country was cut off from the outside world. No one could enter or leave the country for three days. And no one in Nigeria was allowed to move from one place to another between 7 A.M. and 7 P.M. Hundreds of thousands of census takers went from house to house, making a count of the people. The census showed that over 88 million people live in Nigeria, and that the Hausa-Fulani are the country's largest ethnic group. This gives them more political power than other groups.

Over the years, many Nigerians have challenged the census results. In 1963 and 1973, for example, some ethnic groups charged that other ethnic groups had reported too large a number of people. Nigerians hope that by taking accurate censuses, they will be able to hold the many ethnic groups together.

SECTION 1 REVIEW

1. Define (a) multiethnic, (b) census.

2. Identify (a) Lagos, (b) Abuja, (c) Kano.

3. What are the three largest ethnic groups in Nigeria, and where does each group live?

4. Why might taking a census create tension in Nigeria?

Critical Thinking

5. Cause and Effect How did the arrival of Europeans in Nigeria affect the ethnic groups that live in the region?

Activity

6. Writing to Learn Currently, Nigeria does not have one national language. Based on what you have learned about this country, do you think a national language might be useful? Why or why not? Write a paragraph explaining your opinion.

Resource Directory

Teaching Resources

📁 **Section Quiz** in the Chapter and Section Resources booklet, p. 72, covers the main ideas and key terms in the section. Available in Spanish in the Spanish Chapter and Section Resources booklet, p. 45.

📁 **Analyzing Statistics** in the Social Studies and Geography Skills booklet, p. 64, provides additional skill practice.

Ghana

FIRST IN INDEPENDENCE

BEFORE YOU READ

Reach Into Your Background

Think about a turning point in your own life, such as moving to a new community or begin-ning a new school. What was different after that turning point? What remained the same?

Questions to Explore

1. What changes did Kwame Nkrumah bring to Ghana?
2. How has life in Ghana changed since independence?

Key Terms
sovereignty
coup

Key People
Kwame Nkrumah
Jerry Rawlings

Lesson Objectives

1 Identify the circumstances that led to Ghana's gaining its independence.

2 Describe economic and political setbacks and successes following Ghana's independence.

Lesson Plan

1 Engage

Warm-Up Activity

Ask students to think about what an ideal form of government would be. Have them consider what kind of person or persons would lead the government and make decisions.

Activating Prior Knowledge

Tell students that a turning point is an event or situation that triggers change. Then have students read Reach Into Your Background in the Before You Read box.

In 1935, Kwame Nkrumah, a 26-year-old student, sailed from Ghana to the United States. At that time, Ghana was called the Gold Coast. It had been ruled by Great Britain for over 60 years. Nkrumah's visit to the United States was a turning point in his life. He was well aware that the people of his country did not have true freedom or equality. When Nkrumah saw the Statue of Liberty for the first time, it made him determined to bring freedom not only to his country, but to the whole continent. As he looked at the statue, he thought, "I shall never rest until I have carried your message to Africa."

Moving Toward Independence

In 1947, Nkrumah returned to the Gold Coast. The Gold Coast was named for its gold, which is one of the country's most important natural resources. The Country Profile on the next page shows the country's other important resources. But while the Gold Coast had many resources, most of its people were poor. Nkrumah believed that the people should benefit from the wealth of their own country. He began traveling all over the country. He convinced the people to demand independence from Great Britain.

▼ Kwame Nkrumah, the first leader of independent Ghana, showed his respect for African traditions by wearing traditional clothing.

Background

Links Across Place

Kwame Nkrumah in the United States Nkrumah was impressed with the ideals of the United States, but he noticed that reality didn't always match those ideals. During the 1930s, when Nkrumah was studying in the United States, African Americans often endured racial discrimination, and segregation was common. During the 1960s, when Ghana was newly independent, the United States passed laws that made racial discrimination illegal.

Teaching Resources

📁 **Reproducible Lesson Plan** in the Chapter and Section Resources booklet, p. 73, provides a summary of the section lesson.

📁 **Guided Reading and Review** in the Chapter and Section Resources booklet, p. 74, provides a structure for mastering key concepts and reviewing key terms in the section. Available in Spanish in the Spanish Chapter and Section Resources booklet, p. 46.

Program Resources

📁 **Outline Maps** West and Central Africa: Political, p. 34

2 Explore

As students read the section, ask them the following questions: Why did Nkrumah want his country to be independent? How did the British benefit from the Gold Coast's economy? What are Ghana's economy and culture like today?

3 Teach

Have students make a time line of events in Nkrumah's life. Important moments in Ghana's history should also be included. This activity should take about 20 minutes.

4 Assess

See the answers to the Section Review. You may also assess students' time lines.

Acceptable time lines show two key events in Nkrumah's life and in Ghana's history.

Commendable time lines show at least three key events in Nkrumah's life and in Ghana's history.

Outstanding time lines show all key events in Nkrumah's life and highlight Ghana's most significant historical events.

Answers to ...
MAP AND CHART STUDY

The Black Volta, White Volta, Volta, Oti, Tano, and Pra rivers flow into Lake Volta. Accra is located on the Gulf of Guinea, so it is a seaport. Students may suggest that the large number of young people would cause the country to devote much of its budget to education. When young people reach working age, there may be stiff competition for jobs.

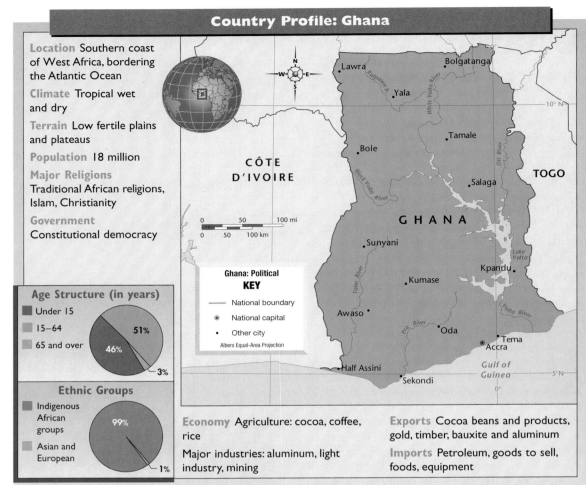

Country Profile: Ghana

Location Southern coast of West Africa, bordering the Atlantic Ocean

Climate Tropical wet and dry

Terrain Low fertile plains and plateaus

Population 18 million

Major Religions Traditional African religions, Islam, Christianity

Government Constitutional democracy

Age Structure (in years)
- Under 15
- 15–64
- 65 and over

51%
46%
3%

Ethnic Groups
- Indigenous African groups
- Asian and European

99%
1%

Ghana: Political
KEY
— National boundary
⊛ National capital
• Other city
Albers Equal-Area Projection

0   50   100 mi
0   50   100 km

Economy Agriculture: cocoa, coffee, rice
Major industries: aluminum, light industry, mining

Exports Cocoa beans and products, gold, timber, bauxite and aluminum

Imports Petroleum, goods to sell, foods, equipment

Map and Chart Study This political map shows Ghana's major cities and waterways. Study Ghana's river systems. Which rivers flow into Lake Volta? **Location** Find Ghana's capital, Accra, on the map. Why does its location make it important? **Critical Thinking** As you can see from the top chart, Ghana has a large number of young people. How might this fact affect education and jobs?

Traditional Government in Ghana During the 1900s, Africans who were ruled by European countries pushed to become independent. But the European countries did not want to give up their colonies. Some Europeans claimed that the colonies were not ready to rule themselves. Kwame Nkrumah answered this with a question.

> "Wasn't the African who is now unprepared to govern himself governing himself before the advent [arrival] of Europeans?"

Resource Directory

Media and Technology

Planet Earth CD-ROM includes an interactive political map of Ghana and thematic maps of Africa.

Color Transparencies 51, 52, 72

The Akan are the largest ethnic group in Ghana. When the Akan give power to a new leader, they also give a warning:

> "Tell him that
> We do not wish greediness
> We do not wish that he should curse us
> We do not wish that his ears should be hard of hearing
> We do not wish that he should call people fools
> We do not wish that he should act on his own initiative
> We do not wish that it should ever be said 'I have no time. I have no time.'
> We do not wish personal abuse
> We do not wish personal violence."

If the leader does not rule fairly, the people can give power to a new ruler. In this way, the Akan are democratic. The people have control over who rules them.

While the Europeans were trading in gold and slaves on the coast, some Akan groups formed the Asante kingdom. This kingdom became very rich from trade. It controlled parts of the northern savanna and the coastal south. The Asante used all their power to try to stop the Europeans from taking over West Africa.

The Influence of Colonialism In 1874, Great Britain made the Gold Coast a colony. But it let the leaders of various ethnic groups continue to rule their people. Even today, there are at least 75 ethnic groups in Ghana, and their leaders are powerful people.

CITIZEN HEROES

To Be a Leader The Asante did not submit to colonial rule without a fight. In 1900, Asante Queen Yaa Asantewa led a war against the British. Although the British were armed with modern rifles and machine guns, it took them more than three months to defeat the queen and her troops. Because of Yaa Asantewa's rebellion, the British began to treat the Asante more respectfully. In her memory, Asante children still sing a song about "Yaa Asantewa, the warrior woman who carries a gun and a sword of state into battle."

All That Glitters is Gold

The current Asantehene, the leader of the Asante, has ruled for more than 25 years. His power is symbolized by the Golden Stool, which sits in a place of honor on a chair beside him. If a leader does something wrong, the people may take the stool away. The Golden Stool is made of wood and decorated with real gold. **Critical Thinking** What does this picture tell you about the economic status of the Asante?

Activity

Interdisciplinary Connections

Language Arts Traditionally, the Akan name their children according to the day of the week on which a child is born. For example, Kwame Nkrumah's first name is the Akan day-name for a boy born on Saturday. Allow students to use the information in the table below to discover and pronounce their Akan day-name. Invite students to make decorated name tags with their day-names.

Day	Girls	Boys
Sun.	Akosua (ah KOS oo uh)	Kwasi (KWAH see)
Mon.	Adwoa (AD joh uh)	Kodwo (KOO joh)
Tues.	Abena (AH beh nuh)	Kwabena (KWAH beh nuh)
Wed.	Akua (ah KOO uh)	Kweku (KWAY koo)
Thurs.	Yaa (yah)	Yaw (YAH oo)
Fri.	Afua (AF oo uh)	Kofi (KOO fee)
Sat.	Amma (AH muh)	Kwame (KWAH mee)

SKILLS MINI LESSON

Recognizing Cause and Effect
To **introduce** the skill, tell students that a cause is the reason an event or development occurs. An effect is the result of the event or development. The words *because, since,* and *as* often indicate causes. The words *therefore, led,* and *as a result* often signal effects. Have students **practice** the skill by looking for cause-and-effect relationships in the text under the heading *The Influence of Colonialism*. Point out that sometimes an effect may become the cause of another effect. Students may **apply** the skill by looking for other cause-and-effect relationships as they read the rest of the section.

Answers to . . .
ALL THAT GLITTERS IS GOLD

They are wealthy.

The End of Colonialism
Ghana's independence was achieved peacefully, but some African countries fought wars to gain their freedom. The Algerians, for example, fought the French for eight years before becoming an independent nation. Angola and Mozambique battled the Portuguese before winning independence in 1975. Britain didn't recognize Zimbabwe's independence until 1980, after years of fighting.

▼ Since colonization, many Ghanaian women purchase machine-made cotton fabrics, instead of traditional kente cloth, for everyday dresses and head scarves.

READ ACTIVELY

Connect How does your community blend traditional ways of life with modern ways?

The British were most interested in controlling the economy of the Gold Coast. They encouraged farmers to grow cocoa. Then, the British sent the cocoa to factories in Britain, where it was made into chocolate. The British also exported timber and gold. As these raw materials left the country, goods from other countries were shipped in. This led to a problem that was typical of much of colonial Africa. People grew fewer food crops because growing cash crops like cocoa brought in more money. Food, therefore, had to be imported. People also spent more time on farming and less on traditional crafts. The British sold food and factory-made goods to the people of the Gold Coast. Soon, they began to depend on these imports.

The British also built schools in the Gold Coast. Foreign missionaries ran the schools. Christianity began to replace traditional religions. By the time Ghana became independent in 1957, many new ideas and lifestyles had come to traditional communities. Many people blended the new ways and the old African ways. Kwame Nkrumah, for example, was a Christian. But he also believed in parts of the traditional African religion. Nkrumah's respect for old and new ways helped him govern when Ghana became independent.

Independence

In 1957, some 22 years after making his pledge to the Statue of Liberty, Nkrumah gave a moving speech to his people. Great Britain, he said, had finally agreed to grant them **sovereignty** (SAHV run tee), or political independence. Cheering, the people carried Nkrumah through the streets. Crowds sang victory songs to celebrate a dream come true.

Nkrumah became the leader of the new country. Later, he became the president. The government changed the country's name from the Gold Coast to Ghana, after an African kingdom that had ruled the region hundreds of years ago. Ghana was the first African colony south of the Sahara to become independent.

Since independence, Ghana has worked to balance new technology with traditional culture. Modern health care, electricity, transportation, and education are things that most Ghanaians want. Sometimes, however, these changes happened too quickly.

Nkrumah's Government Is Overthrown Nine years after being carried through the streets as a hero, Nkrumah was thrown out of office by a military **coup** (koo), or takeover. Army officers led the coup. Most Ghanaian citizens did not protest. In fact, many celebrated. People pulled down statues of Nkrumah.

How did this hero become an enemy? Nkrumah had big plans for Ghana. He borrowed huge amounts of money to make those plans happen fast. He spent millions of dollars to build a conference center. He spent millions more to build a super-highway. In addition, he made a deal with an American company to build a dam on the Volta River. The dam was to provide electricity and irrigation for people in rural areas. But when world prices for cocoa, Ghana's chief export, fell, Ghana could not pay back its loans. Many people blamed Nkrumah for the country's economic problems.

Nkrumah's downfall did not end Ghana's problems. The country alternated between military and democratically elected governments. Few were successful. In the meantime, people began to think better of Nkrumah. Many felt that he had done his best to help the country. When he died in 1972, he was hailed as a national hero. Leaders around the world mourned his death.

Ghana's Economy and Culture Today In the 1980s, Ghana's president, Jerry Rawlings, tried to reform Ghana's politics and economy. Rawlings stressed the traditional African values of hard work and sacrifice. Ghanaians supported Rawlings, and as a result, Ghana's economy began to grow.

Ghana is still dependent on the sale of cocoa. Even so, the economy has grown so much that Ghana has been able to build better roads and irrigation systems. The government plans to improve education and health care. People have formed groups so they can voice concerns about issues that affect their lives.

Ghana's culture, as well as its economy, has benefited from Rawlings's renewal of traditional values. Ghana has special centers that have been

Nkrumah Toppled

Pulled down by angry citizens, the headless statue of Kwame Nkrumah lies on the grounds of the central police station in Accra. Nkrumah was out of the country when he was overthrown, in February 1966. He never returned to Ghana, but lived in exile in the nearby country of Guinea.

Background

Daily Life

Education All children in Ghana are required to attend elementary and junior high school. Students start learning English in first grade. From fourth grade onward, all classes are taught in English, which is the official language of Ghana. Students who choose to continue past junior high may enter a vocational or a commercial program or may prepare for a university.

Talking Drums The talking drums of West Africa are used to send messages. The "language" of the talking drums is characterized by high and low tones. A drummer can relay a message to another drummer up to 20 miles away! In West Africa, news reports on the radio are often preceded by the drum beats that mean news is coming.

set up to keep the country's traditional culture alive. People who visit Ghana may bring new ideas, but they also learn from Ghana's rich traditional culture. Art from Ghana is valued around the world. Ghana's culture can also be seen in daily life. Most people in Ghana live in small villages. Traditional dancing can be found even in the most modern dance clubs. In all forms, traditional Ghanaian culture exists alongside new ideas.

▼ Ghanaian crafts are popular all over the world. Below right is stamped adinkra cloth and woven kente cloth. Below left are hand-crafted beeswax candles.

Section 2 Review

1. (a) political independence (b) a takeover

2. (a) first leader of independent Ghana (b) president of Ghana who established economic reforms

3. The British encouraged farmers to grow cash crops instead of food crops. Food and factory-made goods had to be imported, and the people became dependent on these imports.

4. He believed that the people, not Great Britain, should benefit from the wealth of their country.

5. Nkrumah tried to rush change and spent too much money in the process. Citizens reacted negatively.

6. Answers will vary. Students should write about solutions to one or two community problems, name some possible obstacles, and suggest ways to overcome those obstacles.

SECTION 2 REVIEW

1. Define (a) sovereignty, (b) coup.

2. Identify (a) Kwame Nkrumah, (b) Jerry Rawlings.

3. How did colonization affect Ghana's economy?

4. Why did Kwame Nkrumah believe that Ghana should be independent?

Critical Thinking

5. Recognizing Cause and Effect Kwame Nkrumah went from being a Ghanaian hero to an unpopular figure. What caused this change in people's attitudes?

Activity

6. Writing to Learn Write about one or two changes you would like to see in your country or community. What obstacles might be in the way of this change? How could those obstacles be overcome?

Resource Directory

Teaching Resources

Section Quiz in the Chapter and Section Resources booklet, p. 75, covers the main ideas and key terms in the section. Available in Spanish in the Spanish Chapter and Section Resources booklet, p. 47.

Mali

THE DESERT IS COMING

Section 3

BEFORE YOU READ

Reach Into Your Background
Think about how the environment you live in affects your daily life. How does the clothing you wear reflect the climate? Are there sports or other activities that take place in only certain seasons?

Questions to Explore
1. How does the environment in Mali affect the country's economy?
2. How are the challenges faced by Mali typical of the challenges faced by other countries in the Sahel?

Key Terms
desertification
drought
erode

Key Places
Tombouctou
Sahara
Sahel

Lesson Objectives

1. Identify the relationship between Mali's environment and the way people make their livings.

2. Describe the effects of desertification.

3. Explain how Mali is coping with the problem of desertification.

Outside the Hotel Bouctou in Tombouctou, Mali, sand piles up against buildings. It coats the fur of camels. It gives a yellowish tint to everything in sight. Inside, manager Boubacar Toure (boo buh CAR too RAY) sits in a lobby that is covered with a fine layer of red sand. Only 4 of his hotel's 29 rooms are taken. He is waiting for the river to rise, hoping that it will bring customers.

But each year, the river rises a little later. "Ten years ago the first boat arrived on July 1," says Tombouctou politician Moulaye Haidara (moo LAH ee HY dah rah). "Five years ago it was July 15. Now, we're lucky it's here by early August. In another five years, who knows?"

Mali's Environment

Tombouctou wasn't always so empty. From the 1300s to the end of the 1500s, Tombouctou was an important trade center. Caravans from North Africa crossed the Sahara to trade goods at Tombouctou. The Sahara covers much of West Africa, and it is getting bigger. The Sahara covers almost 60 percent of Mali. Few people live in the Sahara, however. Some Malians live in the savanna, the one area of the country that gets enough rain for farming. Other Malians live in the Sahel, the partly dry lands south of the Sahara. Tombouctou is in the Sahel.

▼ Tombouctou's narrow streets used to attract crowds of tourists and traders. Now the city is slowly being covered with sand.

Lesson Plan

1 Engage

Warm-Up Activity
Remind students that pollution from automobiles is a problem throughout the world. In some cities, air pollution has become so serious that there are regulations to discourage people from driving. Ask students what steps the United States has taken to help the air stay clean.

Activating Prior Knowledge
Ask students to describe how a person in Minnesota would dress during December compared with how a person in Hawaii would dress. Then have students read Reach Into Your Background in the Before You Read box.

2 Explore

Tell students to read the section. Ask them to keep in mind the following questions: What used to be different about life in the Sahel? What is desertification? Why is it important to understand the causes of desertification?

Teaching Resources

📁 **Reproducible Lesson Plan** in the Chapter and Section Resources booklet, p. 76, provides a summary of the section lesson.

📁 **Guided Reading and Review** in the Chapter and Section Resources booklet, p. 77, provides a structure for mastering key concepts and reviewing key terms in the section. Available in Spanish in the Spanish Chapter and Section Resources booklet, p. 48.

Program Resources

📁 **Outline Maps** The Middle East and North Africa: Physical, p. 28; Africa South of the Sahara: Physical, p. 32; West and Central Africa: Political, p. 34

3 Teach

Ask students to write a paragraph explaining how desertification has affected the way Malians make their livings. Have them include information about the business community of Tombouctou and the Tuaregs.

4 Assess

See the answers to the Section Review. You may also use students' completed paragraphs as an assessment.

Acceptable paragraphs discuss at least two effects of desertification on people's livelihoods.

Commendable paragraphs include three or more effects of desertification on people's livelihoods.

Outstanding paragraphs include three or more effects of desertification on people's livelihoods and include an analysis of the consequences of continuing desertification.

Answers to ...
MAP AND CHART STUDY

Students should say that the grasslands to the south appear most habitable and that few people live in Mali because so much of it desert. Tombouctou is on the Niger River and at the edge of the Sahara, so goods transported across the Sahara to Tombouctou could then be shipped elsewhere. Students will have a variety of opinions about what life would be like in a country with a young population.

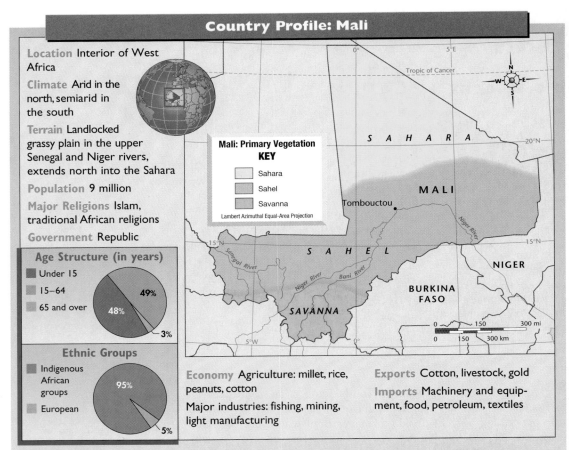

Country Profile: Mali

Location Interior of West Africa

Climate Arid in the north, semiarid in the south

Terrain Landlocked grassy plain in the upper Senegal and Niger rivers, extends north into the Sahara

Population 9 million

Major Religions Islam, traditional African religions

Government Republic

Mali: Primary Vegetation
KEY
- Sahara
- Sahel
- Savanna

Lambert Azimuthal Equal-Area Projection

Age Structure (in years)
- Under 15
- 15–64
- 65 and over

49%
48%
3%

Ethnic Groups
- Indigenous African groups
- European

95%
5%

Economy Agriculture: millet, rice, peanuts, cotton

Major industries: fishing, mining, light manufacturing

Exports Cotton, livestock, gold

Imports Machinery and equipment, food, petroleum, textiles

Map and Chart Study This map shows Mali's major vegetation regions. What part of the country is most liveable? Why do you think the population is so small in a country so large? **Location** Find Mali's major city, Tombouctou. How do you think the city's location contributed to its importance as a trading crossroads? **Critical Thinking** Like many other African countries, Mali has a very young population as the top chart shows. What do you think it would be like to live in a country where almost half the people are under the age of 15?

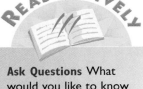

READ ACTIVELY

Ask Questions What would you like to know about life in the Sahel?

Life in the Sahel The Sahel is a zone between the desert and the savanna. Eleven African countries lie partly in the Sahel. The Sahel stretches through the middle of Mali. Look at the map in the Activity Atlas. What other countries are in the Sahel? The large, dry Sahel affects the economy of every country it touches. But people who live in the region have long used the resources of the Sahel to earn their living.

People have lived in the Sahel for thousands of years. For a long time, they did very well and even grew rich. The region's grasslands provide food for animal herds. And the Sahel's location between the Sahara and the savanna is important. People traveling south must pass through the Sahel before reaching the savanna. For this reason, Tombouctou became a wealthy center of learning and business.

Resource Directory

Program Resources

Environmental and Global Issues Topic: Population, pp. 49–53

Media and Technology

Color Transparencies 6, 72, 92, 93

Planet Earth CD-ROM includes an interactive political map of Mali and thematic maps of Africa.

Material World CD-ROM includes a portrait of a family from Mali plus geographic data on Mali.

Once European ships began trading along Africa's coast, trade through the Sahara decreased. Tombouctou and other trade cities declined. But life in Tombouctou still follows certain traditional patterns. As in past times, caravans still carry huge blocks of salt into Tombouctou. And women still bake bread in outdoor ovens in the traditional way.

The Desert Comes Closer Mali has little industry. Most people make their living by trading, farming, and herding. However, all of these kinds of work are being threatened by **desertification**, the change of fertile land into land that is too dry or damaged to support life. In Mali and other countries of the Sahel, the desert is spreading south. Even the wetter lands in southwest Mali are in danger.

The region facing the greatest threat is the Sahel. The people of the Sahel whose way of life is most affected by desertification may be the Tuareg (TWAR ehg). The Tuareg have lived in the desert and the Sahel for hundreds of years. Wrapped from head to toe in blue cloth, with only their eyes showing, the Tuareg gallop across the land on fast camels. They live a nomadic life, moving their herds of goats, sheep, and camels

Dogon Granary Doors
The Dogon live in a wetter part of Mali. They work as farmers. They use granaries to store grain. These granaries are made of twigs and mud but have very stylized wood doors. The Dogon believe the tree from which the wood came contains a spirit that protects the stored grain. Although the rain and sun often wear down the granaries, the Dogon transfer the symbolic door from one granary to another.

◄ Baking bread outside makes sense when average daily temperatures exceed 90°F (32°C). An oven inside would only heat your house up more.

Activity

Journal Writing

From Here to Timbuktu
Tell students that *Timbuktu* is another way of spelling Tombouctou. Students may be surprised to learn that Timbuktu and Tombouctou are one and the same. Ask students to write in their journals about their associations with the place and its name. Invite students to add to their entries after they finish reading the section.

Activity

Interdisciplinary Connections

Math Tell students that not all of the Sahara's surface is covered in sand. In fact, only about 15 percent of the Sahara is sandy. Most of the desert's surface (70 percent) is covered in stone and gravel. Another 15 percent is covered by mountains. Ask students to make a pie graph that shows the proportions of the Sahara that are covered by sand, stone and gravel, and mountains.

SKILLS MINI LESSON

Using the Writing Process
As a way to **introduce** the skill, write the following headings on the chalkboard: *Prewrite, Draft, Revise, Proofread, Publish.* Discuss each step in the context of writing a report about a Sahelian country. In the prewriting stage, writers should use a map to identify a Sahelian country (excluding Mali), conduct research, and record facts and ideas in an outline or a diagram. During drafting, writers shape ideas and facts into sentences and paragraphs focused on a main idea. During revision, writers remove unimportant ideas and rework awkward sentences. Stress that writers then proofread their work, checking for spelling and grammatical errors. Finally, writers publish or share their work. Have students **practice** and **apply** the skill by asking them to use the writing process to prepare a report on a Sahelian country.

Interdisciplinary Connections

Science To demonstrate the compound effects of drought and desertification on plant growth, have students plant bean seeds in two containers. One container should be filled with sand and the other with potting soil. Ask students to predict which plants will fare better. Have students water both containers with the same amounts of water until growth has been established for several weeks. Students should record their observations daily. Then have them simulate a drought by withholding water from the plants for several days and record their observations. Ask students to check their predictions and discuss their findings in the context of the problems that face Sahelian countries. *English Language Learner, Visual*

south in the dry season and north in the wet season. Most Tuareg have never lived permanently in one place. The desertification of countries like Mali and Niger is threatening their way of life.

A Change in Lifestyle Major droughts in the 1970s and 1980s made life very difficult for the Tuareg. A **drought** is a time when there is little or no rain. Facing water and food shortages, some Tuareg settled on farms or in cities. Others built camps outside Tombouctou.

Ibrahim Ag Abdullah and his wife Fatimata are Tuareg. They live in a camp near Tombouctou. In the morning, Ibrahim Abdullah rides his camel into the city. Instead of tending his herds, Ibrahim Abdullah now sells camel rides to tourists. Fatimata Abdullah draws water from a well built by the government and grows vegetables. But the Abdullahs want to return to their nomadic life. "Each time I earn a little money, I buy a goat or a sheep. I save up so I can have enough animals to return to the desert," says Ibrahim Abdullah. But this way of life will only be possible if the Sahel's grasslands are maintained.

Preserving the Environment

Many people around the world are worried about the Sahel. The United Nations has created a committee to fight desertification. First people must understand why the fertile land changes into unusable desert.

Some environmentalists think that overgrazing can cause desertification. They say that grazing large herds of animals **erodes** the soil, or wears it away. That allows the desert to take over. When there are no roots to hold soil in place, the fierce winds of the Sahel blow it around. Yellow dust clouds fill the air. This loose soil is one reason that Tombouctou is slowly being covered in sand.

Other environmentalists say that grazing does not increase desertification. They think that grazing may actually help grasses grow once the area gets enough rain. These scientists think that long periods of

▼ This picture shows a Tuareg man dressed in traditional style. The Tuaregs' name for themselves means "free people." Clustered in small groups throughout the southwest Sahara, these nomads resist being controlled by any government. The Tuareg practice their own form of Islam, which keeps many elements of their original religion.

Teaching Resources

Section Quiz in the Chapter and Section Resources booklet, p. 78, covers the main ideas and key terms in the section. Available in Spanish in the Spanish Chapter and Section Resources booklet, p. 49.

Vocabulary in the Chapter and Section Resources booklet, p. 80, provides a review of key terms in the chapter. Available in Spanish in the Spanish Chapter and Section Resources booklet, p. 51.

Reteaching in the Chapter and Section Resources booklet, p. 81, provides a structure for students who may need additional help in mastering chapter content.

Program Resources

Environmental and Global Issues Topic: Environmental Destruction, pp. 14–19

Desertification and the Economy

This is the West Africa Regional Bank in Bamako, Mali's capital and largest city. Desertification has hurt Mali's economy by making it harder for farmers to grow cash crops. Now Mali's government is trying to encourage people to start their own businesses, as well as encouraging existing businesses to come to Mali.

drought turn land into desert. Over the last 25 years, the Sahel has had much less rain than it did in the 70 years before. If these scientists are right, a few years of good rainfall could stop desertification. The Tuareg would not have to change their way of life.

Currently, Mali's government is studying the problem. Mali is working with the United Nations to educate people in rural areas about better ways to use land. The government is also irrigating and planting in some areas to create a greenbelt. It hopes to have its plan for tackling desertification operating by the year 2000.

SECTION 3 REVIEW

1. **Define** (a) desertification, (b) drought, (c) erode.

2. **Identify** (a) Tombouctou, (b) Sahara, (c) Sahel.

3. How does Mali's geography affect how people make a living?

4. How does desertification affect the people who live in the Sahel?

Critical Thinking

5. **Drawing Conclusions** Many Tuareg living around Tombouctou are now depending on the tourist trade for income. Based on what you have learned about Tombouctou, what will be some of the challenges of this new occupation?

Activity

6. **Writing to Learn** Overgrazing may contribute to the desertification of the Sahel. What common North American activities may present a threat to the environment? Do you think those activities should be discouraged? Why or why not?

1. (a) the change of fertile soil into soil that is too dry or damaged to support life (b) a time when there is little or no rain (c) to wear away soil

2. (a) ancient city of the Sahel, once an important center of trade (b) large desert that covers much of West Africa and about 60 percent of Mali (c) a semiarid zone between the Sahara and the forests

3. Because much of Mali is a desert, most people live in the Sahel where it is possible to farm, trade, and raise livestock.

4. Land affected by desertification cannot support plant life. People who raise livestock cannot graze their animals, and farmers cannot farm.

5. People such as the manager of the Hotel Bouctou have experienced a decline in visitors in recent years, so relying on tourism may not be a very dependable way to make a living.

6. Answers may vary. Possibilities may include the following: Driving cars threatens the environment because exhaust from the cars pollutes the air. People should walk, ride bikes, or use public transportation to cut down on the amount of pollution created by cars.

Teaching Resources

☐ **Enrichment** in the Chapter and Section Resources booklet, p. 82, extends chapter content and enriches students' understanding.

☐ **Spanish Glossary** in the Spanish Chapter and Section Resources, pp. 68–73, provides key terms translated from English to Spanish as well as definitions in Spanish.

☐ **Chapter Summary** in the Chapter and Section Resources booklet, p. 79, provides a summary of chapter content. Available in Spanish in the Spanish Chapter and Section Resources booklet, p. 50.

☐ **Cooperative Learning Activity** in the Activities and Projects booklet, pp. 33–36, provides two student handouts, one page of teacher's directions, and a scoring rubric for a cooperative learning activity on making a relief map.

Media and Technology

🎧 **Guided Reading Audiotapes** (English and Spanish)

SKILLS ACTIVITY

Using Distribution Maps

Do you think in pictures? Most people do. They try to visualize what they read about. For example, if you read a story about a trip along the Niger River, you may imagine a wide river with dense forest along its banks. You may try to picture, in your own mind, what the writer saw. Thinking in pictures is a natural way to make sense of the world.

Geographers think in pictures, too. For them, of course, the pictures are often maps. There is an old saying: "A picture is worth a thousand words." This is especially true when the picture is a distribution map.

Get Ready

A distribution map is a map that shows how something is distributed. In other words, it shows where something is located. A "population distribution map" shows where people live. It is one of the most common distribution maps. A "resource distribution map" shows where resources are found. You can make a distribution map that shows how nearly anything is distributed. The location of ethnic groups, languages, vegetation, schools—and almost anything else you can think of—can all be indicated on distribution maps.

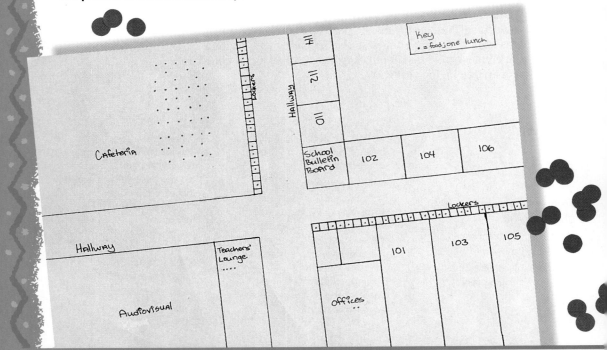

Try It Out

Imagine a map of your school. What would a "food distribution map" of your school look like? Chances are, it would indicate that food is located in the cafeteria, in student lunchboxes, and perhaps in the teacher's lounge.

How would this work exactly? To find out, make that map. Sketch a map, or floor plan, of your school. Make a map key that uses a symbol to indicate "food." One symbol on the map will indicate one food item, two symbols will represent two food items, and so on. Now mark the map with the symbols. When you're done, you'll probably have a map with many symbols in the cafeteria and some others scattered throughout the school.

Every distribution map tells you three basic things:

A. What is distributed Your map shows the distribution of food.

B. Where it is distributed By looking at the symbols, you can see where the food is located.

C. How many are distributed Because each symbol represents a certain number of food items, the map tells you approximately how many food items are located in each room in the house.

Apply the Skill

Now that you see how distribution maps are made and what three things they tell you, you can use what you have learned to read a real distribution map. Use the distribution map on the right to answer the following questions.

1 **Determine what is distributed.** What resource does this map show the distribution of?

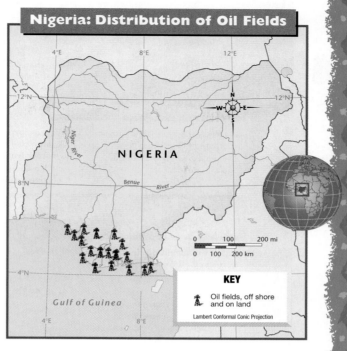

Nigeria: Distribution of Oil Fields

KEY

Oil fields, off shore and on land

Lambert Conformal Conic Projection

2 **Determine where it is distributed.** How is the distribution indicated on the map? In what part or parts of Nigeria is this resource located?

3 **Determine how many are distributed.** How many symbols are shown on the map?

4 **Organize what you have learned.** Using the map as a guide, write a paragraph that explains the information on the map. After you have completed your paragraph, write another paragraph explaining whether or not you think the map is a more useful way of communicating this information than writing.

5 **Make a connection to the real world.** Explain why this map would be useful to each of the following people: the president of an oil company, an officer in the Nigerian armed forces, a member of the Nigerian government, a member of the government of neighboring Cameroon.

3 Teach

Allow students to work in groups as they **practice** using the skill to create the map described in *Try It Out*. Encourage groups to compare their maps. Together, identify and explain any differences.

For additional reinforcement, ask students to map the distribution within the school of another item, such as computers, sports equipment, or musical instruments.

4 Assess

Have students work independently to **apply** the skill by answering the questions asked in *Apply the Skill*. You may **assess** students' work by evaluating their school food distribution maps and their responses to the questions.

Answers to . . .

APPLY THE SKILL

1. oil fields in Nigeria
2. Oil well symbols represent the locations of oil fields. Most oil fields are located near or just off of the southwestern coast of Nigeria.
3. 18
4. Paragraphs should note that Nigeria has significant oil resources, which are mostly located in the southwest. Students may say that the map is a useful communication tool because a quick glance at it reveals the number and location of Nigeria's oil fields.
5. Students' answers should indicate that they recognize that the location of oil, which is one of Nigeria's most important natural resources, has economic and political significance for the public and private sectors and for neighboring countries.

Reviewing Main Ideas

1. the Yoruba, the Ibo, and the Hausa-Fulani

2. A census shows which ethnic group is the largest. The largest group will have the most political power.

3. He traveled all over the country to convince people that they should demand independence from Great Britain. He became the first leader of the independent country.

4. Its economy has grown. The government has been able to build better roads and irrigation systems and has addressed the concerns of the people.

5. They are no longer able to make a living by herding animals, because the land has become unable to support much plant life for grazing. Many Tuareg have had to give up their nomadic lifestyle and settle near towns or cities.

6. overgrazing, which causes the soil to erode, and drought

Reviewing Key Terms

1. b	4. g	7. f
2. e	5. a	8. h
3. d	6. c	

Critical Thinking

1. Mali has no coast and has large areas of desert. Because of these geographic features, Mali's culture has developed around trade and the raising of livestock. A significant proportion of Ghana's land can be farmed. The country also has abundant natural resources. The British government encouraged people to grow cash crops for export. Ghana's independence movement was in part sparked by the people's desire to benefit from the wealth of their country.

2. The British drew boundaries in Nigeria and did not consider the traditional lands of certain ethnic groups. The British government encouraged people to grow cash crops such as cocoa and exported the country's natural resources. The country had to import food and other essentials. Once independent, Ghana continued to rely on cocoa exports as the mainstay of the economy. A drop in cocoa prices caused economic problems.

Reviewing Main Ideas

1. Identify the three largest ethnic groups of Nigeria.
2. Explain how Nigeria's census affects politics.
3. What role did Kwame Nkrumah play in Ghana's move to independence?
4. How has Ghana changed since it became independent?
5. How has desertification affected the life of the Tuareg?
6. Describe two possible causes of desertification.

Reviewing Key Terms

Match the definitions in Column I with the key terms in Column II.

Column I
1. to wear away
2. composed of many ethnic groups
3. a group distinguished by race, language, religion, or cultural traditions
4. the change of fertile land into land that is too dry or damaged to support life
5. a long period of little or no rainfall
6. a systematic counting of the population
7. a sudden overthrow of a ruler or government
8. a country's freedom and power to decide on policies and actions

Column II
a. drought
b. erode
c. census
d. ethnic group
e. multiethnic
f. coup
g. desertification
h. sovereignty

Critical Thinking

1. **Making Comparisons** Compare Ghana's geography to that of Mali. How do you think each country's geography has affected its history?
2. **Recognizing Cause and Effect** How did the colonial histories of Nigeria and Ghana affect those countries after independence?

Graphic Organizer

Copy the chart onto a sheet of paper. Fill it in to show how Nigeria's Hausa-Fulani, Yoruba, and Ibo groups are similar and different.

	Hausa-Fulani	Yoruba	Ibo
Region of Nigeria			
Ways of Making a Living			

Graphic Organizer

	Hausa-Fulani	Yoruba	Ibo
Region of Nigeria	north	southwest	southeast
Ways of Making a Living	traders	farmers	traders

Map Activity

West Africa
For each place listed below, write the letter from the map that shows its location.

1. Nigeria
2. Ghana
3. Sahara
4. Tombouctou
5. Lagos
6. Abuja
7. Sahel
8. Mali

Place Location

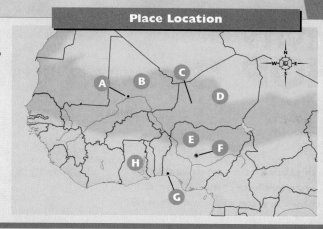

Writing Activity

Writing a News Report
Choose one of the recent events described in this chapter and write a news report about it. Remember to describe these five things for your readers: who, what, where, when, and why.

Internet Activity

Use a search engine to find **Cyberkids.** Click on **Reading Room** and then choose **Previous Issues.** Choose Issue 5. Then click on **TOC.** Choose **My Trip to Ghana.** Read about a girl's trip to her parents' homeland, Ghana. According to the author, how is life in Ghana different from life in the United States?

Skills Review

Turn to the Skills Activity.

Review the three basic types of information a distribution map provides. Then answer the following questions: (a) What would a vegetation distribution map of Mali tell you? (b) What would a natural resources distribution map tell you about Ghana?

How Am I Doing?

Answer these questions to check your progress.

1. Can I describe the main geographic features of West Africa?
2. Do I understand how cultures in West Africa compare to other African cultures I've studied?
3. Can I identify some historic events that have shaped the modern cultures of West Africa?
4. What information from this chapter can I use in my book project?

Internet Activity

If students are having difficulty finding this site, you may wish to have them use the following URL, which was accurate at the time this textbook was published:

http://www.cyberkids.com/

You might also guide students to a search engine. Four of the most useful are Infoseek, Alta Vista, Lycos, and Yahoo. For additional suggestions on using the Internet, refer to the Prentice Hall Social Studies' Educator's Handbook "Using the Internet," in the *Prentice Hall World Explorer Program Resources.*

For additional links to the world history and culture topics, visit the Prentice Hall Home Page at:
http://www.phschool.com

How Am I Doing?

Point out to students that this checklist is a quick reminder for them of what they learned in the chapter. If their answer to any of the questions is *no* or if they are unsure, they may need to review the topic.

Map Activity

1. E	4. A	7. C
2. H	5. G	8. B
3. D	6. F	

Writing Activity

Reports will vary, but should identify an event covered in the chapter, such as the census taken in Nigeria.

Skills Review

(a) The map would show how much vegetation grows in Mali and would also show what types of vegetation grow and where they grow. (b) The map would show the quantities of natural resources found in Ghana and would also show what kinds of resources exist and where they can be found.

Resource Directory

Teaching Resources

Chapter Tests Forms A and B are in the Tests booklet, pp. 26–31.

Program Resources

Writing Process Handbook includes Writing Effective Paragraphs, pp. 27–28, to help students with the Writing Activity.

Media and Technology

Color Transparencies
Color Transparency 174
(Graphic organizer table template)

Prentice Hall Writer's Solution Writing Lab CD-ROM

Computer Test Bank

Resource Pro™ CD-ROM

Desertification

Lesson Objectives

1 Describe the process of desertification.

2 Explain how desertification affects land and its productivity.

Lesson Plan

1 Engage

Warm-Up Activity

Ask: *What would happen to the human and natural environment of our community if the trees and grass disappeared?* Point out, for example, that vegetation supports animal life, shields people and buildings from the wind and the sun, and holds soil in place. Then, point out any places where vegetation once grew but has disappeared, for example, footpaths worn across lawns or empty lots. Ask students to suggest reasons for which vegetation might disappear.

Activating Prior Knowledge

Have a volunteer read Step One of the Activity Lab aloud. Ask students to describe a desert and explain how it might be created from land that was once fertile.

2 Explore

Instruct students to read the remaining Activity Shop directions before proceeding. Then explain that in the Sahara, powerful sandstorm winds may blow for days, radically changing the desert landscape. The sun's light is blocked, and travel becomes extremely dangerous. People must cover their skin or flying sand will cause abrasions.

D esertification occurs when land that was once fertile becomes a desert. The land becomes dry and salty, underground water dries up, erosion occurs, and plant life dies. Changes in climate, such as a long drought, can cause desertification. So can people. For example, people sometimes allow animals to graze so much that most plants are killed.

Purpose

The Sahara is expanding into the edge of the savanna, or the Sahel. The desertification of the Sahel affects not only the environment, but also the people living there. In this activity, you will explore one cause of desertification.

Materials

- three-sided box
- blow-dryer
- piece of sod as wide as the box
- sand
- goggles

Procedure

STEP ONE

Set up your experiment. Place the box so that the open end is in front of you. Put on your goggles. Lay the sod in the box, with some space between the sod and the back of the box.

Resource Directory

Teaching Resources

Activity Shop: Lab in the Activities and Projects booklet, p. 6, provides a structure that helps students complete the lab activity.

Pour the sand in a pile across the open end of the box, directly in front of the sod. Hold the blow-dryer at the open end of the box so that it will blow across the sand toward the sod.

STEP TWO

Create a windstorm over good land. Use the blow-dryer to create "wind." Lift handfuls of sand and let it sift through your fingers in front of the blow-dryer, so that the sand is blown across the grass. This represents the sandy winds that blow across the desert and over grassy lands. Do this for about one minute, holding the blow-dryer no higher than the top of the sod. Note how much sand gets caught in the grass.

STEP THREE

Begin the desertification process. Thin the vegetation by removing about half of the grass in the sod. This is similar to what happens when vegetation is grazed or dies from climate change. Use the blow-dryer and handfuls of sand to create another windstorm, again for one minute. How much sand is in the sod this time? How does the grass look?

STEP FOUR

Continue the desertification process. This time remove almost all of the grass in the sod. This represents more overgrazing and the death of vegetation. Make a final one-minute windstorm. How much sand is in the sod now? How does the sand affect the soil?

Observations

1 What happened to the sand as it blew across the grass?

2 What happened to the remaining grass and topsoil as the sand blew across the "overgrazed" sod?

3 Imagine you are a cattle herder who needs to feed your cattle. You know that if you let your animals graze, you might contribute to desertification. But if your animals do not eat, they will die. What would you do? The agricultural officials in your region want to know your decision. Write them a letter explaining your decision.

ANALYSIS AND CONCLUSION

1. Why do you think that it is important to people living in the Sahel to slow desertification?

2. Pretend you are a journalist on a photo shoot. You see a farmer allowing animals to feed in an area where there is little vegetation. You know the farmer has no other place to let the animals graze. You take a photograph. Write an article to accompany your photograph.

The Distant Talking Drum

POEMS FROM NIGERIA
BY ISAAC OLALEYE

Lesson Objectives

1. Analyze two poems.

2. Link imagery in a literary work to the country of its origin.

Lesson Plan

1 Engage

Building Vocabulary

Point out that the vocabulary terms defined in the margin are *gourd* and *radiant*.

Activating Prior Knowledge

Ask a student to read aloud the *Before You Read* text. Invite volunteers to describe a place where they have lived and why it was special.

2 Develop Student Reading

Direct students to read the two poems. Explain that these poems are written in free verse and do not use rhyme. When reading this kind of poetry, readers should pause at the punctuation rather than at the end of each line. Model this style of reading for students.

Background

About the Author

Isaac Olaleye was born in Nigeria. He has lived in Nigeria and England and currently lives in West Virginia.

About the Selections

The Distant Talking Drum was published in 1995 by Boyds Mills Press, Inc. The poems in the collection describe life in a Yoruban village.

BEFORE YOU READ

Reach Into Your Background

Have you lived in your hometown all your life, or have you moved from place to place? How do you think it would feel to live somewhere far from where you grew up?

Writers who have moved far away from their homes often write about the place where they grew up. Many writers feel that writing helps them deal with their feelings of homesickness. Some writers respond to other changes in their lives, or to the loss of a friend or family member, in the same way.

Isaac Olaleye, the author of these poems, grew up in Nigeria and lived there for many years. He moved to England and lived there for several years. Now he lives in the United States.

Questions to Explore

1. What can you learn from these poems about the ways that many Nigerians make a living?

2. What can these poems teach you about some features of Nigerian culture?

READ ACTIVELY

Visualize How can people make light using palm oil?

gourd *n.*: a fruit with a hard skin, such as a melon or a pumpkin
radiant *adj.*: bright

My Village

Èrín is the name
Of my African village.
Laughter is what Èrín means
In the Yoruba language.

In streams,
Women and children
Still collect water in gourds
and clay pots,
Which they balance on their
heads.

Electric light has not shone in
my village.
With ruby-red palm oil
Poured into a clay vessel
We see at night.

My village of Èrín is peaceful,
Like a hidden world.
It's ringed by radiant green
And surrounded by five
streams.

Like a stream,
The love
For my village
Flows.

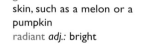

Resource Directory

Program Resources

Material in the **Primary Sources and Literature Readings** booklet provides additional literature selections on the region under study.

Village Weavers

Men and women
Weave cloth
From yarns
Dyed in herbs
In colors of green, blue,
    black, and red.

Thick and heavy cloth
They weave.
Cloth thick for the sun,
Tough for the field,
And fancy for feasts.

In alleys,
Or under the shadow of
    trees,
From morning to evening
Their hands and feet
Are busy weaving.

They work happily,
Singing and laughing,
So their mouths
Also keep busy.

Connect Do you like to keep your mouth busy talking when your hands are busy working? Why or why not?

◀ This Nigerian man is weaving in a workshop.

EXPLORING YOUR READING

Look Back
1. How do the people of the village use the cloth that the weavers weave?

Think It Over
2. Do you think the people in the poems live in rural or urban Nigeria? Why?

3. Why do you think that the author describes Èrín as peaceful?

4. How do you think the people in the village spend most of their time? Why?

Go Beyond
5. No electricity means no televisions, no light bulbs, and no air conditioning. How would your life be different without electricity? How would your life be the same? For example, you would not watch television, but you would still play with your friends. Think of other examples.

Ideas for Writing: Hometown Poem
6. If you were going to write a book of poems about your hometown, what topics would you write about? Make a list. Then choose one topic from your list and write a poem. Use Olaleye's poems as a model.

3 Assess

Work through the *Exploring Your Reading* questions with students.

1. The people make clothes for different purposes out of the cloth.
2. They live in a rural area. Both poems are about a village, which is a small, non-urban community. The activities, such as collecting water from streams and working in fields, describe rural life.
3. The village is remote and therefore probably quiet.
4. They do not have modern conveniences, so they work at tasks and chores required for daily survival in a remote, rural area.
5. Comparisons should accurately identify the role of electricity in students' lives while also recognizing the elements that would remain unchanged if they had no electricity.
6. Poems should describe a hometown, what the community's inhabitants do, and how the poet feels about the community and its people.

Activity

Critical Thinking

Drawing Conclusions
Suitable as either an individual or a whole class activity.
Prompt students to write a brief paragraph describing the poet's feelings about his village. As students share these with the class, discuss the textual clues and personal experiences from which students drew their conclusions.

AFRICA

Exploring East Africa

To help you plan instruction, the chart below shows how teaching resources correspond to chapter content. Use the resources to vary instruction, add activities, or plan block schedules. Where appropriate, resources have **suggested time allotments** for students. Time allotments are approximate.

Managing Time and Instruction

	Africa Teaching Resources Binder		World Explorer Program Resources Binder	
	Resource	**mins.**	**Resource**	**mins.**
SECTION 1 Ethiopia: Churches and Mosques	**Chapter and Section Support** Reproducible Lesson Plan, p. 85 ⓢ Guided Reading and Review, p. 86 ⓢ Section Quiz, p. 87	20 25	**Outline Maps** East and Southern Africa: Political, p. 35 **Nystrom Desk Atlas** Ⓣ **Primary Sources and Literature Readings** **Writing Process Handbook** Using Transitions, p. 30	20 40 25
SKILLS ACTIVITY Using Isolines	**Social Studies and Geography Skills,** Understanding Isolines, p. 29 Reading a Contour Map, p. 30	30 30		
2 SECTION 2 Tanzania: When People Cooperate	**Chapter and Section Support** Reproducible Lesson Plan, p. 88 ⓢ Guided Reading and Review, p. 89 ⓢ Section Quiz, p. 90 **Social Studies and Geography Skills,** Predicting Consequences, p. 50	20 25 30	**Outline Maps** East and Southern Africa: Political, p. 35	20
3 SECTION 3 Skyscrapers in the Savanna	**Chapter and Section Support** Reproducible Lesson Plan, p. 91 ⓢ Guided Reading and Review, p. 92 Critical Thinking Activity, p. 98 ⓢ Section Quiz, p. 93 ⓢ Vocabulary, p. 95 Reteaching, p. 96 Enrichment, p. 97 ⓢ Chapter Summary, p. 94 **Tests** Forms A and B Chapter Tests, pp. 32–37	20 30 25 20 25 25 15 40	**Outline Maps** Africa South of the Sahara: Physical, p. 32 East and Southern Africa: Political, p. 35 **Environmental and Global Issues** Topic: Urbanization, pp. 54–58	20 20 30
LITERATURE *A Promise to the Sun* by Tololwa M. Mollel			Ⓣ **Primary Sources and Literature Readings**	40

134A CHAPTER 6

Block Scheduling Program Support

- Block Scheduling Folder — PROGRAM TEACHING RESOURCES
- Activities and Projects
- Interdisciplinary Links
- Resource Pro™ CD-ROM
- Media and Technology

Media and Technology

Resource	mins.
🔲 📀 ⑤ World Video Explorer	20
📀 Planet Earth CD-ROM	20
📀 Material World CD-ROM	20
⬛ Color Transparencies 72, Historical Map Set 2	20
📀 Planet Earth CD-ROM	20
⬛ Color Transparencies 19, 20, 73	20
📀 Planet Earth CD-ROM	20
⬛ Color Transparencies 4, 19, 24, 51, 52, 73, 93, 151, 159	20
🎧 ⑤ Guided Reading Audiotapes	20
⬛ Color Transparency 171 (Graphic organizer web template)	20
📀 The Writer's Solution CD-ROM	30
🖥 Computer Test Bank	30

- **T Teaming Opportunity** This resource is especially well-suited for teaching teams.
- **⑤ Spanish** This resource is also in Spanish support.
- 📀 CD-ROM
- 📀 Laserdisc
- ⬛ Transparency
- 🖥 Software
- 🔲 Videotape
- 🎧 Audiotape

Assessment Opportunities

From Guiding Questions to Assessment A series of Guiding Questions serves as an organizing framework for this book. The Guiding Questions that relate to this chapter are listed below. Section Reviews and Section Quizzes provide opportunities for assessing students' insights into these Guiding Questions. Additional assessments are listed below.

GUIDING QUESTIONS

- *Why have many Africans been moving to cities in recent years?*
- *What factors influence the ways in which Africans make a living?*

ASSESSMENTS

Section 1

Students should be able to give an oral presentation describing the development of Christianity in Ethiopia.

▶ **RUBRIC** See the Assessment booklet for a rubric on assessing an oral presentation.

Section 2

Students should be able to create a web that shows some of the ways the government of Tanzania is changing.

▶ **RUBRIC** See the Assessment booklet for a rubric on assessing graphic organizers.

Section 3

Students should be able to write a short report describing the reasons why many Africans, especially men, are moving to cities.

▶ **RUBRIC** See the Assessment booklet for a rubric on assessing a report.

Activities and Projects

Mental Mapping

Taking a Trip Suggest that students imagine they will take a trip through East Africa. Write the country names *Ethiopia, Tanzania,* and *Kenya* on the board. Have students attempt to outline these three countries on a blank map of Africa. Then ask students to plan their trip through the three countries. Have students work in pairs. One student can dictate directions for the route of the trip to the other student, who draws the route on his or her map. Have students check their work against a political map of Africa and adjust their routes as necessary.

Links to Current Events

African Tourism National parks and game preserves in Kenya and Tanzania attract many tourists to East Africa. Safari tours allow visitors to see lions, zebras, giraffes, rhinos, leopards, cheetahs, ostriches, and other wild animals. These large animals, and the grasslands of East Africa, are what many North Americans think of when they think of Africa. Although poaching, or the illegal capture of wild animals, is still a problem in East Africa, for the most part Tanzania and Kenya have succeeded in preserving their wild animal population by treating it as an economic resource that attracts tourists.

Suggest that students set the mood for their study of East Africa by creating a mural of animals that might be seen on a safari tour to a national park in this region.

Hands-On Activities

Cities of East Africa List the names of these cities on the chalkboard: Mombasa, Addis Ababa, Nairobi, Dar es Salaam, Dodoma. Ask students to use maps in their books to locate these cities. Have them notice whether the cities are located on the coast, a river, or some other physical feature. Then have them go to a wall map or globe and locate the cities.

Make a simple graphic organizer on the chalkboard listing the countries Ethiopia, Kenya, and Tanzania with the cities listed in the correct columns. (Ethiopia: Addis Ababa; Kenya: Nairobi, Mombasa; Tanzania: Dodoma, Dar es Salaam)

Churches, Mosques, and Temples About 40 percent of Ethiopians are Ethiopian Orthodox Christian; about 40 percent are Muslim. The rest are other types of Christians or practice traditional African religions. There were about 30,000 Falasha, or Ethiopians who practice a form of Judaism, in Ethiopia until most of them relocated to Israel in the mid-1980s and early 1990s. Ask students to make a poster or mural depicting houses of worship in Ethiopia. They may photocopy pictures from books or draw pictures themselves. Ask them to label the buildings. Ask them to discuss the ways these buildings are similar to or different from houses of worship they have seen elsewhere. *English Language Learners*

Respected Leaders Haile Selassie (Ethiopia), Julius Nyerere (Tanzania), and Jomo Kenyatta (Kenya) were all important leaders. Have students prepare a report on the life and achievements of one of these men. Tell students to try to find out something about the childhood of the man they are researching, his achievements, and his impact on Africa as a whole as well as on his own country. *Challenging*

Swahili Swahili is an official language of Tanzania and Kenya. The word *Swahili* comes from an Arabic word for "coast." Swahili uses the structures of an African language with many Arabic influences. It is not the language of a particular group of people but a *lingua franca,* or shared language, throughout much of East and Central Africa. It is also used in parts of Arabia and Pakistan. Invite students to find and use a Swahili phrase book to learn a few common phrases or words in Swahili and practice them with others in the class. *Average*

F.Y.I.

This page can help you extend your own and students' understanding of the concepts in this chapter. You may want to browse through some of the suggestions in the **Bibliography. Interdisciplinary Links** can connect social studies understandings to areas elsewhere in the curriculum through the use of other Prentice Hall products. **National Geography Standards** reflected specifically in this chapter are listed for your convenience. Some hints about appropriate **Internet Access** are also provided. **School to Careers** provides insights into the practical uses of some of the concepts in this chapter as they might pertain to various careers.

BIBLIOGRAPHY

FOR THE TEACHER

Gish, Steven. *Ethiopia.* Cavendish, 1996.

Langley, Myrtle. *Religion.* Knopf, 1996.

Pateman, Robert. *Kenya.* Cavendish, 1993.

Laure, Jason. *Tanzania.* Childrens Press, 1994.

FOR THE STUDENT

Easy

Schur, Maxine Rose. *Day of Delight: A Jewish Sabbath in Ethiopia.* Dial, 1994.

Margolies, Barbara A. *Rehema's Journey: A Visit in Tanzania.* Scholastic, 1990.

Average

Wilkes, Sybella. *One Day We Had to Run! Refugee Children Tell Their Stories in Words and Paintings.* Millbrook, 1995.

Challenging

Smith, Roland. *Thunder Cave.* Hyperion, 1995.

LITERATURE CONNECTION

Kurtz, Jane. *Pulling the Lion's Tale.* Simon & Schuster, 1995.

Grimsdell, Jeremy. *Kalinzu: A Story From Africa.* Kingfisher, 1993.

Levitin, Sonia. *The Return.* Atheneum, 1987.

INTERDISCIPLINARY LINKS

Subject	Theme: Diversity
MATH	Middle Grades Math: Tools for Success Course 1, Lesson 1-7, **Analyzing Graphs**
SCIENCE	Prentice Hall Science *Ecology: Earth's Living Resources,* Chapter 3, **Exploring Earth's Biomes,** Lesson 4-1, **Identifying Problems**
LANGUAGE ARTS	Choices in Literature *Deciding What's Right,* **The Judgment of the Wind** Prentice Hall Literature *Bronze,* **The Magnificent Bull**

NATIONAL GEOGRAPHY STANDARDS

Students explore the 18 National Geography Standards throughout *Africa.* Chapter 6, however, concentrates on investigating the following standards: 1, 3, 4, 5, 6, 9, 11, 12, 13, 15, 16, 17, 18. For a complete list of the standards, see the *Teacher's Flexible Planning Guide.*

SCHOOL TO CAREERS

In Chapter 6, Exploring East Africa, students learn about the countries of Ethiopia, Tanzania, and Kenya. They also learn the skill of using isolines. Knowing about East Africa can help students prepare for careers in many fields such as politics, history, economics, education, business, and so on. Using isolines is a skill used in many careers, including weather forecasting, geology, travel planning, and others. The curriculum presented in this book, as in all eight titles of Prentice Hall's *World Explorer* program, is designed to prepare students not only for careers but also for good citizenship—of the world as well as of this country.

INTERNET ACCESS

Many social studies teachers and students use Internet browsers, or search engines, to investigate particular topics. For the best results, use narrow rather than broad topics. Try these for Chapter 6: Kenya, Dar es Salaam, Kikutu, Nairobis. Finding age-appropriate sites is an important consideration when using the Internet. For links to age-appropriate sites in world studies and geography, visit the Prentice Hall Home Page at:
http://www.phschool.com

Connecting to the Guiding Questions

As students complete this chapter, they will focus on the countries of Ethiopia, Tanzania, and Kenya. Content in this chapter corresponds to the following Guiding Questions:

● Why have many Africans been moving to cities in recent years?

● What factors influence the ways in which Africans make a living?

Using the Map Activities

As students work through the activity, suggest that they compare the political map with the physical maps shown in the Country Profiles of Ethiopia, Tanzania, and Kenya.

- Names may be related to physical or political features shown on the map.

- Access to waterways is important for trade and cultural and economic development.

Heterogeneous Groups

The following Teacher's Edition strategies are suitable for heterogeneous groups.

Critical Thinking
Recognizing Cause and Effect   p. 137

Cooperative Learning
Focus on Zanzibar   p. 144

Interdisciplinary Connections
Art   p. 152

CHAPTER 6

Exploring East Africa

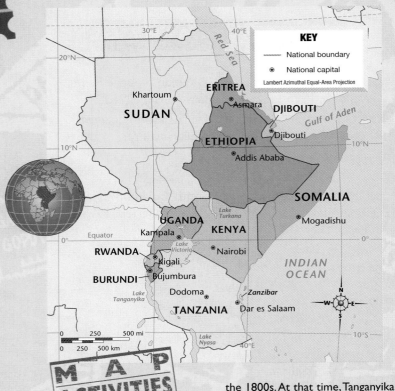

KEY
— National boundary
⊛ National capital
Lambert Azimuthal Equal-Area Projection

MAP ACTIVITIES

The borders of many East African countries were set by the Europeans who started colonies there. Borders often follow rivers and mountains. To get to know this region, do the following:

Rename a lake
Find Lake Victoria on the map. It was named after Queen Victoria of England, who ruled at the end of the 1800s. At that time, Tanganyika and Kenya were ruled by Great Britain. (Tanganyika later became part of the country of Tanzania.) Use features on the map or ideas of your own to help you rename the lake.

Consider location
The countries of East Africa are located between the Red Sea, the Gulf of Aden, and the Indian Ocean. How do you think East Africa's location might have affected its history and cultures?

Resource Directory

Media and Technology

Case Study: Ecotourism, from the World Video Explorer, enhances students' understanding of the ways in which East Africa, like countries worldwide, protects wildlife while benefiting from tourism.

Chapter 8

Ethiopia
CHURCHES AND MOSQUES

BEFORE YOU READ

Reach Into Your Background

Think about the subjects you study in school. Why is it important for you to be able to read and write? Why is it important for you to learn history and math? What might your life be like if you could not go to school? What kind of jobs could you do if you did not go to school?

Questions to Explore

1. What religions can be found in Ethiopia?

2. Why did Christianity in Ethiopia develop in a unique way?

Key Terms
monastery

Key Places
Lalibela
Addis Ababa

As a young boy, Iyasus Moa (ee YAH soos MOH uh) went to school and learned to read and write. But he dreamed of studying music and painting. He also wanted to learn another language, so Iyasus traveled to Tigray (TEE gray), in northern Ethiopia. He walked a distance that today would take three days to drive. Did he plan to enter a university in Tigray? No. The year was A.D. 1220, and there were no universities in Ethiopia. Iyasus entered a Christian **monastery.** This is a place where priests live, work, and study. A priest who lives in a monastery is called a monk.

Iyasus studied hard for many years. He became a monk. He also became a famous teacher and artist. His students built monasteries and schools all over the country.

Religions of Ethiopia

Iyasus Moa lived in Ethiopia, a country in East Africa. He studied Geez (gee EZ), one of the world's oldest languages. Geez is an ancient form of the language spoken by the Amhara, one of Ethiopia's larger ethnic groups. The Amhara were writing their language by 500 B.C. Ethiopia and

▼ The Debre Bizen monastery sits about 8,000 feet (2,438 m) up in the mountains of Eritrea, which was part of Ethiopia until 1993.

Teaching Resources

📁 **Reproducible Lesson Plan** in the Chapter and Section Resources booklet, p. 85, provides a summary of the section lesson.

📁 **Guided Reading and Review** in the Chapter and Section Resources booklet, p. 86, provides a structure for mastering key concepts and reviewing key terms in the section. Available in Spanish in the Spanish Chapter and Section Resources booklet, p. 53.

Program Resources

📁 Material in the **Primary Sources and Literature Readings** booklet extends content with a selection from the region under study.

📁 **Outline Maps** East and Southern Africa: Political, p. 35

Lesson Objectives

1️⃣ Describe how Christianity and Islam reached Ethiopia.

2️⃣ Compare and contrast rural and urban life in Ethiopia.

Lesson Plan

1 Engage
Warm-Up Activity

Display a large world map. Tell students that Ethiopia once included the present-day countries of Eritrea, Djibouti, and Somalia, and have students locate these countries and Ethiopia on the map. Have students identify some possible land or sea routes that people from surrounding regions or countries could have taken to travel to ancient Ethiopia.

Activating Prior Knowledge

Ask students to consider what they have learned since first grade. What skills do they have that first graders have not yet acquired? Then have students read Reach Into Your Background in the Before You Read box.

2 Explore

Have students read the section. Discuss with them the two main religions of Ethiopia. Ask students to consider the following questions as they read: How did Christianity spread to Ethiopia? How did Islam come to Ethiopia? How do the lives of rural Ethiopians differ from the lives of urban Ethiopians?

3 Teach

Have students write a five-question true-or-false quiz about the material covered in the section. Ask students to also make an answer key. For additional reinforcement, have students exchange quizzes. Alternately, you might read selected statements and have the class say whether each is true or false. This activity should take about 20 minutes.

4 Assess

See the answers to the Section Review. You may also use students' completed quizzes and answer keys as an assessment.

Acceptable quizzes contain five statements correctly identified as true or false.

Commendable quizzes include five statements derived from different topics and correctly identified as true or false.

Outstanding quizzes include five statements that reflect a grasp of key points and are correctly identified as true or false.

Answers to ...
MAP AND CHART STUDY

The highest elevations are in northwestern Ethiopia and the most rivers are in the west. The mountains of western Ethiopia make travel difficult. Islam and Christianity have the most followers.

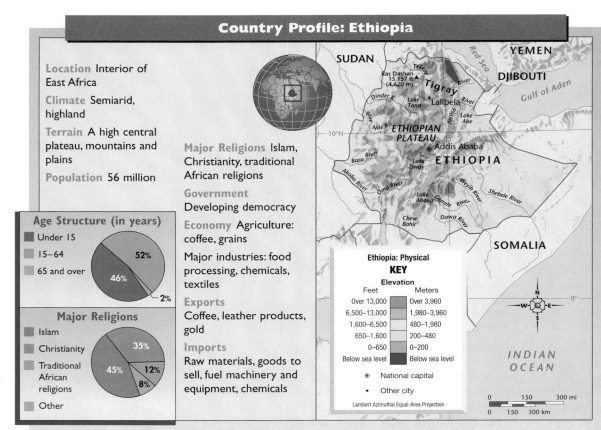

Country Profile: Ethiopia

Location Interior of East Africa

Climate Semiarid, highland

Terrain A high central plateau, mountains and plains

Population 56 million

Major Religions Islam, Christianity, traditional African religions

Government Developing democracy

Economy Agriculture: coffee, grains

Major industries: food processing, chemicals, textiles

Exports Coffee, leather products, gold

Imports Raw materials, goods to sell, fuel machinery and equipment, chemicals

Age Structure (in years)
- Under 15
- 15–64
- 65 and over

52%
46%
2%

Major Religions
- Islam
- Christianity
- Traditional African religions
- Other

35%
45%
12%
8%

Ethiopia: Physical
KEY

Elevation	
Feet	Meters
Over 13,000	Over 3,960
6,500–13,000	1,980–3,960
1,600–6,500	480–1,980
650–1,600	200–480
0–650	0–200
Below sea level	Below sea level

⊛ National capital
• Other city

Lambert Azimuthal Equal-Area Projection

0   150   300 mi
0   150   300 km

Map and Chart Study This map shows land elevation in Ethiopia. **Location** What area of Ethiopia has the highest elevations? **Place** Where are most of Ethiopia's rivers located? **Movement** What physical features might make it hard to travel between western and eastern Ethiopia? **Critical Thinking** Look at the graph of Ethiopia's major religions. What two religions have the most followers?

LINKS
ACROSS TIME

Church History The Egyptian Coptic Church was one of the first to leave the rest of the Christian Church. Later, the Christian Church divided even more. Today, there are many denominations, or types, of Christian churches.

Egypt are the only African countries that have a written history dating back to ancient times. Much of Ethiopia's history was preserved by monks like Iyasus, who copied books by hand.

The religion Iyasus studied was also very old. It had spread to Ethiopia along trade routes. Ethiopia was a center of trade. Look at the map in the Country Profile. Find the Nile River and the Red Sea. The main source of the Nile River is in Ethiopia's highlands. Ethiopia used to include the countries that today are Eritrea, Djibouti, and Somalia. These countries border the Red Sea. As people traded goods along the Nile River and the Red Sea, they also learned about each other's religions.

Ethiopian Christianity Alexandria, a city in Egypt, was one of the first centers of Christianity. Over time, Christians in Alexandria came to differ with Christians in Rome and Constantinople. In A.D. 451,

Resource Directory

Program Resources

Nystrom Desk Atlas

Media and Technology

Planet Earth CD-ROM includes an interactive political map of Ethiopia and thematic maps of Africa.

Material World CD-ROM includes a portrait of an Ethiopian family plus geographic data on Ethiopia.

Color Transparencies 73, Historical Map Set 2

Egyptian Christians separated from the rest of the Christian Church. They formed the Coptic Christian Church. Coptic Christianity slowly spread from Egypt to Ethiopia.

Ethiopian Christians were isolated from Christians in other parts of the world. Ethiopia's mountains made it hard for people in the interior to travel to other areas. Some people traveled along the Nile River and the Red Sea. With the spread of Islam, however, these travel routes were cut off to Ethiopian Christians.

Islam In the 600s, Arabs began to spread across North Africa. They brought their religion, Islam, with them. Muslim Arabs did not take over Ethiopia, but they moved into the areas around it. Over time, Arab traders built cities along trade routes. Eventually, Muslim Arabs came to control trade in the entire region. And, in time, some Ethiopians adopted the Muslim faith.

Christians and Muslims As Muslim Arabs took control of Ethiopia's coastal regions, Ethiopian Christians began moving inland. Finally, Christian Ethiopia was landlocked. It was surrounded by Muslim-controlled areas. As a result, Christians in Ethiopia had little contact with Christians elsewhere. The Ethiopian Christian Church developed into a unique form of Christianity. The Ethiopian Church still uses its own traditions and literary language, Geez.

Throughout Ethiopia's history, Christians and Muslims have sometimes fought over religious issues. They were at war with each other in the 1500s. But, for the most part, Christians and Muslims have lived together peacefully in Ethiopia. Today, about 35 percent of Ethiopians are Christians, and some 45 percent are Muslims. The rest practice traditional African religions.

READ ACTIVELY

Ask Questions What questions do you have about the spread of Islam to Ethiopia?

▼ Ethiopian Christians and Muslims both have histories that are rich in literature and education. The page at left is from the Quran and the page at right is from a hand-painted Christian document.

Activity

Critical Thinking

Recognizing Cause and Effect *Suitable as a whole class activity.* After students have read the segment entitled *Christians and Muslims,* write the following statements on the chalkboard:

1. Muslims took control of Ethiopia's coastal areas.

2. Christian Ethiopia was surrounded by Muslim-controlled areas.

Explain that each of these statements describes an event or a circumstance that caused other events or circumstances. Ask volunteers to identify one or more effects, or results, caused by the circumstances described in the above statements.

Background

Links Across Time

Ethiopia's Long History Ethiopia has suffered drought, famine, and civil war and is one of the poorest countries in the world. However, it holds a unique position in the history of the African continent. It has existed as an independent nation for some 2,000 years and, except for the brief occupation by Italy during World War II, has escaped subjugation by European countries.

SKILLS MINI LESSON

Interpreting Graphs
To **introduce** the skill, point out the two pie graphs in the Country Profile. Tell students that pie graphs are useful for comparing the parts of a whole. Have students **practice** interpreting pie graphs by asking them the following questions: (1) What age group makes up the smallest percentage of Ethiopia's population, and what is that percentage? (2) Which religion has the highest percentage of followers in Ethiopia? Which religion has the second highest? Allow students to **apply** the skill by using information from the graphs to draw some conclusions about Ethiopia. Ask: *What can you say about life expectancy in Ethiopia?* (Not many people live beyond 65, since that age grouping contains only 2 percent of the population.) *Is it likely that one religious group is more powerful than all the others?* (Possible answer: No. Christianity and Islam have roughly the same number of followers.)

Exploring Technology

The Churches of Lalibela

Tell students that the church shown here is known as Beit Giorgis, or the House of St. George. From bottom to top, the enormous cross-shaped church measures about 40 feet (12 m). Like the other 10 churches in Lalibela, Beit Giorgis was carved from solid granite. Granite is a very hard, durable rock and was a popular building material in the days before concrete and steel.

Workers used picks, chisels, and hatchets to carve the hard rock away. Point out to students that builders did all of this work by hand. You might bring in a piece of granite and some other types of rock (sandstone, limestone, quartz, or mica) for students to examine. Ask them to evaluate each as a possible building material. Ask: *Which would crumble easily? How difficult to chip or chisel would each be?* Then ask students to speculate on how long it would have taken workers to complete the 11 churches. *Note:* According to legend, workers (who were kindly assisted by angels) completed the churches in 20 years. Scholars estimate that the churches were built over a period of about 150 years.

Most churches are built from the bottom up. In the 1100s, however, Ethiopians carved 11 churches from the top down. Workers carved the roof first. They worked their way from the top of the church to the bottom. They always left enough rock in place so that they could stand on it and still reach the area, inside or outside, that they were carving. How might carving a church starting at the top be easier than starting at the bottom? How might it be harder?

Because the churches at Lalibela were underground, Ethiopian Christians were able to hide them from invaders by piling earth on the roofs.

Workers carved the roof, windows, and floors of each church on a slight incline, to allow the heavy summer rains to run off.

Each church is connected to other churches by underground passages carved out of rock.

Workers used hand tools to carve each church out of solid underground rock. Some churches took 150 years to complete.

Contrasting Ways of Life

Most Ethiopians, regardless of their religious background, live in rural areas. What is life like for rural Ethiopians? A look at the town of Lalibela (lah lih BEL uh) provides some clues.

Lalibela Lalibela was the capital of Christian Ethiopia for about 300 years. Rural Ethiopia also has many towns with Muslim shrines and tombs.

Services such as electricity and running water are rare in rural Ethiopia. No one in Lalibela has electricity or a telephone, and the town has only one car. The people who live around Lalibela make a living by farming. In some areas, people make a living by herding cattle or fishing. Some families specialize in jobs such as woodworking and beekeeping.

Addis Ababa Some 200 miles (322 km) south of Lalibela lies Ethiopia's capital city, Addis Ababa (ad uh SAB uh buh). It has all the conveniences of city life—running water, electricity, and modern hospitals. The city also has a more traditional, rural side. In some areas, houses are made not of concrete and stone, but of wood and dried mud. And some families still wash their clothes in the river, leaving them to dry on the riverbanks.

Addis Ababa's mix of modern and traditional ways of living illustrates the outlook of many Ethiopians. While expressing great pride in their past, they look toward the future with confidence.

A Growing City

The population of Addis Ababa is growing. New buildings are always being constructed. This one lies near the center of the city.

READ ACTIVELY

Connect How is your community a mix of old and new?

SECTION 1 REVIEW

1. **Define** monastery.
2. **Identify** (a) Lalibela, (b) Addis Ababa.
3. How did Ethiopia's geography affect its role in the ancient world?
4. Why did Christian beliefs in Ethiopia differ from those of Christians in the rest of the world?

Critical Thinking
5. **Making Comparisons** How is life in Ethiopia's rural areas different from life in Addis Ababa? How is life similar in both areas?

Activity
6. **Writing to Learn** Write a paragraph encouraging travelers to visit the historic churches of Ethiopia. In your paragraph, explain how the Ethiopian Christian Church has been affected by the country's history.

Resource Directory

Teaching Resources

📁 **Section Quiz** in the Chapter and Section Resources booklet, p. 87, covers the main ideas and key terms in the section. Available in Spanish in the Spanish Chapter and Section Resources booklet, p. 54.

Section 1 Review

1. a place where priests live, work, and study

2. (a) a famous rural town, once the capital of Christian Ethiopia (b) Ethiopia's capital

3. The Red Sea and Nile River were major trade routes; Ethiopia was a trade center.

4. The Ethiopian Christian Church developed a unique form of Christianity because Ethiopian Christians were surrounded by Muslim-controlled areas and had little contact with Christians elsewhere.

5. In rural areas, modern conveniences like electricity, running water, and cars are rare. Most people are farmers who use traditional methods. Addis Ababa has modern conveniences and services. The city has a rural side, however, where houses are made of wood and dried mud and people continue to live in a traditional way.

6. Students should describe the features of the Lalibela churches and point out that Ethiopian Christians, whose Christianity was derived from Egyptian Coptic Christianity, developed a unique form of the religion because they had little contact with other Christians.

Activity

Journal Writing

Tour of Lalibela Have students write about what they would like to see on a visit to Lalibela. Encourage them to describe specific sights and explain why those sights interest them. Ask them to write about how they might prepare themselves for visiting a city where there are no telephones or electricity.

Tanzania

WHEN PEOPLE COOPERATE

BEFORE YOU READ

Reach Into Your Background

Think about how you feel when things are about to change. Are you excited or nervous? Are you a little unsure about what the future might hold?

Questions to Explore

1. How is Tanzania's government changing?

2. What challenges have these changes produced?

Key Terms

lingua franca
foreign debt
multiparty system

Key People and Places

Julius Nyerere
Dar es Salaam
Zanzibar

▼ In October 1995, happy citizens rallied in Tanzania's capital, Dar es Salaam, as the country prepared to hold its first multiparty general elections.

In October 1995, the capital of Tanzania, Dar es Salaam, looked ready for a celebration. Flags hung from almost every building. Crowds of people chanted and sang in the streets. Why all this joy? Was it a special holiday? Had a Tanzanian sports team won a championship? Neither. An election was about to start. It would be the first election in over 30 years to include more than one political party. Finally, voters would have a real choice among candidates with differing views.

Tanzanians felt joyful, but they did not know what the future might hold. Their feelings were rooted in Tanzania's history.

Tanzania's History

Look at the map of Tanzania in the Country Profile. You can see that Tanzania lies on the Indian Ocean. Its location has made this area a center for trade. The people on the coast of East Africa traded with the ancient Greeks, Romans, Arabs, and Persians.

In the last 2,000 years, this part of East Africa has been ruled mostly by Arabs, who settled here, and by the Germans and the British, who did not. The British named the area Tanganyika. Tanganyika became independent in 1961. In 1964, it joined with the island of Zanzibar to form the nation of Tanzania.

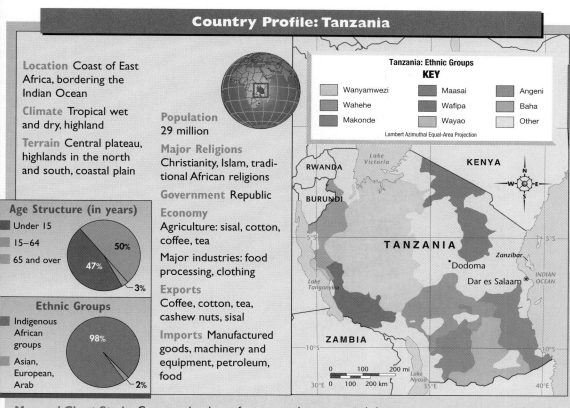

Country Profile: Tanzania

Location Coast of East Africa, bordering the Indian Ocean

Climate Tropical wet and dry, highland

Terrain Central plateau, highlands in the north and south, coastal plain

Population 29 million

Major Religions Christianity, Islam, traditional African religions

Government Republic

Economy Agriculture: sisal, cotton, coffee, tea

Major industries: food processing, clothing

Exports Coffee, cotton, tea, cashew nuts, sisal

Imports Manufactured goods, machinery and equipment, petroleum, food

Age Structure (in years)
- Under 15
- 15–64
- 65 and over

50%
47%
3%

Ethnic Groups
- Indigenous African groups
- Asian, European, Arab

98%
2%

Tanzania: Ethnic Groups
KEY
- Wanyamwezi
- Wahehe
- Makonde
- Maasai
- Wafipa
- Wayao
- Angeni
- Baha
- Other

Lambert Azimuthal Equal-Area Projection

Map and Chart Study Compare the chart of Tanzania's ethnic groups with the map. Although most Tanzanians are descended from Africans, they come from many different African ethnic groups. **Regions** Tanzania has two capitals because it is moving its capital from Dar es Salaam to Dodoma. Based on the distribution of ethnic groups, why do you think the government of Tanzania decided to move its capital?

Nyerere's Changes

When Tanzania became independent, most of its people were poor. Few were literate. Literacy is the ability to read and write. Tanzania's new president was Julius Nyerere. According to Nyerere, the new republic had serious problems:

> "We had 12 medical doctors in a population of 9 million. About 45 percent of children of school-going age were going to school, and 85 percent of the population was illiterate."

Nyerere also worried about keeping the peace among Tanzania's 120 ethnic groups. In many African nations, ethnic groups fought each other after independence. Nyerere wanted to make sure that would not happen in Tanzania.

CITIZEN HEROES

Working Together When Tanzania became independent, it did not have enough educated citizens to run the government. Many people had to moonlight, or work more than one job. For example, Amri Abedi was the mayor of Dar es Salaam, the leader of a regional government, and the Minister of Justice—all at the same time.

Program Resources

📁 **Outline Maps** East and Southern Africa: Political, p. 35

Media and Technology

💿 **Planet Earth** CD-ROM includes an interactive political map of Tanzania and thematic maps of Africa. Plus, it includes World Wonders, Natural: Serengeti, Tanzania.

📽 **Color Transparencies** 19, 20, 73

2 Explore

Have students read the section. Prompt discussion with questions such as these: What were the reasons behind such policies as the one-party political system and *ujamaa*? What improvements came about as a result of Nyerere's policies? Why did some of Nyerere's ideas fail? Why was the idea of a multiparty government a cause for celebration?

3 Teach

Ask students to make a chart with two headings: *One-Party System* and *Multiparty System*. Have students record the features, both positive and negative, of the two systems. This activity should take about 20 minutes.

4 Assess

See the answers to the Section Review. You may also use students' completed charts as an assessment.

Acceptable charts include two features in each column.

Commendable charts include three features in each column.

Outstanding charts include at least three features in each column and demonstrate an understanding that the multiparty system could lead to conflict among ethnic groups.

Answers to ...
MAP AND CHART STUDY

The government decided that Tanzania needed two capitals so that some ethnic groups would not have more access to the capital than others.

Links Across Place

Socialism The ideas set forth by Julius Nyerere were based, in part, on traditional African social systems, but his policies, on a nationwide scale, are recognized as socialism—a system in which land and industry are owned by the community, collectively. The first major socialist state was the Union of Soviet Socialist Republics (U.S.S.R.), formed as a result of the Russian Revolution of 1917. Although socialism in the U.S.S.R. lasted much longer than Nyerere's system, it also eventually failed.

Julius Nyerere—Tanzania's First Leader

After Julius Nyerere became Tanzania's first president, he also became famous for living simply. He drove a tiny compact car and would accept only a small salary. He now lives in a simple home on his family farm.

LINKS TO LANGUAGE ARTS

English and Swahili
Swahili is spoken as a lingua franca by people whose first languages are different. As a result, it contains words from several languages. English, too, contains words from several languages and is used as a lingua franca in some countries. Nyerere called English "the 'Swahili' of the world."

Swahili To help all the ethnic groups feel like part of one country, Nyerere made Swahili the national language. Swahili is a mix of Arab and African words. It is the language of East African trade. Swahili culture mixes African and Arab cultures. As a result, adopting Swahili as the national language made it less likely that the government would be controlled by just one ethnic group.

Many Tanzanians speak Swahili as a second language. It is the country's *lingua franca.* This means that Tanzanians can use it to talk to each other if they speak different first languages.

The One-Party System Nyerere also feared that political parties in Tanzania would be based on ethnic groups. Then, to win an election, a candidate from one party might promote hatred toward an ethnic group whose members belonged to another party. This had happened in other newly independent African nations.

To avoid this situation, Nyerere pushed to have only one political party. In Nyerere's one-party system, voters still chose from more than one candidate. But all the candidates were members of the same party.

Improving the Economy Next, Nyerere turned to the economy. He told Tanzanians that independence meant *uhuru na kazi* (oo HOO roo nah KAH zee)—"freedom and work." This was his way of saying that only hard work could end poverty. Nyerere said that Tanzania should be self-reliant and not depend on other nations.

One part of self-reliance was *ujamaa* (oo JAH mah), which is Swahili for "togetherness" or "being a family." Tanzania's economy is based on farming. Most Tanzanian farmers work on family homesteads. Nyerere asked these farmers to move to ujamaa villages. He knew that it would be easier for the government to provide clean water and education in a few locations, rather than in many scattered places. At first, many people volunteered to move to the villages. Later, many others were forced to move.

Nyerere's Successes and Failures Nyerere's social policies worked. He kept peace in Tanzania. He also greatly improved education. Nyerere was proud of his success. He commented:

Predict Do you think Nyerere's policies helped Tanzania? Why or why not?

> "When I stepped down, 91 percent of the adult population was literate, 100 percent of the children of schoolgoing age were going to school, not just for four years, but for seven years. We did not have enough engineers, but we had thousands of engineers trained by ourselves. We did not have enough doctors, but we had many more than twelve, we had thousands trained by ourselves. That is what we were able to do ourselves in a short period of independence."

Background

Global Perspectives

Kibbutzim A kibbutz is a collective farm in Israel. Land is rented for a small fee from the Jewish National Fund, and all property (except some personal items) is owned in common by the people who choose to live and work on the kibbutz. About 3 percent of Israel's population lives on kibbutzim. One of the main reasons the kibbutz system is successful is the desire of its members to live such a lifestyle.

An Ujamaa Village

The ujamaa villages were supposed to boost farm production. Communities could then sell their surplus produce. Some people, like the women hoeing corn above, were glad to take part in ujamaa. Many other Tanzanians, however, resisted leaving the small family farms where their ancestors were buried. In the long run, Tanzania ended the ujamaa program.

However, Nyerere's ujamaa program failed. Many farm families refused to live in ujamaa villages. They wanted to work their own land. Few crops were produced. Meanwhile, factories produced fewer products, and world prices for many of Tanzania's products fell. By the mid-1980s, the country was poorer than it had been at independence.

Tanzania Today

Nyerere retired in 1985. Now he works with leaders from other countries to study the challenges that face the continent. In 1996, he led an effort to stop a civil war in a nearby country, Burundi.

The End of Ujamaa After Nyerere left office, Tanzania's new leaders changed some of his unsuccessful programs. To begin with, they ended ujamaa. They also decided that farms should put more effort into producing cash crops to sell. They also asked foreign countries for more help. Tanzania is still very poor. It has a huge **foreign debt,** or money owed to foreign countries. But the economy is improving.

A Multiparty System Tanzania's new leaders also changed the election system. In 1992, the government started to allow new political parties to form. When a country has two or more political parties, it has a **multiparty system.** The first elections under the multiparty system were held in October 1995. Members of more than 10 parties

Connect How are elections in the United States like elections in Tanzania today?

A Cash Crop That Smells Sweet

Tanzania's island of Zanzibar is the biggest producer of cloves in the world. People use cloves as a spice. A clove tree must grow for five years before it will begin to flower (right). When it does, farmers pick the buds by hand before the flowers open. They dry the cloves in the sun until they turn dark brown (below).

▲ New farming methods and seeds are helping some Tanzanian farmers to grow more than they could in the past. Changes like these are helping to improve Tanzania's economy.

ran for office. In the end, Nyerere's party won the most votes. But the election raised some issues that divided people. For example, one party suggested that Zanzibar should leave the union with Tanzania. This is exactly what Nyerere worried about.

As Tanzania's leaders face new challenges, they may keep in mind Nyerere's words: "There is a time for planting and a time for harvesting. I am afraid for us it is still a time for planting."

SECTION 2 REVIEW

1. **Define** (a) lingua franca, (b) foreign debt, (c) multiparty system.

2. **Identify** (a) Julius Nyerere, (b) Dar es Salaam, (c) Zanzibar.

3. What changes did Julius Nyerere bring to Tanzania?

4. What challenges faced Tanzania in the 1990s?

Critical Thinking

5. **Identifying Central Issues** Why did Julius Nyerere want a one-party system? Do you think he was right? Why or why not?

Activity

6. **Writing to Learn** How does Nyerere's slogan, "uhuru na kazi," or freedom and work, apply to the kind of independence that comes from growing up? Write a paragraph explaining how you have experienced uhuru na kazi as you have grown older.

Teaching Resources

📁 **Section Quiz** in the Chapter and Section Resources booklet, p. 90, covers the main ideas and key terms in the section. Available in Spanish in the Spanish Chapter and Section Resources booklet, p. 56.

Section 2 Review

1. (a) the ability to read and write (b) a language that is a mix of Arab and African words (c) money owed to foreign countries

2. (a) the first president of Tanzania (b) the capital of Tanzania (c) an island that in 1964 joined Tanganyika to form the nation of Tanzania

3. Nyerere made Swahili the national language, instituted a one-party system, asked farmers to move to ujamaa villages, and improved education and literacy.

4. huge foreign debt; issues that divide the nation, such as one party's suggestion that Zanzibar should leave the union

5. Students will probably suggest that Nyerere wanted to prevent ethnic strife. They may agree or disagree about the effectiveness of the one-party system, but they should base their opinions on facts.

6. Paragraphs will vary. Students may say that as they have grown older, they have worked more independently to complete schoolwork assignments and household tasks and relied less upon adult supervision.

SKILLS ACTIVITY

Using Isolines to Show Elevation

Lesson Objectives

1 Explain the purpose of isolines on a contour map.

2 Visualize the contours of land by reading an isoline map.

Lesson Plan

1 Engage

Warm-Up Activity

Write the term *isoline* on the chalkboard. Then invite two volunteers to **introduce** the skill by reading the opening dialogue.

Activating Prior Knowledge

Ask students to define and describe a contour map. Have them locate an example in a book or draw one on a sheet of paper.

2 Explore

Read the *Get Ready* text aloud. Then write the definition of *isoline* on the chalkboard under the term. Have students trace the isolines shown on the Mt. Kenya contour map as you read aloud the term's definition. Help students understand that every area through which an isoline is drawn has the same elevation. Urge students to trace the isolines as they compare them to the pictured landforms. Explain that more isolines are shown in steeper areas because the elevation is changing rapidly. Then direct students to finish reading the activity.

"**W**hat on Earth is this?"

Alicia stared at the map. She could not imagine the purpose of the strange lines she was looking at.

"Those are isolines," her teacher, Ms. Washington, answered. "And they are not really on Earth. They are imaginary lines that people draw on maps. Think about the borders of countries. You can't see borders in the real world—there are no big, painted lines on the ground. Isolines are like that. They exist only on maps, to show information."

"Okay," Alicia said. "What do they show?"

"These isolines show elevation. By understanding isolines, you can make a flat map stand up! Let me show you how to figure them out."

Get Ready

Ms. Washington is right. Isolines do make flat maps stand up, in a way. How? Start with the word *isolines* itself. It comes from the Greek word *iso,* which means "equal," and the English word *lines*. Isolines outline equal parts of a map. When isolines are used to show elevation, they outline different parts of the map at the same elevation. Isolines that show elevation are also called contour lines because their pattern shows the contour, or shape, of the land. If you understand how to read isolines, you can see a two-dimensional map in three dimensions!

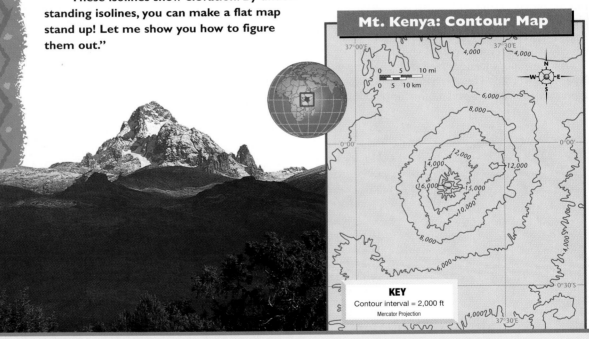

Mt. Kenya: Contour Map

KEY
Contour interval = 2,000 ft
Mercator Projection

Resource Directory

Teaching Resources

Understanding Isolines in the Social Studies and Geography Skills booklet, p. 29, provides additional skill practice.

Reading a Contour Map in the Social Studies and Geography Skills booklet, p. 30, provides additional skill practice.

Look at the opposite page. The picture on the left shows how a landform looks from the side. To the right, the landform is represented by isolines. Do you see how they match? Where the land is steeper, the isolines are closer together. Where the land is flatter, the isolines are farther apart.

Try It Out

You can learn to read isolines by playing a game. All you need are notecards, pens, and a partner.

A. Deal the cards. Deal six notecards to your partner and six to yourself.

B. Draw landforms. You and your partner should each draw a profile, or sideways view, of an imaginary landform on each of your cards.

C. Draw isolines. Now, on your remaining three cards, you and your partner should each draw isolines that represent different imaginary landforms, one per card. The isolines can be any shape you want.

D. Trade Cards. Work with your partner's cards. Draw a profile of the landform based on your partner's isolines, and isolines based on your partner's landforms. When you have finished, check each other's work.

Apply the Skill

The map on this page shows isolines of Ethiopia. Use the map to complete the steps that follow, and try to visualize the contour of the land of Ethiopia.

1 **Remember that isolines connect places of equal elevation.** The isolines on this map are labeled to show elevation. What is the lowest elevation in Ethiopia? What is the highest? What is the difference between each pair of isolines?

2 **Use the isolines to get an idea of landscape.** How would you describe the Ethiopian landscape—hilly, mountainous, flat? Where are the highest parts of the country? Which part of the country is the most rugged?

3 **Use isolines to find the elevation near bodies of water.** Look at the isolines around Lake Tana and Ethiopia's other bodies of water. Which is on higher land, Lake Tana or the rivers in the southeastern part of Ethiopia?

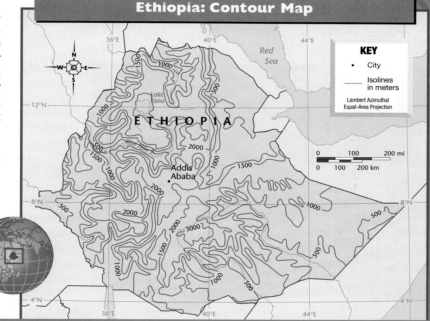

Ethiopia: Contour Map

KEY
- City
— Isolines in meters

Lambert Azimuthal Equal-Area Projection

0   100   200 mi
0   100   200 km

3 Teach

Encourage student pairs to **practice** by playing the *Try It Out* game. You may want to demonstrate one round of the game. Check on pairs as they play to assess understanding. Invite pairs to post their completed cards on the bulletin board for class review and discussion.

For additional reinforcement, have students describe what an isoline map of the area around your community would look like. Would the isolines be close together or far apart?

4 Assess

Students may **apply** the skill by completing the final activity section and answering the questions. You may **assess** by evaluating the accuracy of students' answers to the text questions.

1. Identify the ways people make their livings in rural areas of Kenya.

2. Describe why Kenyans are moving to cities.

3. Explain how people who have moved to the city maintain family ties.

1 Engage

Warm-Up Activity

Ask students to think of ways in which groups sometimes "pull together" to achieve a common goal such as organizing a neighborhood cleanup or raising funds for a charitable purpose. Record students' ideas on the board. Then ask why teamwork and organization are necessary for these activities to be successful.

Activating Prior Knowledge

Have students read Reach Into Your Background in the Before You Read box. Then ask them to consider how they would stay in contact with people if they did not have telephones or computers.

2 Explore

Have students read the section and then discuss questions such as the following: What are the features of rural and urban life in Kenya? What is *harambee*, and what are some examples of it? What kinds of work do women do? Why do men leave their families to find work in Nairobi?

Kenya

SKYSCRAPERS IN THE SAVANNA

BEFORE YOU READ

Reach Into Your Background

How do you stay in touch with friends and family members after one of you moves? How do you cope with feeling homesick when you are away from home?

Questions to Explore

1. How do Kenyans who move to Nairobi from rural areas maintain ties to their homes and families?

2. Why do many more Kenyan men than women move from the country to the city?

Key Terms

harambee

Key People and Places

Jomo Kenyatta
Mount Kenya
Nairobi

▼ This series of buildings is called a shamba. It was built by members of Kenya's Kikuyu ethnic group. The whole shamba is considered the family home.

"Where is your *shamba*?" This is a question that two Kenyans usually ask each other when they first meet. A shamba is a small farm owned and run by a Kenyan family. Even Kenyans who live in the city think of the piece of land where they were born as home. They return to it throughout their lives. Land is very important to Kenyans.

Kenya's Geography and People

Kenya is a country in central East Africa. Mount Kenya, Kenya's highest mountain, lies just south of the Equator. But its twin peaks are covered with snow all year. Find Mount Kenya in the Country Profile map. Southwest of Mount Kenya is a region of highlands. This region has a high elevation. Its average temperature is 67°F (19°C). The area also gets plenty of rain, so the land is good for farming. Most of Kenya's people are farmers, and they live in shambas dotting the countryside in the highlands.

Teaching Resources

📁 **Reproducible Lesson Plan** in the Chapter and Section Resources booklet, p. 91, provides a summary of the section lesson.

📁 **Guided Reading and Review** in the Chapter and Section Resources booklet, p. 92, provides a structure for mastering key concepts and reviewing key terms in the section. Available in Spanish in the Spanish Chapter and Section Resources booklet, p. 57.

Program Resources

📁 **Outline Maps** Africa South of the Sahara: Physical, p. 32
East and Southern Africa: Political, p. 35

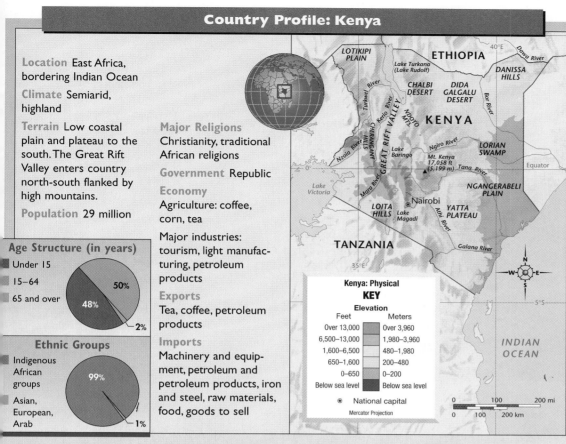

Country Profile: Kenya

Location East Africa, bordering Indian Ocean

Climate Semiarid, highland

Terrain Low coastal plain and plateau to the south. The Great Rift Valley enters country north-south flanked by high mountains.

Population 29 million

Major Religions Christianity, traditional African religions

Government Republic

Economy Agriculture: coffee, corn, tea

Major industries: tourism, light manufacturing, petroleum products

Exports Tea, coffee, petroleum products

Imports Machinery and equipment, petroleum and petroleum products, iron and steel, raw materials, food, goods to sell

Age Structure (in years)

- Under 15
- 15–64
- 65 and over

50%
48%
2%

Ethnic Groups

- Indigenous African groups
- Asian, European, Arab

99%
1%

Kenya: Physical
KEY
Elevation

Feet	Meters
Over 13,000	Over 3,960
6,500–13,000	1,980–3,960
1,600–6,500	480–1,980
650–1,600	200–480
0–650	0–200
Below sea level	Below sea level

⊛ National capital

Mercator Projection

0   100   200 mi
0   100   200 km

Map and Chart Study This map shows land elevation in Kenya. **Location** What areas of Kenya have the highest elevation? **Interaction** Look at the information about Kenya's economy. What parts of the country might be suited to agriculture? **Critical Thinking** Look at the chart showing the age structure of Kenya's population. If you had to guess, what percentage of people in your community would you say are under age 15? How is your community similar to or different from Kenya?

The land near the coast is warmer than the highlands, but the area also has good farmland. Farther inland, plains stretch across Kenya. Here there is little rainfall. Because of this lack of rain, the plains support only bushes, small trees, and grasses. North of the plains lie deserts, where the temperature can sometimes climb as high as 135°F (57°C).

The Diversity of Kenya's People   Nearly all of Kenya's people are indigenous Africans. A few of Kenya's people are of European or Asian descent. Kenyans belong to more than 40 different ethnic groups. Each group has its own culture and language. Most Kenyans are Christian or Muslim.

Media and Technology

Color Transparencies 4, 19, 24, 51, 52, 73, 93, 151, 159

Planet Earth CD-ROM includes an interactive political map of Kenya as well as thematic maps of Africa.

3 Teach

Have students begin two concept webs. They should label one web *Females* and the other *Males*. Encourage students to suggest words or phrases that describe differences and similarities between the ways men and women in Kenya live. Aspects common to both sexes can be connected to both webs. This activity should take about 25 minutes.

4 Assess

See the answers to the Section Review. You may also use students' completed webs as an assessment.

Acceptable webs identify three unique facts each for males and females and three they share.

Commendable webs identify four unique facts each for males and females and three they share.

Outstanding webs identify more than four unique facts each for males and females and more than three they share.

Answers to ...
MAP AND CHART STUDY

The western part of Kenya has the highest elevations. You might explain to students that Kenya's highland region in the southwestern part of the country is the chief farming region. Tea and coffee are some of the main crops grown in the highlands. Students' answers to comparisons of their community with Kenya will vary.

Daily Life

The Samburu Although the vast majority of rural Kenyans are farmers, a small percentage continues to live as nomadic herders. About 70,000 members of the Samburu ethnic group continue to live much as their ancestors did. The Samburu herd cattle, sheep, and goats in northern Kenya. Milk is their main food, but they also augment their diets with the protein-rich blood of their herds. The semidesert land limits farming, but on the Lorogi Plateau and in the Karisia Hills, some Samburu grow small crops of sorghum, corn, and vegetables.

A Typical Day for Young Kenyans

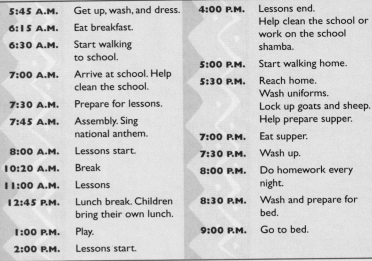

Time	Activity	Time	Activity
5:45 A.M.	Get up, wash, and dress.	4:00 P.M.	Lessons end. Help clean the school or work on the school shamba.
6:15 A.M.	Eat breakfast.		
6:30 A.M.	Start walking to school.	5:00 P.M.	Start walking home.
7:00 A.M.	Arrive at school. Help clean the school.	5:30 P.M.	Reach home. Wash uniforms. Lock up goats and sheep. Help prepare supper.
7:30 A.M.	Prepare for lessons.		
7:45 A.M.	Assembly. Sing national anthem.	7:00 P.M.	Eat supper.
8:00 A.M.	Lessons start.	7:30 P.M.	Wash up.
10:20 A.M.	Break	8:00 P.M.	Do homework every night.
11:00 A.M.	Lessons		
12:45 P.M.	Lunch break. Children bring their own lunch.	8:30 P.M.	Wash and prepare for bed.
1:00 P.M.	Play.	9:00 P.M.	Go to bed.
2:00 P.M.	Lessons start.		

Chart Study Like you, Kenyan children spend most of each day in school. **Critical Thinking** Compare your schedule with this one. How would your day be different if you lived in Kenya? How would it be similar?

LINKS ACROSS THE WORLD

Running from Kenya to Boston Kenyan runners work together to train for athletic events—and it pays off. Kenyan runners won the Boston Marathon four times in a row, from 1992 to 1995. In 1995, they placed first, second, and third. And Kenyan athletes have won numerous Olympic medals. No one is sure why Kenyan runners are so good at their sport, but some people think that training in Kenya's high elevations gives runners more endurance.

Despite the differences among Kenya's people, they have many things in common. As much as they value the land, Kenyans also value their families. Many families have six or more children. People also consider their cousins to be almost like brothers and sisters. An uncle may be called "my other father."

Harambee—Working Together After Kenya gained independence in 1963, the new president, Jomo Kenyatta (JOH moh ken YAH tuh), began a campaign he called *harambee* (hah RAHM bay). The word is Swahili for "let's pull together." One example of harambee is Kenyatta's approach to education. The government pays for some of a child's education, but not all of it. As a result, in many villages, the people have worked together to build and support schools.

Rural Kenya

The people who live in the rural areas of Kenya are farmers. Most of Kenya's farmers, like farmers all over Africa, are women. They grow fruits and vegetables to eat. They also herd livestock. Men also farm, but they usually raise cash crops, such as coffee and tea. Some women also grow cash crops.

Farming in the Highlands The Kikuyu (ki KOO yoo) are Kenya's largest ethnic group. Many Kikuyu live in shambas on the highlands near Mount Kenya. They build round homes with mud walls and thatched roofs. The Kikuyu grow food and cash crops such as coffee and sisal, which is used to make rope.

Children in a farming village have more responsibilities than most children in the United States. They may begin their day by carrying water from a stream to the village. They milk the cattle or goats and clean their homes before going to school. For fun, Kenyan boys play soccer, and the girls play dodgeball. Kenyan children also make toy cars, dolls, and other toys. Occasionally, someone will bring a truck with a generator, a film projector, and a screen to the village, and the people will enjoy a movie. To see what a typical day is like for a Kenyan child, look at the schedule on the previous page.

Moving to the City

The way of life of many Kenyans is changing. As the population increases, many men and some women are moving to the city to find work. Most women and children, however, stay in the rural areas. Women are the primary caretakers for children, and it is expensive for women with children to move from the country to the city. Many find it easier to support their families by farming.

READ ACTIVELY

Visualize Kenyan children spend about half an hour walking to school in the morning. Visualize the scenes they might see on their way to school.

A Nairobi Street Scene

Residents enjoy a stroll in downtown Nairobi, the largest city in East Africa. Nairobi is East Africa's most important business center. Many products are manufactured here. Tourists frequently come to Kenya to visit Nairobi National Park. In addition, much of East African banking and trade is centered in Nairobi. Because Nairobi is a thriving city, many Kenyans come here looking for jobs. **Critical Thinking** What in the picture looks familiar to you? What, if anything, looks unfamiliar?

Background

Biography

Ngugi wa Thiong'o (1938–) Kenya's best-known writer, Ngugi wa Thiong'o, was born into a Kikuyu community in the highlands of Kenya. He attended a colonial school and earned degrees from universities in Uganda and Great Britain. In 1964, he wrote his first novel, *Weep Not, Child*. Though Ngugi wrote in English, the novel tells the story of a Kikuyu family during Kenya's struggle for independence. In his other works, he often deals with the social, moral, and racial issues that confront a young nation. After 1977, Ngugi began publishing works in Swahili or in his native Kikuyu language. This made his writing much more accessible to most Kenyans. Whether writing in English, Swahili, or Kikuyu, however, Ngugi's novels and plays have always been part of the African tradition that calls upon the power of literature to combat injustice.

Teaching Resources

📁 **Section Quiz** in the Chapter and Section Resources booklet, p. 93, covers the main ideas and key terms in the section. Available in Spanish in the Spanish Chapter and Section Resources booklet, p. 58.

📁 **Vocabulary** in the Chapter and Section Resources booklet, p. 95, provides a review of key terms in the chapter. Available in Spanish in the Spanish Chapter and Section Resources booklet, p. 60.

📁 **Reteaching** in the Chapter and Section Resources booklet, p. 96, provides a structure for students who may need additional help in mastering chapter content.

Program Resources

Environmental and Global Issues Topic: Urbanization, pp. 54–58

Answers to . . .

A NAIROBI STREET SCENE

Answers will vary.

Activity

Interdisciplinary Connections

Art The Maasai are well known for the beautiful beaded jewelry they make. Organize students into two or three large groups to make a collection of Maasai jewelry. Show students photographs of the Maasai for guidance. Provide each group with wire and colored beads. Students may make necklaces, bracelets, headbands, or earrings. *English Language Learner, Kinesthetic*

Nairobi: Kenya's Capital City Every day, people arrive in Nairobi (ny ROH bee) by train, bus, or *matatu* (muh TAH too)—a minibus. They are new residents of the city. Nairobi's population grew from one million in 1985 to three million in 1995, making it bigger than the city of Chicago in the United States. By the year 2000, the city is expected to have more than four million residents. Many of Nairobi's newcomers walk to their jobs in the city from the outskirts of town. They may walk as far as 10 miles to work, because they cannot afford the few cents that it costs to take the bus.

When men move to Nairobi without their families, they often feel homesick for their loved ones in rural villages. Meanwhile, the women who are left behind in the villages must do twice as much work. Many people in Kenya have responded to this situation in the spirit of harambee—working together.

Women's Self-Help Groups One of the best examples of harambee in rural Kenya are women's self-help groups. Women in rural areas all over Kenya have formed these groups to solve problems in their communities. The women grow cash crops in addition to the crops they grow for their families to eat. Then they sell the cash crops and save the money as a group. The women meet to decide what to do with the money they have saved.

Matatu Ride

Ian Kamau
Age 16
Kenya

Look carefully at the painting. Notice that, like the British, Kenyans drive on the left side of the road and have their steering wheels on the right side of vehicles. That's because Kenya used to be a colony of Great Britain. **Critical Thinking** This matatu is bound for Nairobi. Do you think the artist considers a visit to Nairobi a happy event? Why or why not?

Answers to ...
MATATU RIDE

Accept all thoughtful responses.

Resource Directory

Teaching Resources

Enrichment in the Chapter and Section Resources booklet, p. 97, extends chapter content and enriches students' understanding.

Spanish Glossary in the Spanish Chapter and Section Resources, pp. 68–72, provides key terms translated from English to Spanish as well as definitions in Spanish.

Chapter Summary in the Chapter and Section Resources booklet, p. 94, provides a summary of chapter content. Available in Spanish in the Spanish Chapter and Section Resources booklet, p. 58.

Cooperative Learning Activity in the Activities and Projects booklet, pp. 37–40, provides two student handouts, one page of teacher's directions, and a scoring rubric for a cooperative learning activity on making a relief map.

Media and Technology

Guided Reading Audiotapes (English and Spanish)

In Mitero, a village in the mountains north of Nairobi, Kikuyu women's groups have built a nursery school and installed water pipes for the community. They also loan money to women who want to start small businesses. Sometimes they give money to women who need to buy such things as a cow or a water tank. They also save money individually and use it to educate their children.

However, it is not easy to grow cash crops, grow vegetables for the family, chop firewood, haul water, and take care of children all in one day. One woman commented, "My children were educated through the sweat of my brow."

Men in the City Men who move to the city also work hard. Many are saving money to buy land in the countryside. Men in Nairobi who are from the same ethnic group often welcome each other, share rooms, and help each other.

Moses Mpoke (MOH zuz uhm POHK ay) is a Maasai. The Maasai of Kenya traditionally make a living farming and herding. Mpoke finished high school and now works in Nairobi. He has land in his home village. But the land is too dry for farming, and he could not move his livestock to find good grazing. He left the village to find work.

Now Mpoke is a filing clerk in the city. Mpoke lives outside the city, where he shares a room with two other Maasai. Their friendship makes his life in the city bearable. Like Mpoke, most newcomers to the city are made welcome by relatives or other members of their ethnic group.

Every weekend, Mpoke returns to his village to see his family and friends. Once, as Mpoke sat in his village home, a visitor asked him which was the real Moses Mpoke, the one in the city or the one in the village. He answered:

"This is the real Moses Mpoke, but the other is also me. In the week, I can live in the city and be comfortable. At weekends, I can live here and be comfortable. The city has not stopped me from being a Maasai."

SECTION 3 REVIEW

1. Define harambee.

2. Identify (a) Jomo Kenyatta, (b) Mount Kenya, (c) Nairobi.

3. Describe the daily life of a child in a rural Kenyan village.

4. Why do so many Kenyan men move to Nairobi?

Critical Thinking

5. Expressing Problems Clearly How are women in rural villages affected when men move to the city?

Activity

6. Writing to Learn Describe an example of harambee in your community.

Drawing Conclusions
To **introduce** the skill, explain that when people draw a conclusion they are making an educated guess, which is based upon available clues and knowledge they already have. Tell students that they may **practice** drawing some conclusions about life in Nairobi as they read the text under the heading *Nairobi: Kenya's Capital City.* Have students look for clues about the size of the population and the distance people travel to get to work and to relate the clues to what they already know about cities. Then ask students to **apply** the skill by writing a short paragraph about what challenges Nairobi will probably need to address in the early 2000s. (Students may conclude that Nairobi will need to build new housing and roads and may need to expand its public transportation system. The country might also need to find ways to provide social services to a large and fairly poor population.)

CHAPTER 6 Review and Activities

Reviewing Main Ideas

1. The main religions are Islam and Christianity. Traders from Egypt brought Christianity to Ethiopia. Islam came to Ethiopia when Islamic Arabs began to conquer North Africa.

2. Urban Ethiopians enjoy conveniences such as running water and electricity. Rural Ethiopians usually make their livings as farmers. Running water and electricity are rare in rural areas.

3. Students may say that Nyerere achieved some of his goals such as increased literacy. Other programs such as the ujamaa collective farms failed.

4. The purpose of an ujamaa village was to provide a setting where people could work together. It was also easier to provide government services to people when they lived in centralized villages.

5. Men are separated from their homes and families and often become homesick. Women have to raise the children and do all of the day-to-day work a household requires.

6. In rural Kenya, some women work together to grow cash crops. They pool the money they earn and use it for projects that will benefit the community.

Reviewing Key Terms

1. harambee

2. true

3. monastery

4. literacy

Critical Thinking

1. In a country where there are many ethnic groups, having only one party might help avoid alignments and divisions along ethnic lines. A multiparty system allows people freedom of choice and makes the election process more democratic.

2. When Muslim Arabs took control of Ethiopia's coastal regions, Ethiopian Christians began moving inland so they could practice their faith without interference. They moved into a landlocked area where they had little contact with Christians elsewhere.

Reviewing Main Ideas

1. What are the main religions in Ethiopia? How did they get there?

2. Compare life in Ethiopia's cities with life in its rural communities.

3. Did Nyerere's one-party system achieve its goals? Why or why not?

4. Explain the purpose of an ujamaa village.

5. How do men's and women's lives change when men move to Nairobi?

6. How are Kenyans in rural areas working together to improve their lives?

Reviewing Key Terms

Decide whether each statement is true or false. If it is true, write "true." If it is false, change the underlined term to make the statement true.

1. The Swahili word that means "let's pull together" is <u>shamba</u>.

2. Tanzania owes a huge <u>foreign debt</u> to other countries.

3. A building where priests live and work is a <u>multiparty system</u>.

4. People who speak different languages often communicate by speaking a <u>lingua franca</u>.

5. A country with two or more political parties has a <u>harambee</u>.

Critical Thinking

1. Making Comparisons What do you think would be the advantages of a one-party political system? What would be the advantages of a multiparty political system?

2. Recognizing Cause and Effect How did the spread of Islam cause Ethiopian Christians to become more isolated?

Graphic Organizer

Copy the web onto a sheet of paper. Then complete the web by filling in the empty circles with the ways that President Nyerere planned to help Tanzania to be self-reliant.

Self-reliance in Tanzania

Graphic Organizer

Students completed webs may vary slightly.

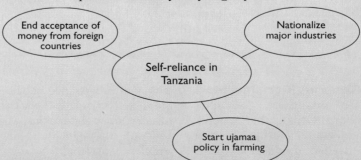

Map Activity

East Africa
For each place listed below, write the letter from the map that shows its location.

1. Ethiopia
2. Nairobi
3. Tanzania
4. Dar es Salaam
5. Zanzibar
6. Kenya
7. Addis Ababa
8. Lalibela

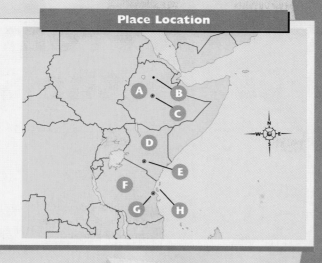

Place Location

Writing Activity

Writing a Newspaper Opinion Article
Think about your community. Is it growing or getting smaller? Hypothesize about why your community has developed in the way that it has. Is it developing in a way that benefits its citizens? What are some good things about the change in growth in your community? What are some bad things? Write a newspaper opinion article explaining your view.

Skills Review

Turn to the Skills Activity.
Review the steps for using isolines. Then complete the following: (a) Explain what information you can discover by using the isolines on a map. (b) How are isolines used on water maps?

Internet Activity
Use a search engine to find **AfricaOnline.** Choose **Kids Only** and then choose **Learn About Africa.** Click on the **Land** icon. Click **Next** two times to get to the **Cities** page. Take an on-line quiz about African cities. Then click **Next** to learn about Kenya. Compare and contrast the top 10 things kids do in Kenya with what kids do in your city or town.

How Am I Doing?

Answer these questions to check your progress.

1. Can I identify the main religions of Ethiopia?
2. Can I explain some of the ways Tanzania's government has changed in recent years?
3. Do I understand why men in Kenya are moving to the cities? Can I explain how their move affects people throughout the country?
4. What information from this chapter can I use in my book project?

Internet Activity

If students are having difficulty finding this site, you may wish to have them use the following URL, which was accurate at the time this textbook was published:

   http://www.africaonline.com/

You might also guide students to a search engine. Four of the most useful are Infoseek, Alta Vista, Lycos, and Yahoo. For additional suggestions on using the Internet, refer to the Prentice Hall Social Studies, Educator's Handbook "Using the Internet," in the *Prentice Hall World Explorer Program Resources.*

For additional links to world history and culture topics, visit the Prentice Hall Home Page at:
   http://www.phschool.com

How Am I Doing?

Point out to students that this checklist is a quick reminder for them of what they learned in the chapter. If their answer is *no* to any of the questions or if they are unsure, they may need to review the topic.

Map Activity

1. A	4. G	7. C
2. E	5. H	8. B
3. F	6. D	

Writing Activity

Students' articles will vary, but should provide well-supported opinions concerning the advantages and disadvantages of either a decrease or an increase in a community's population.

Skills Review

(a) They show elevation and which parts of a landscape are hilly, mountainous, or flat.
(b) to show the elevation of the surface of a body of water

Resource Directory

Teaching Resources

Chapter Tests Forms A and B are in the Tests booklet, pp. 32–37.

Program Resources

Writing Process Handbook includes Using Transitions, p. 30, to help students with the Writing Activity.

Media and Technology

Color Transparencies
Color Transparency 171
(Graphic organizer web template)
Prentice Hall Writer's Solution
Writing Lab CD-ROM
Computer Test Bank

Resource Pro™ CD-ROM

1. Identify the message in an East African fable.

2. Analyze a fable to learn about the culture of its origin.

1 Engage

Building Vocabulary

Point out that notes in the margin can help students understand certain words and can give helpful hints as students read. The vocabulary terms defined in the margin are *maize, shrivel, wilt, withered, horizon, throb, shriek, venture,* and *embrace.* Before reading, you might ask students to take turns reading aloud the definitions of the listed words. Other students can then suggest sentences containing each vocabulary word.

Activating Prior Knowledge

When students have read the text under *Before You Read,* ask them to describe the importance of a promise. Challenge students to consider both promises between people and promises among nations.

2 Develop Student Reading

Direct students to read the story. Encourage students to note answers to the *Questions to Explore* as they read.

A Promise to the Sun

BY TOLOLWA M. MOLLEL

BEFORE YOU READ

Reach Into Your Background

What does a promise mean to you? Have you ever made a promise that you later discovered you could not keep?

Promises are famous around the world for being easy to make but hard to keep. Making a promise is a serious matter, because a person who accepts a promise trusts that it will be kept. In most cultures, breaking a promise is the same as betraying a person's trust. This Maasai story from East Africa is about just such a broken promise.

Questions to Explore

1. What can you learn from this story about how people in East Africa make a living?
2. What does this story tell you about the values of the Maasai people?

maize *n.:* a type of corn
shrivel *v.:* to wrinkle as moisture is lost
wilt *v.:* to droop
withered *adj.:* shriveled and shrunken from drying out

Long ago, when the world was new, a severe drought hit the land of the birds. The savannah turned brown, and streams dried up. Maize plants died, and banana trees shriveled in the sun, their broad leaves wilting away. Even the nearby forest grew withered and pale.

The birds held a meeting and decided to send someone in search of rain. They drew lots to choose who would go on the journey. And they told the Bat, their distant cousin who was visiting, that she must draw, too. "You might not be a bird," they said, "but for now you're one of us."

Everyone took a lot, and as luck would have it, the task fell to the Bat.

Over the trees and the mountains flew the Bat, to the Moon. There she cried, "Earth has no rain, Earth has no food, Earth asks for rain!"

The Moon smiled. "I can't bring rain. My task is to wash and oil the night's face. But you can try the Stars."

On flew the Bat, until she found the Stars at play. "Away with you!" they snapped, angry at being interrupted. "If you want rain, go to the Clouds!"

The Clouds were asleep but awoke at the sound of the Bat

Program Resources

Material in the **Primary Sources and Literature Readings** booklet provides additional literature selections on the region under study.

arriving. "We can bring rain," they yawned, "but the Winds must first blow us together, to hang over the Earth in one big lump."

At the approach of the Bat, the Winds howled to a stop.

"We'll blow the Clouds together," they said, "but not before the Sun has brought up steam to the sky."

As the Bat flew toward the Sun, a sudden scream shook the sky:

"Stop where you are, foolish Bat, before I burn off your little wings!"

The Bat shrank back in terror, and the Sun smothered its fire in rolls of clouds. Quickly the Bat said, "Earth has no rain, Earth has no food, Earth asks for rain!"

"I'll help you," replied the Sun, "in return for a favor. After the rain falls, choose for me the greenest patch on the forest top, and build me a nest there. Then no longer will I have to journey to the horizon at the end of each day but will rest for the night in the cool and quiet of the forest."

The Bat quickly replied, "I'm only a Bat and don't know how to build nests, but the birds will happily make you one. Nothing will be easier—there are so many of them. They will do it right after the harvest, I promise—all in a day!"

And down the sky's sunlit paths the Bat flew, excited to bring the good news to the birds.

The birds readily promised to build the nest.

"The very day after the harvest," said the Sparrow.

"All in a day," said the Owl.

"A beautiful nest it'll be," said the Canary.

"With all the colors of the rainbow," said the Peacock.

So the Sun burnt down upon the earth, steam rose, Winds blew, and Clouds gathered. Then rain fell. The savannah bloomed, and streams flowed. Green and thick and tall, the forest grew until it touched the sky. Crops flourished and ripened—maize, bananas, cassava, millet, and peanuts—and the birds harvested. The morning after the harvest, the Bat reminded the birds about

▲ "After the rain falls, choose for me the greenest patch on the forest top, and build me a nest there," the sun said.

horizon *n.*: the place where the Earth and the sky appear to meet

READ ACTIVELY

Predict Do you think the birds will ever build the nest for the sun?

Background

About the Authors

This story is part of the oral tradition of the Maasai people. In the 1700s and 1800s, the Maasai migrated from the north to what is now Kenya. Like many of the other peoples of East Africa, the Maasai were primarily cattle herders. They traded cattle for food grown by farming peoples.

About the Selection

Many writers have collected and published the oral traditions of people from around the world. Tololwa M. Mollel's retelling of this fable helps preserve the Maasai tradition of oral history. *A Promise to the Sun* was published in 1992 by Little, Brown and Company, Boston, and was illustrated by Beatriz Vidal.

Background

Global Perspectives

Native American History The tradition of oral history is a part of many Native American cultures. The Kiowa song below, for example, honors the oral tradition:

They carried dreams in their voices;
They were the elders, the old ones.
They told us the old stories,
And they sang the spirit songs.

Native Americans continue to transmit history through song, ritual drama, and storytelling.

Activity

Journal Writing

Letter of Apology Suggest that students write a letter from the Bat to the Sun explaining why the Bat's promise was broken. Encourage them to draw on a recent personal experience in which they broke a promise. Remind students that journal writing need not be shared.

Activity

Critical Thinking

Recognizing Cause and Effect *Suitable as a whole class activity.* On the board, begin a cause-and-effect chain diagram by writing *the Sun* inside a circle. Ask students what the Sun must do to bring rain to the Earth (heat the Earth). Invite students to take turns adding characters from the story to the diagram and linking the characters with their actions until they reach the final effect of *rain*.

throb *v.:* to beat

shriek *v.:* to cry out with a sharp, shrill sound

▼ The Sun inched down toward the horizon.

the nest. Suddenly the birds were in no mood for work. All they cared about was the harvest celebrations, which were to start that night and last several days.

"I have to adorn myself," said the Peacock.

"I have to practice my flute," said the Canary.

"I have to heat up my drums," said the Owl.

"I have to help prepare the feast," said the Sparrow.

"Wait until after the celebrations," they said. "We'll do it then." But their hearts were not in it, and the Bat knew they would never build the nest.

What was she to do? A promise is a promise, she believed, yet she didn't know anything about making a nest. Even if she did,

how could she, all on her own, hope to make one big enough for the sun?

The Sun set, and the Moon rose. The celebrations began. The drums throbbed, the flutes wailed, and the dancers pounded the earth with their feet.

Alone with her thoughts and tired, the Bat fell fast asleep.

She awoke in a panic. The Moon had vanished, the Stars faded. Soon the Sun would rise!

Slowly, the Sun peered out over the horizon in search of the nest.

Certain the Sun was looking for her, the Bat scrambled behind a banana leaf. The Sun moved up in the sky. One of its rays glared over the leaf. With a cry of fear, the Bat fled to the forest.

But even there, she was not long at peace. There was a gust of wind, and the forest opened for a moment overhead. The Bat looked up anxiously. Peeking down at her was the Sun.

She let out a shriek and flew away.

As she flew, a cave came into view below. She dived down and quickly darted in.

There, silent and out of reach, she hid from the glare of the Sun.

She hid from the shame of a broken promise, a shame the birds did not feel.

Outside, the celebrations went on. The Owl's drums roared furiously.

The Canary's flute pierced the air. And the Sparrow cheered the Peacock's wild dancing.

The Sun inched down toward the horizon. It lingered over the forest and cast one more glance at the treetops, hoping for a miracle. Then, disappointed, it began to set. The birds carried on unconcerned, the sounds of their festivities reaching into the cave.

But the Bat did not stir from her hiding place that night. Nor the next day. For many days and nights she huddled in the cave. Then gradually she got up enough courage to venture out—but never in daylight! Only after sunset with Earth in the embrace of night.

Days and months and years went by, but the birds didn't build the nest. The Sun never gave up wishing, though. Every day as it set, it would linger to cast one last, hopeful glance at the forest top. Then, slowly, very slowly, it would sink away below the horizon.

Year after year the Sun continued to drag up steam, so the Winds would blow, the Clouds gather, and rain fall. It continues to do so today, hoping that the birds will one day keep their promise and build a nest among the treetops.

As for the Bat, . . . she made a home in the cave, and there she lives to this day. Whenever it rains, though, she listens eagerly. From the dark silence of her perch, the sound of the down-pour, ripening the crops and renewing the forest, is to her a magical song she wishes she could be out dancing to.

And as she listens, the trees outside sway and bow toward the cave. It is their thank-you salute to the hero who helped turn the forests green and thick and tall as the sky.

READ ACTIVELY

Connect How do you feel if you break a promise?

venture *v.:* to move in the face of danger
embrace *v.:* to hug

EXPLORING YOUR READING

Look Back
1. What favor did the Sun ask of the Bat? Why didn't the Bat keep her promise?

Think It Over
2. What natural events are explained by this story?

3. Based on this story, how dependable do you think the Maasai people consider nature to be?

4. Why do you think that the birds did not feel as ashamed as the Bat?

Go Beyond
5. What lesson does this story teach about how all the different parts of the world relate to each other? What lesson does it teach about how the animals relate to each other?

Ideas for Writing: Short Story
6. Using this story as a model, write a story in which the Bat makes her peace with the Sun.

3 Assess

Work through the *Exploring Your Reading* questions with students.

1. The Bat promised that the birds would build the Sun a nest in the forest. She could not keep her promise because the birds did not follow through.
2. The story explains why bats live in caves, why the sun disappears over the horizon, and why the trees sway when it rains.
3. Students may say that the Maasai feel somewhat threatened by nature because the birds and the natural elements do not treat the Bat well. Students may say that the Maasai are *not* threatened by nature, because the story portrays nature as having human characteristics and emotions.
4. Possible answer: The birds did not make the promise themselves.
5. Possible answer: Some parts of the world are, like the birds, only concerned about their own well-being. The birds want the Bat to help them when times are bad, but when the birds get everything they need, they are not willing to help the Bat.
6. Stories should retain the characterizations of the Bat and the Sun and should present a plausible plot.

Exploring Central and Southern Africa

To help you plan instruction, the chart below shows how teaching resources correspond to chapter content. Use the resources to vary instruction, add activities, or plan block schedules. Where appropriate, resources have **suggested time allotments** for students. Time allotments are approximate.

Managing Time and Instruction

	Africa Teaching Resources Binder		World Explorer Program Resources Binder	
	Resource	**mins.**	**Resource**	**mins.**

SECTION 1
Zaire: Rich but Poor
	Chapter and Section Support
	Reproducible Lesson Plan, p. 100
	Ⓢ Guided Reading and Review, p. 101
	Ⓢ Section Quiz, p. 102
		
		20
		25
			Outline Maps
			  Africa South of the Sahara: Physical, p. 32
			  West and Central Africa: Political, p. 34
			Nystrom Desk Atlas
			Ⓣ **Primary Sources and Literature**
			  Readings
			Writing Process Handbook
			  Organizing Material in a Logical
			    Sequence, pp. 23–24
				
				20
				20
				
				40
				
				25

SKILLS ACTIVITY **Organizing Your Time**	**Social Studies and Geography Skills,** Planning Your Time, p. 107	 30		

SECTION 2
South Africa: The End of Apartheid
	Chapter and Section Support
	Reproducible Lesson Plan, p. 103
	Ⓢ Guided Reading and Review, p. 104
	Critical Thinking Activity, p. 110
	Ⓢ Section Quiz, p. 105
	Ⓢ Vocabulary, p. 107
	Reteaching, p. 108
	Enrichment, p. 109
	Ⓢ Chapter Summary, p. 106
	Tests
	Forms A and B Chapter Tests, pp. 38–43
	Forms A and B Final Exams, pp. 44–49
		
		20
		30
		25
		20
		25
		25
		15
		
		40
		40
			Outline Maps
			  East and Southern Africa: Political, p. 35
			Environmental and Global Issues
			  Topic: Human Rights, pp. 25–30
				
				20
				
				30

Block Scheduling
Program Support

- Block Scheduling Folder
  PROGRAM TEACHING RESOURCES
- Activities and Projects
- Interdisciplinary Links
- Resource Pro™ CD-ROM
- Media and Technology

Assessment Opportunities

From Guiding Questions to Assessment   A series of Guiding Questions serves as an organizing framework for this book. The Guiding Questions that relate to this chapter are listed below. Section Reviews and Section Quizzes provide opportunities for assessing students' insights into these Guiding Questions. Additional assessments are listed below.

Media and Technology

Resource	mins.
▧ ⌾ Ⓢ World Video Explorer	20
⌾ Planet Earth CD-ROM	20
⌐ Color Transparencies 9, 11, 72, 93	20
⌾ Planet Earth CD-ROM	20
⌾ Material World CD-ROM	20
⌐ Color Transparencies 73, 160	20
⌂ Ⓢ Guided Reading Audiotapes	20
⌐ Color Transparency 173 (Graphic organizer flow map template)	20
⌾ The Writer's Solution CD-ROM	30
⌸ Computer Test Bank	30

- **T Teaming Opportunity**
  This resource is especially well-suited for teaching teams.
- **Ⓢ Spanish**
  This resource is also in Spanish support.
- ⌾ **CD-ROM**
- ⌾ **Laserdisc**
- ⌐ **Transparency**
- ⌸ **Software**
- ▧ **Videotape**
- ⌂ **Audiotape**

GUIDING QUESTIONS

- **What connections do African nations have with the United States and the world?**
- **What factors influence the ways in which Africans make a living?**

ASSESSMENTS

Section 1

Students should be able to create a natural resources map of Zaire.

▶ **RUBRIC**   See the Assessment booklet for a rubric on assessing a map produced by a student.

Section 2

Students should be able to write an explanation of the effect of apartheid on South Africa.

▶ **RUBRIC**   See the Assessment booklet for a rubric on assessing cause-and-effect statements.

Activities and Projects

Mental Mapping

Southern and Central Africa
Ask students to locate Zaire and South Africa on an unlabeled outlined map. Have them check their ideas on a political map of Africa. Have students note the latitude and longitude of these countries. Point out, for example, that the Equator runs through Zaire. Much of South Africa lies south of the Tropic of Capricorn, placing it outside the tropical zone. Have students locate a U.S. city that lies about as far from the Tropic of Cancer as Johannesburg does from the Tropic of Capricorn. (Miami) Have students discuss what they think the climates are like in Zaire and South Africa.

Links to Current Events

Elections The issue of who can vote, when they can vote, and for whom they can vote has been important in both South Africa and Zaire. Help students understand why elections can be tricky by discussing some of the many factors that determine how democratic elections are. You might relate the issue of who can vote, for example, to U.S. history, which has extended the right to vote to more people over the years. Point out that in South Africa, most of the population could not vote until 1993. Other issues involve how people get on the ballot. In Zaire, the ruler has made opposition parties that would put him out of power illegal. Discuss with students the factors that make elections fair and democratic, such as knowing when an election will be held, knowing that you will not be punished for voting, and knowing that your ballot will be secret.

Hands-On Activities

Trace a River The name *Zaire* comes from an African word for "river." Have students look at a map of Zaire and think about what river might have caused the country to be named this way. (Congo) Ask students to trace the course of the Congo on a wall map or globe.

Ask them to say out loud the names of the cities they see along the river. Explain that on some maps many of the cities have two names. Tell them that the more recent name is African, while the other name was given by European rulers during the colonial period. Ask students to discuss why people might give places different names after independence or a shift in governments.

Rich Resources Zaire produces about two-thirds of the world's cobalt. It leads the world in industrial diamond production and ranks sixth in copper production. South Africa is the world's leading producer of gold, chrome, and vanadium. It is also a leading producer of industrial diamonds. Have students find out how these resources are used. Ask them to make resource maps using symbols to show the mineral resources of Zaire and South Africa. Along the edges of the maps, have them show the way these mineral resources are used. *Average.*

Great Rift Ask students to make a three-dimensional outline model of Zaire

and its immediate surroundings using a salt-and-flour dough, clay, or some other pliable medium. Tell students that Africa is slowly pulling apart at the Great Rift Valley. They may wish to model what the continent might look like in the distant future. *English Language Learners*

New Government Following the elimination of apartheid in 1991, South Africa has started building a new government and a new society. Have students who are able to meet a challenge research the tasks involved in building a new South Africa by reading news articles about the country. Ask them to list some of the challenges facing the government. You might

also ask them to compare the situation in South Africa to the creation of a new government for the United States following the American Revolution. *Challenging*

News Reports Have students prepare and present two television news reports. The first one could have appeared in 1991, just as apartheid began to be dismantled. The second might have appeared in 1995, as the government began the effort to create a new country. *Basic*

F.Y.I.

This page can help you extend your own and students' understanding of the concepts in this chapter. You may want to browse through some of the suggestions in the **Bibliography. Interdisciplinary Links** can connect social studies understandings to areas elsewhere in the curriculum through the use of other Prentice Hall products. **National Geography Standards** reflected specifically in this chapter are listed for your convenience. Some hints about appropriate **Internet Access** are also provided. **School to Careers** provides insights into the practical uses of some of the concepts in this chapter as they might pertain to various careers.

BIBLIOGRAPHY

FOR THE TEACHER

African Religions: Zulu Zion. Time/Life, 1996. Videocassette.

Middleton, Nick. *Southern Africa.* Raintree, 1995.

Pratt, Paula Bryant. *The End of Apartheid in South Africa.* Lucent, 1995.

Zaire in Pictures. Lerner, 1992.

FOR THE STUDENT

Easy
Lewin, Hugh. *Jafta: The Homecoming.* Knopf, 1994.

Average
Nicholson, Robert. *The Zulus.* Chelsea House, 1994.

Siy, Alexandra. *The Efe: People of the Ituri Forest.* Dillon, 1993.

Challenging
Otfinoski, Steven. *Nelson Mandela: The Fight Against Apartheid.* Millbrook, 1992.

LITERATURE CONNECTION

Aardema, Verna. *Traveling to Tonda: A Tale of the Nkundo of Zaire.* Knopf, 1991.

Beake, Lesley. *Song of Be.* Holt, 1993.

Williams, Michael. *Crocodile Burning.* Puffin, 1992.

INTERDISCIPLINARY LINKS

Subject	Theme: Identity
MATH	Middle Grades Math: Tools for Success Course 1, Lesson 3-9, **Metric Length**
SCIENCE	Prentice Hall Science *Parade of Life: Animals*, Lesson 5-4, **Placental Mammals** *Parade of Life: Monerans, Protists, Fungi, and Plants*, Chapter 1 Introduction, **Classification of Living Things**
LANGUAGE ARTS	Choices in Literature *Deciding What's Right,* **Children of Wax, Power**

NATIONAL GEOGRAPHY STANDARDS

Students explore the 18 National Geography Standards throughout *Africa.* Chapter 7, however, concentrates on investigating the following standards: 1, 2, 3, 4, 5, 7, 8, 9, 11, 12, 14, 15, 16. For a complete list of the standards, see the *Teacher's Flexible Planning Guide.*

SCHOOL TO CAREERS

In Chapter 7, Exploring Central and Southern Africa, students learn about Zaire and South Africa. They also learn the skill of organizing your time. Knowing more about Zaire and South Africa can help students prepare for careers in such fields as politics, history, education, and so on. Organizing your time is a skill used in many careers, including sales, teaching, editing, researching, and others. The curriculum presented in this book, as in all eight titles of Prentice Hall's *World Explorer* program, is designed to prepare students not only for careers but also for good citizenship—of the world as well as of this country.

INTERNET ACCESS

Many social studies teachers and students use Internet browsers, or search engines, to investigate particular topics. For the best results, use narrow rather than broad topics. Try these for Chapter 7: apartheid, Shaba, Nelson Mandela, Cape Town. Finding age-appropriate sites is an important consideration when using the Internet. For links to age-appropriate sites in world studies and geography, visit the Prentice Hall Home Page at: **http://www.phschool.com**

Chapter 7

Connecting to the Guiding Questions

In this chapter, students will study Zaire and South Africa. Content in this chapter corresponds to the following Guiding Questions:

● What connections do African nations have with the United States and the world?

● What factors influence the ways in which Africans make a living?

Using the Map Activities

● There are 20 nations in Central and Southern Africa. Zaire is the biggest country; São Tomé and Príncipe is the smallest. Zaire, Central African Republic, Zambia, Malawi, Swaziland, Botswana, Zimbabwe, and Lesotho are landlocked; the rest of the countries in the region have access to an ocean.

● São Tomé and Príncipe is surrounded by the Atlantic Ocean. Comoros, Mauritius, and Madagascar are surrounded by the Indian Ocean.

Heterogeneous Groups

The following Teacher's Edition strategies are suitable for heterogeneous groups.

Interdisciplinary Connections
Science   p. 163
Critical Thinking
Drawing Conclusions   p. 164
Cooperative Learning
Designing Stamps   p. 173

Chapter 9

CHAPTER 7

Exploring Central and Southern Africa

SECTION 1
Zaire
RICH BUT POOR

SECTION 2
South Africa
THE END OF APARTHEID

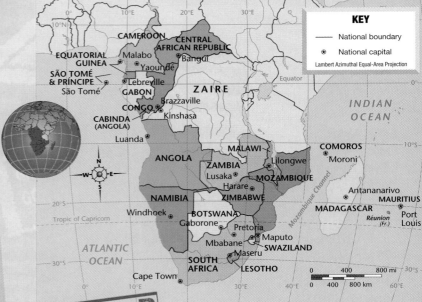

KEY
—— National boundary
⊛ National capital
Lambert Azimuthal Equal-Area Projection

This map shows the nations that make up Central and Southern Africa. To help you get to know this region, do the following activities.

Consider the geography
How many countries can you count on this map? Which country is the biggest? The smallest? Which countries are near water? Which countries are landlocked, or surrounded by other countries?

Find the island countries
Look at the west coast of Central Africa. How many countries are completely surrounded by the Atlantic Ocean? Look at the east coast of Central and Southern Africa. How many countries are completely surrounded by the Indian Ocean?

Resource Directory

Media and Technology

Spotlight On: Apartheid, from the World Video Explorer, enhances students' understanding of the political and social changes resulting from the demise of apartheid in South Africa.

Zaire

RICH BUT POOR

BEFORE YOU READ

Reach Into Your Background

What resources do you think a country needs to provide a good life for its people? Make a list of these resources. Share your list with the rest of the class.

Questions to Explore

1. Why is mining important to Zaire's economy?

2. What economic challenges has Zaire faced since independence?

Key Terms

authoritarian
nationalize

Key People and Places

King Leopold II
Mobutu Sese Seko
Shaba

C opper mining in what today is Zaire began in ancient times. The demand for copper brought Europeans to the area in the early 1900s. In 1930, a mining company found copper in a place called Kolwezi (kohl WAY zee). The company built a mine and hired miners, truck drivers, and a host of other workers. Soon a small city of workers' houses arose. Meanwhile, miners started to tunnel down into the earth to find the copper. They found it, too—right under their houses.

The Kolwezi area proved so rich in copper that, at first, miners found that they barely had to scratch the surface to find the mineral. After time, however, the miners had to dig deeper. Soon, they had dug a huge pit. Miners are still digging for copper there today. The Kolwezi mine in southern Zaire is one of the largest open-pit mines in Africa.

▼ In Zaire, miners take copper out of the ground in layers, leaving an open pit behind.

Zaire's Physical Geography

Since the 1930s, Zaire has become one of the world's main sources of copper. Zaire also has supplies of many other resources, including gold, diamonds, copper, forests, water, and wildlife. Look at the map in the Country Profile and identify these resources. Zaire's minerals and other resources have played an important role in the nation's history.

Teaching Resources

📁 **Reproducible Lesson Plan** in the Chapter and Section Resources booklet, p. 100, provides a summary of the section lesson.

📁 **Guided Reading and Review** in the Chapter and Section Resources booklet, p. 101, provides a structure for mastering key concepts and reviewing key terms in the section. Available in Spanish in the Spanish Chapter and Section Resources booklet, p. 62.

Program Resources

📁 Material in the **Primary Sources and Literature Readings** booklet extends content with a selection from the region under study.

📁 **Outline Maps** Africa South of the Sahara: Physical, p. 32; West and Central Africa: Political, p. 34

Lesson Objectives

1. Describe Zaire's physical geography and the significance of its natural resources.

2. Summarize Zaire's economic and political history.

Lesson Plan

1 Engage

Warm-Up Activity

Tell students that developing countries have little in the way of cash resources and rely upon loans from wealthier countries to finance the building of much-needed transportation systems, communications systems, hospitals, and other services. Help students understand that paying back large loans severely strains a developing country's economy.

Activating Prior Knowledge

Have students read Reach Into Your Background in the Before You Read box. Ask students to decide which resources on their lists are most essential. Suggest that they rank each resource according to its importance.

2 Explore

As students read the section, have them look for answers to the following questions: What are Zaire's most important natural resources? How have Zaire's abundant natural resources affected Zaireans' lives? How do other country's benefit from Zaire's resources? What have been some of the results of Mobutu Sese Seko's rule?

3 Teach

Ask students to make time lines that describe important dates and time periods in the economic and political histories of Zaire. This activity should take about 25 minutes.

4 Assess

See the answers to the Section Review. You may also use students' completed time lines as an assessment.

Acceptable time lines include descriptions of political or economic conditions during three different time periods.

Commendable time lines include descriptions of political or economic conditions during more than three different time periods.

Outstanding time lines include descriptions of political or economic conditions during more than three time periods and indicate that the establishment of control over natural resources is a common thread in Zaire's history.

Answers to ...

MAP AND CHART STUDY

Three power plants are near mineral deposits. Mining processes and operations require large amounts of electrical power. As in many African countries, a large percentage of Zaire's population is under 15.

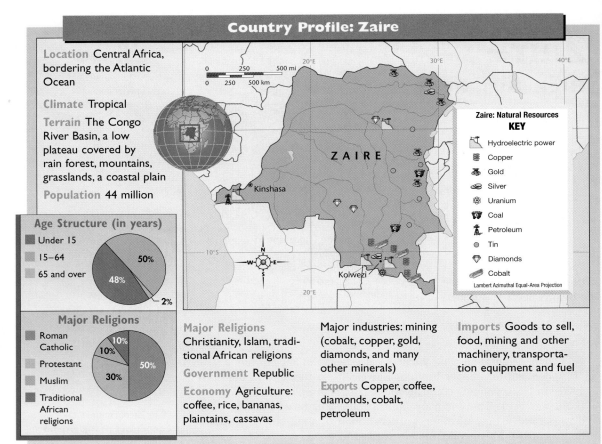

Country Profile: Zaire

Location Central Africa, bordering the Atlantic Ocean

Climate Tropical

Terrain The Congo River Basin, a low plateau covered by rain forest, mountains, grasslands, a coastal plain

Population 44 million

Age Structure (in years)
- Under 15
- 15–64
- 65 and over

50% / 48% / 2%

Major Religions
- Roman Catholic
- Protestant
- Muslim
- Traditional African religions

10% / 10% / 30% / 50%

Zaire: Natural Resources KEY
- Hydroelectric power
- Copper
- Gold
- Silver
- Uranium
- Coal
- Petroleum
- Tin
- Diamonds
- Cobalt

Lambert Azimuthal Equal-Area Projection

Major Religions Christianity, Islam, traditional African religions

Government Republic

Economy Agriculture: coffee, rice, bananas, plaintains, cassavas

Major industries: mining (cobalt, copper, gold, diamonds, and many other minerals)

Exports Copper, coffee, diamonds, cobalt, petroleum

Imports Goods to sell, food, mining and other machinery, transportation equipment and fuel

Map and Chart Study This map shows Zaire's natural resources. **Location** Where are Zaire's copper deposits located? **Interaction** How many hydroelectric power sites are located close to mineral deposits? Why would it be useful to have a power plant near a mine? Read the information about Zaire's economy. Which of its natural resources does Zaire export? **Critical Thinking** Compare Zaire's age structure with that of other countries profiled in this book. How is Zaire's age structure similar to that of other African countries?

READ ACTIVELY

Connect How do people make a living on the grasslands of the United States?

Forests and Grasslands The Republic of Zaire is located in west Central Africa. Equal in size to the United States east of the Mississippi River, it is Africa's third largest country. Zaire has four major physical regions: The Congo Basin, the Northern Uplands, the Eastern Highlands, and the Southern Uplands.

The Congo Basin is covered by a dense rain forest. People who live in this region mostly hunt and fish for a living. Most Zaireans live in the country's other regions. The Northern Uplands, along the country's northern border, are covered with savanna, or grasslands. The Eastern Highlands have grasslands and occasional thick forests. The Southern Uplands are high, flat plains of grasslands and wooded areas. In these regions, most people make a living by subsistence farming.

Resource Directory

Program Resources

Nystrom Desk Atlas

Media and Technology

Planet Earth CD-ROM includes an interactive political map of Zaire as well as thematic maps of Africa.

Color Transparencies 9, 11, 72, 93

A Mineral-Rich Nation While about two thirds of Zaire's people work as farmers, mining produces most of the country's wealth. Zaire has huge copper deposits in the southern province of Shaba (SHAHB uh). (In Swahili, *shaba* means "copper.") The country also has reserves of gold and other minerals. Zaire produces more diamonds than any other country except Australia. And Zaire has enough water power to run many hydroelectric plants. However, as is the case with many of its mineral resources, Zaire has developed only a small part of its potential water power.

Natural Resources in Zaire's History

Resources dominate the history of Zaire. By the 1400s, the kingdoms of Kongo, Luba, and Lunda ruled Central Africa. The power of these kingdoms was based on their knowledge of ironworking. The first Europeans who arrived in the area—the Portuguese in the 1480s—were not interested in iron. They came in search of gold.

Some 400 years later, during the scramble for Africa, Belgium took control of the area, calling it the Congo Free State. King Leopold II of Belgium ruled brutally, forcing Africans to harvest wild rubber. He grew wealthy while Africans suffered and starved. Later, Belgian government officials ruled less harshly. But they still were interested only in the Congo's resources, especially its copper and diamonds.

During the 1950s, calls for independence echoed throughout Africa, including the Congo. After a time of unrest, the Congo won its independence in 1960.

READ ACTIVELY

Predict How do you think that Zaire's mineral resources have affected its history?

Agriculture in Eastern Zaire

Although Zaire is rich in natural resources, not all Zairians make a living as miners. Many Zaireans work as farmers. They grow bananas, cassavas, corn, peanuts, and rice for their families. Others make a living growing cash crops such as cocoa, coffee, cotton, and tea. **Critical Thinking** The fields shown in this photograph are in a hilly area of Zaire. How do you think the shape of the land here creates challenges for farmers?

Background

Daily Life

Zairean Cuisine The preparation of food is an important part of each day's work. Zaireans eat corn and other starchy foods such as cassava, sorghum, and rice. Women and older children pound these foods into meal and then cook the meal with sweet potatoes, yams, or bananas.

Activity

Critical Thinking

Drawing Conclusions *Suitable as a whole class activity.* Write *Democratic System* and *Authoritarian System* on the chalkboard. Give students the following list of events and have them decide whether each event could or could not occur under each of the two types of government systems:
(1) the cancellation of national elections
(2) open criticism of political leaders
(3) the impeachment of a high government official
(4) being arrested without a warrant

Answers to ...
AT WORK IN KINSHASA

Students' answers regarding the employee's occupation will vary. Students will probably say that his office is equipped with a personal computer, as are many offices in the United States.

LINKS ACROSS THE WORLD

Latin American Economies Like Zaire, many Latin American countries used to depend on one resource. These countries have been working to diversify their economies. They are trying to earn more money by growing more types of cash crops. They are also working to build their own industries and mine their own resources without help from foreign countries.

The Congo's first years as an independent country were difficult. Various groups fought each other for power. This worried the foreign companies that controlled many of the Congo's industries. The unrest, they feared, might hurt their businesses. In 1965, these foreign companies helped a military leader, Mobutu Sese Seko (muh BOO too SAY say SAY koh), take power. With a strong ruler in control, they thought, their businesses would thrive.

Zaire Under Mobutu

Mobutu quickly took charge. First he set up an **authoritarian** government. In this form of government, a single leader or small group of leaders have all the power. An authoritarian government is not democratic. Also, Mobutu tried to cut all ties with the colonial past. First, he renamed the country *Zaire*. Then, Mobutu **nationalized,** or took under government control, industries that had been owned by foreign companies. At the same time, he borrowed money from foreign countries to build more industries.

Mobutu's plans to help Zaire's industries failed. Some government officials who ran companies were bad managers. Others simply stole their companies' profits. Then, in the late 1970s, the world price of copper dropped sharply. Suddenly, Zaire was earning less and less from the sale of its major export. It could not pay back the money it had borrowed. The country's economy quickly collapsed.

Mobutu responded by cutting government spending, especially on health services and schools. This hit the poor people of Zaire especially hard. When they protested Mobutu's actions, he cracked down. People who opposed his government were thrown into prison.

Zaire Looks to the Future

Calls for reform came from inside and outside Zaire. Many times, Mobutu promised to improve the economy and to allow the people more say in government. However, he rarely took any action. Meanwhile, ordinary Zaireans grew poorer and poorer. By the

At Work in Kinshasa

At a truck assembly plant in Zaire's capital city, Kinshasa, an employee works on a computer in an air-conditioned office. **Critical Thinking** What kind of work might he be doing? How does this office resemble one in the United States?

Resource Directory

Teaching Resources

📁 **Section Quiz** in the Chapter and Section Resources booklet, p. 102, covers the main ideas and key terms in the section. Available in Spanish in the Spanish Chapter and Section Resources booklet, p. 63.

A Breakaway Province?

In recent years, the province of Eastern Kasai (kuh SY) has thrived while the rest of the country has sunk deeper into poverty. Many people in Eastern Kasai fear that their province's wealth might be used to help the rest of the country climb out of poverty. As a result, they have called for Eastern Kasai to break away from the rest of Zaire. In this picture, residents of Eastern Kasai declare their "independence" by continuing to use Zaire's old currency, even though new currency has been issued.

1990s, the buying power of average wages was only 10 percent of what it was in the 1960s. Some middle-class Zaireans left the country rather than stay and watch their wages and living conditions steadily decline.

Those who stayed looked to the future with both hope and uncertainty. They hoped that the leaders after Mobutu would start a democratic government. And they trusted that these leaders, finally, would find a way to develop Zaire's resources for the benefit of all the people.

SECTION 1 REVIEW

1. **Define** (a) authoritarian, (b) nationalize.

2. **Identify** (a) King Leopold II, (b) Mobutu Sese Seko, (c) Shaba.

3. (a) What are some of Zaire's natural resources? (b) What role have they played in Zaire's development as a nation?

4. (a) What programs did Mobutu Sese Seko introduce when he took power? (b) How successful were these programs?

Critical Thinking

5. **Drawing Conclusions** Why do you think Zaireans' wages and living conditions have declined since independence?

Activity

6. **Writing to Learn** Write a title and short description for a book about the history of Zaire. Design a cover for your book by deciding what images best represent Zaire's history.

SKILLS MINI LESSON

Expressing Problems Clearly

To **introduce** the skill, point out that defining and expressing a problem clearly is the first step in understanding and solving the problem. As students consider the relentless poverty in Zaire, engage them in a discussion about why the country remains so poor, despite its wealth of natural resources. Students may **practice** defining the problem by writing a list of three obstacles to Zaire's economic health. The obstacles should be events or conditions that have occurred or existed only since Zaire became independent. To **apply** the skill, have students summarize the information contained in their lists in a concise statement. For example: Poor management of nationalized industries, a drop in earnings from copper, and a large amount of foreign debt led to the collapse of Zaire's economy.

SKILLS ACTIVITY

Organizing Your Time

Lesson Objectives

1 Explain why time-organizing skills are important.

2 Create a chart to identify and schedule steps needed to complete a school assignment.

Lesson Plan

1 Engage

Warm-Up Activity

Have two students role-play the opening scenario. Then **introduce** the skill by reading the activity title and asking students how Claudia might have avoided her situation by organizing her time.

Activating Prior Knowledge

Invite students to explain some ways in which they organize their time to complete tasks outside of school. For example, how could they draft a schedule for fixing a bicycle or skateboard for use next summer? How would they organize their free time to ensure that the project would be completed in time?

2 Explore

As you read aloud the text under *Get Ready*, ask volunteers to write the two rules of time management on the chalkboard. Compare these rules with the methods students described earlier. Instruct students to read the remaining text.

"**Y**our reports are due Monday," the teacher said on Friday afternoon. To Claudia the teacher's words sounded more like this: "You will not have any fun this weekend. You will not have time to see your friends or play basketball. And if you're lucky, you will finish your report late Sunday night and come to school tired Monday morning."

"There goes the weekend," she muttered to Timothy, who sat at the next desk.

"Oh, I don't know," he responded. "I just need to fix up my final copy, and I'll be done."

"How come you're so far along?"

"Well, I started two weeks ago, when she assigned the reports." He paused. "You haven't started yet?"

"No," Claudia said. "But I guess I'd better get on it."

Has this ever happened to you? Or are you more like Timothy, who got an early start—and then a better grade and free time over the weekend for his efforts? The key is to organize your time.

Resource Directory

Teaching Resources

Planning Your Time in the Social Studies and Geography Skills booklet, p. 107, provides additional skill practice.

Get Ready

Teachers know how long it takes for students to complete assignments. So they make sure to give you a reasonable amount of time. But they expect you to start assignments soon after they make them. This is the first rule of organizing your time—get started early.

But an early start does not guarantee success. You must also organize your time carefully.

Try It Out

First, set a goal. Then identify the steps you need to take to reach it. Put these steps in the form of a chart to make a plan.

A. Set your goal. Include it in the title of your chart. Suppose that your goal is to turn in a one-page report by Friday. The title of your chart might be "Timetable for Report on Zaire's Natural Resources."

B. Identify the first step you will need to take to reach your goal. What do you need to find out about Zaire's natural resources? How can you find the information?

C. Continue toward your goal. Write every single step in your chart. What will you need to do after you find books and magazine articles about your topic? List the steps you need to carry out to end up with your written report.

D. Estimate the time for each step. Look back over the steps you need to take. Think about the time you need to complete each one. Write the amount of time next to each step in the chart.

Timetable for Report on Apartheid

	Steps	Amount of Time
Step 1		
Step 2		
Step 3		
Step 4		
Step 5		

Apply the Skill

To see how your chart can help you organize your time, complete these steps.

1. **Identify the steps.** Suppose you must write a two-page paper on the history of apartheid in South Africa. Make a chart of the steps you will take to reach this goal.

2. **Use your chart to organize your time.** You have two weeks to complete this assignment. Estimate how long each step will take. A step might take a few minutes, a few hours, or several days. Next to each step, write how long you think it will take. Remember, *the total amount of time for this assignment cannot be more than two weeks.*

3. **Transfer this information to a calendar.** Copy each step in the chart onto the proper days on the calendar. If you follow the calendar, you will reach your goal.

3 Teach

Have student pairs **practice** by completing the activity described in *Try It Out*. Encourage pairs to use the illustration as a guide in creating their charts. Then work as a whole class to review and compare all the charts, amending steps as necessary.

For additional reinforcement, have students list the steps necessary to complete one of the outside activities they described earlier.

4 Assess

Challenge students to **apply** their time-organizing skills to the task in the final part of the lesson. To **assess**, allow students to evaluate other classmates' schedules. You might then post a few good examples and invite all students to comment. Evaluate their understanding as they orally review the posted charts, checking for logical steps and reasonable time estimates.

1. Describe the policies and legacy of apartheid.

2. Identify the challenges that face post-apartheid South Africa.

Lesson Plan

1 Engage

Warm-Up Activity

Ask students how many of them are right-handed. Then ask students how they would react to a new school policy that says all right-handed people can occupy only the basement of the school and must always carry special passes. The best learning resources and sports equipment are reserved for left-handed people. Ask students whether they think such a policy would be fair. What would they do to oppose it?

Activating Prior Knowledge

Have students read Reach Into Your Background in the Before You Read box. You might invite students to write in their journals about an experience of being unfairly left out.

2 Explore

Have students read the section. Ask them to consider questions such as the following: What was apartheid? During apartheid, why did black families and white families live so differently? Why was it difficult for black families to improve their lives? What changes were made in South Africa after Nelson Mandela became president?

SECTION 2
South Africa
THE END OF APARTHEID

BEFORE YOU READ

Reach Into Your Background

Have you ever experienced being left out when you should have been included? Maybe you didn't get to do something you had planned, or you weren't chosen for a team. How did you deal with the experience of being unfairly left out?

Questions to Explore

1. How did the people of South Africa change their government and society?

2. How has life changed for the people of South Africa in the years since the end of apartheid?

Key Terms
apartheid
discriminate
homeland

Key People and Places
F. W. de Klerk
Nelson Mandela
Cape Town

▼ Many black South African children go to schools with real classrooms now, but on nice days they enjoy studying outside.

Monique du Preez, a white woman, grew up in a world of white privilege. The only black people she knew were her family's servants. Du Preez admits: "Even very small children in the household would [tell the servants], 'Do this. Do that.' . . . Everything was done for us." Today, du Preez faces a world in which everything has changed.

Her school, for example, once was for whites only. Now, however, it is open to people of all races.

Life has changed for other South Africans, too. Just outside Johannesburg (joh HAN is burg), on a rural settlement called Orange Farm, Mavis Lufhugu teaches reading classes. "[People] want to better themselves," she explains. Black South Africans escaping poor rural areas and crowded cities founded Orange Farm in 1989. The original residents lived in tents. Children attended school in what used to be chicken coops and horses' stables.

Today, more than 900 Orange Farm children attend grade school in real school buildings. A team of health-care workers helps the residents stay healthy. And an adult reading program attracts eager students.

The changes experienced by du Preez and Lufhugu have been a long time coming. For many years, the Republic of South Africa was a divided country.

Resource Directory

Teaching Resources

📁 **Reproducible Lesson Plan** in the Chapter and Section Resources booklet, p. 103, provides a summary of the section lesson.

📁 **Guided Reading and Review** in the Chapter and Section Resources booklet, p. 104, provides a structure for mastering key concepts and reviewing key terms in the section. Available in Spanish in the Spanish Chapter and Section Resources booklet, p. 64.

Media and Technology

💿 **Planet Earth** CD-ROM includes an interactive political map of South Africa as well as thematic maps of Africa.

💿 **Material World** CD-ROM includes a portrait of a family from Soweto plus geographic data on South Africa.

🖥 **Color Transparencies** 73, 160

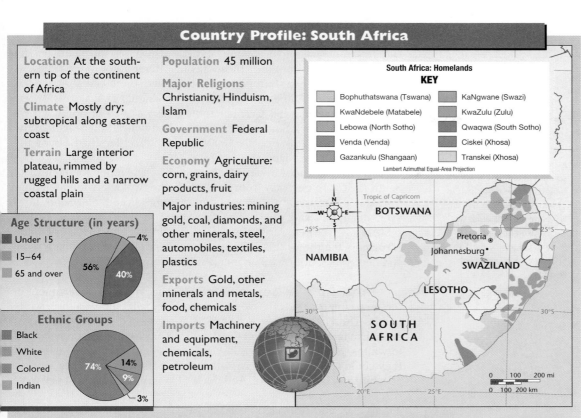

Country Profile: South Africa

Location At the southern tip of the continent of Africa

Climate Mostly dry; subtropical along eastern coast

Terrain Large interior plateau, rimmed by rugged hills and a narrow coastal plain

Population 45 million

Major Religions Christianity, Hinduism, Islam

Government Federal Republic

Economy Agriculture: corn, grains, dairy products, fruit

Major industries: mining gold, coal, diamonds, and other minerals, steel, automobiles, textiles, plastics

Exports Gold, other minerals and metals, food, chemicals

Imports Machinery and equipment, chemicals, petroleum

Age Structure (in years)
- Under 15
- 15–64
- 65 and over

56%
40%
4%

Ethnic Groups
- Black
- White
- Colored
- Indian

74%
14%
9%
3%

South Africa: Homelands
KEY

- Bophuthatswana (Tswana)
- KwaNdebele (Matabele)
- Lebowa (North Sotho)
- Venda (Venda)
- Gazankulu (Shangaan)
- KaNgwane (Swazi)
- KwaZulu (Zulu)
- Qwaqwa (South Sotho)
- Ciskei (Xhosa)
- Transkei (Xhosa)

Lambert Azimuthal Equal-Area Projection

Tropic of Capricorn

BOTSWANA

NAMIBIA

Pretoria
Johannesburg
SWAZILAND

LESOTHO

SOUTH AFRICA

0   100   200 mi
0 100 200 km

Map and Chart Study This map shows South Africa's former homelands. For many years, the white South African government forced thousands of blacks to move to these regions. They generally were far from cities and had few resources and poor soil. The homeland policy was part of a pattern of racial discrimination called apartheid. **Critical Thinking** Look at the graph of South Africa's ethnic groups. Which group forms the majority of the population? **Regions** Notice that most of South Africa's land is not included in the homelands. What do you think it might have been like to live in one of the homelands? **Critical Thinking** Why do you think South Africa's white government created the homelands?

One Country, Two Worlds

South Africa lies at the southern tip of Africa. Look at the map in the Country Profile. Like the United States, South Africa has seacoasts on two oceans—the Atlantic Ocean and the Indian Ocean. The country of South Africa is larger than the states of Texas and California combined. It is one of the wealthiest African countries. Yet, until recently, white people controlled almost all its riches. Society was divided by law along racial and ethnic lines. How did such a system come to be?

Cultures Clash People have lived in southern Africa for millions of years. The ancestors of most of today's black South Africans arrived some 1,500 years ago during the Bantu migrations. White

READ ACTIVELY

Predict How do you think South Africa came to have laws that divided people by race?

Teaching Resources

📁 **Critical Thinking Activity** in the Chapter and Section Resources booklet, p. 110, helps students apply the skill of distinguishing fact from opinion.

Program Resources

📁 **Outline Maps** East and Southern Africa: Political, p. 35

Have students create a chart with three columns: *Life Under Apartheid, Life After Apartheid,* and *Reasons for Change.* Ask students to fill in the chart with facts from the section. Use the completed charts as the basis for a discussion of predictions about South Africa's future. This activity should take about 25 minutes.

4 Assess

See the answers to the Section Review. You may also use students' completed charts as an assessment.

Acceptable charts include three factual entries in each column.

Commendable charts include at least four factual entries in each column.

Outstanding charts include at least four factual entries in each column, some of which are opinions supported by facts from the section.

Answers to ...
MAP AND CHART STUDY

Blacks form the majority of South Africa's population. Students will probably answer that the homelands were created to keep blacks and whites separate.

British and Dutch Rule
In 1814, the British assumed control of South Africa from the Dutch. They began to take steps to liberate black South Africans from judicial inequality and to outlaw racial segregation. In 1834, they declared slavery illegal in all British possessions. Some Afrikaners found these British acts threatening. Between 1835 and the early 1840s, 12,000 to 14,000 *Voortrekkers* (Afrikaans: "Early Migrants") left the colony. After defeating the indigenous black Africans, they established white settlements in what are today the Transvaal and the Orange Free State of South Africa.

ACROSS THE WORLD

The San Language South Africa is home to several different languages. The people of the San ethnic group of Southern Africa speak what many scientists believe is the world's oldest language. In addition to using sounds such as those used to say the letters T, S, or B, the San language also uses click sounds.

▼ Under apartheid, blacks and whites were even forced to sit separately at sports events.

Europeans first arrived in South Africa about 400 years ago. In 1652, Dutch settlers set up a colony at Cape Town on the southern tip of the continent. In time, these people thought of themselves as Africans rather than Europeans. They called themselves *Afrikaners* (af rih KAHN erz). And they spoke their own language, Afrikaans.

British, French, and German settlers also settled in South Africa. For years, the black South Africans who already lived there battled the white settlers. But by the late 1800s, the white settlers had forced the Africans off the best land.

The British and Afrikaners also fought each other for control of South Africa. To get away from the British, the Afrikaners founded their own states, Transvaal (tranz VAHL) and Orange Free State. Soon, however, diamonds and gold were discovered in the Transvaal. British prospectors pushed Afrikaners off their farms. The British and the Afrikaners fought for three years over the territory. Britain finally won, and declared South Africa an independent country in 1910.

White Rule in South Africa   The white-led government of the new country passed several laws to keep land and wealth in white hands. The Natives Land Act of 1913, for example, stated that blacks could live in only 8 percent of the country. The rest of the land belonged to whites. Blacks could work in white areas—for very low wages. But they could not own land there. Other laws passed in the 1920s separated white and black workers. And the best jobs and the highest pay were reserved for whites.

In 1948, the Afrikaners' political party, the National Party, won the election and took over the country. Afrikaner leaders added new laws to the system of white power. And they gave the system a new name—**apartheid** (uh PAHR tayt), which is an Afrikaans word meaning "separateness." Apartheid laws placed every South African into a category based on race. The laws also made it legal to discriminate on the basis of race. To **discriminate** means to treat people differently, and often unfairly, based on race, religion, or sex.

Apartheid separated South Africans into four groups—blacks, whites, coloreds, and Asians. Blacks included all

Resource Directory

Teaching Resources

📁 **Distinguishing Fact From Opinion** in the Social Studies and Geography Skills booklet, p. 50, provides additional skill practice.

Program Resources

📁 **Environmental and Global Issues** Topic: Human Rights, pp. 25–30

Africans. Whites included people of European heritage. Coloreds were people of mixed race. The term Asians usually meant people from India. Coloreds and Asians had a few rights. Blacks had practically no rights at all.

Apartheid forced thousands of South African blacks to move to 10 poor rural areas called **homelands.** These homelands had the driest and least fertile land. There, black South Africans lived in poverty.

Apartheid affected not only where blacks could live but every aspect of their lives. It denied them citizenship rights, including the right to vote. The system kept blacks and coloreds in low-paying jobs. It put them in poor schools. It barred blacks and coloreds from white restaurants, schools, and hospitals. Apartheid also strengthened the pass laws that required all blacks to carry identification. In short, apartheid kept whites in control of the country.

First Multiracial Elections, 1994

Women in Johannesburg joyously displayed the identification papers that allowed them to vote in the historic election on April 26, 1994. Blacks had to wait in line for as long as eight hours to cast ballots for the first time in their lives. As a 93-year-old woman finally reached the polling booth, she said, "I am happy this day has come. I never thought it could happen here."

The Deadly Struggle Against Apartheid Many South Africans fought apartheid. During the 1950s and 1960s, blacks and some whites took to the streets in peaceful protest against it. The well-armed South African police met them with deadly force. Hundreds of men, women, and children were wounded or killed. Thousands more were thrown in jail. In the 1970s, black students and black workers protested against inequality. The government tried to end these protests with more force. But the demonstrations kept growing.

Countries around the world joined the movement against apartheid. Many nations stopped trading with South Africa. Its athletes were banned from the Olympic Games and other international sports events.

In 1990, these struggles began to have an effect. Faced with a weakening economy and continuing protests, South Africa's president, F. W. de Klerk, pushed through laws that tore down the apartheid system.

In April 1994, for the first time, South Africans of all colors peacefully elected a president. They chose Nelson Mandela, a black man who had spent 28 years in prison for fighting apartheid.

To Be a Leader The end of apartheid inspired Ivy Nonqayi to make a change. She made $80 a month tending the big house of a white town councilor, Peb Saunders. Nonqayi wanted jobs and housing for blacks, so in 1995 she took a brave step. She ran for her boss's seat—and easily ousted her. Despite her win, Nonqayi stayed on as Saunders' maid.

Background

Global Perspectives

Gandhi in South Africa In 1893, Indian attorney Mohandas K. Gandhi came to South Africa and stayed for 21 years. While in South Africa, he developed the strategy of passive resistance. Passive resistance later proved instrumental in the liberation of black and Indian South Africans. It was also one of the strategies African Americans used in the 1960s to gain civil rights in the United States.

Activity

Journal Writing

In Protest Music and poetry were two ways in which black South Africans expressed their opposition to apartheid. Invite students to record their own ideas about the unfairness of apartheid or of an aspect of American society in the form of a protest song or poem. Remind students that their journals are private and will not be graded or judged by others.

Teaching Resources

Section Quiz in the Chapter and Section Resources booklet, p. 105, covers the main ideas and key terms in the section. Available in Spanish in the Spanish Chapter and Section Resources booklet, p. 65.

Vocabulary in the Chapter and Section Resources booklet, p. 107, provides a review of key terms in the chapter. Available in Spanish in the Spanish Chapter and Section Resources booklet, p. 67.

Reteaching in the Chapter and Section Resources booklet, p. 108, provides a structure for students who may need additional help in mastering chapter content.

Enrichment in the Chapter and Section Resources booklet, p. 109, extends chapter content and enriches students' understanding.

Nadine Gordimer (1923–)
Though novelist and short-story writer Nadine Gordimer is a member of the South African white minority, she has always been adamantly against the policy of apartheid. From an early age, she supported outlawed black political groups that sought the end of apartheid and enforced racism. Gordimer voiced opposition to her country's racial policies in her novels and stories, and the South African government responded by banning her books. Elsewhere, however, Gordimer's writing has been crucial in drawing international attention to the destructive effects of apartheid on the lives of all South Africans. In 1991, Gordimer was awarded the Nobel Prize for Literature; during that same year, as South Africa took its first tentative steps toward ending apartheid, the government lifted its ban on Gordimer's books.

Answers to ...
FLYING AWAY

Accept any thoughtful answer.

New Challenges

Under Nelson Mandela's government, legal discrimination on the basis of race finally ended. Blacks and some whites welcomed the changes. But many whites who had grown up with the privileges of apartheid were not as happy.

Despite new opportunities for millions of blacks, South Africa remained a divided society. Blacks and whites usually lived in different neighborhoods. Whites still controlled most of the country's biggest businesses and newspapers. Compared to blacks, whites had better-paying jobs and owned more property.

Even though they still held a lot of power, many whites did not like the recent changes in South Africa. Some opposed government plans to help blacks get jobs. Monique du Preez, for example, wondered whether her white skin would be a drawback when she looks for a job. Other whites feared their children's education would suffer in schools attended by all races. Mandela's government had to find ways to reassure whites while making certain that blacks had an equal chance for a good life. To meet its challenges, South Africa's government will need the help of all its citizens, regardless of race.

READ ACTIVELY

Connect What do you think South Africans could learn from people who remember integration in the United States?

STUDENT ART

Children of the Orlando Children's Home
Ages 8-15
Soweto, South Africa

In 1989, the children of the Orlando Children's Home in Soweto painted this mural on the wall that surrounds their home. Apartheid had not yet ended. **Critical Thinking** This mural shows many ways of flying away from South Africa. However, it also shows people with parachutes jumping out of the airplanes. What feelings about South Africa do you think the children meant to express when they painted this mural?

Flying Away

Resource Directory

Teaching Resources

📁 **Spanish Glossary** in the Spanish Chapter and Section Resources, pp. 68–73, provides key terms translated from English to Spanish as well as definitions in Spanish.

📁 **Chapter Summary** in the Chapter and Section Resources booklet, p. 106, provides a summary of chapter content. Available in Spanish in the Spanish Chapter and Section Resources booklet, p. 66.

📁 **Cooperative Learning Activity** in the Activities and Projects booklet, pp. 41–44, provides two student handouts, one page of teacher's directions, and a scoring rubric for a cooperative learning activity on making a relief map.

Media and Technology

🎧 **Guided Reading Audiotapes** (English and Spanish)

Building a New Nation

Nearly every day, television, radio, and newspapers report on the changes that have taken place in South Africa. But the new South Africa has yet to be built. Both black and white South Africans are struggling to replace white rule and apartheid with something better.

David Bailes, a white South African, left the country in the early 1970s because he hated apartheid. Since then, he has been living in the United States. Today, Bailes is thinking about returning to South Africa to live. After a recent visit to Cape Town, he said:

> "There's still a lot of inequality there. Whites still own most of the wealth, and they still have the best jobs and homes. On the surface, things don't appear much different. But you know they are—you can feel it. The laws have changed, and that's a big deal. I can hang out with my black and Indian friends in public places. South Africa is becoming a brand new country. There's still a lot of pain there, but to me, it's the most beautiful country in the world."

▼ In 1993, South Africa's president, F. W. de Klerk, and Nelson Mandela—soon to be elected the first black president of South Africa—share a triumphant moment.

SECTION 2 REVIEW

1. Define (a) apartheid, (b) discriminate, (c) homeland.

2. Identify (a) F. W. de Klerk, (b) Nelson Mandela, (c) Cape Town.

3. How did apartheid affect South Africans?

4. What changes have taken place in South Africa since the collapse of apartheid?

Critical Thinking

5. Expressing Problems Clearly What challenges must the South African government meet in order to build a new nation based on equality for all?

Activity

6. Writing to Learn Write a letter to a friend, explaining your view of the changes in South Africa.

SKILLS MINI LESSON

Organizing Information

To **introduce** the skill, explain that it is often helpful to organize information in a graphic such as a chart, table, or time line. Organizing information in one of these ways is useful when studying for a test or writing a report. Have students **practice** the skill by asking them to extract and paraphrase separately the histories of black Africans, the Dutch (Afrikaners), and the British. Then, have students **apply** the skill by making a time line for each of the three groups, using the same scale, beginning in the year A.D. 500 (the period of the Bantu migration) and ending in 1994. Students should then compare their three time lines. Ask them to identify how political power has shifted over time among the three.

Activity

Cooperative Learning

Designing Stamps Have students work in pairs to brainstorm some ideas for a postage stamp design that commemorates an aspect of the end of apartheid. After students have compiled a list of ideas, have them choose one and work together to create their design. *English Language Learner, Visual*

Section 2 Review

1. (a) the legal policy of racial separation (b) to treat people differently based upon their race, religion, or sex (c) a poor, rural area where black South Africans were forced to live

2. (a) president of South Africa who helped bring about the end of apartheid (b) South Africa's first black president, who spent 28 years in prison for fighting apartheid (c) city on the southern tip of Africa where Dutch settlers established a colony in 1652

3. The system kept blacks and coloreds in low-paying jobs and inferior schools. Whites had control of the government and the economy.

4. Legal racial discrimination has ended.

5. Possible answer: The government must find ways of reassuring whites that the new system can work, while making sure that blacks have an equal chance for a good life.

6. Students' letters will vary. They will probably express their approval of the move toward political equality for all South Africans.

Reviewing Main Ideas

1. (a) The Congo Basin is dense rain forest; the Northern Uplands are a savanna; the Eastern Highlands are grasslands and forests; and the Southern Uplands contain flat grassland plains and wooded areas. (b) the Southern Uplands, where there are huge copper deposits

2. By the 1400s, several Central African kingdoms had grown powerful through their knowledge of ironworking. Foreign powers were attracted to the area because they wanted to mine gold, copper, and diamonds. As an independent nation, Zaire relied too heavily on its copper mines and, when world copper prices fell, the country's economy suffered.

3. He nationalized industries and borrowed money from foreign countries.

4. (a) Apartheid divided South Africans into categories according to their race. (b) Some South Africans held protests and demonstrations against apartheid.

5. (a) Today, South Africans of all races have the rights of citizenship. They can vote and are legally allowed to live where they wish. Under apartheid, black and colored South Africans had none of these rights. (b) Apartheid has not been over for very long. White people have already been well educated and still retain a good deal of economic power. Most black people have not been well educated and do not yet have the skills they need to rise out of poverty.

6. The new South African government must help improve education and housing for black people. It must also find ways to reassure whites while making certain that blacks have an equal chance for a good life.

Reviewing Key Terms

1. b	**3.** e	**5.** a
2. d	**4.** c	

Reviewing Main Ideas

1. (a) Describe Zaire's four main geographic regions. (b) Which region brings in the most income?

2. How has mining affected the history of Zaire?

3. What actions did Mobutu Sese Seko take after coming to power?

4. (a) How did the system of apartheid affect South Africans in their daily lifes? (b) How did South Africans struggle against apartheid?

5. (a) How is life in today's South Africa different than it was under apartheid? (b) How are people still divided by race?

6. What are some challenges faced by the new government of South Africa?

Reviewing Key Terms

Match the definitions in Column I with the key terms in Column II.

Column I

1. form of government in which a single leader or small group of leaders have all the power

2. a system of laws that legalized racial discrimination

3. rural areas in which black South Africans were forced to live

4. to treat people in a different way based on their race, religion, or sex

5. to put under government control

Column II

a. nationalize

b. authoritarian

c. discrimination

d. apartheid

e. homelands

Critical Thinking

1. Recognizing Cause and Effect How have the actions of Mobutu Sese Seko affected Zaire's economy?

2. Drawing Conclusions South Africa's new government is trying to persuade its skilled white workers to remain in the country. Based on what you know about apartheid, why do you think much of South Africa's population lacks these skills?

Graphic Organizer

Copy the flowchart onto a sheet of paper. Then, fill in the empty boxes to show the impact of resources on Zaire's history, from the first contacts with Europeans to the present.

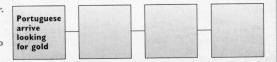

| Portuguese arrive looking for gold | | | |

Graphic Organizer

Answers will vary. Correct student responses may resemble those shown below.

| Portuguese arrive looking for gold. | King Leopold of Belgium takes over and forces Africans to harvest rubber. | Belgium controls and benefits from the Congo's resources. | A drop in the world price of copper harms Zaire's economy. |

Map Activity

Central and Southern Africa

For each place listed below, write the letter from the map that shows its location.

1. Cape Town
2. Johannesburg
3. Kinshasa
4. Zaire
5. South Africa

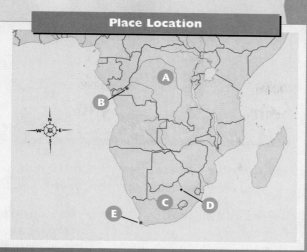

Place Location

Writing Activity

Writing Interview Questions

Choose either South Africa or Zaire. Write a list of five interview questions you would ask someone who is running for president. Consider the challenges the new president will face. Then exchange questions with a partner. Pretend that you are the presidential candidate. Write answers to your partner's questions.

Internet Activity

Use a search engine to find the **Abwenzi** site. Choose the **Abwenzi** home page icon at the bottom. Explore the links and pictures to learn what penpals in Malawi and Aspen, Colorado, learned about each other. Make a class portfolio on daily life in Malawi. Include photos, recipes, writings, and information on games and dances.

Skills Review

Turn to the Skills Activity. Review the steps for organizing your time. Then, in your own words, explain how a flowchart can help you to organize your time.

How Am I Doing?

Answer these questions to check your progress.

1. Can I explain the part that resources have played in Zaire's history?
2. Do I understand the impact of Mobutu Sese Seko's actions on Zaire's economy?
3. Do I understand what apartheid was and how it came to an end?
4. Can I describe how life has changed for black and white South Africans following the collapse of apartheid?

Internet Activity

If students are having difficulty finding this site, you may wish to have them use the following URL, which was accurate at the time this textbook was published:

http://aspen.com/ aspenonline/directory/ business/sponsors/ abwenzi/

You might also guide students to a search engine. Four of the most useful are Infoseek, Alta Vista, Lycos, and Yahoo. For additional suggestions on using the Internet, refer to the Prentice Hall Social Studies' Educator's Handbook "Using the Internet," in the *Prentice*

Hall World Explorer Program Resources.
For additional links to world history and culture topics, visit the Prentice Hall Home Page at:
http://www.phschool.com

How Am I Doing?

Point out to students that this checklist is a quick reminder for them of what they learned in the chapter. If their answer to any of the questions is *no* or if they are unsure, they may need to review the topic.

Critical Thinking

1. President Mobutu borrowed money from foreign countries and nationalized many industries. When nationalized businesses failed, Zaire was left with large debts.

2. Since nonwhites were denied good educations and business opportunities, they have not had the chance to develop the skills necessary to support an economy.

Map Activity

1. E   3. B   5. C
2. D   4. A

Writing Activity

Students' lists of questions will vary, but should reflect an understanding of the current political and economic issues facing Zaire and South Africa.

Skills Review

Possible answer: A flowchart helps you identify the steps you need to take and estimate the amount of time needed to complete the project.

Resource Directory

Teaching Resources

📁 **Chapter Tests** Forms A and B are in the Tests booklet, pp. 38–43.
📁 **Final Exams** Forms A and B are in the Tests booklet, pp. 44–49.

Program Resources

📁 **Writing Process Handbook** includes Organizing Material in a Logical Sequence, pp. 23–24, to help students with the Writing Activity.

Media and Technology

🖥 **Color Transparencies**
Color Transparency 173 (Graphic organizer flow map)
💿 **Prentice Hall Writer's Solution** Writing Lab CD-ROM
💾 **Computer Test Bank**
 Resource Pro™ CD-ROM

Lesson Objectives

1 Display knowledge of Africa in dramatic pre-sentations, art exhibits, conferences, or other projects.

2 Demonstrate an under-standing of the Guiding Questions and their answers by preparing and presenting projects.

Lesson Plan

1 Engage

Warm-Up Activity

Have volunteers post the Guiding Questions on the chalkboard. Ask students to suggest projects that could explore and answer these questions. Explain to students that the *Project Menu* contains several such projects. Students will choose a project to work on during their study of Africa.

Activating Prior Knowledge

Ask students to list five research sources and to describe the kinds of informa-tion each might yield. Compile a classroom list on the chalkboard. Then return to the Guiding Questions and challenge students to tell which resources would be best suited to answering each question.

AFRICA
PROJECT POSSIBILITIES

As you study the vast continent of Africa, you will be reading and thinking about these important questions.

- ☞ **What are the main physical features of Africa?**
- ☞ **What factors have shaped Africa's cultures?**
- ☞ **Why have Africans been moving to cities in recent years?**

- ☞ **What connections do African nations have with the United States and the world?**
- ☞ **What factors influence the ways in which Africans make a living?**

Show what you know by doing a project!

GEO CLEO

Project Menu

The chapters in this book have some answers to these questions. Now it's time for you to find your own answers by doing projects on your own or with a group. Here are some ways to make your own discov-eries about Africa.

Africa on Stage Write a play about growing up in a country in Africa. Set the scene for your play in one of the African countries you have studied. Choose three or four characters. Next think about plot. What situation, serious or humorous, will the main character face? How will he or she react to the situa-tion? How will the other characters affect the plot?

Write a script for your play that shows the lines each character will speak. Then present your play. Ask class-mates to read aloud the parts of your characters. You may wish to videotape your live performance and show it to other classes or your family.

176 AFRICA

Resource Directory

Teaching Resources

📁 **Book Projects** in the Activities and Projects booklet, pp. 8–16, provide a guide to completing the projects described on these two pages. Each project is supported by three pages of structured guidance.

From Questions to Careers
AGRICULTURE

Farmers have always wanted to be able to produce more food. More and more, they face the newer problem of using up too much of the Earth's resources—good soil, land, or grazing material. In some places, people need to farm differently than before because of a changing climate. In Africa and all over the world, people are working on new and different ways of farming that will solve these problems.

Agricultural scientists and farmers work together to develop and try out different farming methods. It may take much time and patience to figure out whether a method works over one or several growing seasons. Engineers invent new machinery, fertilizer, and other products for farmers. Machinists and technicians help manufacture these products. Ecologists study the effects of farming on the surrounding environment.

Agricultural scientists, engineers, and ecologists all go to college. Farmers, technicians, and machinists may go to college or they may have training in specific skills for their jobs. Many farmers learn much of what they know through direct experience.

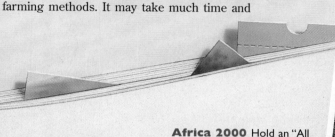

Africa in Art The tradition of mask-making has special meaning in some African cultures. Look through books and magazines for information about different mask-making traditions in Africa. Research the kinds of masks people make, the ways of making them, and the meanings that they have. Prepare a mini-museum display with pictures or examples and detailed explanations of the masks and traditions you research.

You may want to try making a mask of your own. Use papier-mâché and your imagination.

Africa 2000 Hold an "All Africa" conference about life in Africa in the twenty-first century. Decide on several major topics for the conference, such as economic growth, agriculture, literature, and arts. Form committees to plan the conference. For example, a speakers' committee can find speakers to discuss the topics. Speakers can be students who have done research on these topics. A scheduling committee can plan the agenda for the conference. A publicity committee can make posters to let other students know about the conference. A food committee can make and serve African foods. A press committee can write news reports. Invite other classes to attend the conference.

▲ This modern Nigerian farmer is using equipment suitable for his crops and his land.

2 Explore

Have students take turns reading the projects described on the two pages. Begin a discussion of agricultural careers. If possible, invite a visitor from an agricultural college, a farm, or an agricultural business to visit the class. Allow students with agricultural experience to share their knowledge with the class. Then focus on the *Project Menu*. Have student pairs create flowcharts showing the steps and time necessary for each project.

3 Teach

Let students choose a project from the menu or help them develop an alternative project. If you wish, assign projects to students. *Africa 2000* may be best accomplished as a whole class activity. Encourage students to record the completion of each step on their flowcharts. Monitor students at regular intervals.

4 Assess

Allow time for students to present their projects, inviting other classes to attend, if possible.

Rubric

Acceptable projects follow the listed directions and provide accurate information about Africa.

Commendable projects show able research and are creatively presented.

Outstanding projects reflect insight into the issues facing Africa and its people.

Reference

TABLE OF CONTENTS

This Map and Globe Handbook is designed to help you develop some of the skills you need to be a world explorer. These can help you whether you explore from the top of an elephant in India or from a computer at school.

You can use the information in this handbook to improve your map and globe skills. But the best way to sharpen your skills is to practice. The more you practice the better you'll get.

GEO CLEO and GEO LEO

Table of Contents

Using the Map and Globe Handbook

You may choose to present the Map and Globe Handbook as a special unit of study at the beginning of the year or at another point in the school year. As an alternative, you might prefer to choose among the activities in the Map and Globe Handbook to meet the specific needs of your class or of individual students.

Point out to students that they already know a great deal about maps. Ask them to sketch a quick map of the route from their house to school. Discuss the map elements that students include on their maps.

Read through the page with students.

Lesson Objective

Identify and define the five themes of geography.

Lesson Plan

1 Engage

Warm-Up Activity

Work with students to define the word *theme*. (An underlying idea built into or expanded upon in a work of art or study.)

Activating Prior Knowledge

Have students work in small groups for five minutes to write a definition of *geography*. Discuss their definitions. Then write the five themes on the chalkboard and ask students to break up their definitions, putting phrases under the proper headings. For example, if students wrote "studying where other countries are," that would fall under the theme of location. Add to students' definitions as needed.

2 Explore

Read the first verse of the poem "Midwest Town" by Ruth De Long Peterson to the class:

Farther east it wouldn't be on
    the map—
Too small—but here it rates a
    dot and a name.
In Europe it would wear a
    castle cap
Or have a cathedral rising like
    a flame.

Ask students to identify the geography themes in the verse (location and place).

Studying the geography of the entire world can be a huge task. You can make that task easier by using the five themes of geography: location, place, human-environment interaction, movement, and regions. The themes are tools you can use to organize information and to answer the where, why, and how of geography.

1 Location answers the question, "Where is it?" You can think of the location of a continent or a country as its address. You might give an absolute location such as "22 South Lake Street" or "40°N and 80°W." You might also use a relative address, telling where one place is by referring to another place. "Between school and the mall" and "eight miles east of Pleasant City" are examples of relative locations.

2 Place identifies the natural and human features that make one place different from every other place. You can identify a specific place by its landforms, climate, plants, animals, people, or cultures. You might even think of place as a geographic signature. Use the signature to help you understand the natural and human features that make one place different from every other place.

1. Location
Chicago, Illinois, occupies one location on the Earth. No other place has exactly the same absolute location.

2. Place
Ancient cultures in Egypt built distinctive pyramids. Use the theme of place to help you remember features that exist only in Egypt.

3 Human-Environment Interaction

focuses on the relationship between people and the environment. As people live in an area, they often begin to make changes to it, usually to make their lives easier. For example, they might build a dam to control flooding during rainy seasons. Also, the environment can affect how people live, work, dress, travel, and communicate.

4 Movement

answers the question "How do people, goods, and ideas move from place to place?" Remember that, often, what happens in one place can affect what happens in another. Use the theme of movement to help you trace the spread of goods, people, and ideas from one location to the next.

5 Regions

is the last geographic theme. A region is a group of places that share common features. Geographers divide the world into many types of regions. For example, countries, states, and cities are political regions. The people in these places live under the same type of government. Other features can be used to define regions. Places that have the same climate belong to a particular climate region. Places that share the same culture belong to a cultural region. The same place can be found in more than one region. The state of Hawaii is in the political region of the United States. Because it has a tropical climate, Hawaii is also part of a tropical climate region.

PRACTICE YOUR WORLD EXPLORER SKILLS

1. What is the absolute location of your school? What is one way to describe its relative location?

2. What might be a "geographic signature" of the town or city you live in?

3. Give an example of human-environment interaction where you live.

4. Name at least one thing that comes into your town or city and one that goes out. How is each moved? Where does it come from? Where does it go?

5. What are several regions you think your town or city belongs in?

3. Human-Environment Interaction
Peruvians have changed steep mountain slopes into terraces suitable for farming. Think how this environment looked before people made changes.

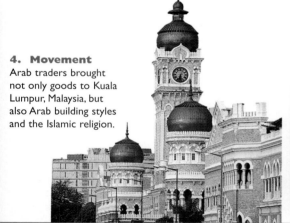

4. Movement
Arab traders brought not only goods to Kuala Lumpur, Malaysia, but also Arab building styles and the Islamic religion.

5. Regions
Wheat farming is an important activity in Kansas. This means that Kansas is part of a farming region.

3 Teach

After students have read the definitions of the themes of geography, begin discussion. Encourage students to relate the themes to what they already know about the Earth and its people. Invite them to provide additional examples for each theme.

4 Assess

Have students work in pairs to create a geographic description of where they live. Descriptions should include one or more items for each of the five themes of geography. Students may need an atlas to find the absolute location of your community. If your community is not in the atlas, accept the absolute location of the nearest city, or other political landmark.

As an alternative, have students complete the Practice Your World Explorer Skills. Assess students' understanding by the accuracy of their answers.

Answers to . . .

PRACTICE YOUR WORLD EXPLORER SKILLS

Sample answers are given for Chicago, Illinois.

1. 33 North Green street, between Green Park and the highway
2. It's along the shore of Lake Michigan.
3. The city built bridges over the river.
4. Manufactured goods leave the city on railroads to other parts of the country. Fruits and vegetables from nearby farms come into the city on trucks.
5. the Midwest, the Great Lakes region

Lesson Objective

Explain how the movement of the Earth causes night and day, as well as the seasons.

Lesson Plan

1 Engage

Warm-Up Activity

To introduce the skill, remind students that the movement of the Earth accounts for some of the differences between places.

Activating Prior Knowledge

Ask students how we know that the Earth moves.

2 Explore

Read the page with students. Discuss anything they have difficulty understanding.

3 Teach

Darken the room and put a lighted lamp on a table. Hold a globe close enough to the lamp to catch the light. Slowly turn the globe to show the movement from day to night. Hold the globe in the positions shown in the diagram to show the changing seasons. Have students practice manipulating the lamp and the globe.

4 Assess

Ask students to apply the skill by explaining why days are longer in the summer in most places in the world—except around the Equator. (The sun's rays hit the Earth most directly near the Equator year-round.)

You may also assess students' understanding by asking them to complete the Practice Your World Explorer Skills.

1. the Earth's tilt
2. March and December

Understanding Movements of the Earth

Planet Earth is part of our solar system. The Earth revolves around the sun in a nearly circular path called an orbit. A revolution, or one complete orbit around the sun, takes 365 1/4 days, or a year. As the Earth revolves around the sun, it is also spinning around in space. This movement is called a rotation. The Earth rotates on its axis—an invisible line through the center of the Earth from the North Pole to the South Pole. The Earth makes one full rotation about every 24 hours. As the Earth rotates, it is daytime on the side facing the sun. It is night on the side away from the sun.

The Earth's axis is tilted at an angle. Because of this tilt, sunlight strikes different parts of the Earth at certain points in the year, creating different seasons.

Earth's Revolution and the Seasons

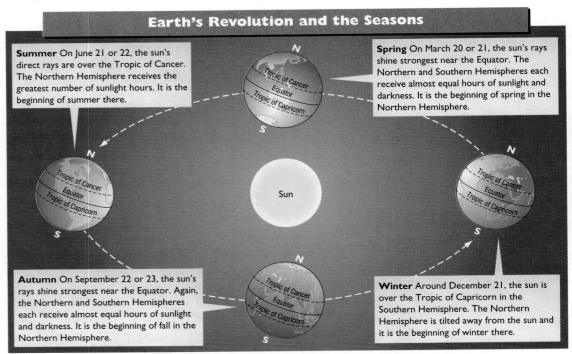

Summer On June 21 or 22, the sun's direct rays are over the Tropic of Cancer. The Northern Hemisphere receives the greatest number of sunlight hours. It is the beginning of summer there.

Spring On March 20 or 21, the sun's rays shine strongest near the Equator. The Northern and Southern Hemispheres each receive almost equal hours of sunlight and darkness. It is the beginning of spring in the Northern Hemisphere.

Autumn On September 22 or 23, the sun's rays shine strongest near the Equator. Again, the Northern and Southern Hemispheres each receive almost equal hours of sunlight and darkness. It is the beginning of fall in the Northern Hemisphere.

Winter Around December 21, the sun is over the Tropic of Capricorn in the Southern Hemisphere. The Northern Hemisphere is tilted away from the sun and it is the beginning of winter there.

▲ **Location** This diagram shows how the Earth's tilt and orbit around the sun combine to create the seasons. Remember, in the Southern Hemisphere the seasons are reversed.

PRACTICE YOUR WORLD EXPLORER SKILLS

1. What causes the seasons in the Northern Hemisphere to be the opposite of those in the Southern Hemisphere?

2. During which two months of the year do the Northern and Southern Hemispheres have about equal hours of daylight and darkness?

Maps and Globes Represent the Earth

Globes

A globe is a scale model of the Earth. It shows the actual shapes, sizes, and locations of all the Earth's landmasses and bodies of water. Features on the surface of the Earth are drawn to scale on a globe. This means a smaller unit of measure on the globe stands for a larger unit of measure on the Earth.

Because a globe is made in the true shape of the Earth, it offers these advantages for studying the Earth.

- The shape of all land and water bodies are accurate.
- Compass directions from one point to any other point are correct.
- The distance from one location to another is always accurately represented.

However, a globe presents some disadvantages for studying the Earth. Because a globe shows the entire Earth, it cannot show small areas in great detail. Also, a globe is not easily folded and carried from one place to another. For these reasons, geographers often use maps to learn about the Earth.

Maps

A map is a drawing or representation, on a flat surface, of a region. A map can show details too small to be seen on a globe. Floor plans, mall directories, and road maps are among the maps we use most often.

While maps solve some of the problems posed by globes, they have some disadvantages of their own. Maps flatten the real round world. Mapmakers cut, stretch, push, and pull some parts of the Earth to get it all flat on paper. As a result, some locations may be distorted. That is, their size, shape, and relative location may not be accurate. For example, on most maps of the entire world, the size and shape of the Antarctic and Arctic regions are not accurate.

PRACTICE YOUR WORLD EXPLORER SKILLS

1. What is the main difference between a globe and a map?

2. What is one advantage of using a globe instead of a map?

Global Gores

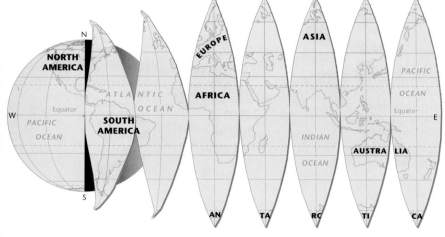

◄ **Location**
When mapmakers flatten the surface of the Earth, curves become straight lines. As a result, size, shape, and distance are distorted.

Lesson Objective

Compare maps and globes as representations of the Earth.

Lesson Plan

1 Engage
Warm-Up Activity
Ask students what it might be like to see the Earth from the inside of a large stained glass globe.

Activating Prior Knowledge
Ask students whether they would use a map or a globe to plan a vacation. Discuss how they might use both.

2 Explore
Have students read the page and study the illustrations. Discuss with them similarities in and differences between maps and globes.

3 Teach
Roughly sketch the continents on a large grapefruit with a ballpoint pen. Explain that the grapefruit is like the Earth. Carefully peel the grapefruit and then challenge students to reassemble the continents into a flat map.

4 Assess
Assess students' understanding by asking them to complete the Practice Your World Explorer Skills.

Answers to . . .

PRACTICE YOUR WORLD EXPLORER SKILLS

1. a globe is a scale model of the Earth; a map is a drawing of a region.
2. Students should be able to support their choices of either accurate shape, true direction, or accurate distance.

The Hemispheres

Another name for a round ball like a globe is a sphere. The Equator, an imaginary line halfway between the North and South Poles, divides the globe into two hemispheres. (The prefix *hemi* means "half.") Land and water south of the Equator are in the Southern Hemisphere. Land and water north of the Equator are in the Northern Hemisphere.

Mapmakers sometimes divide the globe along an imaginary line that runs from North Pole to South Pole. This line, called the Prime Meridian, divides the globe into the Eastern and Western Hemispheres.

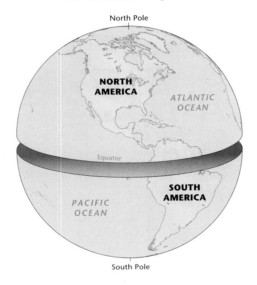

Western Hemisphere   **Eastern Hemisphere**

▲ The Prime Meridian divides the Eastern Hemisphere from the Western Hemisphere.

Southern Hemisphere

▲ The Equator divides the Northern Hemisphere from the Southern Hemisphere.

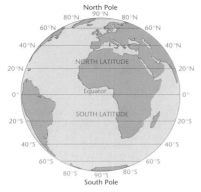

Parallels of Latitude

The Equator, at 0° latitude, is the starting place for measuring latitude or distances north and south. Most globes do not show every parallel of latitude. They may show every 10, 20, or even 30 degrees.

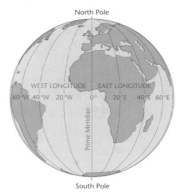

Meridians of Longitude

The Prime Meridian, at 0° longitude, runs from pole to pole through Greenwich, England. It is the starting place for measuring longitude or distances east and west. Each meridian of longitude meets its opposite longitude at the North and South Poles.

The Global Grid

Two sets of lines cover most globes. One set of lines runs parallel to the Equator. These lines, including the Equator, are called *parallels of latitude*. They are measured in degrees (°). One degree of latitude represents a distance of about 70 miles (112 km). The Equator has a location of 0°. The other parallels of latitude tell the direction and distance from the Equator to another location.

The second set of lines runs north and south. These lines are called *meridians of longitude*. Meridians show the degrees of longitude east or west of the Prime Meridian, which is located at 0°. A meridian of longitude tells the direction and distance from the Prime Meridian to another location. Unlike parallels, meridians are not the same distance apart everywhere on the globe.

Together the pattern of parallels of latitude and meridians of longitude is called the global grid. Using the lines of latitude and longitude, you can locate any place on Earth. For example, the location of 30° north latitude and 90° west longitude is usually written as 30°N, 90°W. Only one place on Earth has these coordinates—the city of New Orleans, in the state of Louisiana.

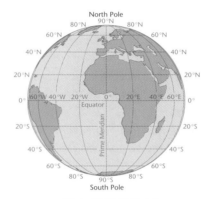

The Global Grid

By using lines of latitude and longitude, you can give the absolute location of any place on the Earth.

PRACTICE YOUR WORLD EXPLORER SKILLS

1 Which continents lie completely in the Northern Hemisphere? The Western Hemisphere?

2 Is there land or water at 20°S latitude and the Prime Meridian? At the Equator and 60°W longitude?

2 Explore

Read through these two pages with students. Using a large map, have students begin at the Prime Meridian and put their fingers on each of the meridians of longitude as they move east and then west. Do the same with the parallels of latitude, moving from the Equator to the North Pole and then to the South Pole. Some students may need help in understanding the definition of *parallel*. (Parallel lines are lines that never meet.)

3 Teach

Ask a volunteer to work with a large map or globe. Have other students name cities around the world. The volunteer must locate them and state their coordinates.

4 Assess

To assess students' understanding, give students coordinates that you have found in an atlas and ask them to locate the city. Have students discuss the process. Use students' discussion to assess their understanding of how to locate places on maps and globes.

1 Compare maps of different projections.

2 Describe distortions in map projections.

Lesson Plan

1 Engage

Warm-Up Activity

Ask students to look at the maps on these two pages. To introduce the skill of understanding map distortions, ask them to find as many differences as they can between the maps.

Activating Prior Knowledge

Ask students whether a person traveling in space could ever see the entire Earth at one time. Ask them why people want or need to use maps that show the entire world.

Map Projections

*I*magine trying to flatten out a complete orange peel. The peel would split. The shape would change. You would have to cut the peel to get it to lie flat. In much the same way, maps cannot show the correct size and shape of every landmass or body of water on the Earth's curved surface. Maps shrink some places and stretch others. This shrinking and stretching is called distortion—*a change made to a shape.*

To make up for this disadvantage, mapmakers use different map projections. Each map projection is a way of showing the round Earth on flat paper. Each type of projection has some distortion. No one projection can accurately show the correct area, shape, distance, and direction for the Earth's surface. Mapmakers use the projection that has the least distortion for the information they are studying.

Same-Shape Maps

Some map projections can accurately show the shapes of landmasses. However, these projections often greatly distort the size of landmasses as well as the distance between them.

One of the most common same-shape maps is a Mercator projection, named for the mapmaker who invented it. The Mercator projection accurately shows shape and direction, but it distorts distance and size. In this projection, the northern and southern areas of the globe appear stretched more than areas near the Equator. Because the projection shows true directions, ships' navigators use it to chart a straight line course between two ports.

Mercator Projection

Equal-Area Maps

Some map projections can show the correct size of landmasses. Maps that use these projections are called equal-area maps. In order to show the correct size of landmasses, these maps usually distort shapes. The distortion is usually greater at the edges of the map and less at the center.

Robinson Maps

Many of the maps in this book use the Robinson projection. This is a compromise between the Mercator and equal-area projections. It gives a useful overall picture of the world. The Robinson projection keeps the size and shape relationships of most continents and oceans but does distort size of the polar regions.

Azimuthal Maps

Another kind of projection shows true compass direction. Maps that use this projection are called azimuthal maps. Such maps are easy to recognize—they are usually circular. Azimuthal maps are often used to show the areas of the North and South Poles. However, azimuthal maps distort scale, area, and shape.

1. What feature is distorted on an equal-area map?

2. Would you use a Mercator projection to find the exact distance between two locations? Tell why or why not.

3. Which would be a better choice for studying the Antarctic—an azimuthal projection or a Robinson projection? Explain.

Equal-Area Projection

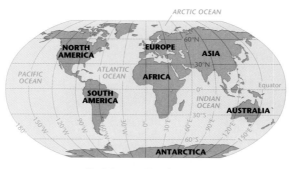

Robinson Projection

Azimuthal Projection

2 Explore

After students have read the two pages, have them look up the word *distortion* in a dictionary. Ask them why we use maps that we know are distorted. (All maps are somewhat distorted.)

3 Teach

Students can practice the skill by comparing the maps to a globe. Ask them to note especially the sizes and positions of Greenland and Antarctica.

To apply their understanding of the skill, students can suggest reasons why many of the maps in this book use the Robinson projection. (It shows the sizes and shapes of the continents with the least amount of distortion.)

4 Assess

Assess students' understanding by the accuracy of their answers.

Lesson Objective

Identify and use the parts of a map.

Lesson Plan

1 Engage

Warm-Up Activity

If possible, show students several maps, such as subway or bus route maps and road maps. To introduce the skill, ask students to describe several parts that all of the maps seem to have in common (probably titles, legends, scales, and compasses).

Activating Prior Knowledge

Ask students why they should pay attention to different parts of a map. (They help the user locate places on it.)

2 Explore

Read the page with students. Help them identify the title, compass, scale, and legend on several different maps.

3 Teach

Show students several maps, including those in the Atlas of this book. Students can practice and apply using the parts of a map by asking each other questions such as What is this map about? Which city is north of the river? How far apart are these two cities?

4 Assess

Assess students' understanding by the accuracy of their answers.

Answers to ...

PRACTICE YOUR WORLD EXPLORER SKILLS

1. the title
2. legend
3. scale

Mapmakers provide several clues to help you understand the information on a map. As an explorer, it is your job to read and interpret these clues.

Compass
Many maps show north at the top of the map. One way to show direction on a map is to use an arrow that points north. There may be an N shown with the arrow. Many maps give more information about direction by displaying a compass showing the directions, north, east, south, and west. The letters N, E, S, and W are placed to indicate these directions.

Title
The title of a map is the most basic clue. It signals what kinds of information you are likely to find on the map. A map titled *West Africa: Population Density* will be most useful for locating information about where people live in West Africa.

West Africa: Population Density

KEY

Persons per sq mi	Persons per sq km
520 and over	200 and over
260–519	100–199
130–259	50–99
25–129	10–49
1–24	1–9
Under 1	Under 1

Cities
- ○ 2,000,000–4,999,999
- ⊙ 1,000,000–1,999,999
- ● 250,000–999,999
- ○ Under 250,000

Lambert Azimuthal Equal-Area Projection

Scale
A map scale helps you find the actual distances between points shown on the map. You can measure the distance between any two points on the map, compare them to the scale, and find out the actual distance between the points. Most map scales show distances in both miles and kilometers.

Key
Often a map has a key, or legend, that shows the symbols used on the map and what each one means. On some maps, color is used as a symbol. On those maps, the key also tells the meaning of each color.

PRACTICE YOUR WORLD EXPLORER SKILLS

1. What part of a map tells you what the map is about?

2. Where on the map should you look to find out the meaning of this symbol? ●

3. What part of the map can you use to find the distance between two cities?

Comparing Maps of Different Scale

Here are three maps drawn to three different scales. The first map shows Moscow's location in the northeastern portion of Russia. This map shows the greatest area—a large section of northern Europe. It has the smallest scale (1 inch = about 900 miles) and shows the fewest details. This map can tell you what direction to travel to reach Moscow from Finland.

Find the red box on Map 1. It shows the whole area covered by Map 2. Study Map 2. It gives a closer look at the city of Moscow. It shows the features around the city, the city's boundary, and the general shape of the city. This map can help you find your way from the airport to the center of town.

Now find the red box on Map 2. This box shows the area shown on Map 3. This map moves you closer into the city. Like the zoom on a computer or camera, Map 3 shows the smallest area but has the greatest detail. This map has the largest scale (1 inch = about 0.8 miles). This is the map to use to explore downtown Moscow.

Map 1

KEY

—— National boundary

| 0 | 500 | 1,000 mi |
| 0 | 500 | 1,000 km |

One inch = about 900 miles

Map 2

KEY

▨ Built-up area

--- Road or street

| 0 | 5 | 10 mi |
| 0 | 5 | 10 km |

One inch = about 12.5 miles

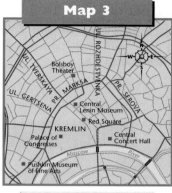

Map 3

KEY

===== Road or street

■ Point of interest

| 0 | .5 | 1 mi |
| 0 | .5 | 1 km |

One inch = about 0.8 miles

PRACTICE YOUR WORLD EXPLORER SKILLS

1. Which map would be best for finding the location of Red Square? Why?

2. Which map best shows Moscow's location relative to Poland? Explain.

3. Which map best shows the area immediately surrounding the city?

Lesson Objective

Compare maps with different scales.

Lesson Plan

1 Engage

Warm-Up Activity

To introduce the skill, ask students why they cannot find the exact location of their school on a world map. Ask them what kind of map would show the exact location of their school.

Activating Prior Knowledge

Ask students what the zoom on a video camera does. Tell students that changing a map scale can help them "zoom in" on a small area.

2 Explore

Have students read the page and study the maps. How are the maps alike? How are they different?

3 Teach

To practice and apply the skill, work with students to identify the steps in drawing a map of their classroom to the scale of 1 inch = 1 foot. Ask students how the map would be different if the scale were 1 inch = 3 foot.

4 Assess

Have students complete the Practice Your World Explorer Skills. Assess their understanding by the accuracy of their answers.

Answers to...

PRACTICE YOUR WORLD EXPLORER SKILLS

1. map 3 2. map 1 3. map 2

Political Maps

1 Engage

Warm-Up Activity

To introduce the skill, tell students that American writer Mark Twain once wrote about people in a hot-air balloon who were confused because the ground below them was not colored like maps.

Activating Prior Knowledge

Point out that the word *political* comes from a Greek word meaning "citizen." A political map is one that emphasizes the boundaries of an area established by its citizens.

2 Explore

Read through the page with students. Make sure they realize that a political map mainly shows how people have divided and named the land.

3 Teach

Ask students to practice using a political map by locating a boundary between countries, the capital of Russia, and a river that is also a boundary.

4 Assess

Have students complete the Practice Your World Explorer Skills. Assess their understanding by the accuracy of their answers.

Answers to ...

PRACTICE YOUR WORLD EXPLORER SKILLS

1. red line   2. star in a circle
3. solid circle

Mapmakers create maps to show all kinds of information. The kind of information presented affects the way a map looks. One type of map is called a political map. Its main purpose is to show continents, countries, and divisions within countries such as states or provinces. Usually different colors are used to show different countries or divisions within a country. The colors do not have any special meaning. They are used only to make the map easier to read.

Political maps also show where people have built towns and cities. Symbols can help you tell capital cities from other cities and towns. Even though political maps do not give information that shows what the land looks like, they often include some physical features such as oceans, lakes, and rivers.

Political maps usually have many labels. They give country names, and the names of capital and major cities. Bodies of water such as lakes, rivers, oceans, seas, gulfs, and bays are also labeled.

1 What symbol shows the continental boundary?

2 What symbol is used to indicate a capital city? A major city?

3 What kinds of landforms are shown on this map?

▲ The keys of political maps may include symbols. Study the key to learn what the symbols on this map mean.

Physical Maps

Like political maps, physical maps show country labels and labels for capital cities. However, physical maps also show what the land of a region looks like by showing the major physical features such as plains, hills, plateaus, or mountains. Labels give the names of features such as mountain peaks, mountains, plateaus, and river basins.

In order to tell one landform from another, physical maps often show elevation and relief.

Elevation is the height of the land above sea level. Physical maps in this book use color to show elevation. Browns and oranges show higher lands while blues and greens show lands that are at or below sea level.

Relief shows how quickly the land rises or falls. Hills, mountains, and plateaus are shown on relief maps using shades of gray. Level or nearly level land is shown without shading. Darkly shaded areas indicate steeper lands.

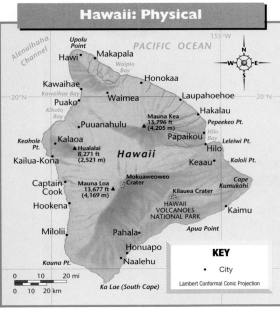

Hawaii: Physical

PRACTICE YOUR WORLD EXPLORER SKILLS

1. How is relief shown on the map to the left?

2. How can you use relief to decide which areas will be the most difficult to climb?

3. What information is given with the name of a mountain peak?

▲ On a physical map, shading is sometimes used to show relief. Use the shading to locate the mountains in Hawaii.

▼ Mauna Kea, an extinct volcano, is the highest peak in the state of Hawaii. Find Mauna Kea on the map.

Lesson Objective

Use physical maps.

Lesson Plan

1 Engage
Warm-Up Activity

To introduce the skill, tell students that they are going for a hike in the mountains. Encourage them to consider that a map showing the heights of the mountains might be useful.

Activating Prior Knowledge

Remind students that political maps do not necessarily show features of the landscape.

2 Explore

Have students read the page. Point out that a physical map makes the physical features of a place clearer than a political map does.

3 Teach

Students can practice using a physical map by checking this one for the highest mountain it shows. Have students apply the skill by pointing out other physical features on the map.

4 Assess

Have students complete the Practice Your World Explorer Skills. Assess their understanding by the accuracy of their answers.

Answers to . . .

PRACTICE YOUR WORLD EXPLORER SKILLS

1. shading
2. Darkly shaded areas are steep and more difficult to climb.
3. its elevation

Lesson Objectice

Use special-purpose maps.

Lesson Plan

1 Engage

Warm-Up Activity

Discuss with students the tools they would need during an archaeological dig in the desert of South Asia. Ask what kinds of maps they would need.

Activating Prior Knowledge

Ask students to think of as many meanings for the word *special* as they can. Have them define special-purpose map, and then read the lesson to check their definitions.

2 Explore

When students have read the page, ask them to offer other examples of special-purpose maps.

3 Teach

Review the importance of the map title and the map legend. Discuss the purposes of the map on the page. How is it different from political maps and physical maps?

4 Assess

Have students complete the Practice Your World Explorer Skills. Assess their understanding by the accuracy of their answers.

Answers to . . .

PRACTICE YOUR WORLD EXPLORER SKILLS

1. its title
2. the legend

As you explore the world, you will encounter many different kinds of special purpose maps. For example, a road map is a special purpose map. The title of each special purpose map tells the purpose and content of the map. Usually a special purpose map highlights only one kind of information. Examples of special purpose maps include land use, population distribution, recreation, transportation, natural resources, or weather.

The key on a special purpose map is very important. Even though a special purpose map shows only one kind of information, it may present many different pieces of data. This data can be shown in symbols, colors, or arrows. In this way, the key acts like a dictionary for the map.

Reading a special purpose map is a skill in itself. Look at the map below. First, try to get an overall sense of what it shows. Then, study the map to identify its main ideas. For example, one main idea of this map is that much of the petroleum production in the region takes place around the Persian Gulf.

PRACTICE YOUR WORLD EXPLORER SKILLS

1. What part of a special purpose map tells what information is contained on the map?

2. What part of a special purpose map acts like a dictionary for the map?

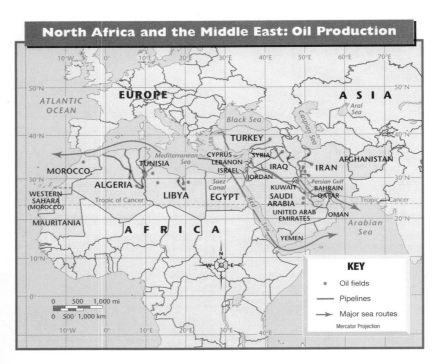

North Africa and the Middle East: Oil Production

KEY
- Oil fields
- Pipelines
- Major sea routes

Mercator Projection

◄ The title on a special purpose map indicates what information can be found on the map. The symbols used on the map are explained in the map's key.

Landforms, Climate Regions, and Natural Vegetation Regions

Maps that show landforms, climate, and vegetation regions are special purpose maps. Unlike the boundary lines on a political map, the boundary lines on these maps do not separate the land into exact divisions. A tropical wet climate gradually changes to a tropical wet and dry climate. A tundra gradually changes to an ice cap. Even though the boundaries between regions may not be exact, the information on these maps can help you understand the region and the lives of people in it.

Landforms

Understanding how people use the land requires an understanding of the shape of the land itself. The four most important landforms are mountains, hills, plateaus, and plains. Human activity in every region in the world is influenced by these landforms.

- **Mountains** are high and steep. Most are wide at the bottom and rise to a narrow peak or ridge. Most geographers classify a mountain as land that rises at least 2,000 feet (610 m) above sea level. A series of mountains is called a mountain range.

- **Hills** rise above surrounding land and have rounded tops. Hills are lower and usually less steep than mountains. The elevation of surrounding land determines whether a landform is called a mountain or a hill.
- A **plateau** is a large, mostly flat area of land that rises above the surrounding land. At least one side of a plateau has a steep slope.
- **Plains** are large areas of flat or gently rolling land. Plains have few changes in elevation. Many plains areas are located along coasts. Others are located in the interior regions of some continents.

▶ A satellite view of the Earth showing North and South America. What landforms are visible in the photograph?

Lesson Plan

1 Engage

Warm-Up Activity

Ask students how they would describe their community to someone moving to their area from Australia. What words would they use to describe the land, the general climate, and the kinds of trees and plants?

Activating Prior Knowledge

Invite volunteers who have moved to your area from a different region to explain how the climate and vegetation are different.

Climate Regions

Another important influence in the ways people live their lives is the climate of their region. Climate is the weather of a given location over a long period of time. Use the descriptions in the table below to help you visualize the climate regions shown on maps.

Climate	Temperatures	Precipitation
Tropical		
Tropical wet	Hot all year round	Heavy all year round
Tropical wet and dry	Hot all year round	Heavy when sun is overhead, dry other times
Dry		
Semiarid	Hot summers, mild to cold winters	Light
Arid	Hot days, cold nights	Very light
Mild		
Mediterranean	Hot summers, cool winters	Dry summers, wet winters
Humid subtropical	Hot summers, cool winters	Year round, heavier in summer than in winter
Marine west coast	Warm summers, cool winters	Year round, heavier in winter than in summer
Continental		
Humid continental	Hot summers, cold winters	Year round, heavier in summer than in winter
Subarctic	Cool summers, cold winters	Light
Polar		
Tundra	Cool summers, very cold winters	Light
Ice Cap	Cold all year round	Light
Highlands	Varies, depending on altitude and direction of prevailing winds	Varies, depending on altitude and direction of prevailing winds

Natural Vegetation Regions

Natural vegetation is the plant life that grows wild without the help of humans. A world vegetation map tells what the vegetation in a place would be if people had not cut down forests or cleared grasslands. The table below provides descriptions of natural vegetation regions shown on maps. Comparing climate and vegetation regions can help you see the close relationship between climate and vegetation.

Vegetation	Description
Tropical rain forest	Tall, close-growing trees forming a canopy over smaller trees, dense growth in general
Deciduous forest	Trees and plants that regularly lose their leaves after each growing season
Mixed forest	Both leaf-losing and cone-bearing trees, no type of tree dominant
Coniferous forest	Cone-bearing trees, evergreen trees and plants
Mediterranean vegetation	Evergreen shrubs and small plants
Tropical savanna	Tall grasses with occasional trees and shrubs
Temperate grassland	Tall grasses with occasional stands of trees
Desert scrub	Low shrubs and bushes, hardy plants
Desert	Little or no vegetation
Tundra	Low shrubs, mosses, lichens; no trees
Ice Cap	No vegetation
Highlands	Varies, depending on altitude and direction of prevailing winds

PRACTICE YOUR WORLD EXPLORER SKILLS

1. How are mountains and hills similar? How are they different?
2. What is the difference between a plateau and a plain?

Atlas

The World: Political

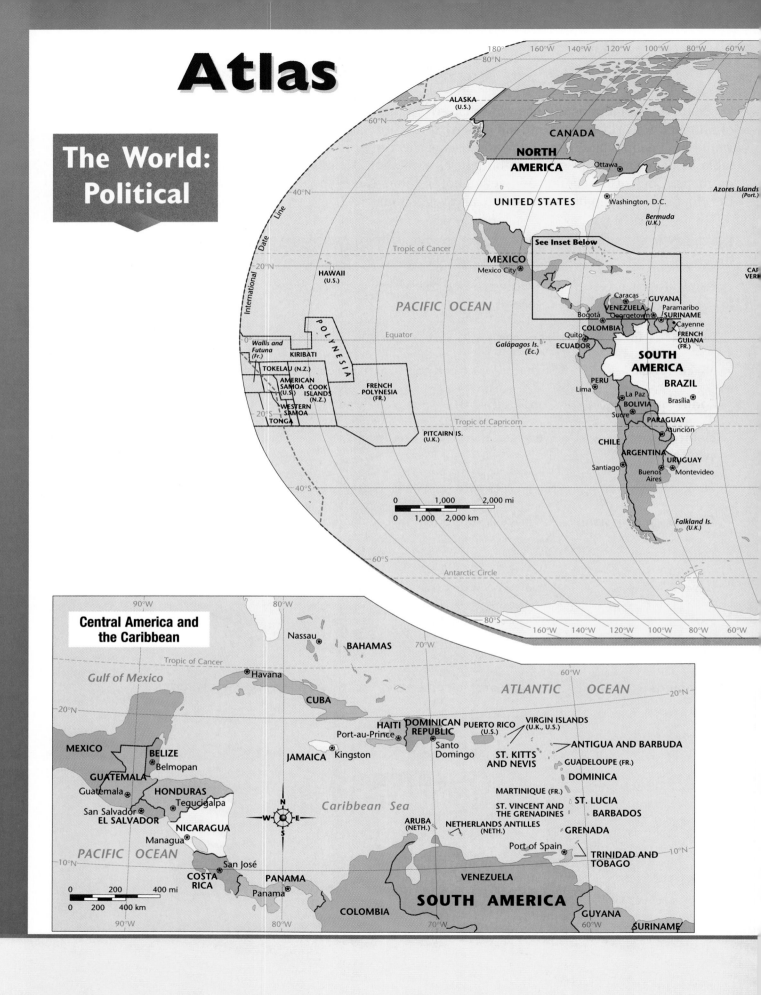

80°N

ALASKA (U.S.)

60°N

CANADA

NORTH AMERICA

Ottawa ⊛

40°N

UNITED STATES

⊛ Washington, D.C.

Azores Islands (Port.)

Bermuda (U.K.)

Tropic of Cancer

See Inset Below

MEXICO

Mexico City ⊛

CAP VER‖

HAWAII (U.S.)

PACIFIC OCEAN

Caracas
VENEZUELA **GUYANA**
Bogotá ⊛ Georgetown ⊛ Paramaribo
COLOMBIA **SURINAME**
✕ Cayenne
Quito ⊛ **FRENCH GUIANA (FR.)**

Equator

Galápagos Is. (Ec.) **ECUADOR**

Wallis and Futuna (Fr.)
KIRIBATI

SOUTH AMERICA

PERU **BRAZIL**
Lima ⊛

International Date Line

P O L Y N E S I A

TOKELAU (N.Z.)

AMERICAN SAMOA (U.S) **COOK ISLANDS (N.Z.)**

FRENCH POLYNESIA (FR.)

La Paz ⊛
BOLIVIA Brasília ⊛
Sucre ⊛ **PARAGUAY**
Asunción ⊛

20°S

WESTERN SAMOA

TONGA

Tropic of Capricorn

PITCAIRN IS. (U.K.)

CHILE **ARGENTINA** **URUGUAY**
Santiago ⊛ Buenos Montevideo
Aires

40°S

| 0 | 1,000 | 2,000 mi |
| 0 | 1,000 | 2,000 km |

Falkland Is. (U.K.)

60°S

Antarctic Circle

80°S

160°W 140°W 120°W 100°W 80°W 60°W

Central America and the Caribbean

90°W **80°W**

Nassau ⊛
BAHAMAS **70°W**

Tropic of Cancer

60°W

ATLANTIC OCEAN
20°N

Gulf of Mexico

⊛ Havana

20°N

CUBA

HAITI **DOMINICAN REPUBLIC** **PUERTO RICO (U.S.)** **VIRGIN ISLANDS (U.K., U.S.)**
Port-au-Prince ⊛
Santo Domingo

ANTIGUA AND BARBUDA

MEXICO

BELIZE
⊛ Belmopan

JAMAICA Kingston

ST. KITTS AND NEVIS **GUADELOUPE (FR.)**

DOMINICA

GUATEMALA
Guatemala ⊛ **HONDURAS**
Tegucigalpa ⊛

Caribbean Sea

MARTINIQUE (FR.) **ST. LUCIA**

ST. VINCENT AND THE GRENADINES **BARBADOS**

San Salvador ⊛
EL SALVADOR

NICARAGUA

Managua ⊛

W ✦ E
S

ARUBA (NETH.) **NETHERLANDS ANTILLES (NETH.)**

GRENADA

Port of Spain ⊛

PACIFIC OCEAN

San José ⊛
COSTA RICA **PANAMA**
Panama ⊛

VENEZUELA

TRINIDAD AND TOBAGO
10°N

10°N

COLOMBIA **SOUTH AMERICA**

GUYANA

SURINAME

| 0 | 200 | 400 mi |
| 0 | 200 | 400 km |

90°W **80°W** **70°W** **60°W**

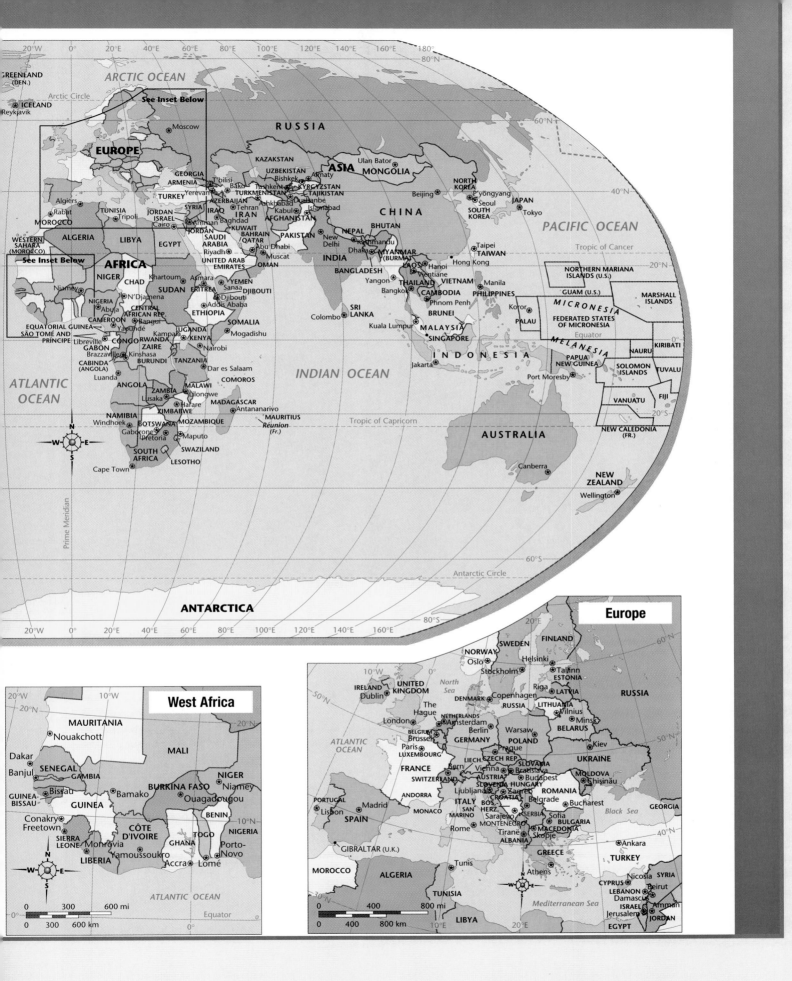

Main World Map

ARCTIC OCEAN

GREENLAND (DEN.)

ICELAND
Reykjavik

Arctic Circle

See Inset Below

EUROPE

Moscow

RUSSIA

ASIA

Ulan Bator

MONGOLIA

KAZAKHSTAN

GEORGIA
ARMENIA
T'bilisi
UZBEKISTAN
Bishkek
Almaty
Baku
Tashkent
KYRGYZSTAN
NORTH KOREA
P'yŏngyang

TURKEY
Yerevan
AZERBAIJAN
TURKMENISTAN
TAJIKISTAN
Dushanbe
Beijing
Seoul
JAPAN
SOUTH KOREA
Tokyo

Algiers
Rabat
TUNISIA
Tripoli
JORDAN
ISRAEL
SYRIA
IRAQ
Tehran
IRAN
Ashkhabad
Islamabad
Kabul
AFGHANISTAN
CHINA
PACIFIC OCEAN

MOROCCO
Cairo
JORDAN
Amman
Baghdad
KUWAIT
CHINA

WESTERN SAHARA (MOROCCO)
ALGERIA
LIBYA
EGYPT
SAUDI ARABIA
Riyadh
BAHRAIN
QATAR
Abu Dhabi
Muscat
OMAN
PAKISTAN
New Delhi
NEPAL
Kathmandu
BHUTAN
Dhaka
Taipei
TAIWAN
Tropic of Cancer

See Inset Below
AFRICA
UNITED ARAB EMIRATES
INDIA
BANGLADESH
MYANMAR (BURMA)
Hong Kong

NIGER
CHAD
Khartoum
Asmara
YEMEN
Sanaa
DJIBOUTI
Yangon
LAOS
Hanoi
Vientiane
VIETNAM
Manila
NORTHERN MARIANA ISLANDS (U.S.)

Niamey
NIGERIA
Abuja
SUDAN
ERITREA
Djibouti
THAILAND
Bangkok
CAMBODIA
PHILIPPINES
GUAM (U.S.)
MARSHALL ISLANDS

N'Djamena
CENTRAL AFRICAN REP.
ETHIOPIA
Addis Ababa
SRI LANKA
Colombo
Phnom Penh
BRUNEI
MICRONESIA
FEDERATED STATES OF MICRONESIA

EQUATORIAL GUINEA
SÃO TOMÉ AND PRÍNCIPE
CAMEROON
Bangui
Yaoundé
SOMALIA
Mogadishu
Kuala Lumpur
MALAYSIA
SINGAPORE
Koror
PALAU
Equator

Libreville
GABON
CONGO
ZAIRE
RWANDA
UGANDA
KENYA
Kampala
Nairobi
INDONESIA
Jakarta
NAURU
KIRIBATI

ATLANTIC OCEAN
Brazzaville
Kinshasa
CABINDA (ANGOLA)
BURUNDI
TANZANIA
Dar es Salaam
COMOROS
INDIAN OCEAN
MELANESIA
PAPUA NEW GUINEA
SOLOMON ISLANDS
TUVALU

Luanda
ANGOLA
ZAMBIA
MALAWI
Lilongwe
Lusaka
Harare
MADAGASCAR
Antananarivo
Port Moresby
VANUATU
FIJI

NAMIBIA
Windhoek
BOTSWANA
ZIMBABWE
MOZAMBIQUE
MAURITIUS
Réunion (Fr.)
Tropic of Capricorn
NEW CALEDONIA (FR.)

Gaborone
Pretoria
Maputo
SWAZILAND
AUSTRALIA

SOUTH AFRICA
LESOTHO
Canberra

Cape Town
NEW ZEALAND
Wellington

Prime Meridian
Antarctic Circle

ANTARCTICA

West Africa (inset)

West Africa

MAURITANIA
Nouakchott
MALI

Dakar
SENEGAL
Banjul
GAMBIA
NIGER
Niamey

GUINEA-BISSAU
Bissau
Bamako
BURKINA FASO
Ouagadougou

Conakry
Freetown
GUINEA
BENIN
NIGERIA

SIERRA LEONE
Monrovia
CÔTE D'IVOIRE
TOGO
GHANA
Porto-Novo

LIBERIA
Yamoussoukro
Accra
Lomé

ATLANTIC OCEAN
Equator

0   300   600 mi
0   300   600 km

Europe (inset)

Europe

SWEDEN
FINLAND
NORWAY
Oslo
Stockholm
Helsinki

IRELAND
Dublin
UNITED KINGDOM
North Sea
DENMARK
Copenhagen
Tallinn
ESTONIA
Riga
LATVIA
RUSSIA

The Hague
NETHERLANDS
Amsterdam
Berlin
RUSSIA
LITHUANIA
Vilnius
Minsk
BELARUS

London
BELGIUM
Brussels
GERMANY
Warsaw
POLAND
Kiev
UKRAINE

ATLANTIC OCEAN
Paris
LUXEMBOURG
Prague
LIECH.
CZECH REP.
SLOVAKIA
Bratislava

FRANCE
Bern
Vienna
AUSTRIA
Budapest
MOLDOVA
Chişinău

SWITZERLAND
SLOVENIA
HUNGARY
ROMANIA
GEORGIA

ANDORRA
Ljubljana
Zagreb
CROATIA
Belgrade
Bucharest

PORTUGAL
MONACO
ITALY
SAN MARINO
BOS. HERZ.
Sarajevo
SERBIA
MONTENEGRO
Sofia
BULGARIA
Black Sea

Lisbon
Madrid
SPAIN
Rome
Tirané
MACEDONIA
Skopje
ALBANIA
Ankara

GIBRALTAR (U.K.)
GREECE
TURKEY
Nicosia
CYPRUS
SYRIA

MOROCCO
ALGERIA
Tunis
Athens
LEBANON
Beirut
Damascus

TUNISIA
Mediterranean Sea
ISRAEL
Jerusalem
Amman
JORDAN

LIBYA
EGYPT

0   400   800 mi
0   400   800 km

The World: Physical

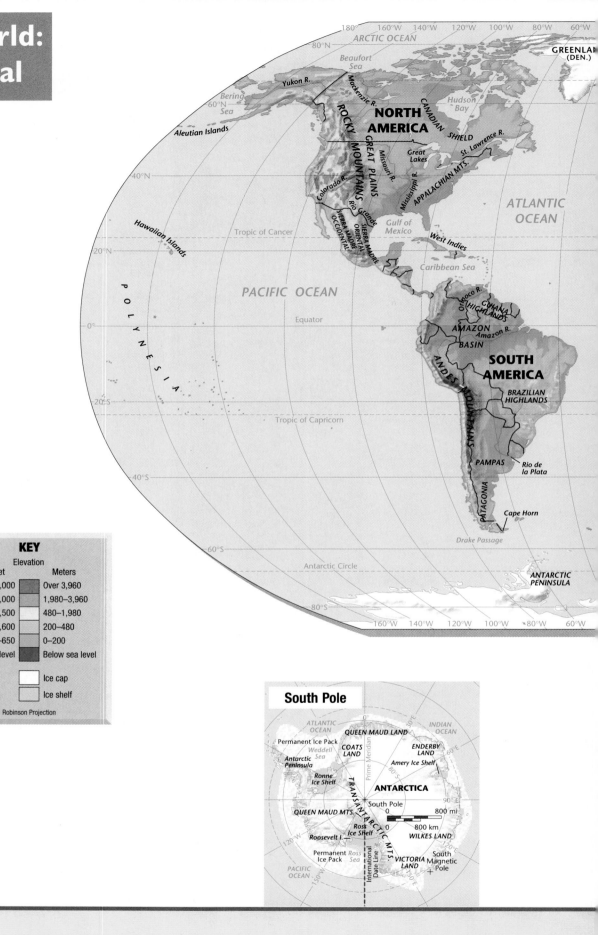

KEY

Elevation

Feet	Meters
Over 13,000	Over 3,960
6,500–13,000	1,980–3,960
1,600–6,500	480–1,980
650–1,600	200–480
0–650	0–200
Below sea level	Below sea level

Ice cap

Ice shelf

Robinson Projection

South Pole

ATLANTIC OCEAN

INDIAN OCEAN

QUEEN MAUD LAND

Permanent Ice Pack

Weddell Sea

COATS LAND

ENDERBY LAND

Antarctic Peninsula

Ronne Ice Shelf

Amery Ice Shelf

ANTARCTICA

Prime Meridian

TRANSANTARCTIC MTS.

QUEEN MAUD MTS.

South Pole

0   800 mi

0   800 km

Roosevelt I.

Ross Ice Shelf

WILKES LAND

Permanent Ice Pack

Ross Sea

VICTORIA LAND

South Magnetic Pole

PACIFIC OCEAN

International Date Line

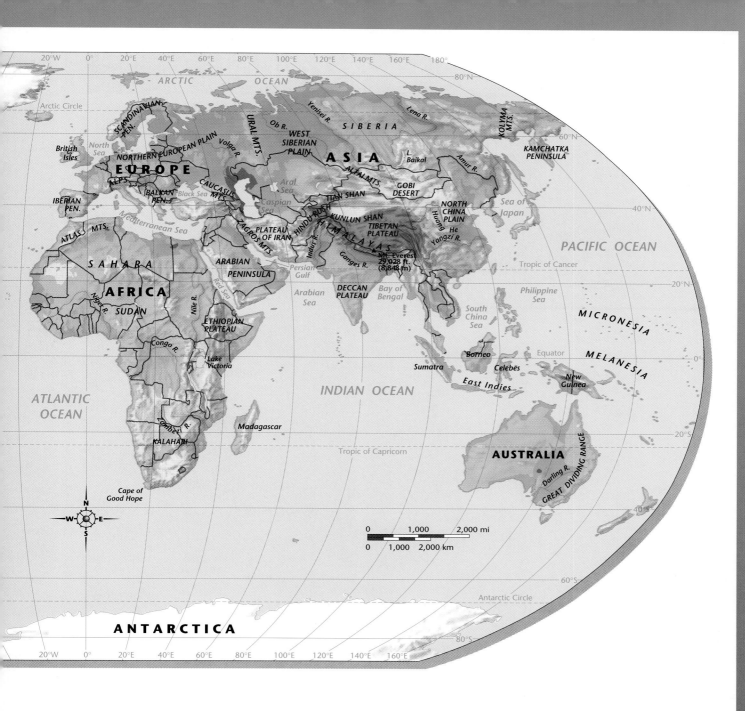

ARCTIC OCEAN

Arctic Circle

SCANDINAVIAN PEN.

British Isles

North Sea

NORTHERN EUROPEAN PLAIN

EUROPE

ALPS

IBERIAN PEN.

BALKAN PEN.

Black Sea

ATLAS MTS.

Mediterranean Sea

SAHARA

AFRICA

Niger R.

SUDAN

Nile R.

ETHIOPIAN PLATEAU

Congo R.

Lake Victoria

ATLANTIC OCEAN

Zambezi R.

KALAHARI

Cape of Good Hope

URAL MTS.

Ob R.

WEST SIBERIAN PLAIN

Volga R.

CAUCASUS MTS.

Caspian Sea

Aral Sea

ZAGROS MTS.

PLATEAU OF IRAN

HINDU KUSH

Indus R.

ARABIAN PENINSULA

Persian Gulf

Red Sea

Arabian Sea

SIBERIA

Yenisei R.

Lena R.

ASIA

ALTAI MTS.

TIAN SHAN

KUNLUN SHAN

TIBETAN PLATEAU

HIMALAYAS

Mt. Everest 29,028 ft. (8,848 m)

Ganges R.

DECCAN PLATEAU

Bay of Bengal

INDIAN OCEAN

Madagascar

L. Baikal

GOBI DESERT

Amur R.

NORTH CHINA PLAIN

Huang He

Yangzi R.

KOLYMA MTS.

KAMCHATKA PENINSULA

Sea of Japan

PACIFIC OCEAN

Tropic of Cancer

Philippine Sea

South China Sea

Sumatra

East Indies

Borneo

Celebes

New Guinea

MICRONESIA

MELANESIA

Equator

Tropic of Capricorn

AUSTRALIA

Darling R.

GREAT DIVIDING RANGE

N W E S

| 0 | 1,000 | 2,000 mi |
| 0 | 1,000 | 2,000 km |

Antarctic Circle

ANTARCTICA

20°W 0° 20°E 40°E 60°E 80°E 100°E 120°E 140°E 160°E 180°

80°N

60°N

40°N

20°N

0°

20°S

40°S

60°S

80°S

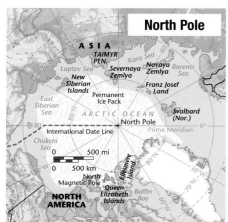

North Pole

ASIA

TAIMYR PEN.

Kara Sea

Laptev Sea

New Siberian Islands

Severnaya Zemlya

Novaya Zemlya

Barents Sea

Franz Josef Land

East Siberian Sea

Permanent Ice Pack

ARCTIC OCEAN

North Pole

Svalbard (Nor.)

Prime Meridian

Chukchi Sea

International Date Line

| 0 | 500 mi |
| 0 | 500 km |

North Magnetic Pole

NORTH AMERICA

Queen Elizabeth Islands

Ellesmere Island

Baffin Bay

United States: Political

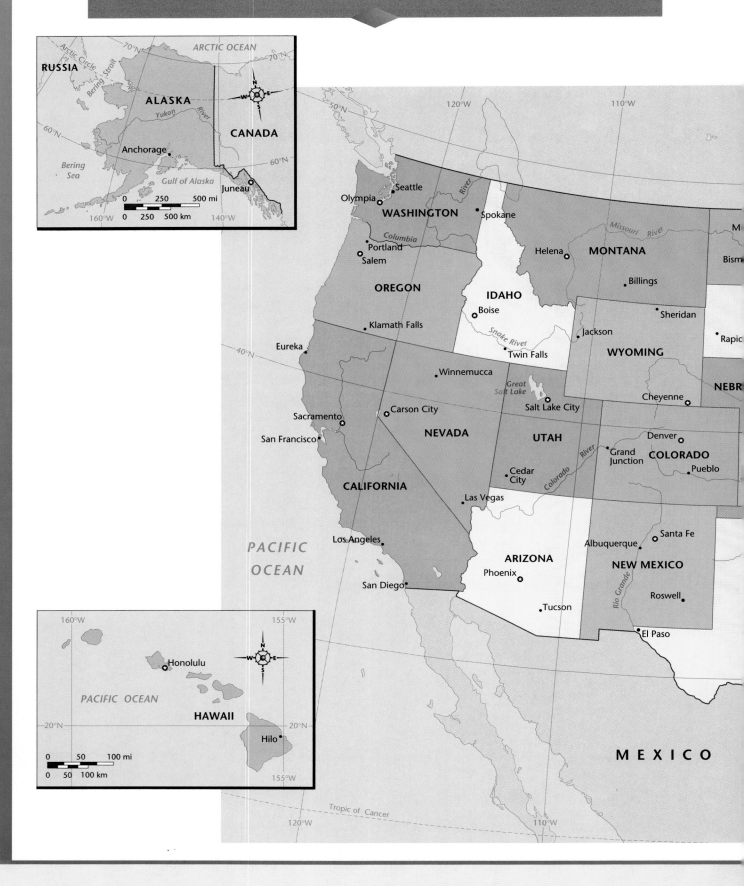

RUSSIA

ARCTIC OCEAN

ALASKA

CANADA

Anchorage

Bering Sea

Gulf of Alaska

Juneau

Yukon River

Arctic Circle

Bering Strait

| 0 | 250 | 500 mi |
| 0 | 250 | 500 km |

ARCTIC OCEAN

CANADA

WASHINGTON
Olympia • Seattle
Spokane
Columbia
Portland
Salem

OREGON

Klamath Falls

Eureka

IDAHO
Boise
Snake River
Twin Falls

MONTANA
Helena
Billings

Bism

WYOMING
Sheridan
Jackson

Rapic

Winnemucca

Great Salt Lake

Salt Lake City

Cheyenne

NEBR

Sacramento
Carson City

San Francisco

NEVADA

UTAH

Denver
Grand Junction

COLORADO
Pueblo

Cedar City

Colorado River

CALIFORNIA

Las Vegas

Los Angeles

PACIFIC OCEAN

San Diego

ARIZONA
Phoenix

Tucson

Albuquerque
Santa Fe

NEW MEXICO

Roswell

Rio Grande

El Paso

MEXICO

Missouri River

Tropic of Cancer

PACIFIC OCEAN

Honolulu

HAWAII

Hilo

| 0 | 50 | 100 mi |
| 0 | 50 | 100 km |

CANADA

Presque Isle

MAINE
Augusta

Portland

Montpelier

VERMONT

NEW HAMPSHIRE
Concord

Boston

NEW YORK

Albany

MASSACHUSETTS
Providence

Buffalo

Hartford

RHODE ISLAND
CONNECTICUT

New Haven

New York City

PENNSYLVANIA

Trenton

NEW JERSEY

Harrisburg

Philadelphia

Pittsburgh

NORTH DAKOTA

Duluth

Sault Ste. Marie

MINNESOTA

MICHIGAN

Lake Superior

Lake Huron

Lake Ontario

Lake Erie

Cleveland

Minneapolis

St. Paul

WISCONSIN

Lake Michigan

Lansing

SOUTH DAKOTA

Milwaukee

Madison

Detroit

Missouri

Chicago

Mississippi River

Baltimore

Dover

DELAWARE

IOWA

Cedar Rapids

INDIANA

OHIO

Columbus

Washington, D.C.

Annapolis

Omaha

Des Moines

MARYLAND

Lincoln

ILLINOIS

Indianapolis

WEST VIRGINIA

Richmond

Springfield

Cincinnati

Norfolk

Topeka

Kansas City

Louisville

Frankfort

Charleston

VIRGINIA

KANSAS

St. Louis

River

Jefferson City

Ohio River

KENTUCKY

Tennessee River

Raleigh

Wichita

MISSOURI

NORTH CAROLINA

Charlotte

Nashville

Tulsa

TENNESSEE

Columbia

OKLAHOMA

ARKANSAS

Memphis

SOUTH CAROLINA

Oklahoma City

Atlanta

Charleston

Little Rock

Birmingham

Pine Bluff

GEORGIA

Red River

MISSISSIPPI

ALABAMA

Columbus

Savannah

Dallas

Montgomery

Jackson

Shreveport

Hattiesburg

Tallahassee

Jacksonville

TEXAS

Baton Rouge

Austin

LOUISIANA

FLORIDA

New Orleans

Houston

San Antonio

Tampa

Lake Okeechobee

Rio Grande

Gulf of Mexico

Miami

ATLANTIC OCEAN

90°W

80°W

70°W

40°N

30°N

90°W

80°W

0   150   300 mi
0   150   300 km

N
W   E
S

KEY
—— National boundary
—— State boundary
⊕ National capital
⊙ State capital
• Other city

Transverse Mercator Projection

North and South America: Political

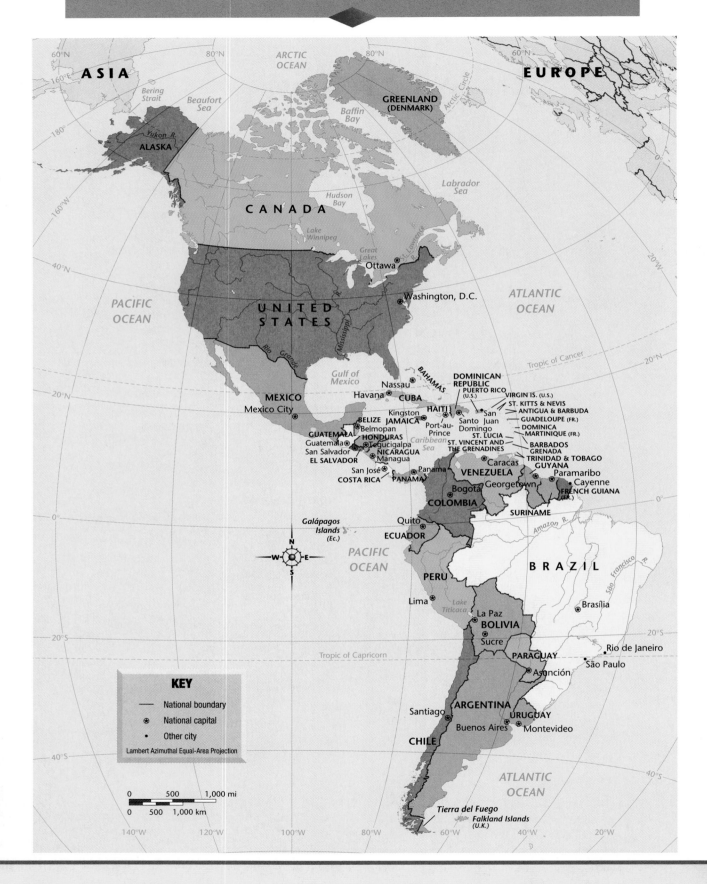

ASIA

ARCTIC OCEAN

EUROPE

Bering Strait

Beaufort Sea

Baffin Bay

GREENLAND (DENMARK)

Arctic Circle

ALASKA

Yukon R.

CANADA

Lake Winnipeg

Hudson Bay

Labrador Sea

Great Lakes

Ottawa

St. Lawrence R.

PACIFIC OCEAN

UNITED STATES

Washington, D.C.

ATLANTIC OCEAN

Rio Grande

Mississippi R.

Gulf of Mexico

Tropic of Cancer

MEXICO

Mexico City

Nassau

Havana

CUBA

BAHAMAS

DOMINICAN REPUBLIC

PUERTO RICO (U.S.)

VIRGIN IS. (U.S.)

ST. KITTS & NEVIS

ANTIGUA & BARBUDA

GUADELOUPE (FR.)

DOMINICA

MARTINIQUE (FR.)

ST. LUCIA

BARBADOS

GRENADA

TRINIDAD & TOBAGO

Kingston

HAITI

JAMAICA

Port-au-Prince

San Juan

Santo Domingo

BELIZE

Belmopan

GUATEMALA

Guatemala

HONDURAS

Tegucigalpa

San Salvador

NICARAGUA

EL SALVADOR

Managua

San José

COSTA RICA

Panama

PANAMA

Caribbean Sea

ST. VINCENT AND THE GRENADINES

Caracas

VENEZUELA

GUYANA

Georgetown

Paramaribo

Cayenne

FRENCH GUIANA (FR.)

Bogotá

COLOMBIA

SURINAME

Galápagos Islands (Ec.)

Quito

ECUADOR

Amazon R.

BRAZIL

São Francisco R.

PACIFIC OCEAN

PERU

Lima

Lake Titicaca

La Paz

BOLIVIA

Sucre

Brasília

Rio de Janeiro

Tropic of Capricorn

PARAGUAY

São Paulo

Asunción

ARGENTINA

URUGUAY

Santiago

Buenos Aires

Montevideo

CHILE

ATLANTIC OCEAN

Tierra del Fuego

Falkland Islands (U.K.)

KEY

— National boundary

⊛ National capital

• Other city

Lambert Azimuthal Equal-Area Projection

0   500   1,000 mi

0   500   1,000 km

North and South America: Physical

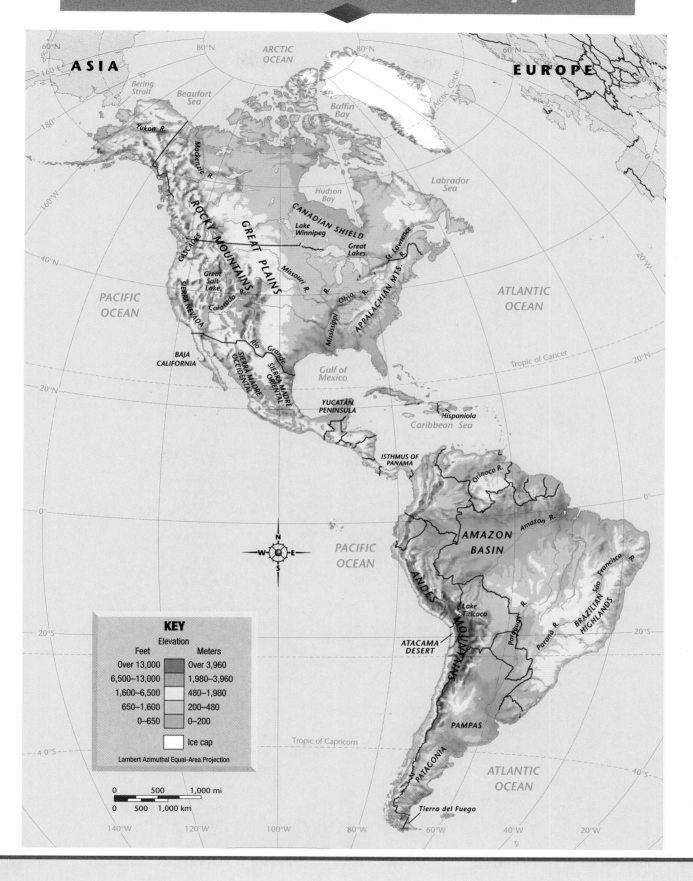

ASIA

EUROPE

ARCTIC OCEAN

Bering Strait

Beaufort Sea

Baffin Bay

Yukon R.

Mackenzie R.

ROCKY MOUNTAINS

GREAT PLAINS

CASCADES

SIERRA NEVADA

Great Salt Lake

Colorado R.

BAJA CALIFORNIA

SIERRA MADRE OCCIDENTAL

SIERRA MADRE ORIENTAL

Rio Grande

Hudson Bay

CANADIAN SHIELD

Lake Winnipeg

Great Lakes

Missouri R.

Mississippi R.

Ohio R.

APPALACHIAN MTS.

St. Lawrence R.

Labrador Sea

ATLANTIC OCEAN

PACIFIC OCEAN

Gulf of Mexico

YUCATÁN PENINSULA

Hispaniola

Caribbean Sea

ISTHMUS OF PANAMA

Tropic of Cancer

Arctic Circle

Orinoco R.

AMAZON BASIN

Amazon R.

ANDES MOUNTAINS

Lake Titicaca

ATACAMA DESERT

Paraguay R.

Paraná R.

São Francisco R.

BRAZILIAN HIGHLANDS

PACIFIC OCEAN

PAMPAS

Tropic of Capricorn

PATAGONIA

Tierra del Fuego

ATLANTIC OCEAN

KEY

Elevation

Feet		Meters
Over 13,000		Over 3,960
6,500–13,000		1,980–3,960
1,600–6,500		480–1,980
650–1,600		200–480
0–650		0–200

Ice cap

Lambert Azimuthal Equal-Area Projection

0   500   1,000 mi

0   500   1,000 km

Europe: Political

KEY

— National boundary
⊛ National capital
• Other city

Lambert Azimuthal Equal-Area Projection

30°W 20°W 10°W 0° 10°E 20°E 30°E 40°E 50°E

ARCTIC OCEAN

Arctic Circle

Reykjavik • ⊛ **ICELAND**

ATLANTIC OCEAN

60°N

Faeroe Is. (Den.)

Shetland Is. (U.K.)

Prime Meridian

Gulf of Bothnia

FINLAND

SWEDEN

NORWAY
Lillehammer •

Turku • • Helsinki • St. Petersburg

Oslo ⊛ • Stockholm
Tallinn ⊛ **ESTONIA** **RUSSIA**

Moscow ⊛

Riga ⊛ **LATVIA**

• Göteborg

North Sea

Baltic Sea

LITHUANIA
Vilnius ⊛ **BELARUS**

DENMARK
Copenhagen ⊛

RUSSIA
Gdańsk • Minsk ⊛

IRELAND
Dublin ⊛

UNITED KINGDOM

• Manchester

50°N

POLAND
Warsaw ⊛
Łódź •

Kiev ⊛

50°N

Berlin ⊛

Amsterdam ⊛
The Hague ⊛
NETHERLANDS

London ⊛

GERMANY

Katowice • Kraków •

UKRAINE

English Channel

Brussels ⊛
BELGIUM
• Cologne
• Bonn
• Frankfurt

Prague ⊛ **CZECH REPUBLIC**
Brno •

SLOVAKIA

LUXEMBOURG
Luxembourg ⊛

Munich •

Bratislava ⊛

MOLDOVA
Chişinău ⊛

Danube R.

LIECHTENSTEIN

Vienna ⊛
Bern ⊛

AUSTRIA

Budapest ⊛
HUNGARY

• Cluj

FRANCE

Paris ⊛

Bay of Biscay

SWITZERLAND

Milan •

Ljubljana ⊛
SLOVENIA
Zagreb ⊛

Bucharest ⊛

ROMANIA

Black Sea

CROATIA

BOSNIA & HERZEGOVINA
Sarajevo ⊛

Belgrade ⊛

SERBIA

BULGARIA

PORTUGAL

40°N

SAN MARINO

Marseille •
MONACO

ITALY

Corsica

Podgorica ⊛
MONTENEGRO

Adriatic Sea

Skopje ⊛
ALBANIA **MACEDONIA**

• Sophia

ANDORRA

• Madrid

• Barcelona

VATICAN CITY
Rome ⊛

Tiranë ⊛

Lisbon ⊛

SPAIN

Balearic Is.

Sardinia

• Naples

Tyrrhenian Sea

Ionian Sea

Aegean Sea

GREECE

Athens ⊛

Strait of Gibraltar

GIBRALTAR (U.K.)

Mediterranean

Sicily

Sea

MALTA

Crete

N
W E
S

0 250 500 mi
0 250 500 km

AFRICA

0° 10°E 20°E

Europe: Physical

ARCTIC OCEAN

Arctic Circle

LAPLAND

Norwegian Sea

0   250   500 mi
0   250   500 km

Faeroe Is. (Den.)

Glittertind
8,110 ft
(2,472 m) ▲

KJØLEN MTS.

SCANDINAVIAN PENINSULA

Gulf of Bothnia

Lake Ladoga

Shetland Is. (U.K.)

ATLANTIC OCEAN

Ben Nevis
4,406 ft ▲
(1,343 m)

Lake Vänern

JUTLAND PENINSULA

Baltic Sea

North Sea

BRITISH ISLES

Dnieper R.

NORTHERN EUROPEAN PLAIN

Vistula R.

Thames R.

Elbe River

Oder River

RUHR VALLEY

English Channel

Seine River

Rhine R.

Danube River

Dniester River

CARPATHIAN MTS.

Bay of Biscay

Loire River

Mont Blanc
15,771 ft.
(4,807 m)

A L P S

Po River

TRANSYLVANIAN ALPS

Black Sea

Garonne R.

MASSIF CENTRAL

Rhône River

DINARIC ALPS

Danube River

BALKAN MTS.

Bosporus

PYRENEES

Ebro R.

A P E N N I N E S

Adriatic Sea

BALKAN PENINSULA

Douro R.

MESETA

Corsica

ITALIAN PENINSULA

Dardanelles

ASIA

Tagus River

Sardinia

Tyrrhenian Sea

Ionian Sea

PINDUS MTS.

Aegean Sea

IBERIAN PENINSULA

Balearic Is.

Sicily

PELOPONNESE

Strait of Gibraltar

Crete

AFRICA

Mediterranean Sea

KEY
Elevation

Feet		Meters
Over 13,000		Over 3,960
6,500-13,000		1,980-3,960
1,600-6,500		480-1,980
650-1,600		200-480
0-650		0-200
Below sea level		Below sea level
	Ice cap	

Lambert Azimuthal Equal-Area Projection

Africa: Political

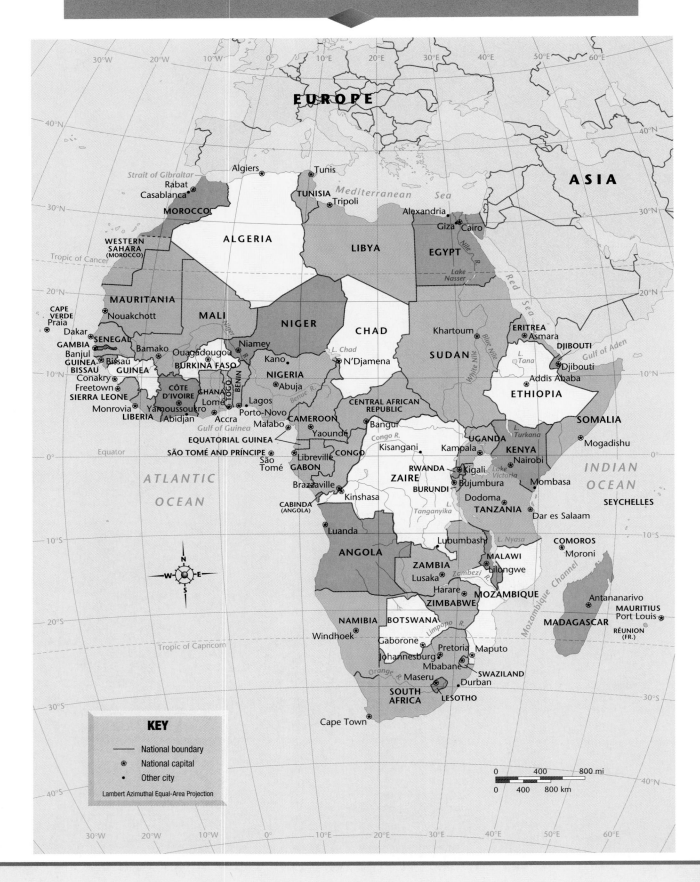

EUROPE

ASIA

Strait of Gibraltar
Algiers ⊛
Tunis ⊛

Rabat ⊛
Casablanca •
MOROCCO
TUNISIA
Tripoli •
Mediterranean Sea

Alexandria •
Giza • Cairo ⊛

WESTERN
SAHARA
(MOROCCO)
ALGERIA
LIBYA
EGYPT
Lake
Nasser
Tropic of Cancer

Nile R.

MAURITANIA
Red Sea

CAPE
VERDE
Praia
Nouakchott ⊛
MALI
NIGER
CHAD
Khartoum ⊛
ERITREA
Asmara •
DJIBOUTI
Gulf of Aden

Dakar ⊛
SENEGAL
L. Chad
L. Tana
Djibouti •

GAMBIA
Banjul ⊛
Bamako ⊛
Ouagadougou ⊛
Niamey ⊛
Kano •
SUDAN

GUINEA-
BISSAU
Bissau ⊛
GUINEA
BURKINA FASO
N'Djamena ⊛
White Nile
Blue Nile
Addis Ababa ⊛

Conakry ⊛
NIGERIA
Abuja ⊛
ETHIOPIA

SIERRA LEONE
CÔTE
D'IVOIRE
GHANA
TOGO
BENIN
Niger R.

Monrovia ⊛
Yamoussoukro ⊛
Lomé
Lagos •
CENTRAL AFRICAN
REPUBLIC
SOMALIA

LIBERIA
Abidjan •
Accra ⊛
Porto-Novo ⊛
CAMEROON
Bangui ⊛
L. Turkana
Mogadishu •

Gulf of Guinea
Malabo ⊛
Yaoundé ⊛
UGANDA
KENYA

EQUATORIAL GUINEA
Congo R.
Kisangani •
Kampala ⊛
Nairobi ⊛

SÃO TOMÉ AND PRÍNCIPE ⊛
Libreville ⊛
CONGO
RWANDA
Kigali ⊛
Lake
Victoria
INDIAN

Equator
São
Tomé
GABON
Brazzaville ⊛
ZAIRE
Bujumbura ⊛
BURUNDI
Dodoma •
Mombasa •
OCEAN

Kinshasa ⊛
Benue R.

CABINDA
(ANGOLA)
L.
Tanganyika
TANZANIA
Dar es Salaam •
SEYCHELLES

Luanda ⊛
Lubumbashi •
COMOROS

ANGOLA
L. Nyasa
Moroni ⊛

ZAMBIA
MALAWI
Lilongwe ⊛
Antananarivo ⊛

ATLANTIC
OCEAN
Lusaka ⊛
Zambezi R.
Mozambique Channel
MAURITIUS
Port Louis ⊛

Harare ⊛
MOZAMBIQUE
MADAGASCAR
RÉUNION
(FR.)

ZIMBABWE
NAMIBIA
BOTSWANA
Windhoek ⊛
Limpopo R.
Gaborone ⊛
Pretoria ⊛
Maputo ⊛

Tropic of Capricorn
Johannesburg •
Mbabane ⊛
SWAZILAND

Orange R.
Maseru ⊛
Durban •

SOUTH
AFRICA
LESOTHO

Cape Town ⊛

KEY

— National boundary
⊛ National capital
• Other city

Lambert Azimuthal Equal-Area Projection

0   400   800 mi
0   400   800 km

Africa: Physical

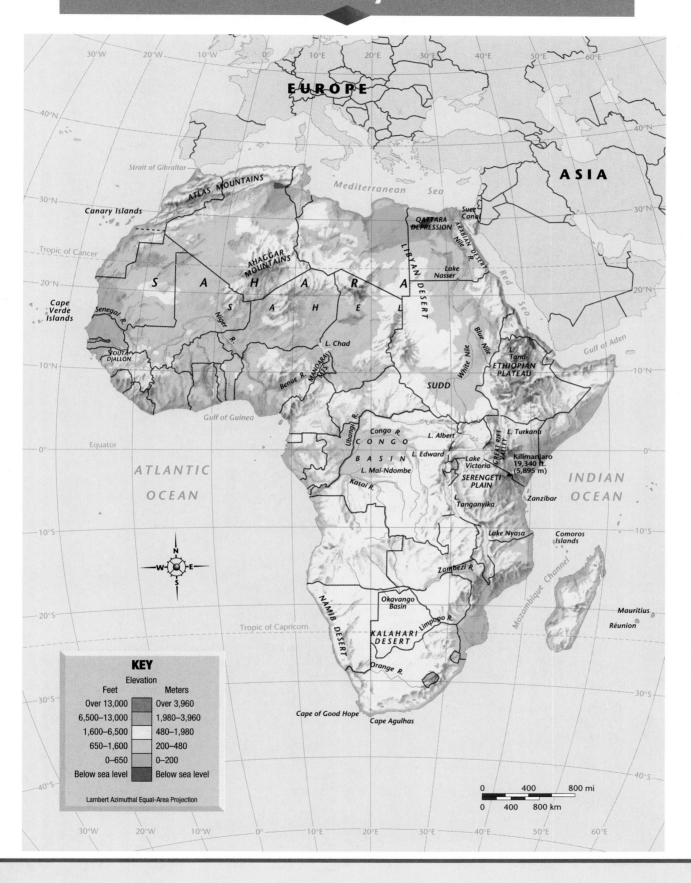

EUROPE

Strait of Gibraltar

ATLAS MOUNTAINS

Canary Islands

Tropic of Cancer

Cape Verde Islands

Senegal R.

FOUTA DJALLON

Niger R.

S A H A R A

A H A G G A R MOUNTAINS

S A H E L

L. Chad

MANDARA MTS.

Benue R.

Gulf of Guinea

Mediterranean Sea

ASIA

QATTARA DEPRESSION

Suez Canal

LIBYAN DESERT

ARABIAN DESERT

Nile R.

Lake Nasser

Red Sea

Gulf of Aden

White Nile

Blue Nile

L. Tana

ETHIOPIAN PLATEAU

SUDD

Ubangi R.

Congo R.

C O N G O

B A S I N

L. Mai-Ndombe

L. Albert

L. Edward

Lake Victoria

GREAT RIFT VALLEY

L. Turkana

Kilimanjaro 19,340 ft. (5,895 m)

SERENGETI PLAIN

Kasai R.

L. Tanganyika

Zanzibar

Equator

ATLANTIC OCEAN

INDIAN OCEAN

Lake Nyasa

Comoros Islands

Zambezi R.

Mozambique Channel

Mauritius

Réunion

NAMIB DESERT

Okavango Basin

Limpopo R.

Tropic of Capricorn

KALAHARI DESERT

Orange R.

Cape of Good Hope

Cape Agulhas

KEY

Elevation

Feet		Meters
Over 13,000		Over 3,960
6,500–13,000		1,980–3,960
1,600–6,500		480–1,980
650–1,600		200–480
0–650		0–200
Below sea level		Below sea level

Lambert Azimuthal Equal-Area Projection

0   400   800 mi
0   400   800 km

Asia: Political

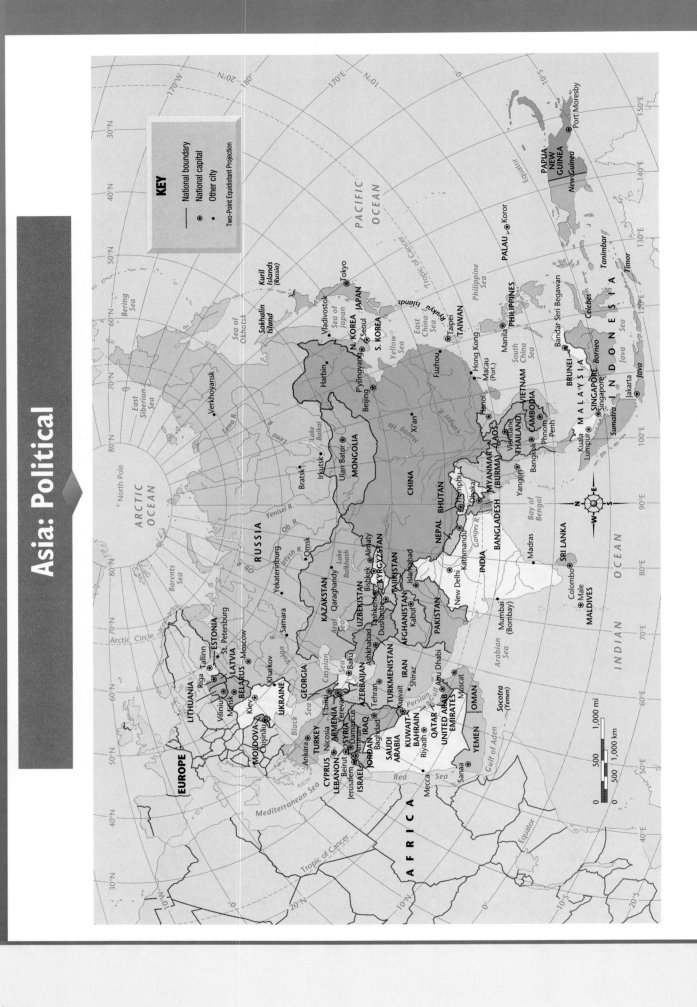

KEY
— National boundary
⊛ National capital
• Other city
Two-Point Equidistant Projection

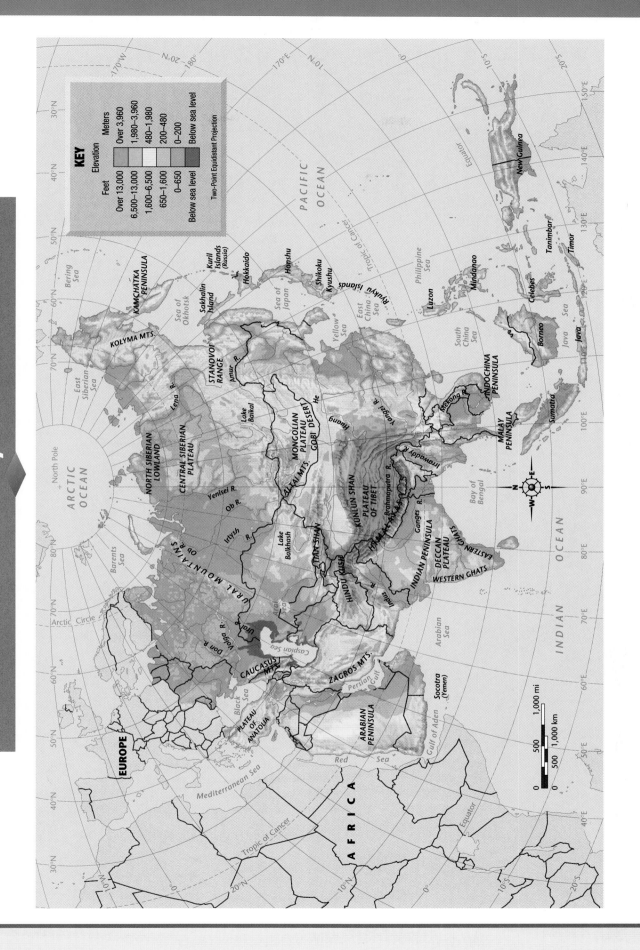

Asia: Physical

KEY

Elevation

Feet	Meters
Over 13,000	Over 3,960
6,500–13,000	1,980–3,960
1,600–6,500	480–1,980
650–1,600	200–480
0–650	0–200
Below sea level	Below sea level

Two-Point Equidistant Projection

PACIFIC OCEAN

New Guinea

Bering Sea

KAMCHATKA PENINSULA

KOLYMA MTS.

Sea of Okhotsk

Sakhalin Island

Kuril Islands (Russia)

Hokkaido

Honshu

Shikoku

Kyushu

Sea of Japan

Ryukyu Islands

East China Sea

Philippine Sea

Luzon

Mindanao

Celebes

Borneo

Java Sea

Java

Sumatra

Tanimbar

Timor

STANOVOI RANGE

Amur R.

He

Huang

Yangzi R.

MONGOLIAN PLATEAU

GOBI DESERT

ALTAI MTS.

Lake Baikal

Lena R.

NORTH SIBERIAN LOWLAND

CENTRAL SIBERIAN PLATEAU

ARCTIC OCEAN

North Pole

East Siberian Sea

INDOCHINA PENINSULA

Mekong R.

MALAY PENINSULA

South China Sea

Yenisei R.

Ob R.

Irtysh R.

KUNLUN SHAN

PLATEAU OF TIBET

Brahmaputra R.

Irrawaddy R.

Ganges R.

TIAN SHAN

Lake Balkhash

HINDU KUSH

Indus R.

HIMALAYAS

INDIAN PENINSULA

DECCAN PLATEAU

EASTERN GHATS

WESTERN GHATS

Bay of Bengal

URAL MOUNTAINS

Ob R.

Barents Sea

Arctic Circle

Aral Sea

Volga R.

Ural R.

Don R.

Caspian Sea

CAUCASUS MTS.

Black Sea

ZAGROS MTS.

Persian Gulf

PLATEAU OF ANATOLIA

Mediterranean Sea

Socotra (Yemen)

ARABIAN PENINSULA

Arabian Sea

INDIAN OCEAN

Gulf of Aden

Red Sea

EUROPE

AFRICA

Tropic of Cancer

Equator

Tropic of Cancer

N W E S

1,000 mi
1,000 km

0   500
0   500   1,000 km

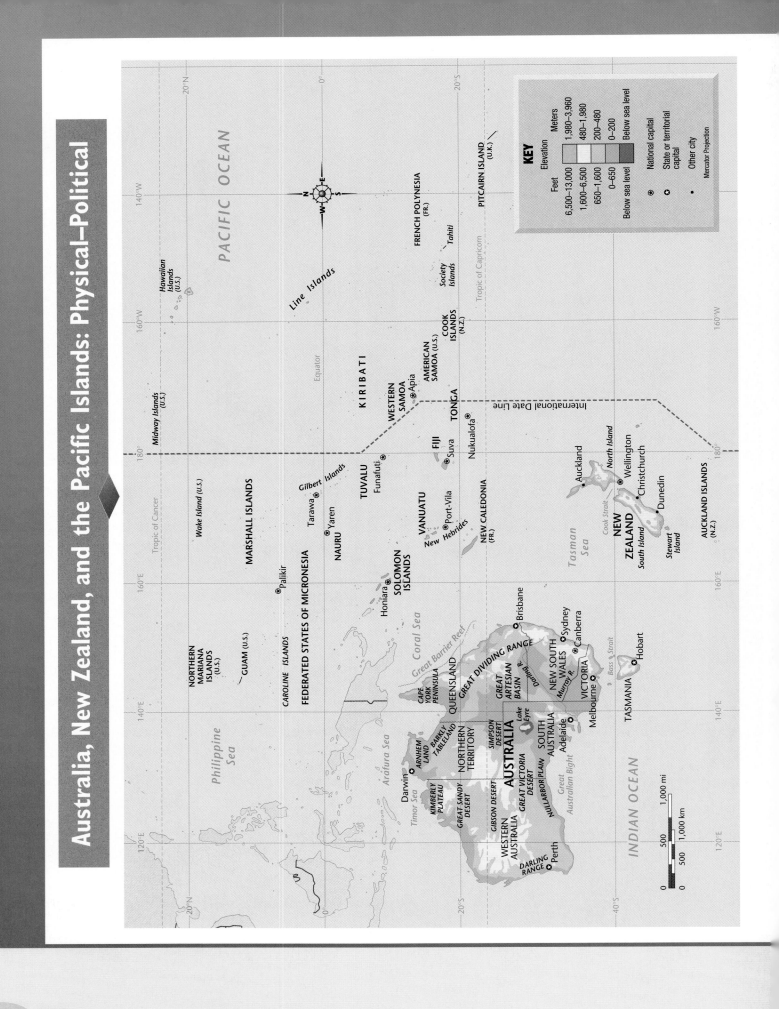

PACIFIC OCEAN

Hawaiian Islands (U.S.)

Line Islands

French Polynesia (FR.)

Society Islands

Tahiti

PITCAIRN ISLAND (U.K.)

Tropic of Capricorn

Midway Islands (U.S.)

Equator

KIRIBATI

WESTERN SAMOA

Apia

AMERICAN SAMOA (U.S.)

COOK ISLANDS (N.Z.)

TONGA

Nukualofa

International Date Line

Wake Island (U.S.)

Tropic of Cancer

MARSHALL ISLANDS

Gilbert Islands

Tarawa

NAURU

Yaren

TUVALU

Funafuti

FIJI

Suva

VANUATU

Port-Vila

New Hebrides

NEW CALEDONIA (FR.)

Auckland

North Island

Wellington

Christchurch

Dunedin

NEW ZEALAND

South Island

Stewart Island

Cook Strait

AUCKLAND ISLANDS (N.Z.)

NORTHERN MARIANA ISLANDS (U.S.)

GUAM (U.S.)

CAROLINE ISLANDS

FEDERATED STATES OF MICRONESIA

Palikir

Honiara

SOLOMON ISLANDS

Coral Sea

Great Barrier Reef

Brisbane

Sydney

Canberra

NEW SOUTH WALES

GREAT DIVIDING RANGE

GREAT ARTESIAN BASIN

QUEENSLAND

CAPE YORK PENINSULA

Darling R.

Murray R.

VICTORIA

Melbourne

Bass Strait

TASMANIA

Hobart

Tasman Sea

Philippine Sea

Arafura Sea

Timor Sea

Darwin

ARNHEM LAND

NORTHERN TERRITORY

BARKLY TABLELAND

SIMPSON DESERT

Lake Eyre

AUSTRALIA

SOUTH AUSTRALIA

Adelaide

KIMBERLEY PLATEAU

GREAT SANDY DESERT

GIBSON DESERT

GREAT VICTORIA DESERT

NULLARBOR PLAIN

WESTERN AUSTRALIA

Great Australian Bight

DARLING RANGE

Perth

INDIAN OCEAN

KEY

Elevation		
Feet		Meters
6,500–13,000		1,980–3,960
1,600–6,500		480–1,980
650–1,600		200–480
0–650		0–200
Below sea level		Below sea level

⊛ National capital

✪ State or territorial capital

• Other city

Mercator Projection

500

1,000 mi

1,000 km

500

1,000 km

0

The Arctic

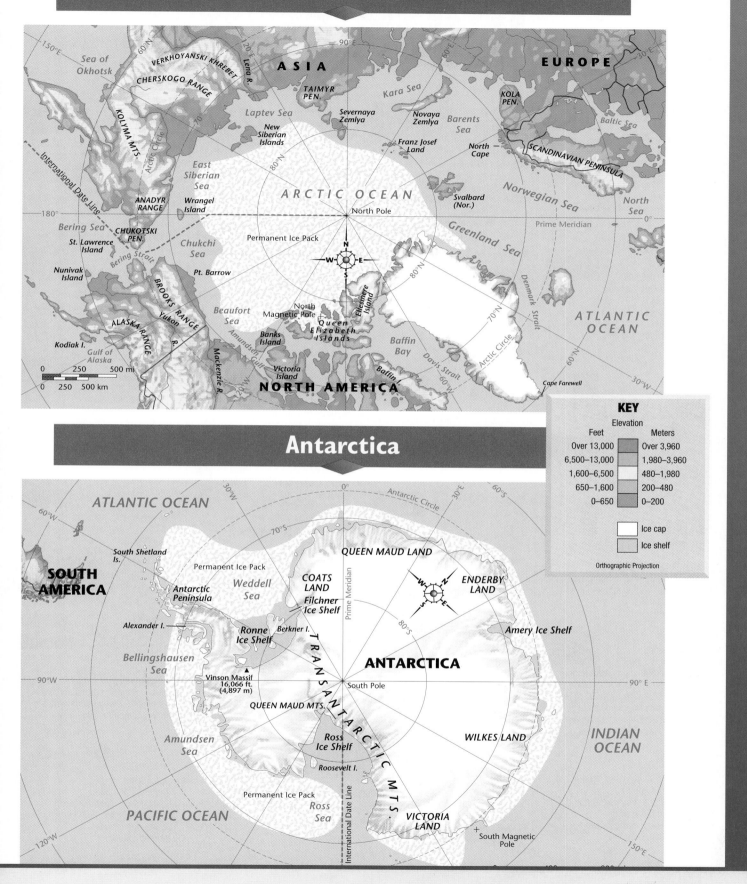

The Arctic (map labels)

Sea of Okhotsk
VERKHOYANSKI KHREBET
CHERSKOGO RANGE
Lena R.
ASIA
EUROPE
KOLYMA MTS.
TAIMYR PEN.
Kara Sea
KOLA PEN.
Laptev Sea
Severnaya Zemlya
Novaya Zemlya
Barents Sea
Baltic Sea
New Siberian Islands
Franz Josef Land
North Cape
SCANDINAVIAN PENINSULA
Arctic Circle
East Siberian Sea
Svalbard (Nor.)
Norwegian Sea
International Date Line
ANADYR RANGE
Wrangel Island
ARCTIC OCEAN
Greenland Sea
North Sea
Bering Sea
CHUKOTSKI PEN.
Chukchi Sea
North Pole
Prime Meridian
St. Lawrence Island
Bering Strait
Permanent Ice Pack
ATLANTIC OCEAN
Nunivak Island
Pt. Barrow
Denmark Strait
BROOKS RANGE
Beaufort Sea
North Magnetic Pole
Ellesmere Island
Queen Elizabeth Islands
Arctic Circle
Kodiak I.
ALASKA RANGE
Yukon R.
Banks Island
Baffin Bay
Gulf of Alaska
Mackenzie R.
Victoria Island
Baffin I.
Davis Strait
Cape Farewell
Amundsen Gulf
NORTH AMERICA

0 250 500 mi
0 250 500 km

Antarctica

Antarctica (map labels)

ATLANTIC OCEAN
Antarctic Circle
South Shetland Is.
Permanent Ice Pack
QUEEN MAUD LAND
SOUTH AMERICA
Weddell Sea
COATS LAND
ENDERBY LAND
Antarctic Peninsula
Filchner Ice Shelf
Prime Meridian
Alexander I.
Ronne Ice Shelf
Berkner I.
Amery Ice Shelf
Bellingshausen Sea
TRANSANTARCTIC MTS.
ANTARCTICA
Vinson Massif
16,066 ft.
(4,897 m)
QUEEN MAUD MTS.
South Pole
Amundsen Sea
WILKES LAND
INDIAN OCEAN
Ross Ice Shelf
Roosevelt I.
International Date Line
PACIFIC OCEAN
Permanent Ice Pack
Ross Sea
VICTORIA LAND
South Magnetic Pole

KEY

Elevation

Feet	Meters
Over 13,000	Over 3,960
6,500–13,000	1,980–3,960
1,600–6,500	480–1,980
650–1,600	200–480
0–650	0–200

Ice cap

Ice shelf

Orthographic Projection

World View

Afghanistan
CAPITAL: Kabul
POPULATION: 21,251,821
MAJOR LANGUAGES: Pashtu, Afghan Persian, Turkic, and 30 various languages
AREA: 250,010 sq mi; 647,500 sq km
LEADING EXPORTS: fruits and nuts, handwoven carpets, and wool
CONTINENT: Asia

Albania
CAPITAL: Tiranë
POPULATION: 3,413,904
MAJOR LANGUAGES: Albanian, Tosk dialect, and Greek
AREA: 11,101 sq mi; 28,750 sq km
LEADING EXPORTS: asphalt, metals and metallic ores, and electricity
CONTINENT: Europe

Algeria
CAPITAL: Algiers
POPULATION: 28,539,321
MAJOR LANGUAGES: Arabic (official), French, and Berber dialects
AREA: 919,626 sq mi; 2,381,740 sq km
LEADING EXPORTS: petroleum and natural gas
CONTINENT: Africa

Andorra
CAPITAL: Andorra La Vella
POPULATION: 65,780
MAJOR LANGUAGES: Catalan (official), French, and Castilian
AREA: 174 sq mi; 450 sq km
LEADING EXPORTS: electricity, tobacco products, and furniture
CONTINENT: Europe

Angola
CAPITAL: Luanda
POPULATION: 10,069,501
MAJOR LANGUAGES: Portuguese (official), Bantu, and various languages
AREA: 481,370 sq mi; 1,246,700 sq km
LEADING EXPORTS: oil, diamonds, and refined petroleum products
CONTINENT: Africa

Anguilla
CAPITAL: The Valley
POPULATION: 7,099
MAJOR LANGUAGE: English (official)
AREA: 35 sq mi; 91 sq km
LEADING EXPORTS: lobster and salt
LOCATION: Caribbean Sea

Antigua and Barbuda
CAPITAL: Saint John's
POPULATION: 65,176
MAJOR LANGUAGES: English (official) and various dialects
AREA: 170 sq mi; 440 sq km
LEADING EXPORTS: petroleum products and manufactures
LOCATION: Caribbean Sea

Argentina
CAPITAL: Buenos Aires
POPULATION: 34,292,742
MAJOR LANGUAGES: Spanish (official), English, Italian, German, and French
AREA: 1,068,339 sq mi; 2,766,890 sq km
LEADING EXPORTS: meat, wheat, corn, oilseed, and manufactures
CONTINENT: South America

Armenia
CAPITAL: Yerevan
POPULATION: 3,557,284
MAJOR LANGUAGES: Armenian and Russian
AREA: 11,506 sq mi; 29,800 sq km
LEADING EXPORTS: gold and jewelry, and aluminum
CONTINENT: Asia

Australia
CAPITAL: Canberra
POPULATION: 18,322,231
MAJOR LANGUAGES: English and various languages
AREA: 2,968,010 sq mi; 7,686,850 sq km
LEADING EXPORTS: coal, gold, meat, wool, and alumina
CONTINENT: Australia

Austria
CAPITAL: Vienna
POPULATION: 7,986,664
MAJOR LANGUAGE: German
AREA: 32,376 sq mi; 83,850 sq km
LEADING EXPORTS: machinery and equipment, and iron and steel
CONTINENT: Europe

Azerbaijan
CAPITAL: Baku
POPULATION: 7,789,886
MAJOR LANGUAGES: Azeri, Russian, Armenian, and various languages
AREA: 33,438 sq mi; 86,600 sq km
LEADING EXPORTS: oil and gas, chemicals, and oil field equipment
CONTINENT: Europe and Asia

Bahamas
CAPITAL: Nassau
POPULATION: 256,616
MAJOR LANGUAGES: English and Creole
AREA: 5,382 sq mi; 13,940 sq km
LEADING EXPORTS: pharmaceuticals, cement, rum, and crawfish
LOCATION: Caribbean Sea

Bahrain
CAPITAL: Manama
POPULATION: 575,925
MAJOR LANGUAGES: Arabic, English, Farsi, and Urdu
AREA: 239 sq mi; 620 sq km
LEADING EXPORTS: petroleum and petroleum products
CONTINENT: Asia

Bangladesh
CAPITAL: Dhaka
POPULATION: 128,094,948
MAJOR LANGUAGES: Bangla and English
AREA: 55,600 sq mi; 144,000 sq km
LEADING EXPORTS: garments, jute and jute goods, and leather
CONTINENT: Asia

Barbados
CAPITAL: Bridgetown
POPULATION: 256,395
MAJOR LANGUAGE: English
AREA: 166 sq mi; 430 sq km
LEADING EXPORTS: sugar and molasses, and rum
LOCATION: Caribbean Sea

Belarus
CAPITAL: Minsk
POPULATION: 10,437,418
MAJOR LANGUAGES: Byelorussian and Russian
AREA: 79,926 sq mi; 207,600 sq km
LEADING EXPORTS: machinery and transportation equipment
CONTINENT: Europe

Belgium
CAPITAL: Brussels
POPULATION: 10,081,880
MAJOR LANGUAGES: Dutch, French, and German
AREA: 11,780 sq mi; 30,510 sq km
LEADING EXPORTS: iron and steel, and transportation equipment
CONTINENT: Europe

Belize
CAPITAL: Belmopan
POPULATION: 214,061
MAJOR LANGUAGES: English (official), Spanish, Maya, and Garifuna
AREA: 8,865 sq mi; 22,960 sq km
LEADING EXPORTS: sugar, citrus fruits, bananas, and clothing
LOCATION: Caribbean Sea

Benin
CAPITAL: Porto-Novo
POPULATION: 5,522,677
MAJOR LANGUAGES: Fon, Yoruba, and at least 6 various languages
AREA: 43,484 sq mi; 112,620 sq km
LEADING EXPORTS: cotton, crude oil, palm products, and cocoa
CONTINENT: Africa

Bermuda
CAPITAL: Hamilton
POPULATION: 61,629
MAJOR LANGUAGE: English
AREA: 19.3 sq mi; 50 sq km
LEADING EXPORTS: semitropical produce and light manufactures
CONTINENT: North America

Bhutan
CAPITAL: Thimphu
POPULATION: 1,780,638
MAJOR LANGUAGES: Dzongkha (official), Tibetan dialects, and Nepalese dialects
AREA: 18,147 sq mi; 47,000 sq km
LEADING EXPORTS: cardamon, gypsum, timber, and handicrafts
CONTINENT: Asia

Bolivia
CAPITAL: La Paz
POPULATION: 7,896,254
MAJOR LANGUAGES: Spanish, Quechua, and Aymara
AREA: 424,179 sq mi; 1,098,580 sq km
LEADING EXPORTS: metals, natural gas, soybeans, jewelry, and wood
CONTINENT: South America

Bosnia and Herzegovina

CAPITAL: Sarajevo
POPULATION: 3,201,823
MAJOR LANGUAGE: Serbo-Croatian
AREA: 19,782 sq mi; 51,233 sq km
LEADING EXPORTS: none
CONTINENT: Europe

Botswana

CAPITAL: Gaborone
POPULATION: 1,392,414
MAJOR LANGUAGES: English and Setswana
AREA: 231,812 sq mi; 600,370 sq km
LEADING EXPORTS: diamonds, copper and nickel, and meat
CONTINENT: Africa

Brazil

CAPITAL: Brasília
POPULATION: 160,737,489
MAJOR LANGUAGES: Portuguese, Spanish, English, and French
AREA: 3,286,600 sq mi; 8,511,965 sq km
LEADING EXPORTS: iron ore, soybean, bran, and orange juice
CONTINENT: South America

British Virgin Islands

CAPITAL: Road Town
POPULATION: 13,027
MAJOR LANGUAGE: English
AREA: 58 sq mi; 150 sq km
LEADING EXPORTS: rum, fresh fish, gravel, sand, and fruits
LOCATION: Caribbean Sea

Brunei

CAPITAL: Bandar Seri Begawan
POPULATION: 292,266
MAJOR LANGUAGES: Malay, English, and Chinese
AREA: 2,228 sq mi; 5,770 sq km
LEADING EXPORTS: crude oil and liquefied natural gas
CONTINENT: Asia

Bulgaria

CAPITAL: Sofia
POPULATION: 8,775,198
MAJOR LANGUAGE: Bulgarian
AREA: 42,824 sq mi; 110,910 sq km
LEADING EXPORTS: machinery and agricultural products
CONTINENT: Europe

Burkina

CAPITAL: Ouagadougou
POPULATION: 10,422,828
MAJOR LANGUAGES: French (official) and Sudanic languages
AREA: 105,873 sq mi; 274,200 sq km
LEADING EXPORTS: cotton, gold, and animal products
CONTINENT: Africa

Burundi

CAPITAL: Bujumbura
POPULATION: 6,262,429
MAJOR LANGUAGES: Kirundi, French, and Swahili
AREA: 10,746 sq mi; 27,830 sq km
LEADING EXPORTS: coffee, tea, cotton, and hides and skins
CONTINENT: Africa

Cambodia

CAPITAL: Phnom Penh
POPULATION: 10,561,373
MAJOR LANGUAGES: Khmer and French
AREA: 69,902 sq mi; 181,040 sq km
LEADING EXPORTS: timber, rubber, soybeans, and sesame
CONTINENT: Asia

Cameroon

CAPITAL: Yaounde
POPULATION: 13,521,000
MAJOR LANGUAGES: 24 various languages, English, and French
AREA: 183,574 sq mi; 475,440 sq km
LEADING EXPORTS: petroleum products and lumber
CONTINENT: Africa

Canada

CAPITAL: Ottawa
POPULATION: 28,434,545
MAJOR LANGUAGES: English and French
AREA: 3,851,940 sq mi; 9,976,140 sq km
LEADING EXPORTS: newsprint, wood pulp, timber, and crude petroleum
CONTINENT: North America

Cape Verde

CAPITAL: Praia
POPULATION: 435,983
MAJOR LANGUAGES: Portuguese and Crioulo
AREA: 1,556 sq mi; 4,030 sq km
LEADING EXPORTS: fish, bananas, and hides and skins
CONTINENT: Africa

Cayman Islands

CAPITAL: George Town
POPULATION: 33,192
MAJOR LANGUAGE: English
AREA: 100 sq mi; 260 sq km
LEADING EXPORTS: turtle products and manufactured goods
LOCATION: Caribbean Sea

Central African Republic

CAPITAL: Bangui
POPULATION: 3,209,759
MAJOR LANGUAGES: French, Sangho, Arabic, Hunsa, and Swahili
AREA: 240,542 sq mi; 622,980 sq km
LEADING EXPORTS: diamonds, timber, cotton, coffee, and tobacco
CONTINENT: Africa

Chad

CAPITAL: N'Djamena
POPULATION: 5,586,505
MAJOR LANGUAGES: French, Arabic, Sara, Songo, and over 100 various languages and dialects
AREA: 495,772 sq mi; 1,284,000 sq km
LEADING EXPORTS: cotton, cattle, textiles, and fish
CONTINENT: Africa

Chile

CAPITAL: Santiago
POPULATION: 14,161,216
MAJOR LANGUAGE: Spanish
AREA: 292,269 sq mi; 756,950 sq km
LEADING EXPORTS: copper and other metals and minerals
CONTINENT: South America

China

CAPITAL: Beijing
POPULATION: 1,203,097,268
MAJOR LANGUAGES: Mandarin, Putonghua, Yue, Wu, Minbei, Minnan, Xiang, and Gan and Hakka dialects
AREA: 3,705,533 sq mi; 9,596,960 sq km
LEADING EXPORTS: textiles, garments, footwear, and toys
CONTINENT: Asia

Colombia

CAPITAL: Bogota
POPULATION: 36,200,251
MAJOR LANGUAGE: Spanish
AREA: 439,751 sq mi; 1,138,910 sq km
LEADING EXPORTS: petroleum, coffee, coal, and bananas
CONTINENT: South America

Comoros

CAPITAL: Moroni
POPULATION: 549,338
MAJOR LANGUAGES: Arabic, French, and Comoran
AREA: 838 sq mi; 2,170 sq km
LEADING EXPORTS: vanilla, ylang-ylang, cloves, and perfume oil
LOCATION: Indian Ocean

Congo

CAPITAL: Brazzaville
POPULATION: 2,504,996
MAJOR LANGUAGES: French, Lingala, Kikongo, and other languages
AREA: 132,051 sq mi; 342,000 sq km
LEADING EXPORTS: crude oil, lumber, plywood, sugar, and cocoa
CONTINENT: Africa

Cook Islands

CAPITAL: Avarua
POPULATION: 19,343
MAJOR LANGUAGES: English and Maori
AREA: 95 sq mi; 240 sq km
LEADING EXPORTS: copra, fresh and canned fruit, and clothing
LOCATION: Pacific Ocean

Costa Rica

CAPITAL: San José
POPULATION: 3,419,114
MAJOR LANGUAGES: Spanish and English
AREA: 19,730 sq mi; 51,100 sq km
LEADING EXPORTS: coffee, bananas, textiles, and sugar
CONTINENT: Central America

Côte d'Ivoire

CAPITAL: Yamoussoukro
POPULATION: 14,791,257
MAJOR LANGUAGES: French, Dioula, and 59 other dialects
AREA: 124,507 sq mi; 322,460 sq km
LEADING EXPORTS: cocoa, coffee, tropical woods, and petroleum
CONTINENT: Africa

Croatia

CAPITAL: Zagreb
POPULATION: 4,665,821
MAJOR LANGUAGE: Serbo-Croatian
AREA: 21,830 sq mi; 56,538 sq km
LEADING EXPORTS: machinery and transportation equipment
CONTINENT: Europe

Cuba

CAPITAL: Havana
POPULATION: 10,937,635
MAJOR LANGUAGE: Spanish
AREA: 42,805 sq mi; 110,860 sq km
LEADING EXPORTS: sugar, nickel, shellfish, and tobacco
LOCATION: Caribbean Sea

Cyprus

CAPITAL: Nicosia
POPULATION: 736,636
MAJOR LANGUAGES: Greek, Turkish, and English
AREA: 3,572 sq mi; 9,250 sq km
LEADING EXPORTS: citrus, potatoes, grapes, wines, and cement
LOCATION: Mediterranean Sea

Czech Republic

CAPITAL: Prague
POPULATION: 10,432,774
MAJOR LANGUAGES: Czech and Slovak
AREA: 30,388 sq mi; 78,703 sq km
LEADING EXPORTS: manufactured goods
CONTINENT: Europe

Denmark

CAPITAL: Copenhagen
POPULATION: 5,199,437
MAJOR LANGUAGES: Danish, Faroese, Greenlandic, and German
AREA: 16,630 sq mi; 43,070 sq km
LEADING EXPORTS: meat and meat products, and dairy products
CONTINENT: Europe

Djibouti

CAPITAL: Djibouti
POPULATION: 421,320
MAJOR LANGUAGES: French, Arabic, Somali, and Afar
AREA: 8,495 sq mi; 22,000 sq km
LEADING EXPORTS: hides and skins, and coffee (in transit)
CONTINENT: Africa

Dominica

CAPITAL: Roseau
POPULATION: 82,608
MAJOR LANGUAGES: English and French patois
AREA: 290 sq mi; 750 sq km
LEADING EXPORTS: bananas, soap, bay oil, and vegetables
LOCATION: Caribbean Sea

Dominican Republic

CAPITAL: Santo Domingo
POPULATION: 7,511,263
MAJOR LANGUAGE: Spanish
AREA: 18,815 sq mi; 48,730 sq km
LEADING EXPORTS: ferronickel, sugar, gold, coffee, and cocoa
LOCATION: Caribbean Sea

Ecuador

CAPITAL: Quito
POPULATION: 10,890,950
MAJOR LANGUAGES: Spanish, Quechua, and various languages
AREA: 109,487 sq mi; 283,560 sq km
LEADING EXPORTS: petroleum, bananas, shrimp, and cocoa
CONTINENT: South America

Egypt

CAPITAL: Cairo
POPULATION: 62,359,623
MAJOR LANGUAGES: Arabic, English, and French
AREA: 386,675 sq mi; 1,001,450 sq km
LEADING EXPORTS: crude oil and petroleum products
CONTINENT: Africa

El Salvador
CAPITAL: San Salvador
POPULATION: 5,870,481
MAJOR LANGUAGES: Spanish and Nahua
AREA: 8,124 sq mi; 21,040 sq km
LEADING EXPORTS: coffee, sugar cane, and shrimp
CONTINENT: Central America

Equatorial Guinea

CAPITAL: Malabo
POPULATION: 420,293
MAJOR LANGUAGES: Spanish, Pidgin English, Fang, Bubi, and Ibo
AREA: 10,831 sq mi; 28,050 sq km
LEADING EXPORTS: coffee, timber, and cocoa beans
CONTINENT: Africa

Eritrea

CAPITAL: Asmara
POPULATION: 3,578,709
MAJOR LANGUAGES: Tigre, Kunama, Cushitic dialects, Nora Bana, and Arabic
AREA: 46,844 sq mi; 121,320 sq km
LEADING EXPORTS: salt, hides, cement, and gum arabic
CONTINENT: Africa

Estonia

CAPITAL: Tallinn
POPULATION: 1,625,399
MAJOR LANGUAGES: Estonian, Latvian, Lithuanian, and Russian
AREA: 17,414 sq mi; 45,100 sq km
LEADING EXPORTS: textiles, food products, vehicles, and metals
CONTINENT: Europe

Ethiopia

CAPITAL: Addis Ababa
POPULATION: 55,979,018
MAJOR LANGUAGES: Amharic, Tigrinya, Orominga, Guaraginga, Somali, Arabic, English, and various languages
AREA: 435,201 sq mi; 1,127,127 sq km
LEADING EXPORTS: coffee, leather products, and gold
CONTINENT: Africa

Fiji

CAPITAL: Suva
POPULATION: 772,891
MAJOR LANGUAGES: English, Fijian, and Hindustani
AREA: 7,054 sq mi; 18,270 sq km
LEADING EXPORTS: sugar, clothing, gold, processed fish, and lumber
LOCATION: Pacific Ocean

Finland
CAPITAL: Helsinki
POPULATION: 5,085,206
MAJOR LANGUAGES: Finnish, Swedish, Lapp, and Russian
AREA: 130,132 sq mi; 337,030 sq km
LEADING EXPORTS: paper and pulp, machinery, and chemicals
CONTINENT: Europe

France

CAPITAL: Paris
POPULATION: 58,109,160
MAJOR LANGUAGES: French and regional dialects and languages
AREA: 211,217 sq mi; 547,030 sq km
LEADING EXPORTS: machinery and transportation equipment
CONTINENT: Europe

Gabon

CAPITAL: Libreville
POPULATION: 1,185,749
MAJOR LANGUAGES: French, Fang, Myene, Bateke, Bapounou/Eschira, and Bandjabi
AREA: 103,351 sq mi; 267,670 sq km
LEADING EXPORTS: crude oil, timber, manganese, and uranium
CONTINENT: Africa

The Gambia

CAPITAL: Banjul
POPULATION: 989,273
MAJOR LANGUAGES: English, Mandinka, Wolof, Fula, and various languages
AREA: 4,363 sq mi; 11,300 sq km
LEADING EXPORTS: peanuts and peanut products, and fish
CONTINENT: Africa

Georgia

CAPITAL: T'bilisi
POPULATION: 5,725,972
MAJOR LANGUAGES: Armenian, Azeri, Georgian, Russian, and various languages
AREA: 26,912 sq mi; 69,700 sq km
LEADING EXPORTS: citrus fruits, tea, and wine
CONTINENT: Asia

Germany
CAPITAL: Berlin
POPULATION: 81,337,541
MAJOR LANGUAGE: German
AREA: 137,808 sq mi; 356,910 sq km
LEADING EXPORTS: machines and machine tools, and chemicals
CONTINENT: Europe

Ghana
CAPITAL: Accra
POPULATION: 17,763,138
MAJOR LANGUAGES: English, Akan, Moshi-Dagomba, Ewe, Ga, and various languages
AREA: 92,104 sq mi; 238,540 sq km
LEADING EXPORTS: cocoa, gold, timber, tuna, and bauxite
CONTINENT: Africa

Greece

CAPITAL: Athens
POPULATION: 10,647,511
MAJOR LANGUAGES: Greek, English, and French
AREA: 50,944 sq mi; 131,940 sq km
LEADING EXPORTS: manufactured goods, foodstuffs, and fuels
CONTINENT: Europe

Grenada

CAPITAL: Saint George's
POPULATION: 94,486
MAJOR LANGUAGES: English and French patois
AREA: 131 sq mi; 340 sq km
LEADING EXPORTS: bananas, cocoa, nutmeg, and fruits and vegetables
LOCATION: Caribbean Sea

Guatemala

CAPITAL: Guatemala
POPULATION: 10,998,602
MAJOR LANGUAGES: Spanish, Quiche, Cakchiquel, Kekchi, and various languages and dialects
AREA: 42,044 sq mi; 108,890 sq km
LEADING EXPORTS: coffee, sugar, bananas, cardamom, and beef
CONTINENT: Central America

Guinea

CAPITAL: Conakry
POPULATION: 6,549,336
MAJOR LANGUAGES: French and various languages
AREA: 94,930 sq mi; 245,860 sq km
LEADING EXPORTS: bauxite, alumina, diamonds, gold, and coffee
CONTINENT: Africa

Guinea Bissau

CAPITAL: Bissau
POPULATION: 1,124,537
MAJOR LANGUAGES: Portuguese, Criolo, and various languages
AREA: 13,946 sq mi; 36,210 sq km
LEADING EXPORTS: cashews, fish, peanuts, and palm kernels
CONTINENT: Africa

Guyana

CAPITAL: Georgetown
POPULATION: 723,774
MAJOR LANGUAGES: English and various dialects
AREA: 83,003 sq mi; 214,970 sq km
LEADING EXPORTS: sugar, bauxite/alumina, rice, and shrimp
CONTINENT: South America

Haiti

CAPITAL: Port-au-Prince
POPULATION: 6,539,983
MAJOR LANGUAGES: French and Creole
AREA: 8,784 sq mi; 22,750 sq km
LEADING EXPORTS: light manufactures and
   coffee
LOCATION: Caribbean Sea

Holy See (Vatican City)

CAPITAL: Vatican City
POPULATION: 830
MAJOR LANGUAGES: Italian, Latin, and
   various languages
AREA: 17 sq mi; 44 sq km
LEADING EXPORTS: none
CONTINENT: Europe

Honduras

CAPITAL: Tegucigalpa
POPULATION: 5,549,743
MAJOR LANGUAGES: Spanish and various
   dialects
AREA: 43,280 sq mi; 112,090 sq km
LEADING EXPORTS: bananas, coffee, shrimp,
   lobsters, and minerals
CONTINENT: Central America

Hungary

CAPITAL: Budapest
POPULATION: 10,318,838
MAJOR LANGUAGES: Hungarian and various
   languages
AREA: 35,920 sq mi; 93,030 sq km
LEADING EXPORTS: raw materials and semi-
   finished goods
CONTINENT: Europe

Iceland

CAPITAL: Reykjavik
POPULATION: 265,998
MAJOR LANGUAGE: Icelandic
AREA: 39,770 sq mi; 103,000 sq km
LEADING EXPORTS: fish and fish products,
   and animal products
CONTINENT: Europe

India

CAPITAL: New Delhi
POPULATION: 936,545,814
MAJOR LANGUAGES: English, Hindi, Bengali,
   Telugu, Marathi, Tamil, Urdu,
   Gujarati, Malayam, Kannada, Oriya,
   Punjabi, Assamese, Kashmiri, Sindhi,
   Sanskrit, and Hindustani (all official)
AREA: 1,269,389 sq mi; 3,287,590 sq km
LEADING EXPORTS: clothing, and gems and
   jewelry
CONTINENT: Asia

Indonesia

CAPITAL: Jakarta
POPULATION: 203,583,886
MAJOR LANGUAGES: Bahasa Indonesia,
   English, Dutch, Javanese, and
   various dialects
AREA: 741,052 sq mi; 1,919,251 sq km
LEADING EXPORTS: manufactures, fuels, and
   foodstuffs
CONTINENT: Asia

Iran

CAPITAL: Tehran
POPULATION: 64,625,455
MAJOR LANGUAGES: Farsi (official) and
   Turkic languages
AREA: 634,562 sq mi; 1,643,452 sq km
LEADING EXPORTS: petroleum, carpets, fruit,
   nuts, and hides
CONTINENT: Asia

Iraq

CAPITAL: Baghdad
POPULATION: 20,643,769
MAJOR LANGUAGES: Arabic, Kurdish,
   Assyrian, and Armenian
AREA: 168,760 sq mi; 437,072 sq km
LEADING EXPORTS: crude oil and refined
   products, and fertilizers
CONTINENT: Asia

Ireland

CAPITAL: Dublin
POPULATION: 3,550,448
MAJOR LANGUAGES: Irish Gaelic and English
AREA: 27,136 sq mi; 70,280 sq km
LEADING EXPORTS: chemicals and data
   processing equipment
CONTINENT: Europe

Israel

CAPITAL: Jerusalem
POPULATION: 7,566,447
MAJOR LANGUAGES: Hebrew, Arabic, and
   English
AREA: 10,421 sq mi; 26,990 sq km
LEADING EXPORTS: machinery and
   equipment, and cut diamonds
CONTINENT: Asia

Italy

CAPITAL: Rome
POPULATION: 58,261,971
MAJOR LANGUAGES: Italian, German,
   French, and Slovene
AREA: 116,310 sq mi; 301,230 sq km
LEADING EXPORTS: metals, and textiles and
   clothing
CONTINENT: Europe

Jamaica

CAPITAL: Kingston
POPULATION: 2,574,291
MAJOR LANGUAGES: English and Creole
AREA: 4,243 sq mi; 10,990 sq km
LEADING EXPORTS: alumina, bauxite, sugar,
   bananas, and rum
LOCATION: Caribbean Sea

Japan

CAPITAL: Tokyo
POPULATION: 125,506,492
MAJOR LANGUAGE: Japanese
AREA: 145,888 sq mi; 377,835 sq km
LEADING EXPORTS: machinery, motor
   vehicles, and electronics
CONTINENT: Asia

Jordan

CAPITAL: Amman
POPULATION: 4,100,709
MAJOR LANGUAGES: Arabic and English
AREA: 34,447 sq mi; 89,213 sq km
LEADING EXPORTS: phosphates, fertilizers,
   and potash
CONTINENT: Asia

Kazakhstan

CAPITAL: Almaty
POPULATION: 17,376,615
MAJOR LANGUAGES: Kazakh and Russian
AREA: 1,049,191 sq mi; 2,717,300 sq km
LEADING EXPORTS: oil, and ferrous and
   nonferrous metals
CONTINENT: Asia

Kenya

CAPITAL: Nairobi
POPULATION: 28,817,227
MAJOR LANGUAGES: English, Swahili, and
   various languages
AREA: 224,970 sq mi; 582,650 sq km
LEADING EXPORTS: tea, coffee, and
   petroleum products
CONTINENT: Africa

Kiribati

CAPITAL: Tarawa
POPULATION: 79,386
MAJOR LANGUAGES: English and Gilbertese
AREA: 277 sq mi; 717 sq km
LEADING EXPORTS: copra, seaweed, and fish
LOCATION: Pacific Ocean

Korea, North

CAPITAL: P'yongyang
POPULATION: 23,486,550
MAJOR LANGUAGE: Korean
AREA: 46,542 sq mi; 120,540 sq km
LEADING EXPORTS: minerals and
   metallurgical products
CONTINENT: Asia

Korea, South

CAPITAL: Seoul
POPULATION: 45,553,882
MAJOR LANGUAGES: Korean and English
AREA: 38,025 sq mi; 98,480 sq km
LEADING EXPORTS: electronic and electrical
   equipment
CONTINENT: Asia

Kuwait

CAPITAL: Kuwait
POPULATION: 1,817,397
MAJOR LANGUAGES: Arabic and English
AREA: 6,881 sq mi; 17,820 sq km
LEADING EXPORT: oil
CONTINENT: Asia

Kyrgyzstan

CAPITAL: Bishkek
POPULATION: 4,769,877
MAJOR LANGUAGES: Kyrgyz and Russian
AREA: 76,644 sq mi; 198,500 sq km
LEADING EXPORTS: wool, chemicals, cotton,
   metals, and shoes
CONTINENT: Asia

Laos

CAPITAL: Vientiane
POPULATION: 4,837,237
MAJOR LANGUAGES: Lao, French, English,
   and various languages
AREA: 91,432 sq mi; 236,800 sq km
LEADING EXPORTS: electricity, wood
   products, coffee, and tin
CONTINENT: Asia

Latvia

CAPITAL: Riga
POPULATION: 2,762,899
MAJOR LANGUAGES: Lettish, Lithuanian,
   Russian, and various languages
AREA: 24,750 sq mi; 64,100 sq km
LEADING EXPORTS: oil products, timber, and
   ferrous metals
CONTINENT: Europe

Lebanon

CAPITAL: Beirut
POPULATION: 3,695,921
MAJOR LANGUAGES: Arabic, French,
   Armenian, and English
AREA: 4,016 sq mi; 10,400 sq km
LEADING EXPORTS: agricultural products,
   chemicals, and textiles
CONTINENT: Asia

Lesotho

CAPITAL: Maseru
POPULATION: 1,992,960
MAJOR LANGUAGES: Sesotho, English, Zulu,
   and Xhosa
AREA: 11,719 sq mi; 30,350 sq km
LEADING EXPORTS: wool, mohair, wheat,
   cattle, and peas
CONTINENT: Africa

Liberia

CAPITAL: Monrovia
POPULATION: 3,073,245
MAJOR LANGUAGES: English and Niger-
   Congo
AREA: 43,002 sq mi; 111,370 sq km
LEADING EXPORTS: iron ore, rubber, timber,
   and coffee
CONTINENT: Africa

Libya

CAPITAL: Tripoli
POPULATION: 5,248,401
MAJOR LANGUAGES: Arabic, Italian, and English
AREA: 679,385 sq mi; 1,759,540 sq km
LEADING EXPORTS: crude oil and refined petroleum products
CONTINENT: Africa

Liechtenstein

CAPITAL: Vaduz
POPULATION: 30,654
MAJOR LANGUAGES: German and Alemannic
AREA: 62 sq mi; 160 sq km
LEADING EXPORTS: small specialty machinery and dental products
CONTINENT: Europe

Lithuania

CAPITAL: Vilnius
POPULATION: 3,876,396
MAJOR LANGUAGES: Lithuanian, Polish, and Russian
AREA: 25,175 sq mi; 65,200 sq km
LEADING EXPORTS: electronics, petroleum products, and food
CONTINENT: Europe

Luxembourg

CAPITAL: Luxembourg
POPULATION: 404,660
MAJOR LANGUAGES: Luxembourgisch, German, French, and English
AREA: 998 sq mi; 2,586 sq km
LEADING EXPORTS: finished steel products and chemicals
CONTINENT: Europe

Macedonia

CAPITAL: Skopje
POPULATION: 2,159,503
MAJOR LANGUAGES: Macedonian, Albanian, Turkish, Serb, Gypsy, and various languages
AREA: 9,781 sq mi; 25,333 sq km
LEADING EXPORTS: manufactured goods and machinery
CONTINENT: Europe

Madagascar

CAPITAL: Antananarivo
POPULATION: 13,862,325
MAJOR LANGUAGES: French and Malagasy
AREA: 226,665 sq mi; 587,040 sq km
LEADING EXPORTS: coffee, vanilla, cloves, shellfish, and sugar
CONTINENT: Africa

Malawi

CAPITAL: Lilongwe
POPULATION: 9,808,384
MAJOR LANGUAGES: English, Chichewa, and various languages
AREA: 45,747 sq mi; 118,480 sq km
LEADING EXPORTS: tobacco, tea, sugar, coffee, and peanuts
CONTINENT: Africa

Malaysia

CAPITAL: Kuala Lumpur
POPULATION: 19,723,587
MAJOR LANGUAGES: Malay, English, Mandarin, Tamil, Chinese dialects, and various languages and dialects
AREA: 127,322 sq mi; 329,750 sq km
LEADING EXPORTS: electronic equipment
CONTINENT: Asia

Maldives

CAPITAL: Male
POPULATION: 261,310
MAJOR LANGUAGES: Divehi dialect and English
AREA: 116 sq mi; 300 sq km
LEADING EXPORTS: fish and clothing
CONTINENT: Asia

Mali

CAPITAL: Bamako
POPULATION: 9,375,132
MAJOR LANGUAGES: French, Bambara, and various languages
AREA: 478,783 sq mi; 1,240,000 sq km
LEADING EXPORTS: cotton, livestock, and gold
CONTINENT: Africa

Malta

CAPITAL: Valletta
POPULATION: 369,609
MAJOR LANGUAGES: Maltese and English
AREA: 124 sq mi; 320 sq km
LEADING EXPORTS: machinery and transportation equipment
CONTINENT: Europe

Marshall Islands

CAPITAL: Majuro
POPULATION: 56,157
MAJOR LANGUAGES: English, Marshallese dialects, and Japanese
AREA: 70 sq mi; 181.3 sq km
LEADING EXPORTS: coconut oil, fish, live animals, and trichus shells
LOCATION: Pacific Ocean

Mauritania

CAPITAL: Nouakchott
POPULATION: 2,263,202
MAJOR LANGUAGES: Hasaniya Arabic, Wolof, Pular, and Soninke
AREA: 397,969 sq mi; 1,030,700 sq km
LEADING EXPORTS: iron ore, and fish and fish products
CONTINENT: Africa

Mauritius

CAPITAL: Port Louis
POPULATION: 1,127,068
MAJOR LANGUAGES: English (official), Creole, French, Hindi, Urdu, Hakka, and Bojpoori
AREA: 718 sq mi; 1,860 sq km
LEADING EXPORTS: textiles, sugar, and light manufactures
LOCATION: Indian Ocean

Mayotte

CAPITAL: Mamoutzou
POPULATION: 97,088
MAJOR LANGUAGES: Mahorian and French
AREA: 145 sq mi; 375 sq km
LEADING EXPORTS: ylang-ylang and vanilla
CONTINENT: Africa

Mexico

CAPITAL: Mexico City
POPULATION: 93,985,848
MAJOR LANGUAGES: Spanish and Mayan dialects
AREA: 761,632 sq mi; 1,972,550 sq km
LEADING EXPORTS: crude oil, oil products, coffee, and silver
CONTINENT: North America

Micronesia

CAPITAL: Federated states of Kolonia (on the Island of Pohnpei)
*a new capital is being built about 10 km southwest in the Palikir Valley
POPULATION: 122,950
MAJOR LANGUAGES: English, Turkese, Pohnpeian, Yapese, and Kosrean
AREA: 271 sq mi; 702 sq km
LEADING EXPORTS: fish, copra, bananas, and black pepper
LOCATION: Pacific Ocean

Moldova

CAPITAL: Chisinau
POPULATION: 4,489,657
MAJOR LANGUAGES: Moldovan (official), Russian, and Gagauz dialect
AREA: 13,012 sq mi; 33,700 sq km
LEADING EXPORTS: foodstuffs, wine, and tobacco
CONTINENT: Europe

Monaco

CAPITAL: Monaco
POPULATION: 31,515
MAJOR LANGUAGES: French (official), English, Italian, and Monegasque
AREA: .73 sq mi; 1.9 sq km
LEADING EXPORTS: exports through France
CONTINENT: Europe

Mongolia

CAPITAL: Ulaanbaatar
POPULATION: 2,493,615
MAJOR LANGUAGES: Khalkha Mongol, Turkic, Russian, and Chinese
AREA: 604,270 sq mi; 1,565,000 sq km
LEADING EXPORTS: copper, livestock, animal products, and cashmere
CONTINENT: Asia

Morocco

CAPITAL: Rabat
POPULATION: 29,168,848
MAJOR LANGUAGES: Arabic (official), Berber dialects, and French
AREA: 172,420 sq mi; 446,550 sq km
LEADING EXPORTS: food and beverages
CONTINENT: Africa

Mozambique

CAPITAL: Maputo
POPULATION: 18,115,250
MAJOR LANGUAGES: Portuguese and various dialects
AREA: 309,506 sq mi; 801,590 sq km
LEADING EXPORTS: shrimp, cashews, cotton, sugar, copra, and citrus
CONTINENT: Africa

Myanmar (Burma)

CAPITAL: Rangoon
POPULATION: 45,103,809
MAJOR LANGUAGE: Burmese
AREA: 261,979 sq mi; 678,500 sq km
LEADING EXPORTS: pulses and beans, teak, rice, and hardwood
CONTINENT: Asia

Namibia

CAPITAL: Windhoek
POPULATION: 1,651,545
MAJOR LANGUAGES: English (official), Afrikaans, German, Oshivambo, Herero, Nama, and various languages
AREA: 318,707 sq mi; 825,418 sq km
LEADING EXPORTS: diamonds, copper, gold, zinc, and lead
CONTINENT: Africa

Nauru

CAPITAL: Government offices in Yaren District
POPULATION: 10,149
MAJOR LANGUAGES: Nauruan and English
AREA: 8 sq mi; 21 sq km
LEADING EXPORTS: phosphates
LOCATION: Pacific Ocean

Nepal

CAPITAL: Kathmandu
POPULATION: 21,560,869
MAJOR LANGUAGES: Nepali (official) and 20 various languages divided into numerous dialects
AREA: 54,365 sq mi; 140,800 sq km
LEADING EXPORTS: carpets, clothing, and leather goods
CONTINENT: Asia

Netherlands

CAPITAL: Amsterdam
POPULATION: 15,452,903
MAJOR LANGUAGE: Dutch
AREA: 14,414 sq mi; 37,330 sq km
LEADING EXPORTS: metal products and chemicals
CONTINENT: Europe

New Caledonia

CAPITAL: Noumea
POPULATION: 184,552
MAJOR LANGUAGES: French and 28 Melanesian-Polynesian dialects
AREA: 7,359 sq mi; 19,060 sq km
LEADING EXPORTS: nickel metal and nickel ore
LOCATION: Pacific Ocean

New Zealand

CAPITAL: Wellington
POPULATION: 3,407,277
MAJOR LANGUAGES: English and Maori
AREA: 103,741 sq mi; 268,680 sq km
LEADING EXPORTS: wool, lamb, mutton, beef, fish, and cheese
LOCATION: Pacific Ocean

Nicaragua

CAPITAL: Managua
POPULATION: 4,206,353
MAJOR LANGUAGES: Spanish (official), English, and various languages
AREA: 50,000 sq mi; 129,494 sq km
LEADING EXPORTS: meat, coffee, cotton, sugar, seafood, and gold
LOCATION: Caribbean Sea

Niger

CAPITAL: Niamey
POPULATION: 9,280,208
MAJOR LANGUAGES: French (official), Hausa, and Djerma
AREA: 489,208 sq mi; 1,267,000 sq km
LEADING EXPORTS: uranium ore and livestock products
CONTINENT: Africa

Nigeria

CAPITAL: Abuja
POPULATION: 101,232,251
MAJOR LANGUAGES: English (official), Hausa, Yoruba, Ibo, and Fulani
AREA: 356,682 sq mi; 923,770 sq km
LEADING EXPORTS: oil, cocoa, and rubber
CONTINENT: Africa

Niue

CAPITAL: (Free association with New Zealand)
POPULATION: 1,837
MAJOR LANGUAGES: Polynesian and English
AREA: 100 sq mi; 260 sq km
LEADING EXPORTS: canned coconut cream, copra, and honey
LOCATION: Pacific Ocean

Norway

CAPITAL: Oslo
POPULATION: 4,330,951
MAJOR LANGUAGES: Norwegian (official), Lapp, and Finnish
AREA: 125,186 sq mi; 324,220 sq km
LEADING EXPORTS: petroleum and petroleum products
CONTINENT: Europe

Oman

CAPITAL: Muscat
POPULATION: 2,125,089
MAJOR LANGUAGES: Arabic (official), English, Baluchi, Urdu, and Indian dialects
AREA: 82,034 sq mi; 212,460 sq km
LEADING EXPORTS: petroleum, re-exports, and fish
CONTINENT: Asia

Pakistan

CAPITAL: Islamabad
POPULATION: 131,541,920
MAJOR LANGUAGES: Urdu (official), English (official), Punjabi, Sindhi, Pashtu, Urdu, Balochi, and other languages
AREA: 310,414 sq mi; 803,940 sq km
LEADING EXPORTS: cotton, textiles, clothing, rice, and leather
CONTINENT: Asia

Palau

CAPITAL: Koror
POPULATION: 16,661
MAJOR LANGUAGES: English (official), Sonsorolese, Angaur, Japanese, Tobi, and Palauan
AREA: 177 sq mi; 458 sq km
LEADING EXPORTS: trochus, tuna, copra, and handicrafts
LOCATION: Pacific Ocean

Panama

CAPITAL: Panama
POPULATION: 2,680,903
MAJOR LANGUAGES: Spanish (official) and English
AREA: 30,194 sq mi; 78,200 sq km
LEADING EXPORTS: bananas, shrimp, sugar, clothing, and coffee
CONTINENT: Central America

Papua New Guinea

CAPITAL: Port Moresby
POPULATION: 4,294,750
MAJOR LANGUAGES: English, pidgin English, and Motu
AREA: 178,266 sq mi; 461,690 sq km
LEADING EXPORTS: gold, copper ore, oil, logs, and palm oil
LOCATION: Pacific Ocean

Paraguay

CAPITAL: Asuncion
POPULATION: 5,358,198
MAJOR LANGUAGES: Spanish (official) and Guarani
AREA: 157,052 sq mi; 406,750 sq km
LEADING EXPORTS: cotton, soybeans, timber, and vegetable oils
CONTINENT: South America

Peru

CAPITAL: Lima
POPULATION: 24,087,372
MAJOR LANGUAGES: Spanish (official), Quechua (official), and Aymara
AREA: 496,243 sq mi; 1,285,220 sq km
LEADING EXPORTS: copper, zinc, and fish meal
CONTINENT: South America

Philippines

CAPITAL: Manila
POPULATION: 73,265,584
MAJOR LANGUAGES: Pilipino and English (official)
AREA: 115,834 sq mi; 300,000 sq km
LEADING EXPORTS: electronics, textiles, and coconut products
CONTINENT: Asia

Poland

CAPITAL: Warsaw
POPULATION: 38,792,442
MAJOR LANGUAGE: Polish
AREA: 120,731 sq mi; 312,680 sq km
LEADING EXPORTS: intermediate goods
CONTINENT: Europe

Portugal

CAPITAL: Lisbon
POPULATION: 10,562,388
MAJOR LANGUAGE: Portuguese
AREA: 35,553 sq mi; 92,080 sq km
LEADING EXPORTS: clothing and footwear, and machinery
CONTINENT: Europe

Qatar

CAPITAL: Doha
POPULATION: 533,916
MAJOR LANGUAGES: Arabic (official) and English
AREA: 4,247 sq mi; 11,000 sq km
LEADING EXPORTS: petroleum products, steel, and fertilizers
CONTINENT: Asia

Romania

CAPITAL: Bucharest
POPULATION: 23,198,330
MAJOR LANGUAGES: Romanian, Hungarian, and German
AREA: 91,702 sq mi; 237,500 sq km
LEADING EXPORTS: metals and metal products, and mineral products
CONTINENT: Europe

Russia

CAPITAL: Moscow
POPULATION: 149,909,089
MAJOR LANGUAGES: Russian and various languages
AREA: 6,952,996 sq mi; 17,075,200 sq km
LEADING EXPORTS: petroleum and petroleum products
CONTINENT: Europe and Asia

Rwanda

CAPITAL: Kigali
POPULATION: 8,605,307
MAJOR LANGUAGES: Kinyarwanda (official), French (official), and Kiswahili
AREA: 10,170 sq mi; 26,340 sq km
LEADING EXPORTS: coffee, tea, cassiterite, and wolframite
CONTINENT: Africa

Saint Kitts and Nevis

CAPITAL: Basseterre
POPULATION: 40,992
MAJOR LANGUAGE: English
AREA: 104 sq mi; 269 sq km
LEADING EXPORTS: machinery, food, and electronics
LOCATION: Caribbean Sea

Saint Lucia

CAPITAL: Castries
POPULATION: 156,050
MAJOR LANGUAGES: English and French patois
AREA: 239 sq mi; 620 sq km
LEADING EXPORTS: bananas, clothing, cocoa, and vegetables
LOCATION: Caribbean Sea

Saint Vincent and the Grenadines

CAPITAL: Kingstown
POPULATION: 117,344
MAJOR LANGUAGES: English and French patois
AREA: 131 sq mi; 340 sq km
LEADING EXPORTS: bananas, and eddoes and dasheen (taro)
LOCATION: Caribbean Sea

San Marino

CAPITAL: San Marino
POPULATION: 24,313
MAJOR LANGUAGE: Italian
AREA: 23 sq mi; 60 sq km
LEADING EXPORTS: building stone, lime, wood, and chestnuts
CONTINENT: Europe

Sao Tome and Principe

CAPITAL: Sao Tome
POPULATION: 140,423
MAJOR LANGUAGE: Portuguese (official)
AREA: 371 sq mi; 960 sq km
LEADING EXPORTS: cocoa, copra, coffee, and palm oil
CONTINENT: Africa

Saudi Arabia

CAPITAL: Riyadh
POPULATION: 18,729,576
MAJOR LANGUAGE: Arabic
AREA: 757,011 sq mi; 1,960,582 sq km
LEADING EXPORTS: petroleum and petroleum products
CONTINENT: Asia

Senegal

CAPITAL: Dakar
POPULATION: 9,007,080
MAJOR LANGUAGES: French (official), Wolof, Pulaar, Diola, and Mandingo
AREA: 75,752 sq mi; 196,190 sq km
LEADING EXPORTS: fish, ground nuts, and petroleum products
CONTINENT: Africa

Serbia and Montenegro

CAPITAL: Belgrade
POPULATION: 11,101,833
MAJOR LANGUAGES: Serbo-Croatian and Albanian
AREA: 39,436 sq mi; 102,350 sq km
LEADING EXPORTS: none
CONTINENT: Europe

Seychelles

CAPITAL: Victoria
POPULATION: 72,709
MAJOR LANGUAGES: English (official), French (official), and Creole
AREA: 176 sq mi; 455 sq km
LEADING EXPORTS: fish, cinnamon bark, and copra
CONTINENT: Africa

Sierra Leone

CAPITAL: Freetown
POPULATION: 4,753,120
MAJOR LANGUAGES: English (official), Mende, Temne, and Krio
AREA: 27,700 sq mi; 71,740 sq km
LEADING EXPORTS: rutile, bauxite, diamonds, coffee, and cocoa
CONTINENT: Africa

Singapore

CAPITAL: Singapore
POPULATION: 2,890,468
MAJOR LANGUAGES: Chinese, Malay, Tamil, and English
AREA: 244 sq mi; 633 sq km
LEADING EXPORTS: computer equipment
CONTINENT: Asia

Slovakia

CAPITAL: Bratislava
POPULATION: 5,432,383
MAJOR LANGUAGES: Slovak and Hungarian
AREA: 18,860 sq mi; 48,845 sq km
LEADING EXPORTS: machinery and transportation equipment
CONTINENT: Europe

Slovenia

CAPITAL: Ljubljana
POPULATION: 2,051,522
MAJOR LANGUAGES: Slovenian, Serbo-Croatian, and various languages
AREA: 7,837 sq mi; 20,296 sq km
LEADING EXPORTS: machinery and transportation equipment
CONTINENT: Europe

Solomon Islands

CAPITAL: Honiara
POPULATION: 399,206
MAJOR LANGUAGES: Melanesian pidgin and English
AREA: 10,985 sq mi; 28,450 sq km
LEADING EXPORTS: fish, timber, palm oil, cocoa, and copra
LOCATION: Pacific Ocean

Somalia

CAPITAL: Mogadishu
POPULATION: 7,347,554
MAJOR LANGUAGES: Somali (official), Arabic, Italian, and English
AREA: 246,210 sq mi; 637,660 sq km
LEADING EXPORTS: bananas, live animals, fish, and hides
CONTINENT: Africa

South Africa

CAPITAL: Pretoria (administrative), Cape Town (legislative), Bloemfontein (judicial)
POPULATION: 45,095,459
MAJOR LANGUAGES: Afrikaans, English, Ndebele, Pedi, Sotho, Swazi, Tsonga, Tswana, Venda, Xhosa, and Zulu (all official)
AREA: 471,027 sq mi; 1,219,912 sq km
LEADING EXPORTS: gold, other minerals and metals, and food
CONTINENT: Africa

Spain

CAPITAL: Madrid
POPULATION: 39,404,348
MAJOR LANGUAGES: Spanish, Catalan, Galician, and Basque
AREA: 194,892 sq mi; 504,750 sq km
LEADING EXPORTS: cars and trucks, and semifinished goods
CONTINENT: Europe

Sri Lanka

CAPITAL: Colombo
POPULATION: 18,342,660
MAJOR LANGUAGES: Sinhala (official) and Tamil
AREA: 25,333 sq mi; 65,610 sq km
LEADING EXPORTS: garments and textiles, teas, and diamonds
CONTINENT: Asia

Sudan

CAPITAL: Khartoum
POPULATION: 30,120,420
MAJOR LANGUAGES: Arabic (official), Nubian, Ta Bedawie, Nilotic, Nilo-Hamitic, and Sudanic dialects
AREA: 967,532 sq mi; 2,505,810 sq km
LEADING EXPORTS: gum arabic, livestock/meat, and cotton
CONTINENT: Africa

Suriname

CAPITAL: Paramaribo
POPULATION: 429,544
MAJOR LANGUAGES: Dutch (official), English, Sranang, Tongo, Hindustani, and Japanese
AREA: 63,041 sq mi; 163,270 sq km
LEADING EXPORTS: alumina, aluminum, and shrimp and fish
CONTINENT: South America

Swaziland

CAPITAL: Mbabane
POPULATION: 966,977
MAJOR LANGUAGES: English (official) and SiSwati (official)
AREA: 6,641 sq mi; 17,360 sq km
LEADING EXPORTS: sugar, edible concentrates, and wood pulp
CONTINENT: Africa

Sweden

CAPITAL: Stockholm
POPULATION: 8,821,759
MAJOR LANGUAGES: Swedish, Lapp, and Finnish
AREA: 173,738 sq mi; 449,964 sq km
LEADING EXPORTS: machinery, motor vehicles, and paper products
CONTINENT: Europe

Switzerland

CAPITAL: Bern
POPULATION: 7,084,984
MAJOR LANGUAGES: German, French, Italian, Romansch, and various languages
AREA: 15,943 sq mi; 41,290 sq km
LEADING EXPORTS: machinery and equipment
CONTINENT: Europe

Syria

CAPITAL: Damascus
POPULATION: 15,451,917
MAJOR LANGUAGES: Arabic (official), Kurdish, Armenian, Aramaic, Circassian, and French
AREA: 71,501 sq mi; 185,180 sq km
LEADING EXPORTS: petroleum, textiles, cotton, and fruits
CONTINENT: Asia

Taiwan

CAPITAL: Taipei
POPULATION: 21,500,583
MAJOR LANGUAGES: Mandarin Chinese (official), Taiwanese, and Hakka dialects
AREA: 13,892 sq mi; 35,980 sq km
LEADING EXPORTS: electrical machinery and electronics
CONTINENT: Asia

Tajikistan
CAPITAL: Dushanbe
POPULATION: 6,155,474
MAJOR LANGUAGES: Tajik (official) and Russian
AREA: 55,253 sq mi; 143,100 sq km
LEADING EXPORTS: cotton, aluminum, fruits, and vegetable oil
CONTINENT: Asia

Tanzania
CAPITAL: Dar Es Salaam
POPULATION: 28,701,077
MAJOR LANGUAGES: Swahili, English, and various languages
AREA: 364,914 sq mi; 945,090 sq km
LEADING EXPORTS: coffee, cotton, tobacco, tea, and cashew nuts
CONTINENT: Africa

Thailand
CAPITAL: Bangkok
POPULATION: 60,271,300
MAJOR LANGUAGES: Thai and English
AREA: 198,463 sq mi; 511,770 sq km
LEADING EXPORTS: machinery and manufactures
CONTINENT: Asia

Togo
CAPITAL: Lome
POPULATION: 4,410,370
MAJOR LANGUAGES: French, Ewe and Mina, Dagomba, and Kabye
AREA: 21,927 sq mi; 56,790 sq km
LEADING EXPORTS: phosphates, cotton, cocoa, and coffee
CONTINENT: Africa

Tonga
CAPITAL: Nukualofa
POPULATION: 105,600
MAJOR LANGUAGES: Tongan and English
AREA: 289 sq mi; 748 sq km
LEADING EXPORTS: squash, vanilla, fish, root crops, and coconut oil
LOCATION: Pacific Ocean

Trinidad and Tobago
CAPITAL: Port-of-Spain
POPULATION: 1,271,159
MAJOR LANGUAGES: English, Hindu, French, and Spanish
AREA: 1,981 sq mi; 5,130 sq km
LEADING EXPORTS: petroleum and petroleum products
LOCATION: Caribbean Sea

Tunisia
CAPITAL: Tunis
POPULATION: 8,879,845
MAJOR LANGUAGES: Arabic and French
AREA: 63,172 sq mi; 163,610 sq km
LEADING EXPORTS: hydrocarbons and agricultural products
CONTINENT: Africa

Turkey
CAPITAL: Ankara
POPULATION: 63,405,526
MAJOR LANGUAGES: Turkish, Kurdish, and Arabic
AREA: 301,394 sq mi; 780,580 sq km
LEADING EXPORTS: manufactured products, and foodstuffs
CONTINENT: Europe and Asia

Turkmenistan
CAPITAL: Ashgabat
POPULATION: 4,075,316
MAJOR LANGUAGES: Turkmen, Russian, Uzbek, and various languages
AREA: 188,463 sq mi; 488,100 sq km
LEADING EXPORTS: natural gas, cotton, and petroleum products
CONTINENT: Asia

Tuvalu
CAPITAL: Fongafale, on Funafuti atoll
POPULATION: 9,991
MAJOR LANGUAGES: Tuvaluan and English
AREA: 10 sq mi; 26 sq km
LEADING EXPORT: copra
LOCATION: Pacific Ocean

Uganda
CAPITAL: Kampala
POPULATION: 19,573,262
MAJOR LANGUAGES: English, Luganda, Swahili, Bantu languages, and Nilotic languages
AREA: 91,139 sq mi; 236,040 sq km
LEADING EXPORTS: coffee, cotton, and tea
CONTINENT: Africa

Ukraine
CAPITAL: Kiev
POPULATION: 51,867,828
MAJOR LANGUAGES: Ukranian, Russian, Romanian, Polish, and Hungarian
AREA: 233,098 sq mi; 603,700 sq km
LEADING EXPORTS: coal, electric power, and metals
CONTINENT: Europe

United Arab Emirates
CAPITAL: Abu Dhabi
POPULATION: 2,924,594
MAJOR LANGUAGES: Arabic, Persian, English, Hindi, and Urdu
AREA: 29,183 sq mi; 75,581 sq km
LEADING EXPORTS: crude oil, natural gas, re-exports, and dried fish
CONTINENT: Asia

United Kingdom

CAPITAL: London
POPULATION: 58,295,119
MAJOR LANGUAGES: English, Welsh, and Scottish Gaelic
AREA: 94,529 sq mi; 244,820 sq km
LEADING EXPORTS: manufactured goods, machinery, and fuels
CONTINENT: Europe

United States
CAPITAL: Washington, D.C.
POPULATION: 263,814,032
MAJOR LANGUAGES: English and Spanish
AREA: 3,618,908 sq mi; 9,372,610 sq km
LEADING EXPORTS: capital goods and automobiles
CONTINENT: North America

Uruguay
CAPITAL: Montevideo
POPULATION: 3,222,716
MAJOR LANGUAGES: Spanish and Brazilero
AREA: 68,041 sq mi; 176,220 sq km
LEADING EXPORTS: wool and textile manufactures
CONTINENT: South America

Uzbekistan
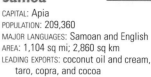
CAPITAL: Tashkent
POPULATION: 23,089,261
MAJOR LANGUAGES: Uzbek, Russian, Tajik, various languages
AREA: 172,748 sq mi; 447,400 sq km
LEADING EXPORTS: cotton, gold, natural gas, and minerals
CONTINENT: Asia

Vanuatu
CAPITAL: Port-Vila
POPULATION: 173,648
MAJOR LANGUAGES: English, French, pidgin, and Bislama
AREA: 5,699 sq mi; 14,760 sq km
LEADING EXPORTS: copra, beef, cocoa, timber, and coffee
LOCATION: Pacific Ocean

Venezuela
CAPITAL: Caracas
POPULATION: 21,004,773
MAJOR LANGUAGES: Spanish and various languages
AREA: 352,156 sq mi; 912,050 sq km
LEADING EXPORTS: petroleum, bauxite and aluminum, and steel
CONTINENT: South America

Vietnam
CAPITAL: Hanoi
POPULATION: 74,393,324
MAJOR LANGUAGES: Vietnamese, French, Chinese, English, Khmer, and various languages
AREA: 127,248 sq mi; 329,560 sq km
LEADING EXPORTS: petroleum, rice, and agricultural products
CONTINENT: Asia

Western Samoa
CAPITAL: Apia
POPULATION: 209,360
MAJOR LANGUAGES: Samoan and English
AREA: 1,104 sq mi; 2,860 sq km
LEADING EXPORTS: coconut oil and cream, taro, copra, and cocoa
LOCATION: Pacific Ocean

Yemen
CAPITAL: Sanaa
POPULATION: 14,728,474
MAJOR LANGUAGE: Arabic
AREA: 203,857 sq mi; 527,970 sq km
LEADING EXPORTS: crude oil, cotton, coffee, hides, and vegetables
CONTINENT: Asia

Zaire
CAPITAL: Kinshasa
POPULATION: 44,060,636
MAJOR LANGUAGES: French, Lingala, Swahili, Kingwana, Kikongo, and Tshiluba
AREA: 905,599 sq mi; 2,345,410 sq km
LEADING EXPORTS: copper, coffee, diamonds, cobalt, and crude oil
CONTINENT: Africa

Zambia
CAPITAL: Lusaka
POPULATION: 9,445,723
MAJOR LANGUAGES: English (official) and about 70 various languages
AREA: 290,594 sq mi; 752,610 sq km
LEADING EXPORTS: copper, zinc, cobalt, lead, and tobacco
CONTINENT: Africa

Zimbabwe
CAPITAL: Harare
POPULATION: 11,139,961
MAJOR LANGUAGES: English, Shona, and Sindebele
area: 150,809 sq mi; 390,580 sq km
LEADING EXPORTS: agricultural products and manufactures
CONTINENT: Africa

Glossary of Geographic Terms

basin
a depression in the surface of the land; some basins are filled with water

bay
a part of a sea or lake that extends into the land

butte
a small raised area of land with steep sides

▲ butte

canyon
a deep, narrow valley with steep sides; often has a stream flowing through it

cataract
a large waterfall; any strong flood or rush of water

◀ cataract

delta
a triangular-shaped plain at the mouth of a river, formed when sediment is deposited by flowing water

flood plain
a broad plain on either side of a river, formed when sediment settles on the riverbanks

glacier
a huge, slow-moving mass of snow and ice

hill
an area that rises above surrounding land and has a rounded top; lower and usually less steep than a mountain

island
an area of land completely surrounded by water

isthmus
a narrow strip of land that connects two larger areas of land

mesa
a high, flat-topped landform with cliff-like sides; larger than a butte

mountain
an area that rises steeply at least 2,000 feet (300 m) above surrounding land; usually wide at the bottom and rising to a narrow peak or ridge

▶ glacier

◄ delta

mountain pass
a gap between mountains

peninsula
an area of land almost completely surrounded by water and connected to the mainland by an isthmus

plain
a large area of flat or gently rolling land

plateau
a large, flat area that rises above the surrounding land; at least one side has a steep slope

river mouth
the point where a river enters a lake or sea

strait
a narrow stretch of water that connects two larger bodies of water

tributary
a river or stream that flows into a larger river

volcano
an opening in the Earth's surface through which molten rock, ashes, and gasses from the Earth's interior escape

► volcano

Gazetteer

A

Abuja (9.12°N, 7.11°E) the federal capital of Nigeria, p. 110

Addis Ababa (9°N, 38.44°E) the capital city of Ethiopia, p. 139

Aksum an ancient city in northern Ethiopia, a powerful kingdom and trade center from about A.D. 200 to A.D. 600, p. 35

C

Cairo (30°N, 31°E) the capital of Egypt and most populous city in Africa, p. 93

Cape of Good Hope (34°S, 18°E) a province of the Republic of South Africa; the cape at the southern end of Cape Peninsula, South Africa, p. 42

Cape Town (33.48°S, 18.28°E) the legislative capital of the Republic of South Africa; the capital of Cape Province, p. 170

Central and Southern Africa countries in the central and southern region of Africa, p. 84

Congo River (2°S, 17°E) a river in Central Africa that flows into the Atlantic Ocean, p. 12

D

Dar es Salaam (6.48°S, 39.17°E) the capital and largest city in Tanzania, an industrial center and major port on the Indian Ocean, p. 140

E

East Africa countries in the eastern region of Africa, p. 76

Egypt (26.58°S, 27.01°E) a country in North Africa, officially Arab Republic of Egypt, p. 33

G

Ghana (8°N, 2°W) a country in West Africa, officially Republic of Ghana, p. 37

Gorée an island off the coast of Senegal, p. 41

Great Rift Valley the major branch of the East African Rift System, p. 11

K

Kalahari Desert (23°S, 22.03°E) a desert region in Southern Africa, p. 19

Kano (12°N, 8.30°E) a city and the capital of Kano state in northern Nigeria; a historic kingdom in northern Nigeria, p. 111

Kilwa late tenth-century Islamic city-state located on an island off the coast of present-day Tanzania, p. 39

L

Lagos (6.27°N, 3.24°E) a city and chief Atlantic port of Nigeria; a state in Nigeria, p. 110

Lalibela a town in Ethiopia famous for its stone churches carved in the 1100s, p. 139

M

Mali (15.45°N, .15°W) an early African empire; a present-day country in West Africa, officially Republic of Mali, p. 37

Mediterranean Sea (36.22°N, 13.25°E) the large sea separating Europe and Africa, p. 67

Mount Kenya (.10°S, 37.20°E) a volcano in central Kenya, p. 148

N

Nairobi (1.17°S, 36.49°E) the capital of Kenya, p. 152

Namib Desert (18.45°S, 12.45°E) a desert extending along the Atlantic Coast of South Africa, p. 19

Niger (18.02°N, 8.30°E) a country in West Africa, officially Republic of Niger, p. 53

Niger River (8°N, 6°E) the river in West Africa that flows from Guinea into the Gulf of Guinea, p. 13

Nile River (27.30°N, 31°E) the longest river in the world, flows through northeastern Africa into the Mediterranean Sea, p. 12

North Africa countries in the northern region of Africa, p. 63

Nubia an ancient region in North Africa, p. 33

R

Republic of South Africa (28°S, 24.50°E) southernmost country in Africa, p. 81

S

Sahara (23.44°N, 1.40°W) largest tropical desert in the world, covers almost all of North Africa, p. 9

Sahel (15°N, 7°E) the region in West and Central Africa that forms a changing climate zone between the dry Sahara to the north and humid savannas to the south, p. 19

Senegal (14.53°N, 14.58°W) a country in West Africa, officially Republic of Senegal, p. 55

Shaba a southern province in Zaire, p. 163

Songhai an empire and trading state in West Africa founded in the 1400s, p. 38

Southern Africa countries in the southern region of Africa, p. 82

T

Tombouctou (16.46°N, 3.01°W) city in Mali near the Niger River; in the past an important center of Islamic education and a trans-Saharan caravan stop (also spelled Timbuktu), p. 38

W

West Africa countries in the western region of Africa, p. 69

Z

Zaire (1°S, 22.15°E) a country in Central Africa, officially Republic of Zaire, p. 84

Zambezi River (16°S, 29.45°E) a river in Central and Southern Africa that flows into the Indian Ocean, p. 13

Zanzibar (6.20°S, 39.37°E) an island in the Indian Ocean off the coast of East Africa, part of Tanzania, p. 140

Zimbabwe (17.50°S, 29.30°E) a country in Southern Africa, officially Republic of Zimbabwe, p. 40

Glossary

A

apartheid the South African system in which racial groups were separated and racial discrimination was legal, p. 170

authoritarian controlled by one person or a small group, p. 164

B

bazaar a traditional open-air market with rows of shops or stalls, p. 97

boycott a refusal to buy or use certain products or services, p. 51

C

casbah an old, crowded section of a North African city, p. 103

cash crop a crop that is raised for sale, p. 23

cataract a rock-filled rapid, p. 11

census a count of the people in a country, p. 113

city-state a city that controls much of the land around it and has its own government, p. 39

civilization a society with cities, a government, and social classes; a civilization also has architecture, writing, and art, p. 32

clan a group of lineages, p. 72

colonize to settle an area and take over or create a government, p. 46

commercial farming the large-scale production of crops for sale, often coffee, cocoa, or bananas, p. 54

coup the takeover of a government, often done by military force, p. 119

D

cultural diffusion the movement of customs and ideas from one culture to another, p. 67

cultural diversity a wide variety of cultures, p. 69

culture the way of life of people who share similar customs and beliefs, p. 64

D

democracy a government in which citizens have power through their elected representatives, p. 51

desertification the changing of fertile land into land that is too dry for crops, p. 123

discriminate to treat people unfairly based on race, religion, or gender, p. 170

diversify to add variety; a country can diversify its economy by producing more products, p. 25

domesticate to adapt wild plants and animals for human use, p. 32

drought a long period of little or no rainfall, p. 124

E

economy all the things people do to make a living in a particular place, p. 24

elevation the height of land above sea level, p. 10

erode to wear away slowly, p. 124

escarpment a steep cliff about 100 stories high, p. 11

ethnic group a group that shares a language, a religion, family ties, and customs, p. 34

extended family a family that includes relatives other than parents and children, p. 71

F

fellaheen peasants or agricultural workers in an Arab country, p. 97

fertile able to grow a lot of plants; productive, p. 12

foreign debt money owed to foreign countries, p. 144

G

griot an African storyteller, p. 73

H

harambee the Swahili word for "let's pull together"; the campaign in Kenya begun by President Jomo Kenyatta in 1963, after the country became independent, p. 150

homeland South African lands where blacks were forced to live during apartheid; driest and least fertile parts of the country, p. 171

hunter-gatherer person who gathers wild food and hunts animals to survive, p. 31

hybrid a plant that is a combination of two or more types of the same plant, p. 55

I

irrigate to artificially water crops, p. 17

K

kinship a family relationship, p. 71

L

life expectancy how long an average person will live, p. 56

lineage a group of families with a common ancestor, p. 72

literacy the ability to read and write, p. 56

M

migrant worker a person who moves from place to place to find work, p. 82

migrate to move from one place to another, p. 33

monastery a place where monks or nuns live, work, and study, p. 135

multiethnic containing many ethnic groups, p. 109

N

nationalism a feeling of pride in one's homeland; a group's identity as members of a nation, p. 47

nationalize to put a once-private industry under national control, p. 164

nomad a person who moves around to make a living, usually by herding animals, trading, hunting, or gathering food, p. 19

nuclear family a family that includes parents and children, p. 71

O

oasis a fertile place in a desert where there is water and vegetation, p. 17

P

Pan-Africanism a movement that stressed unity among all Africans, p. 48

pilgrimage a religious journey; for Muslims, the journey to Mecca, p. 38

plantation a large farm where cash crops are grown, p. 78

plateau a large, mostly flat area that rises above the surrounding land, p. 10

Q

Quran the holy book of the religion of Islam, p. 38

R

rift a deep crack in the Earth's surface, p. 11

S

silt bits of rock and dirt on river bottoms, p. 12

souq an open-air marketplace, p. 103

sovereignty political independence, p. 118

subsistence farming raising just enough crops to support one's family, p. 22

surplus more than is needed, p. 32

Swahili an African language that includes some Arabic words, p. 38

T

terrace a platform cut into the side of a mountain, used for growing crops in steep places, p. 101

tributary a small stream or river that flows into a larger river, p. 13

The *italicized* page numbers refer to illustrations. The *m, c, p,* or *t* preceding the number refers to maps *(m),* charts *(c),* pictures *(p),* or tables *(t).*

Index

Acknowledgments

Program Development, Design, Illustration, and Production
Proof Positive/Farrowlyne Associates, Inc.

Cover Design
Olena Serbyn and Bruce Bond

Cover Photo
Jon Chomitz

Maps
GeoSystems Global Corp.

Text
19, From *Sand and Fog: Adventures in Southern Africa,* by Jim Brandenburg. Copyright © 1994 by Jim Brandenburg. Reprinted with permission of Walker Publishing Company, Inc. 21, From *Cocoa Comes to Mampong,* by Dei Anang. Copyright © 1949. Reprinted with the permission of Methodist Book Depot. 80, From "African Statesman Still Sowing Seeds for Future," by James C. McKinley, Jr., *New York Times,* September 1, 1996. Copyright © 1996 by *The New York Times.* Reprinted by permission. 87, From *The Africans,* by David Lamb. Copyright © 1982 by David Lamb. Reprinted with the permission of Random House, Inc. 99, From "The World in Its Extreme," by William Langewiesche. Copyright © 1991 by William Langewiesche as first published in *The Atlantic Monthly,* November 1991. 117, From *Ghana in Transition,* by David E. Apter. Copyright © 1955, '63, and '72 by Princeton University Press. Used with permission. 132, "My Village" from *The Distant Talking Drum.* Text copyright © 1995 by Isaac Olaleye. Reprinted with permission of Wordsong/Boyds Mills Press, Inc. 133, "Village Weavers" from *The Distant Talking Drum.* Text copyright © 1995 by Isaac Olaleye. Reprinted with permission of Wordsong/Boyds Mills Press, Inc. 141, 143, From "Three Leaders," by Andrew Meldrum, *Africa Report,* September–October 1994. Copyright © 1994 by *Africa Report.* Reprinted by permission. 150, From *Baricho - A Village in Kenya,* by Richard Wright. Copyright © 1993 by Warwickshire World Studies Centre. Distributed by DEDU, 153, Cardigan Road, Leeds, LS6 1LJ, United Kingdom. Reprinted with permission of Warwickshire World Studies Centre. 153, From "Back to No Man's Land," by George Monbiot, *Geographical Magazine,* July 1994. Copyright © 1994 by *Geographical Magazine.* Reprinted by permission. 156, From *A Promise to the Sun* by Tololwa M. Mollel. Text Copyright © 1991 by Tololwa M. Mollel; Illustrations Copyright © 1991 by Beatriz Vidal. By permission of Little, Brown and Company.

Photos
1 T, © John Chasson/Gamma Liaison International, 1 BL, © Jason Laure'/Laure' Communications, 1 BR, © Robert Frerck/Odyssey Productions, 5, © Mark Thayer, Boston, 7, ©, Kjell B. Sandved/Visuals Unlimited, 9, © Paul C. Sereno/Paul C. Sereno, 10 ©, Robert Frerck/Odyssey Productions, 10 (inset), © Wendy Stone/Odyssey Productions, 11, © G. Winters/Trip Photographic, 12, © SuperStock International, 13, © Comstock, 14, © Steve McCutcheon/Visuals Unlimited, 15, © Frans Lanting/Minden Pictures, 17, © Don W. Fawcett/Visuals Unlimited, 19, © Nicholas Parfitt/Tony Stone Images, 20, © Penny Tweedie/Tony Stone Images, 21, © Victor Englebert/Victor Englebert Photography, 21 (inset), © Cabisco/Visuals Unlimited, 22 L, © Victor Englebert/Victor Englebert Photography, 22 M, © Brian Seed/Tony Stone Images, 22 R, © Wendy Stone/Odyssey Productions, 25, © Ian Murphy/Tony Stone Images, 26–27, © David Young-Wolff/PhotoEdit, 31, © The Granger Collection, 32 L, TR, BR, © Lee Boltin/Boltin Picture Library, 33, © Courtesy of Museum of Fine Arts Boston, 35, © H. Rogers/Trip Photographic, 37, © The Granger Collection, 39 L, © SuperStock International, 39 R, © The Granger Collection, 40, © Jason Laure'/Laure' Communications, 41, © Erich Lessing/Art Resource, 42, © Robert Frerck/Odyssey Productions, 44 L, R, © The Granger Collection, 47, © Jason Laure'/Laure' Communications, 48, © L. P. Winfrey/Woodfin Camp & Associates, 49, 51, © UPI/Corbis-Bettmann, 52, © Wolfgang Kaehler/Wolfgang Kaehler Photography, 53, © W. Jacobs/Trip Photographic, 56, © Jason Laure'/Laure' Communications, 55, © M. & V. Birley/Tropix Photographic Library, 57, © Marc & Evelyn Bernheim/Woodfin Camp & Associates, 58, © Bill Aron/PhotoEdit, 62, © M. & E. Bernheim/Woodfin Camp & Associates, 63, © Glen Allison/Tony Stone Images, 64, © Robert Frerck/Woodfin Camp & Associates, 65, © Robert Azzi/Woodfin Camp & Associates, 66 L, © Bob Smith/Trip Photographic, 66 R, © Ben Nakayama/Tony Stone Images, 68, © Lorne Resnick/Tony Stone Images, 69, © Jason Laure'/Laure' Communications, 70, 71 L, © Wolfgang Kaehler/Wolfgang Kaehler Photography, 71 R, © M. & V. Birley/Tropix Photographic Library, 72, © Wolfgang Kaehler/Wolfgang Kaehler Photography, 73, © Betty Press/Woodfin Camp & Associates, 74, © M. & E. Bernheim/Woodfin Camp & Associates, 75, © Victor Englebert/Victor Englebert Photography, 76, © Robert Frerck/Odyssey Productions, 77, © P. Joynson-Hicks/Trip Photographic, 78–79, © D. Saunders/Trip Photographic, 80, © Boyd Norton/Boyd Norton, 81, 82, 83, © Jason Laure'/Laure' Communications, 84, © D. Davis/Tropix Photographic Library, 85, © Robert Caputo/Aurora & Quanta Productions, 86, © Betty Press/Woodfin Camp & Associates, 87, © Michael Newman/PhotoEdit, 90, © M. & E. Bernheim/Woodfin Camp & Associates, 91, © Adam Novick/Village Pulse, 93, © P. Mitchell/Trip Photographic, 95, © Roland & Sabrina Michaud/Woodfin Camp & Associates, 96, © Donna DeCesare/Impact Visuals, 97, © Israel Talby/Woodfin Camp & Associates, 98, © Don Smetzer/Tony Stone Images, 99, © Victor Englebert/Victor Englebert Photography, 101, © Sylvain Grandadam/Tony Stone Images, 102, © Sean Sprague/Impact Visuals, 103 L, © Wendy Stone/Odyssey Productions, 103 R, © Victor Englebert/Victor Englebert Photography, 111, © Marc & Evelyn Bernheim/Woodfin Camp & Associates, 112, © Robert Frerck/Odyssey Productions, 113 T, © Sylvan Wittwer/Visuals Unlimited, 113 B, © J. Highet/Trip Photographic, 114, © Trip/Trip Photographic, 115, © AP/Wide World Photos, 117, © Frank Fournier/Woodfin Camp & Associates, 118, © Tim Beddow/Tony Stone Images, 119, © AP/Wide World Photos, 120 L, R, © M. & V. Birley/Tropix Photographic Library, 121, © M. Jelliffe/Trip Photographic, 123, © Norman Myers/Bruce Coleman Inc., 124, © Wolfgang Kaehler/Wolfgang Kaehler Photography, 125, © Betty Press/Woodfin Camp & Associates, 126, © Michael Newman/PhotoEdit, 130, 131, © David Young-Wolff/PhotoEdit, 132, © Betty Press/Woodfin Camp & Associates, 133, © Lawrence Manning/Tony Stone Images, 135, © Robert Caputo/Aurora & Quanta Productions, 137 L, R, © The Granger Collection, 139, © R. Ashford/Tropix Photographic Library, 140, © AP/Wide World Photos, 142, © Reuters/Corbis-Bettmann, 143, © M. & V. Birley/Tropix Photographic Library, 144 L, R, © Gerald Cubitt/Gerald Cubitt Photographer, 145, © AP/Wide World Photos, 146, © James P. Rowan/Tony Stone Images, 148, © M. & E. Bernheim/Woodfin Camp & Associates, 150, © Betty Press/Woodfin Camp & Associates, 151, © Victor Englebert/Victor Englebert Photography, 152, Matutu Ride, by Ian Kamau, Kenya. Courtesy of the International Children's Art Museum, 157, © Marc Chamberlain/Tony Stone Images, 158, © Tim Davis/Tony Stone Images, 161, © Jason Laure'/Laure' Communications, 163, © M. Jelliffe/Trip Photographic, 164, © Betty Press/Woodfin Camp & Associates, 165, © Robert Grossman/New York Times Rights & Royalties, 166, © Michael Newman/PhotoEdit, 168, © B. Mnguni/Trip Photographic, 170, © Jason Laure'/Laure' Communications, 171, © Paula Bronstein/Impact Visuals, 172, © African Institute of Art, Funda Art Centre in Soweto, 173, © Reuters/Corbis-Bettman, 176, © Mark Thayer, Boston, 177, © Betty Press/Woodfin Camp & Associates, 179, © Mark Thayer, Boston, 180 T, © Steve Leonard/Tony Stone Images, 180 B, Robert Frerck/Odyssey Productions, 181 T, © Wolfgang Kaehler/Wolfgang Kaehler Photography, 181 BL, © John Elk/Tony Stone Images, 181 BR, Will & Deni McIntyre/Tony Stone Images, 191, © G. Brad Lewis/Tony Stone Images, 193, © Nigel Press/Tony Stone Images, 220 T, © A. & L. Sinibaldi/Tony Stone Images, 220 BL, © John Beatty/Tony Stone Images, 221 T, © Hans Strand/Tony Stone Images, 221 BL, © Spencer Swanger/Tom Stack & Associates, 221 BR, © Paul Chesley/Tony Stone Images.

Teacher's Notes

Teacher's Notes

Teacher's Notes

Teacher's Notes

Teacher's Notes